Becoming Buddhist

Continuum Advances in Religious Studies

Series Editors: James Cox and Peggy Morgan

This groundbreaking series offers original reflections on theory and method in the study of religions, and demonstrates new approaches to the way religious traditions are studied and presented. Studies published under its auspices look to clarify the role and place of Religious Studies in the academy, but not in a purely theoretical manner. Each study will demonstrate its theoretical aspects by applying them to the actual study of religions, often in the form of front-line research.

Other titles available in the series:

Becoming Buddhist

Experiences of Socialization and Self-Transformation in Two Australian Buddhist Centres

Glenys Eddy

Continuum Advances in Religious Studies

Continuum International Publishing Group

The Tower Building
11 York Road
London, SE1 7NX

80 Maiden Lane
Suite 704
New York, NY 10038

www.continuumbooks.com

British Library Cataloguing-in-Publication Data
A catalogue record for this book is available from the British Library.

ISBN: HB: 978-1-4411-1846-2

Library of Congress Cataloguing-in-Publication Data
Eddy, Glenys.
Becoming Buddhist : experiences of socialization and self-transformation in two
Australian Buddhist centres/Glenys Eddy. – 1st.
     p. cm. – (Continuum advances in religious studies)
Includes bibliographical references and index.
ISBN 978-1-4411-1846-2 (hardcover)
1. Buddhism–Social aspects–Australia. 2. Buddhist converts–Australia.
I. Title. II. Series.
BQ772.E33 2011
294.30994–dc23   2011031363

Typeset by Deanta Global Publishing Services, Chennai, India
Printed and bound in Great Britain

This work is dedicated to the well-being and happiness
of all sentient beings.

Contents

Foreword

This book is an outgrowth of my Doctoral thesis (2007b). Although during its preparation I was privileged to have the advice and intellectual support of many people from the University of Sydney and beyond—which I happily acknowledge—of course I bear the responsibility for the finished work.

My grateful thanks are due to the practitioners, teachers and administrators of the two Buddhist Centres—the Blue Mountains Insight Meditation Centre at Medlow Bath, in the Blue Mountains west of Sydney, and Vajrayana Institute in Ashfield, in Sydney's Inner West—that permitted me to conduct the research for my thesis. Not only did their kindness enable me to pursue an academic analysis of a subject of interest to me, but also it gained me stimulating discourse and friendly encounters. For their support, in particular I must thank Venerable Tenzin Chönyi from Vajrayana Institute, Patrick Kearney—formerly a resident teacher at the Blue Mountains Insight Meditation Centre—and Danny Taylor. No less gratitude is due to the practitioners who willingly gave their time, experiences and insights during interview.

The fundamental purpose of this book is to explore and articulate what it means—for the practitioners and adherents of two forms of Western Buddhism—to *be* a *Western Buddhist*. It accomplishes this by exploring individual encounters with, socialization into and appropriation of the worldview of a Buddhist centre as a taken-for-granted reality, leading to a coherent picture of reality as if it were an object existing prior to our awareness of it, and which an individual acquires through socialization.

Throughout, my intention is to articulate the subjective experience of being a Western Buddhist, in a largely Anglo-Australian context, and of how Buddhist doctrine and practice, as it is mediated by the organization, is understood and applied by the individual.

Because this book deals with the *import* to Western English-speaking minds of the Pali and Sanskrit words mentioned rather than with their philology, I have used the relevant English terms where those are likely to be in common use. The original terms are therefore given in their transliterated forms, but without their romanized diacriticals. The equivalences between Pali, Sanskrit and English terms of significance appear in the Glossary.

Permission to use published material has been graciously given by Dr Cristina Rocha, Managing Editor of the Journal of Global Buddhism; Dr Maureen Miner Bridges, former Chair of the University of Western Sydney Psychology and Spirituality Society; and by Associate Professor Douglas Pratt, President of the Australian Association for the Study of Religion, and is hereby gratefully acknowledged.

Sydney, 2011

Acknowledgements

Special thanks are due to Associate Professor Carole Cusack, my supervisor and friend, for her endless encouragement and support during and since my candidature at the University of Sydney; to my associate supervisor Dr Jadran Mimica from the Department of Social Anthropology; and to my former supervisor Dr Edward Crangle, for their enthusiasm and support.

My warm thanks go also to staff-members in the University's Department of Studies in Religion: Honorary Professor Gary Trompf, Professor Iain Gardner, Dr Jay Johnston and Dr Chris Hartney, for their constructive comment. Similarly, my thanks go to Dr Peter Oldmeadow and other members of the Australasian Association of Buddhist Studies (AABS) for their encouragement, and to my fellow doctoral candidates and friends—especially Dr Katharine Buljan, Dr Andrew McGarrity, Dr John Wu and Dr Sarah Penicka-Smith—whose inspiration I value. I wish also to thank Dr Sally McAra from Auckland University's Department of Anthropology for her friendship and support.

And finally, thank you Denis for being always there for me, for the endless hours that you devoted to listening to my deliberations, and—in their final phases—for providing the support that I needed during the writing of my thesis and this book.

Glossary

Term	Use
Aggregates	Khandha (Pali). Skandha (Skt). The five heaps or components that collectively constitute the human being: form, feeling, perception, volitional factors, and consciousness
BMIMC	The Blue Mountains Insight Meditation Centre, at Medlow Bath, NSW, Australia
Bodhicitta (Skt)	The state-of-mind of a bodhisattva. A key term in Mahayana Buddhism, and one of the three principal aspects of the Mahayana path *(The Three Principals of the Path)*: renunciation, bodhicitta, and wisdom-realizing emptiness.
Bodhisattva (Skt)	The embodiment of the spiritual ideal of Mahayana Buddhism. The bodhisattva generates the aspiration to achieve enlightenment for the sake of all sentient beings, and cultivates the six perfections.
Brahmaviharas (Pali, Skt)	The four sublime states of mind: compassion, lovingkindness, sympathetic joy and equanimity.
Concentration	Samatha (Pali, Skt). The meditation technique used to achieve the state of one-pointedness of mind.
Dana (Pali)	Generosity. An Asian-derived practice that involves giving to others.
Deity Yoga	A key meditative practice of Tantric Buddhism in which the visualized image of the deity is used as a model of the enlightened attributes within oneself.
Dependent Origination	The Buddhist doctrine that teaches that all phenomena arise in dependence on causes and conditions, and lack intrinsic being.
Dhamma (Pali) Dharma (Skt)	Denotes three things: the natural order that underpins the physical and moral spheres, the Buddhist teachings, and the phenomena that constitute the word. It refers mainly to the fourth satipatthana in this work.
Dukkha (Pali) Duhkha (Skt)	There is no direct English translation, although 'suffering' is most commonly used. While I prefer the terms 'unsatisfactoriness' or 'unrest', I have used suffering throughout the book, following the way the term is most commonly understood by vipassana and Vajrayana practitioners.

(Continued)

Term	Use
Emptiness	Sunnata (Pali). Sunyata (Skt). The Mahayana doctrine that all phenomena are empty of intrinsic existence.
Five Lay Precepts	To abstain from killing, stealing, false speech, sexual misconduct and taking intoxicants
Four Noble Truths	The four foundational propositions of Buddhist doctrine: the truth of suffering; suffering arises because of craving; the end of suffering is Nirvana (Skt); the way to Nirvana is the Noble Eight-fold Path.
FPMT	The Foundation for the Preservation of the Mahayana Tradition, a world-wide Gelugpa Tibetan organization
Gelugpa (Tib.)	One of the four main schools of Tibetan Buddhism, founded by Tsong-kha-pa in the Fourteenth Century CE
Gompa (Tib.)	A meditation-room or -hall
Hindrances	The five mental states held to be the main impediments to the development of both concentration and insight meditation: sense-desire, aversion, sloth and torpor, restlessness and doubt
Impression Point	Dilthey's notion of a symbolic phenomenon in which a new understanding of self and symbol system, and a feeling of commitment are all generated at once
Lam Rim	A class of Tibetan literature which outlines the stages of the path to enlightenment. Tsong-kha-pa's work Lam-rim Chenmo is the foundational text for the FPMT.
Madhyamaka (Skt)	The Middle School, which advocates a middle course between extreme practices and theories. It was founded by Nagarjuna in the Second Century CE, and later transmitted from India to Tibet.
Mahayana	One of the three vehicles of Buddhism, emphasizing the values of compassion and insight, and the ideal of the bodhisattva
Merit	Punna (Pali). Punya (Skt). Good karma; the result or potential result of right or wholesome action
Metta (Pali)	A meditation based on generation of lovingkindness to all beings equally, in order to develop equanimity
Mindfulness	Sati (Pali). Smrti (Skt). An alert state of mind cultivated as the foundation for insight
Nibbana (Pali) Nirvana (Skt)	The goal of the Eightfold Path, attainment of which marks the end of samsaric existence
Noble Eightfold Path	The path that leads from samsara to nirvana. The eight factors are placed in three groups: wisdom, ethics and concentration. In teachings at VI these three are referred to as the three higher trainings.

(Continued)

Term	Use
Principals, The Three	The Three Principals (*principal aspects*) of the (Mahayana) Path to enlightment: renunciation, bodhicitta, and wisdom-realizing emptiness.
Samsara (Pali, Skt)	The cycle of repeated birth and death that human beings undergo until they attain Nirvana (Skt)
Sangha (Pali)	The community of ordained nuns and monks
Satipatthana Sutta	The foundational sutta for the Vipassana method of Mahasi Sayadaw, outlining the practice of the Four Foundations of Mindfulness
Satipatthanas (Pali)	The foundations of mindfulness: body, feelings, mind, and dhammas
Sutta (Pali) Sutra (Skt)	A discourse of the Buddha. In the Pali Canon, texts are grouped in the second of the three pitakas.
Tantra	A class of Mahayana treatise claiming to provide a rapid means of attaining enlightenment. Within the Mahayana, enlightenment may be gained by sutric or tantric practice.
Theravada	One of the three vehicles of Buddhism. It is characterized by fidelity to the texts of the Pali Canon.
Three Marks of Existence	Dukkha, anicca, anatta (Pali). Duhkha, anitya, anatman (Skt). Translated as suffering, impermanence, not-self.
Vajrayana (Skt)	Tantric Buddhism: one of the three vehicles of Buddhism, although sometimes thought of as a branch of the Mahayana
VI	The Vajrayana Institute at Ashfield, NSW, Australia, affiliated with the FPMT
Vipassana (Pali) Vipasyana (Skt)	Insight Meditation: the form of meditation predominantly practised at BMIMC

Chapter 1

Approaching the *Western Buddhist* Experience

Introduction

The fundamental purpose of this book is to explore and articulate what it means, for the practitioners and adherents of the two forms of Western Buddhism, to be a Western Buddhist. It accomplishes this by exploring practitioners' engagement with the religious activity at two Australian Buddhist Centres: the Blue Mountains Insight Meditation Centre (BMIMC) at Medlow Bath in the Blue Mountains, west of Sydney, and Vajrayana Institute (VI) at Ashfield, in Sydney's Inner West.

By 'religious engagement', I mean the nature of religious belief, practice, experience, personal transformation and commitment of the affiliates of both Centres, and the shaping and maintenance of these by the religious cultures of the Centres. The book also aims to describe the way in which Buddhism meets the expectations and needs of the practitioners affiliated with the Centres. Throughout, the study maintains a synchronic perspective. An exploration of the way in which these two Buddhist Centres were founded and developed, while historically significant, would distract the study from the exploration of contemporary Anglo-Australian Buddhist discourse, practice and sensibilities as they are embodied in the activity of the Centres. The history of Buddhism in the West is well documented in other works, as is information about demographics, ethnic identity and migrant history. Notable Australian publications in this vein are Paul Croucher's *Buddhism in Australia 1848–1988*,[1] a historical survey, and the more recent publication by Enid Adam and Phillip Hughes, *The Buddhists in Australia*, based on 1996 Census-data[2] of the Commonwealth of Australia. By comparison, Patricia Sherwood's *The Buddha Is in the Street: Engaged Buddhism in Australia* explores more of the ethos of Australia's Western Buddhists.[3]

Through this book, it is my intention to add to the understanding of the subjective experience of being a Buddhist in a Western—and largely Anglo-Australian—context, and of how Buddhist doctrine and practice, as it is mediated by the organization, is understood and applied by the individual. In this, I hope to complement studies with a more pragmatic demographic, social, historical or political focus and address the lack of research about the 'mental cultures' of Western Buddhist centres in Australia noted by Michelle Barker (nee Spuler) in 2000.[4] The current work concerns itself with an individual's encounter with, socialization into and appropriation of the worldview of a Buddhist centre as a taken-for-granted reality,[5] a coherent picture of reality as if it were an object existing prior to our awareness of it, and which an individual acquires through socialization into it.

In so doing, this study corresponds to the last of Tweed's four phases of Buddhist studies in the West, i.e. contemporary expressions.[6] Much has been written about the shaping effects of globalization and cross-cultural translation on contemporary Buddhist forms, organizations and their local centres in the West: for instance, by Baumann in Germany[7] and Waterhouse,[8] Bell[9] and Kay[10] in Britain. While I am sensitive to concern about the tendency of some Western scholars both to privilege studies of the Western-convert experience of Buddhist traditions over those of Buddhism's historical development and cross-cultural translation—and thereby to endow the Buddhism currently practised by Westerners with the reputation of authenticity[11]—a work of this scope is necessarily limited in its capacity to explore the shaping effects of historical and cross-cultural factors, and notably of Western modernization, on the two Centres in this study. The foregrounding of attainment of states of consciousness through disciplined meditation practice as a Western development—notably critiqued by Sharf[12]—is a strong characteristic of the activity of both Centres. For this reason, a recurring theme throughout this book is the practitioner's appreciation of the transformation of mental states through meditation.

The Nature of Western Buddhism and the Western-Buddhist Identity

Scholars distinguish the form of Buddhism emergent among its Western adherents from forms practised in Asia and by immigrant groups in Western countries.[13] According to Conze, Prebish, Coleman and Rocha, it is characterized by a strong emphasis on doctrinal study and meditation practice.[14] By contrast, according to Rocha, ethnic practices are generally defined as devotional and merit-making, and the repository of the group's cultural identity.[15] This Western Buddhism also draws on three principal Asian-Buddhist traditions: Zen from East Asia, vipassana from the Theravadin tradition, and Vajrayana from Tibet,[16] and also on the common foundations of all Buddhist schools:[17] the *Four Noble Truths*, the *Noble Eight-Fold Path* and the meditative practices of *mindfulness, concentration* and *lovingkindness*.[18] Coleman adds that the central focus of Western Buddhists is 'direct religious experience and the personal transformation it produces'.[19] Layman refers to a meditational Buddhism. She refers to the North Americans who practise because of the personality changes they attribute to meditation: increased warmth and friendliness, spontaneity, improved disposition, alleviated anxiety and depression, better physical health, a sense of purpose and direction, improved concentration, better self-control, awakening of creativity, a reduction in ego-centredness and a lessened attachment to material things.[20]

Drawing a distinction between Western 'convert' Buddhists and Asian 'ethnic' Buddhists highlights basic differences in the function of religious identity. Ethnic Buddhism functions to maintain a stable identity through the maintenance of an ethnic group's cohesive way of life and heritage, whereas convert Buddhism's function is transformative, providing an alternative religious identity to the one provided by one's primary religious socialization.[21] Although Baumann and Rocha argue for a more-nuanced approach, citing evidence to demonstrate shifting boundaries,[22] the distinction is useful in illuminating a functional characteristic of the Western Buddhist identity. However, I believe that Cadge's conceptions of *ascribed* and *achieved* identities[23] have more to recommend them for the current purpose than the terms 'ethnic' and 'convert', in that the sense of religious change as an achievement rather than as a conversion is in agreement with other theoretical approaches to religious change supported by my data, as I discuss below. Despite this, the nature of one's identity as a Western Buddhist is thought to be complex. Bryant and Lamb raise the complexities introduced by the phenomena of serial conversion and religious pluralism.[24] Add to which, Layman, Nattier and Tweed draw attention to the large number of self-defined Buddhists with no formal Buddhist affiliation, a category of Buddhist sympathizer that Tweed refers to as 'night-stands', i.e. those who read and incorporate Buddhist ideas into their life.[25] A variety of means has been suggested: using criteria such as taking refuge or the five lay vows, holding certain beliefs, meditating and chanting, or active membership in a specific organization.[26] Rather than utilizing objective means for the determination of identity, I have allowed the participants in this study to speak for themselves. The question of how religious identity is determined, while relevant, is secondary to my research concern of how changes to one's inner life and sense-of-self, and to one's sense of reality, are effected by one's involvement in Buddhism.

The attraction of Westerners to doctrinal, practical and experiential elements of traditional Buddhist systems[27] suggests that any successful explanation of conversion in the Western Buddhist context must account for the role of Buddhist doctrine, practice and the experience it produces. In other words, what are the substantive elements, the *substance* of belief as well as the functional,[28] in the conversion and commitment process? Although the beliefs and practices of Western Buddhist organizations are Asian-derived,[29] the choice is thought to be shaped by Western freedom and liberty to select what appeals—amongst the variety of Buddhist traditions and schools currently available—under the direction of Westerners' own needs, tastes and sentiments. Fronsdal notes that giving

American vipassana students pragmatic and experiential goals—without the support of traditional Theravadin doctrinal frameworks and motivations—appears to reduce vipassana in the West to a form of therapy.[30] Similarly, Urban maintains that Tantra may be reduced to a hedonistic and pleasure-affirming spirituality in the West.[31] The current Western preoccupation with self can be seen in various aspects of the contemporary religious counter-culture. Numerous scholars have written about the relationship between religious-identity construction and the consumer-culture;[32] the growth of self-religion facilitated by the 'religious supermarket'; the aim at the heart of New Age religion of sacralizing the self and the cosmos;[33] and the self-constructing activity observed in Neo-Paganism.[34] I feel that, given the amount of freedom to choose and the seemingly limitless number of options provided in the current climate, it is all the more relevant to determine how Buddhism is approached and understood by those who are 'trying it out'. As I found when I began to consider which Buddhist organizations might be suited to the aims of my study, in Sydney alone there are so many different Buddhist centres that it was hard to know where to begin.

The Western Buddhist Ethnographic field in Sydney

On conducting an initial survey of the Western-convert Buddhist milieu in Sydney,[35] I found it to be at once diffuse and complex, comprising many organizations from various Buddhist traditions, and some—such as the Buddhist Library in Camperdown, Sydney—that were not affiliated with any specific form of Buddhism. Two ways of viewing the field were suggested: the first as a single religious subculture with many manifestations, and the second as a collection of institutions or organizations, each with its own comparatively separate religious culture. A related consideration was whether my research should evenly represent the three most popular forms of Buddhism in the West: vipassana from the Theravadin tradition, and Zen and Tibetan Buddhism from the Mahayana.[36] However, this posed more decisions about which of the multitude of organizations representing these forms to approach. Some preliminary fieldwork conducted with BMIMC (Theravadin), VI and Rigpa[37] (Tibetan Buddhist, but Gelugpa and Nyingma respectively), and *Friends of the Western Buddhist Order* (FWBO), which draws upon the entire Buddhist tradition,[38] gave me an understanding of the individual organizations' beliefs, practices, teaching activities and social structure. It also demonstrated the diversity of Buddhist doctrine, practice, social organization and teaching formats that could be found in different Buddhist organizations.

The second view, of organizations as discrete religious cultures, seemed more true to the Western Buddhist reality. Also, taking into account the needs of a comparative study, it seemed more methodologically sound to compare material from two or more groups that could be compared along doctrinal, practical and experiential lines, rather than to interview individuals from a diffuse religious culture wherein lines of comparison would be difficult to draw. As outlined above, Western Buddhists are, in the main, 'convert' Buddhists. Conversion models are frequently generated from single-group studies wherein the nature of the group's shared reality is assumed to be shared by all participants. Comparing Buddhist groups with commonalities and differences in doctrinal, practical and experiential approach should provide two levels of comparison: between participants affiliated with the same centre, and between the respective religious cultures of the centres selected. This enabled me to narrow my choice of organizations to what was both manageable for and relevant to the aims of my study.

BMIMC and VI were selected for several significant reasons. First, with the exception of tantric initiation at VI, both Centres allowed access to their full range of activities. This had to be borne in mind; I needed to access and understand the nature and range of religious and social activity, and its role in maintaining and propagating the Centre's shared reality, within the time-constraints imposed by researching and writing a Ph.D. thesis. Conversely, Rigpa appeared to be designed to field newcomers into a program of introductory meditation courses that would occupy them for a year or so. Second, the FWBO appeared to be somewhat eclectic in its mix of Buddhist ideas and practices compared with the adherence, at BMIMC and VI, to the writings of one founder. This was despite that the inclusion of the FWBO would have provided an interesting contrast with the other two. With consideration for the limitations of time and space, I decided to focus on the two organizations that came to provide the subject matter for this study, viz. BMIMC, as which it is succinctly known, and VI, as it is affectionately known amongst its participants. Hereafter, I cite both Centres by their initials only.

Vipassana and Vajrayana settings: The Two Centres

In addition to the brief comments above with respect to the influence of Western modernization on the two centres, the BMIMC and VI, discussion here pertains to the ways in which the two centres can be *compared and contrasted* for the purposes of the study. First, the religious activity of each draws on traditional textual material to inform the teachings of its practices. The teaching and religious activities of both Centres exhibit a consistent adherence to their doctrinal foundations. While not initially apparent to a new participant, the teachings and practices of both organizations offer a slow, structured progression on the path to enlightenment. Rawlinson's model of experiential comparative religion categorizes the nature of Eastern traditions embraced in the West according to two pairs of opposites: 'hot and cool' and 'structured and unstructured'. 'Hot and cool' contrast otherness and numinosity with self-realization, while 'structured and unstructured' contrast an inherent order in the cosmos that needs to be discovered.[39] According to this model, both groups are classified as structured, but Theravada is classified as cool and Vajrayana as hot.[40] Of the list of characteristics that Rawlinson outlines for each, a comparison of hot and cool structured with respect to soteriology appears to hold for the two traditions, at least superficially. Hot structured Buddhist soteriology sees 'everything in *samsara* as sacred, and that one should live as though this is true', while cool structured sees 'learning how samsara operates' as the way to liberation.

However, Rawlinson's description of cool structured, 'Liberation is within oneself but it must be uncovered by disciplined practice'[41] is more subtantially applicable to both. As discussion in Chapters 2 and 4 show, the gradual step-wise approach taken to the acquisition of insight into the nature of reality is explained in the textual sources for the practice in each case, namely, Mahasi Sayadaw's Thirteen Stages of Insight Knowledge[42] and Tsong-kha-pa's Lam Rim Chen Mo.[43] Despite the apparent differences between the *Foundation for the Preservation of the Mahayana Tradition* (FPMT) and the vipassana Buddhism of Mahasi Sayadaw, it seems that the essentially structured nature of both appeals to those individuals, including myself, who take the experimental approach to religious involvement, and facilitates their gradual comprehension of the *meaning-system* of each organization. However, these similarities would be evident to a participant/practitioner only after some involvement—from weeks to months—with the group and after exposure to its range of teachings and activities. From the perspective of the potential participant, the most obvious difference between the two is the retreat format at BMIMC and the classroom-style of VI. With exposure, differences in meditation practices and the different Theravada and Mahayana doctrinal emphases would become apparent, as would differences in the nature of religious activity and social organization and interaction.

The BMIMC is Theravadin, and it facilitates teaching and practice of vipassana meditation in the method of Mahasi Sayadaw of Burma. This practice is doctrinally based on the *Satipatthana Sutta* from the *Majjhima Nikaya* of the Pali Canon.[44] BMIMC primarily offers meditation retreats ranging from two days' to one month's duration, and also some one- or two-day workshops.

In distinction, VI is affiliated with the worldwide FPMT under the directorship of Lama Thubten Zopa Rinpoche, the successor to Lama Thubten Yeshe. The FPMT takes the writings of Lama Tsong-kha-pa, the acknowledged founder of the Tibetan Gelugpa Order who drew on the work of Lama Atisha and the earlier *Kadampa* Order, as its scriptural authority. Besides Tsong-kha-pa's *Lam Rim, The Great Treatise on the Stages of the Path to Enlightenment*, the FPMT also draws on a variety of Mahayana sutric and tantric literature, including root texts composed by key figures of the lineage. VI offers a variety of beginners and advanced courses in various aspects of the Gelugpa path to Enlightenment. Because of the difference in teaching styles, the nature of social engagement differs between the two Centres. These characteristics are explored in Chapters 2 and 4, which outline how teaching and learning occurs at the two Centres.

A difference in orientation to practice and the motivation behind it is highlighted by a consideration of the traditionalist–modernist distinction, made by Baumann and others, based on the adherence to the doctrine of karma and rebirth as a rationale for thought and practice. Traditionalist forms retain the performance of devotional practices and merit-making as a means to acquire better conditions in this and future lives, whereas the modernist emphasis on personal cultivation through study and meditation appears to be for improving one's conditions in this life.[45] BMIMC, being devoted to the vipassana meditation method of Mahasi Sayadaw, itself a revitalization movement in Burma,[46] is more modernist in its orientation than VI. While the doctrine of karma and rebirth is present in religious discourse, BMIMC's activity consists mainly of meditation and doctrinal study, with ritual limited to chanting the precepts in Pali at the beginning of retreats, and in the mornings on most retreats. Conversely, a traditionalist orientation is exhibited by VI's merit-making activities, and the centrality of the doctrine of karma and rebirth to its teachings. More precisely, however, VI's emphasis on doctrinal study and meditation alongside traditional ritual such as pujas and sadhanas, and prayers and chanting before and after teachings, shows it to have characteristics of both orientations, traditionalist and modernist. An interesting effect of this, as I observe in Chapter 4, is that participants appear to engage initially in VI's religious activity from a modernist orientation, and through their exposure to merit-making activities and their interpretive framework based on the doctrine of karma and rebirth, attempt to accommodate these more traditional notions into their thinking.

Approaches to Understanding Religious Change

As convert Buddhists, Western Buddhists come to worldviews, and methods of engagement therewith, to which they are not native. I have chosen to use the term *commitment* to denote the stage of change in affiliation most typically taken to indicate a religious conversion, to separate it from the 'theoretical problematics' traditionally associated with the term religious conversion. Most notable is its definition as radical personal change, and as something that 'happens to' a convert rather than as something sought after by the individual. The term religious conversion is presently understood to refer to religious change in a general sense.[47] However, it is understood and accepted to be a complex process involving personal, cultural, social and religious dimensions.[48] Of the many models formulated in response to the almost infinite number of views of conversion, possibly the most universally applicable is Rambo's seven-stage model, which attempts to account for the field of influences that bear on the phenomenon.[49]

Most conversion models appear to be generated from single-group studies,[50] and cannot be assumed to have general applicability. In my search for models that might provide an initial approach with which to make some preliminary interpretations of the data at hand, two were found to be appropriate, and were pressed into service as precursors to theoretical elaboration of the data concerned. These were Berger's principle of conversion as *religious resocialization*,[51] and Lofland and Skonovd's *experimental motif*,[52] both of which are to be outlined presently. Apart from this, the thoughts of a number of other scholars tend to express the sentiments and manner of approach to Buddhism held by the Western Buddhists concerned. Chief among these is the notion of participants as active seekers, and their exploration as a process of experimental participation. Others are conversion as a self-transformation,[53] a change in the self-concept,[54] and as a trend towards treating religions 'less as systems of truth than as efforts to discover a ground of being that orients and orders experience more generally'.[55] The last of these accurately reflects the spirit in which the Buddhist view of reality and salvation appears to be embraced by the adherents of both forms of Buddhism in this study.

Historically, the essential nature of conversion has been seen as change to one's self or identity and to one's worldview, often denoted by the term 'universe of discourse', from *symbolic interactionism*. Travisano's definition of conversion as a 'radical reorganization of identity, meaning, and life',[56] and Heirich's as 'the process of changing a sense of root reality',[57] were frequently employed in scholarly research during the 1970s and 1980s.[58] Categorizations of conversion types based on the distinction between complete or partial internal movement typically take Nock's conversion-adhesion distinction,[59] or symbolic interactionist Richard Travisano's conversion-alternation distinction[60] as their foundation. Categorizations of this type are based first on whether the transformation is complete or partial, and on whether the new universe of discourse is at the centre or the periphery of the individual's reality-picture. Second, they employ the substantive relation between the old and new universes of discourse and how such movement facilitates identity-change.[61] Much research has been based on the traditional implication of radical personal change at the heart of conversions. In 1984, Snow and Machalek drew attention to the scholarly debate about whether conversion involves sudden, gradual or multiple and serial changes, but noted that the notion of radical change remained central to all conceptions of conversion. They and Richardson observed that the term was used in different ways, without clear definition.[62]

Over the previous few decades, notably since the 1970s, the radical-change thesis has decreased in influence for two reasons. First, scholars maintain that such radical internal transformation is not easily observed.[63] Second is the acceptance of the active conversion paradigm. Based on James's identification of two conversion types according to the active or passive nature of the convert, 'volitional conversion and the conversion of self-surrender',[64] in 1985 Richardson posited the existence of an alternative active paradigm which questioned 'the traditional assumption of a passive subject and a deterministic model'.[65] This paradigm, as Granqvist notes, describes conversions as being more gradual and less transforming of the self.[66] Amongst others to question these prior assumptions were Downton, who theorized conversion as an evolutionary process as opposed to a radical change,[67] and Gussner and Berkowitz who questioned the disruption-neediness-belongingness thesis that dominated much of the literature on new religious movements in the 1980s.[68] Similarly, Volinn expressed the search for answers and meditative experience by those who participated in eastern meditation groups as a sense for the experiential, as a 'going towards' rather than as a 'fleeing from'.[69]

The view of the active convert, the religious seeker who experiments with religious beliefs and practices in order to effect processual identity-change, is currently widely accepted.[70] The conceptualization of the active participant possibly reaches its zenith in the thinking of Dawson, who sees self-definition and change at the heart of rational conversions which are reflectively monitored, based on the principle that rational actions are their own explanation. Dawson also argues for self-affirmation as opposed to the self-surrender implicit not only in the traditional view in the West, the *Pauline paradigm*—an imposition of a Christian conversion model onto all conversion data[71]—but also in models of conversion based on coercion, deprivation and neediness,[72] and on the assumption of psychological pathology or unstable identity.[73] This includes literature devoted to the study of the recruitment mechanisms utilized by religious groups to ensure commitment,[74] such as the forming of cult-affective bonds and the severment of beyond-group ties.[75]

From the understanding that conversions differ in a number of significant ways, several researchers have devised models that attempt to account for the phenomenological variations found in different religious contexts. These schemas aimed to account for large differences, highlighted by much research of the previous few decades, in both mainstream religion and new religious movements. Both classification schemes arrange conversion process types along a passive–active axis which attempts to account for the somewhat competing forces of the individual's set of needs and interests, and the socioreligious interests of the group.[76] A notable example is Lofland and Skonovd's conception of six conversion motifs,[77] conceived as salient thematic elements and key experiences combined with objective situations. They define *motif experience* itself as 'those aspects of a conversion which are most memorable and orienting to the person undergoing personal transformation'.[78]

Lofland and Skonovd's *experimental motif*

My early fieldwork-experience suggested the appropriateness of Lofland and Skonovd's experimental motif to the interpretation of the process of engagement and change exhibited by affiliates of both Centres. The experimental motif consists of 'a pragmatic, *show me* attitude', learning to act like a convert, and withholding judgement for a considerable length of time after taking up the life style of the fully committed participant. There is a relatively low level of social pressure and transformation of identity, behaviour and worldview that takes place over a relatively prolonged period, i.e. from months to years. It is held to operate in New Age, metaphysical types of groups and others where the prospective convert is encouraged to take an experimental attitude towards the group's ritual and organizational activities.[79] Their formulation draws on the work of Balch and Taylor with the Human Individual Metamorphosis (HIM) Movement, later renamed Heaven's Gate. Balch and Taylor's essential observation involved the way in which HIM participants did not exhibit signs of radical personal change, but saw their own involvement as a logical extension of their spiritual quest, as prescribed by the epistemological individualism of the cultic milieu.[80]

These passages come about as something allowed within Western religious culture itself. Much has been written about an alternative religious stream in the West. According to Campbell, while cultic groups are transitory, the cultic milieu is a constant feature of society, and is united and identified by the existence of an ideology of seekership and by seekership institutions.[81] This current has existed alongside Christianity since antiquity, in Ellwood's view.[82] Ellwood's view of the *Western Alternative Reality Tradition* is the most inclusive view of this current historically and substantively, which he sees as continuous with a current alternative to mainstream religion in Western culture since the Hellenic period, which includes Asian shamanistic influences. Its more-recent expression is in the religious counterculture that synthesizes and reinterprets earlier streams of religious thought.[83] Described by this culture are the religious seekers who effect exploration and change, thereby negotiating their own religious identities. Participants at both centres unanimously fit the profile of the religious seeker in that they undergo a process of trying out and evaluating belief structures and practices, both in their religious exploration *before* encounter with Buddhism, and as *part of their exploration*. The process is active and long, from months to years, and when commitment ensues, it is either a decision made privately or stated publicly by individuals, of their own volition.[84]

While the experimental motif accurately models the means of approach to religious change, it does not explain or define the nature of the change itself. Lofland and Skonovd themselves note that their motifs adduce types of change, but do not 'delineate steps, phases or processes within each type'.[85] Respondents' narratives illustrated the processual nature of personal change leading to commitment, and the outcome of experimental immersion to be the gradual acquisition of knowledge of the worldview and its frameworks of meaning. However, while socialization into a religious reality is facilitated by a variety of factors, including intellectual, emotional, experiential, aesthetic and social characteristics, the point of decision to commit to the religion appears to be fundamentally cognitive or intellectual in nature. Respondents from both Centres described a gradual intellectual process of evaluation and acceptance that included experiential and emotional components and that was marked or signposted by more than one point of apprehension, evaluation and decision. Significantly, these descriptions exhibited a correspondence to James' definition of volitional conversion as the regenerative, usually gradual building up of a new set of moral and spiritual habits, containing critical points where movement is more rapid.[86]

Respondents' descriptions of these points or moments also bear a striking resemblance to Stromberg's borrowing of Dilthey's impression point, 'the moment in the perceptual process when a complex phenomenon becomes a graspable, coherent unity to the perceiver'.[87] Stromberg's adaptation of Dilthey's conception to the understanding of conversion experiences, is rendered as: 'a symbolic phenomenon in which a new understanding of self, a new understanding of a symbol system, and a feeling of commitment are all generated at once'. In a sense, these three developments are inseparable, and better understood as three different perspectives on the same change than as separate processes. Stromberg successfully describes the central and ideal transformation process of the more intense of respondents' experiences when he states that 'as the actor forges a commitment to a set of symbols—elements of culture—those symbols reform the actor by becoming part of his or her new understanding of self'.[88] As a model for the conception of the instant of change that appears to elude theorists, it has some explanatory power for the two Western Buddhist contexts of interest, if two conditions are borne in mind. First, Stromberg's theoretical approach is generated from Christian conversion accounts, viz. from the experiences of St Paul and St Augustine and from other accounts collected during fieldwork. These accounts appear to convey much more of an intense emotional response to the moment in question than do the Buddhist accounts of interest.

The second condition is related. According to the interview data, these moments varied with respect to the effect on self, and the nature of the symbol involved. There is no one dominant symbol, set of symbols or symbolic representation of ideas that features in commitment accounts. Unlike conversion accounts offered by Jehovah's Witnesses that had to follow a standard symbolic rhetoric,[89] a standard symbolic representation of change is absent from the accounts at hand. Practitioners who reported this kind of experience cited a symbolic moment or a grasp of a symbolic representation that appears to be peculiar to them. Two further points of difference exist. Some respondents reported having more than one point or moment of this nature, and some added that their experience overall was more akin to an extended process with several of these markers. Each one was accompanied by the realization that they felt more involved with the new meaning-system than previously. In addition to this, some respondents did not appear to experience these moments of relative intensity. While they had invested effort in study, personal meditation practice and contemplation and were committed to the endeavour of learning and application of the new material, their descriptions convey the sense that their actions in exploration were intended to bring about transformation, but for most, their actions in commitment were the result of transformation.[90] This point is discussed in Chapter 6, which provides a comparative overview of the process.

Berger's phenomenological sociology

Lofland and Skonovd's approach can be seen to be phenomenological in that they attempt to 'adduce types of change' to isolate the essential types of conversion process from the mass of data generated by research. Two other phenomenological perspectives are found to be highly applicable to the task of 'delineating the steps, phases and processes' within the experimental type itself,[91] and this study utilizes the theoretical positions and frameworks of the two: the phenomenology of religion as a disciplinary outlook utilized in Religious Studies, and the phenomenological sociology of Peter Berger. The Phenomenology of Religion provides a useful frame from which to explore the elements of a meaning-system with which religious seekers may engage. One such frame is Smart's dimensional analysis of worldviews, consisting of seven dimensions of religious activity: the doctrinal, ritual, narrative, experiential, ethical, social and material.[92] The advantage of this disciplinary approach over others, e.g. the sociology or psychology of religion—wherein religious conversion studies constitute a subfield of enquiry[93]—is its manner of exploration and articulation of the modes and forms in which religion manifests itself,[94] rather than interpreting religion reductively in terms of psychological or social function. This morphological approach is employed throughout the study in the analysis, interpretation and reporting of data, an approach that is rendered more conducive to the aims of this book by the conscious attempt to empathize with the experiences and orientations of the religious participants.[95]

Towards similar ends, Berger's phenomenological sociology is employed to provide useful theoretical constructs within a theoretical frame of reference that facilitates articulation of the individual's manner of engagement with and appropriation of the new meaning-system. Central to the theoretical position of social-constructionist theories in general, to which Berger's approach belongs—notably socialization-theory, symbolic interaction,[96] role-theory and reference-group theory[97]—is the notion of socialization.[98] It is defined by Berger and Luckmann as 'the comprehensive and consistent induction of an individual into the objective world of a society or a sector of it'.[99] Berger explains the social world—in the ideal situation of a closed system or culture—in terms of a three-step dialectic, namely externalization, objectivation and internalization. Respectively, these refer to the ongoing outpouring of the human being into the social world in terms of physical and mental activity; by the products of this activity, the attainment of a reality that appears as a facticity external to its original producers; and the reappropriation of the same reality, transforming it from structures of the objective world into structures of the subjective consciousness.[100] Berger and Luckmann refer to processes of resocialization as they occur in a religious setting as alternations, or instances of near-total transformation,[101] which Berger defines as 'the possibility to choose between varying and sometimes contradictory systems of meaning'.[102]

According to Berger and Luckmann, complete movement between world-views or meaning-systems is not possible for two reasons. First, the authors maintain that subjective reality is never totally socialized.[103] Second, although alternations are held to resemble primary socialization—one's initial childhood socialization into society—because they need to replicate the childhood affective ties with significant others responsible for socialization, as distinct from the original socialization process, they need to dismantle the preceding structure of subjective reality. According to the authors' perspective, the most complete case of alternation as resocialization into a new meaning-system would involve a near-total transformation of subjective consciousness, which they see as impossible.[104] This, considered together with Paloutzian's view that socialization into a tradition takes place over a lifespan,[105] suggests that just as the preceding structure of subjective reality is never completely dismantled, so is it never completely built.

The comparison of religious biographies in Chapter 6 shows that nearly all respondents are from Christian backgrounds. Although two common routes of passage from Christianity to Buddhism are apparent—the first from Christianity straight into a form of Buddhism before involvement with either BMIMC or VI, and the second from original Christianity into some form of Western alternative religious or spiritual subculture—all respondents had been exposed to an alternative meaning-system of some type, and all had taken an experimental attitude to their spiritual, religious or self-growth involvements and affiliations. It was found that the alternative religious field provides access to Buddhism both in terms of passage through organizations and groups, and in terms of the intellectual and experiential structures of their shared reality.

As noted above, these passages come about as something allowed within Western religious culture itself. Dawson draws attention to the human existential dilemma of human autonomy versus socialization underlying the postulate 'rational action is its own explanation'. For people's actions to be seen as self-directed and expressive of their authentic preferences, they must be able to stand apart from the products of their own socialization. Because, as many besides Dawson hold, our thoughts, feelings and actions are the products of primary and secondary socializations, this capacity to be objective or reflexive is itself part of one's socialization, and therefore present as an idea in one's culture.[106] To recapitulate the theoretical argument to this point, two issues are accorded centrality. First, one can never entirely transform the imprint of one's original interpretive frameworks through religious change,[107] and second, passage from Christianity to Buddhism appears to be facilitated by passage through forms of Western alternative spirituality, a passage prescribed by the surrounding culture. A third consideration at this point indicates what can be realistically determined about the nature of such religious passage.

Fieldwork data gathered by participation and interview highlight the impossibility of determining the substantive constitution of complete internalization of either Buddhist perspective. The doctrinal foundations and textual material are vast for both forms of Buddhism. Vipassana meditation, including the Satipatthana vipassana of Mahasi Sayadaw, draws on the entire Pali Canon for its doctrinal and philosophical foundations. Similarly, the Gelugpa lineage draws on much Mahayana material, besides the writings of lineage leaders such as Lama Tsong-kha-pa, Lama Atisha, Lamas Yeshe and Zopa and the fourteenth Dalai Lama, Tenzin Gyatso. What can be demonstrated from the fieldwork data is what practitioners typically learn, apply to their own understandings of experience and accept. There is a clear indication of the religious material involved in the socialization and commitment process. As stated above, what can be demonstrated is the role that specific doctrines and practices appear to play in acculturation to and acceptance of the Buddhist meaning-system. It will be shown that commitment is conditional upon accepting and employing the three marks of samsaric existence, *dukkha,* 'suffering' and *anatman,* 'no essentially existing self' (in Sanskrit) as an interpretive framework for lived reality; the three groups of the Eight-Fold Path, ethics, concentration and wisdom as a strategy for negotiating lived experience; and meditation techniques specific to the particular Buddhist orientation as a method for applying doctrinal principles to one's own transformation. What is thereby demonstrated, by determining the role of doctrine and practice in these processes, is the way in which Westerners are socialized into a Western Buddhist shared reality.

Commitment to a Buddhist perspective can be seen as a response to the way in which these doctrines and practices facilitate comprehension of the worldview, and in turn promote self-transformation in the practitioners. In this sense, commitment can be seen as one's response to the knowledge that one acquires through interaction with the meaning-system of the Buddhist centre of one's affiliation. Further, this response has a quality of intention and 'orientation towards', as if respondents' commitment is the expression of an intensification of intention towards internalization, rather than as a result of it as the end-point of socialization. As the discussion in Chapter 6 shows, adherents' accounts indicate that they adopt the Buddhist perspective as their primary authority, but in the sense conveyed by Heirich in his reference to scholarly literature 'which treats religion less as systems of truth than as efforts to discover a ground of being that orients and orders experience more generally'.[108] This reflects the way in which the Buddhist meaning-system is viewed and utilized by practitioners. It is not accepted as an absolute internal authority, but more as a guide to interpretation of personal experience.

Heirich's view is useful in one other respect, viz. his view of conversion and commitment as two qualitatively different processes. The former is a dramatic turnabout, either adopting a new belief system or returning to a former one with new intensity, and the latter a qualitatively different process where 'there is qualitative change in experience and in level of commitment, regardless of previous mindset'.[109] This usage must be distinguished from others that do not convey the same qualitative difference. Harrison's distinction between 'conversion' and 'commitment', where the latter is the renewal or regeneration of existing beliefs as opposed to the adoption of new beliefs,[110] is similar to Snow and Machalek's use of 'alternation' and 'regeneration' to denote processes of change where there is no disruption to an individual's existing worldview.[111] Ultimately, my use of the term commitment is determined by the quality of activity presented in research data, irrespective of other researchers' use of the term. The term commitment is used in this book to denote the process of comprehension and adoption of the Buddhist perspective by Western practitioners of the two forms of Buddhism explored.

The resocialization thesis and the problem of *internalization*

Religious change is understood to occur through the interaction of a range of forces, individual and collective as well as intellectual and emotional, that serve ideological and existential needs. Berger and Luckmann maintain that a successful religious resocialization has to include both social and conceptual conditions, with 'the social serving as the matrix for the conceptual'. They see the availability of an effective plausibility structure as the most important social condition, which is mediated to the individual by means of significant others. This is because significant others represent the plausibility structure in the roles they play with regard to the individual, roles that are defined in terms of their resocializing function. Berger and Luckmann maintain that, in this way, the cognitive and affective focus of the individual's world is the plausibility structure.[112] Symbolic interactionists are divided over the question of which is the dominant factor in people's choice of religious group: the worldview or perspective of the group, or the individuals (one's new significant others) who share the perspective. Some appear to emphasize the role of significant others or one's *reference group* above the appeal of the belief system for the individual undergoing religious change.[113]

I suggest that truly active, intellectual-type conversions are apparent only in religious environments where social pressures are minimal, and where the cognitive process is free to function unencumbered by social moulding as distinct from social facilitation. While there is no doubt that differences exist between individuals in terms of response style,[114] I suggest that the religious change itself, as distinct from the surrounding social forces and processes that facilitate it, is essentially a cognitive process. At BMIMC, vipassana meditation is taught under retreat conditions with the observance of *Noble Silence* for much of the time. It is highly probable that this religious environment allows for individual exploration to occur under the least amount of social influence or pressure. By comparison, this process, as it takes place in the environment of VI, is more open to social influence and shaping because of the style of social interaction and the performance of the refuge ceremony, and the rationale it offers as to why taking refuge helps one's progress. However, this is to be interpreted as encouragement rather than as pressure.

Speaking in terms of primary socialization, where internalization is defined as 'the reabsorption into consciousness of the objectivated world so that its structures come to determine the subjective structures of consciousness itself', Berger maintains that one is socialized through the effectiveness of internalization. On the basis of his distinction between apprehension of the social world as an external facticity and its internalization as 'the formative influence on the subjective structures of consciousness', Berger maintains that a crucial dimension of socialization is missed by seeing it as a learning process without the subsequent step of internalization.[115] Wentworth, supporting his own argument for a 'socialization as interaction' model to replace the 'socialization as internalization' model, reframes socialization as 'the process of acquisition' and 'what the novice does to accept experience' to avoid both confusing 'the social-nurturing activity with a cognitive process' and the 'connotation of a purely passive subject'.[116] Of the two approaches, Wentworth's is the more theoretically tenable in the light of my findings, which support the active conversion paradigm. Participants do not passively absorb religious beliefs as if they were merely injected into consciousness, but actively question and assess the information before them. Further, in religious environments that allow for experimental participation, the distinction between learning and internalization becomes a methodological consideration. The researcher must be sensitive to the difference between the participant's acquiring knowledge about beliefs, and taking them on as their own, a distinction made by Spiro in his study of the acquisition of the meaning of culturally-constituted beliefs.[117]

According to Spiro, the process of acquisition of doctrinal meanings as personal beliefs, i.e. propositions 'concerning human beings, society and the world that are held to be true', happens in five stages. D'Andrade refers to these as five levels of internalization, which he defines as 'the process by which cultural representations become a part of the individual'.[118] These are: (1) to learn about them, become acquainted with them, (2) to understand their traditional meanings as they are interpreted in authoritative texts or by recognized specialists, (3) to believe doctrines so defined to be true, (4) the same as (3), but doctrines also inform the behavioural environment of social actors, serving to structure their perceptual worlds and guide their actions, and (5) the same as (4), but also serve to instigate action, and therefore have motivational as well as cognitive properties.[119] As discussion throughout the next five chapters show, it is possible to become conversant in the doctrinal meanings that comprise the taken-for-granted reality of the group without necessarily believing them to be true for oneself, as represented by level 2 of Spiro's model. One can come to understand doctrinal meanings as they are interpreted in authoritative texts or by a centre's teachers. I accomplished this by participant observation, that is, by attending the religious activities at each Centre and learning the doctrinal meanings and meditation techniques, but at the end, remained sympathetic rather than committed.

Spiro's six-fold method for investigating a culturally constituted belief involves the following: (1) describe the cultural doctrine which is the basis for the belief, (2) ascertain the doctrine's traditional meanings, (3) delineate its relationship to the other doctrines comprising the system, (4) explicate the structure of the system, (5) uncover the grounds for the actor's accepting the doctrine as their own belief, and (6) discover the functions of holding this belief, the consequences, either for the social actors or their society.[120] My methodological point is this. Stages 1 and 2 of Spiro's internalization model can be studied by participant observation, utilizing steps 1–4 of his investigative method, which involves uncovering the framework of ideas that comprise a group's shared reality, the meanings of individual doctrines or concepts, and the inter-relationships between them. This is the language that participants communicate with. Beyond this, the other stages involve the manner in which the individual appropriates the belief system as their own, and their own reasons for doing so. Levels 3–5 of internalization refer to a doctrine being held as true and having both cognitive and motivational properties, and steps 5 and 6 of the investigative model refer to the grounds for and consequences of holding the belief. I found these aspects of participants' engagement with the belief system much more effectively uncovered by interview wherein respondents were better placed to answer questions about their reasons for accepting particular doctrines. Even so, I maintain that it is impossible to determine whether complete internalization has taken place. Although Spiro's fourth level of internalization, where doctrines serve to structure the perceptual worlds of individuals and guide their actions, may indicate the point at which a belief can be said to have been internalized, without reference to follow-up data concerning long-term belief-maintenance, it is difficult to state whether complete belief-commitment has been attained. What can be reported is what the respondent believes in—what they are committed to as the truth—at the time of interview.

The *experimental* model of commitment

The contribution of role-theory to the active paradigm posits the participant as adopting the role of the adherent by outwardly conforming to a prescribed set of role-expectations, values and norms of a group, and by learning the group's language and interpretive schemes.[121] This approach reaches its zenith in Dawson's combination of rational choice theory and role-theory, which he calls reflexive role re-enactment, where role-taking becomes increasingly about role-making: fashioning one's self-concept.[122] Notable among researchers who in the 1980s applied a role-theory approach to the understanding of learning and transformation processes in Asian-based meditation groups are Wilson,[123] Preston[124] and Volinn.[125] These studies focus on the participant's approach to learning the behaviours of the meditator and the associated meanings of the practice(s) in order to access experiential states prescribed by the group's meaning-system. Wilson explores the way in which personal change is effected by the giving up of assumed rigid role-expectations of being a yogi, and instead freeing the impulsive and spontaneous elements of the personality from the socially conditioned component.[126] Preston's study of American Zen examines, among other inter-related issues, the process of learning to produce and label experiential states as a way of gaining membership status in a group.[127] Similarly, McIntyre describes the learning process for vipassana practitioners as their assuming the role of the meditator, but as his theorization takes place within the context of adult education, it does not explore the learning of doctrine in any depth except to say that in acquiring the meditator's perspective, one learns the practice and understandings associated with the learning-context.[128] In each of these cases, the researcher does not attempt to deal with comprehension of the meaning-system underpinning the practice beyond what was directly associated with the technical aspects of learning the practice.

Conversely, the aim of this study is to explain how meaning is attributed to experiences generated in meditation by the application of doctrine, and further, how meanings are accessed and selected from the range of doctrinal material available to the practitioner. This is accomplished by the role theoretical approach to the understanding of how participants access, begin to make sense of, and apply the religious material that they encounter, with the limitation that while it models the actor's orientation towards the transformation event, it cannot describe the exact point of change but only indicate the manner of approach. It is at this point that other theoretical approaches are necessary to understand the change itself. In terms of the overall process, apprehension, validation and acceptance of the meaning-system is gradual. One's commitment to learning and application increases in intensity from the time of engagement until the decision point is reached.

Based on my interpretation of the data collected through fieldwork conducted at the two Centres, I propose a model of commitment consisting of three cumulative stages: (1) apprehension and engagement, (2) comprehension and (3) commitment. The decisions about appropriate terms for these stages take the difference in meaning between apprehension and comprehension into account. According to the Concise Oxford English Dictionary, to apprehend is 'to understand or perceive', and to comprehend is 'to grasp mentally, to understand, to include, comprise, encompass'.[129] Both terms have the meaning to 'take hold', and thence 'to understand', but the difference is in perceiving one or several discrete meanings as opposed to an understanding that encompasses a field of meanings and their inter-relationships. In other words, apprehension really refers to the acquisition of a stock of knowledge, the term used by Greil to designate that which an individual perceives at a given point in time to be true about the social or physical world,[130] while comprehension refers to the acquisition of a framework for organizing this stock of knowledge. As the analysis of respondents' accounts will show throughout this book, practitioners feel committed to their Buddhist practice once they have apprehended some of the key meanings, and have then comprehended them as a set of inter-related meanings. Apprehension engenders engagement and deeper, more intense exploration. Commitment is engendered by increasing comprehension of the meaning-system and validation of life experience.

Accordingly, the apprehension and engagement stage describes initial encounter with the new group and its meaning-system, and how one begins to learn the concepts, practices and experiential states that comprise it. The comprehension stage describes the point at which one begins to form a framework of concepts or notions and to understand how key ideas fit together within it. Feelings of being committed or wanting to commit do not occur until one has begun to understand how aspects of the framework relate to each other. This commitment is conditional upon ongoing validation of the meaning-system through its capacity to interpret life-experience. Despite the organizational differences in the propagation of religious belief and activity promoted by the two Centres, certain consistencies of orientation to Buddhist engagement are exhibited by both kinds of practitioners. They are referred to hereafter as vipassana- and vajrayana-practitioners, or vipassana- and vajrayana-respondents, according to the context. The orientations are outlined here in brief so as to indicate the nature of those elements found to be central to Buddhist engagement in the forms of vipassana and vajrayana that were explored.

Commitment, as opposed to conversion, is based on the recognition that one has internalized the beliefs, values and expectations of the new religious reality. This occurs after a process of religious experimentation in which the claims of a religious reality are experientially validated against one's inner understandings and convictions, which themselves become clearer as a result of experimental participation in religious activity. Functionally, the adopted worldview is seen to frame personal experience in a manner that renders it more meaningful. Meditative experience and its interpretation according to doctrine must be applicable to the improvement of quality of lived experience. It must be relevant to current life-challenges, and ethically sustainable. A theoretical and methodological strength of the social constructionist approach of Berger's sociological phenomenology is its explanatory power for the way in which a Buddhist Centre's shared reality is maintained and perpetuated by the engagement of the experimental participant with its teachings and practices.

As discussed above, it can be seen that the two centres represent two very different Buddhist perspectives, and yet, strong similarities exist between the two types of Buddhist practitioners in terms of their general orientation and commitment to Buddhism. Substantively, commitment is conditional upon accepting and employing *the three marks* of samsaric existence: *duhkha*, 'suffering', *anitya*, 'impermanence' and anatman, 'no essentially-existing self', as an *interpretive framework* for lived reality; the three groups of the Eight-Fold Path, *sila*, 'ethics', *samadhi*, 'concentration' and *panna*, 'wisdom', as a *strategy for negotiating lived experience*; and meditation techniques specific to the particular Buddhist orientation as a *method for applying doctrinal principles* to one's own transformation. A central aim of this book is to outline how these consistencies occur despite the different Western Buddhist grounds that foster them.

Methodological Considerations

This section is devoted to those methodological considerations that can be seen to affect the gathering and reporting of, and the drawing of meaningful conclusions from, the available data obtained by the fieldwork undertaken. Of utmost importance to the quality of data obtained is the successful acquisition of respondents that accurately represent participant and adherent characteristics of both centres. I have not included a separate section on respondent characteristics, but refer the reader to Appendix 1: Interview-Respondents. Beyond this, individual respondent characteristics are discussed, where relevant, throughout.

Methods of data-gathering

There were three methods of data-gathering: examination of relevant sources and teaching material, participant observation and interview. Both Centres recommend a range of relevant teaching material to students, and have these on hand. They include primary texts; recommended writings by Sangha members, Western teachers and interpreters; and handouts for classes or workshops at VI. Both Centres also keep a collection of recordings of previous teachings, which students can borrow. There is also access to some teachings via the Internet. The first challenge was to satisfy myself that my fieldwork participation and observations were as representative as possible of the activities of the two organizations.

VI was then in Newtown, Sydney, and the BMIMC was and is still in Medlow Bath in the Blue Mountains. My research with both groups involved both fieldwork, by participant observation, and interview. Dividing my time between the two organizations meant that some fieldwork opportunities had to be sacrificed. For example, both groups held their weekly meditation sessions on Monday nights, although both changed their nights subsequent to my fieldwork. These sessions were valuable sources of information about teaching the techniques, and beginners' access to the tradition's worldview through instruction in and explanation of meditative practice. The result was that my attention was divided between the two classes.

My way around this was to attend a range of classes, courses, workshops, retreats and other activities from each group, and to take my cues from interview material describing how the practitioners themselves decided what to try. Crucial information was revealed in the practitioner interview material. For example, in the case of the BMIMC, interviews conducted with long-term practitioners revealed the nature of differences between teaching styles and approaches to the practice between teachers associated with the Centre. I therefore participated in a range of workshops and retreats in order to establish the range of religious material explored, and the variations in teaching styles that are representative of the activities that the Centre offers practitioners. Establishing this range is vital to the exposition of the nature of the teaching and learning processes involved in practitioners' socialization into the practice and its worldview. Similarly, at VI I was confronted with a large range of literature and courses to become familiar with, although the familiarization process was easier in this setting because of the social nature of the Centre. Participants spoke freely about their choice of courses and reading material. After some involvement with both centres, I established a knowledge of the scope of teachings and practices on offer.

However, each Centre presented its own challenges to participant observation. Most of the teaching and meditation activity at BMIMC takes place in Noble Silence, except for instruction and private interviews given by the teachers. With my participation in the activities of BMIMC I faced the problem of gathering data from a group whose primary activities take place in silence, and where personal interaction is minimal. Primary source materials available were formal instruction, *dhamma-talks*, group interviews during retreats, everyday activity at the beginning and end of retreats, and interviews with practitioners. Generally, the nature of the activities at VI made participant observation easier. VI has a broader range of teaching formats, and allows for more verbal interaction between people. I got to know people, joined in conversations, helped set up chairs for class, and participated in other activities. However, my interaction in both groups was more than as a passive participant observer. In order to empathize with the practitioners, I had to take on the role and perspective of a religious explorer, and I found this easy to do.

During instruction, dhamma talks and group interviews at BMIMC I took notes as discreetly and as unobtrusively as I could, and similarly during meditation sessions at VI. Although I had permission from both organizations to conduct participant observation, there were still times when it seemed intrusive to keep writing, to take down every word being said. This seemed especially so in group interviews at BMIMC when individual responses to points of technique or progress reports were called for, and during classes at VI when people were discussing a personal problem from the Buddhist perspective. In situations where it seemed insensitive to keep writing, I attempted to note the main points mentally, the important trends of response, some indicative examples or some differences from the norm, and to record them later. When I needed to rely on memory until I had access to my tape recorder or notepad, it is likely that pieces of information may have been lost, or that people may have been paraphrased incorrectly. This was true of the Monday night meditation sessions for both organizations. One way around this was to observe a number of sessions in order to extract the main points. Increasing familiarity with and understanding of the two discourses and their techniques, terms, concepts and belief structures, as well as familiarity with the style of and structure used by the teacher, also helped. Another way was to check my impressions against practitioners' understandings and memories.

Interview-respondents were selected by three means. At both Centres some volunteers were gained by word-of-mouth, and in response to posters outlining the nature of my thesis and asking for volunteers for interview. At BMIMC, by prior arrangement with teachers, I asked for volunteers during the closing talk at the end of some workshops and retreats. Many committee members and volunteer workers at the Centre were receptive to the aims of my study and gladly gave of their time. Respondent-selection at VI was more reliant on word-of-mouth and to an almost negligible extent, on responses to the poster. The spread of information by word-of-mouth was surprisingly slow. Teachers did not want to be seen to endorse any particular individual's research, and so I did not ask for volunteers during or at the end of teachings, but waited until suitable opportunities presented themselves during social occasions. In the end, I approached individuals of my acquaintance from teachings and study group attendance, many of whom had been coming to the Centre for only a small number of years by comparison with those at BMIMC.

In all, twenty vipassana and nineteen vajrayana practitioners were interviewed. For both groups of practitioners, the average age was in the mid-forties, with a range from mid-thirties to late fifties. Almost all respondents were either highly skilled or university-educated, and engaged in occupations that made use of their qualifications. A difference in the male-to-female ratio existed: of the twenty vipassana-practitioners responding, nine were male; of the nineteen vajrayana-practitioners, five were male. Roundly, males constituted one-half and one-quarter respectively of the respondents from BMIMC and VI. However, there was no evidence to suggest that either the different absolute numbers or the ratios had any bearing on the nature of the data collected. Significantly, however, accompanying the differing effectiveness of the three selection methods in each Centre was the finding that the two groups of respondents differed also in their cumulative practical experience of Buddhism. Of the twenty vipassana respondents, nine had been meditating for a period of twenty to thirty years, and most had been attracted by the poster placed in the dining room at BMIMC. Conversely, almost all of the vajrayana respondents had been involved with Buddhism for fewer than ten years.

A set of interview questions was formulated to obtain information about the relevant dimensions of religious activity and engagement, and paid particular attention to the doctrinal, practical, experiential and social aspects.[131] Aesthetic aspects, if relevant, emerged from the interview material. Other questions addressed specific issues to do with conversion theory, such as testing for the existence of a crisis or turning point in one's conversion process. During interviews, which were semi-structured, I used the questions as a guide to discussion, and would blend them with letting the interview go where it was taken by my respondent. I asked for further detail at times, or asked the participant to go in a particular direction. In order to get clarification of a point, or to elicit further response, I would sum up their previous response, as if asking them a question. As has been suggested by Snow *et al.*,[132] this proved an effective means of gathering information.

I am aware that the under-representation of experiential accounts of vajrayana practitioners with periods of involvement equal to that of the vipassana practioners limits the potential for understanding the nature of the experiential dimension as it is constituted within the FPMT. Consequently, I am more confident in the validity of conclusions drawn about the nature of the experiential dimension as it is produced through practice at BMIMC. However, this does not diminish the significance of the results of the study with respect to its analysis of the role of doctrine and orientation to practice maintained in the commitment process for the vajrayana respondents, who at the time of interview, were confident in their recall of events, and clear about why they had or had not made a commitment to the Buddhist path.

According to social constructionist views of meaning-making, experience is always interpreted in terms of concepts that belong to the individual's stock of knowledge, and therefore, my endeavour to isolate the conceptual and doctrinal from the experiential base in accounts of meditative experience and its interpretation is idealistic. However, the purely intellectual learning of and reflection on doctrinal material in daily life, and the understanding of meditative experience according to this doctrine, may be seen as the two modes of learning at the student's disposal.

The attempt to isolate these dimensions is simply to understand how they are put together by students who are directed to 'observe their experience', and it of necessity relied heavily on the use of data from interview. Data from participant observation are limited because, during silent retreats, one can observe outward behaviour only; one is not privy to the internal states of others. In interviews I aimed to get first-hand accounts of the bare experiential level of the practice in order to determine how particular concepts are applied to experience. This was done to get an overview of the experiences and experience-concept relationships reported by practitioners so as to determine how interpretive frameworks are acquired. In order to achieve this, I asked respondents a series of questions to do with the doctrinal concepts or notions they found significant and why, about the kinds of experience both typical and significant for the practitioner, how these were interpreted and how the understandings were applied to daily life. Where possible, I encouraged practitioners to describe their experience in their own words, with minimal doctrinal elaboration, so that relationships between experiences and their attribution of meaning in Buddhist terms were as visible as possible. This line of questioning was designed to reveal the nature and order of acquisition of specific meaning structures, as well as their relative significance.

It is interesting that immediate responses sometimes consisted of descriptions of experience already contextualized in Buddhist terms. For example, in interviews, practitioners might say 'On retreats I have experiences of dukkha'. When asked about what actually happened, they might answer 'I felt pain in my legs', which is typically noted as 'feeling' or 'pain'. Conversely, transcripts showed this barest level of experiential reporting more likely to be found in dialogue between the teacher and practitioner during teacher–student interviews on retreats, where teachers ask the students to describe their experience at its barest level of observation, and how it was noted. However, I was able to ameliorate this in interview by asking more specific questions. For example, I asked, "When you say that you experienced impermanence, do you mean that the observation of changing mental states lent itself to interpretation as impermanence?" This being said, the comparison of the relevant sections of interview transcripts highlighted commonalities in terms of the range of objects and mental states noted by practitioners during meditation, but common in everyday experience.

Methods of interpretation and exposition

Throughout my period of fieldwork, two interrelated methodological concerns dominated my thinking: the concern for accurate representation of practitioners' experiences, and for a treatment of the experience-interpretation relationship that did justice to the material at hand. A consideration related to both is the way in which respondents were obtained for interview and how accurately they can be taken to represent the range of learning, practice and experience possible through the activity of each Centre.

With respect to the first, my discussion of significant trends and their variations has attempted to mirror the data as closely as possible. Whilst every interview contained important information, such as an account of the individual's religious history and exploration of and experience with Buddhism, particular interview transcripts seemed to lend themselves easily to particular topics. A comparison of the interview transcripts of two vajrayana practitioners highlights the point. One practitioner was good at recalling factual information such as the books that he had read, the courses that he had done, and the order of acquisition of concepts and their significance. A feature of the second transcript is the clarity with which the practitioner recounts her experiences of self-transformation, and the significance she attributes to them. Where material from one interview transcript is given prominence in this way, I shall make this obvious, and indicate how it compares to similar material, so that single instances are not taken as necessarily representative of the whole.

My interview questions reflected a set of concerns related to the understanding of conversion and commitment in Western Buddhism. Initially I had no structure in mind for reporting the data. After several interviews had been conducted with practitioners of both groups, significant features of the whole field of religious activity for each organization became apparent. First was how features of the organization and teaching structure facilitated access to the perspective. Second were features of individuals' own religious exploration, viz. how they encountered the organization and its perspective, and how they made choices about what to engage in. Many practitioners were able to evaluate what they had learned through their exploration by reviewing the changes that had occurred within themselves through the application of the principles and techniques.

Finally, the decision to accept the Buddhist perspective and commit to its practices was linked to the appreciation of what had been learned and the self-transformation that it had produced. However, these processes—learning doctrine and practice, testing their validity, applying them to effect self-transformation and making the decision to commit to the perspective—did not occur as a linear set of discrete steps, but were somewhat concurrent and definitely mutually reinforcing. Because of this, the division of the material into chapters that, for convenience of exposition, treat these significant features sequentially should not be understood as implying a fixed sequence in participants' journeys towards commitment.

The chapter order and content is intended for ease of reporting and clarity of exposition. The fieldwork data for each Centre are divided into three aspects: engagement and learning, self-transformation, and socialization and commitment. The first two aspects are treated in individual chapters for both Centres: Chapters 2 and 3 for the BMIMC, and Chapters 4 and 5 for VI. Chapters 2 and 4 explore the nature of the interaction between the experimental participant and the religious activity of a Centre. They explore the scriptural foundations of the Centre's worldview, the nature of religious authority, methods of teaching, content in terms of doctrine and practice, how participants begin to engage with and work with the material, and finally, what they learn. Chapters 3 and 5 explore the significance of personal application of the interpretive frameworks and techniques to the project of self-transformation. This is essentially a study of the way in which concepts, doctrines, practices—and the experiential states that they facilitate—become meaningful for the practitioner through their efforts in their private practice, study and self-reflection. One of the trends to emerge early in the interview process was the effect on practitioners of their recognition that they had undergone personal change as a result of their Buddhist involvement. This resulted in a definite decision either to commit to Buddhism or to keep investigating it with new energy. These chapters explore the nature of the self-transformations involved, and the doctrinal frameworks and practices employed to effect this change.

I believe that it is this approach that uncovers an aspect of the nature of the construction, maintenance and change, where possible, of a shared reality. Distinguishing between what one learns through interaction at a Buddhist Centre and what one applies in personal practice reveals what is selected from the range of material accessed through the Centre's activity, and therefore what one holds as personally valuable and useful. This distinction has explanatory power for understanding how the shaping of a Western Buddhism is affected by the tastes and needs of the practitioners.

Finally, Chapter 6 encapsulates the previous exploration of the socialization process within the gamut of its exposition by taking a more holistic view of the socialization process that, from an examination of the prior religious histories of the respondents, proceeds to an establishment of the relationships between their religious backgrounds, experimental pathways and current choices of Buddhist affiliation. Their biographies offer insights into the ways in which religious explorers make use of concepts, interpretive frameworks, practices—and the experiential states that these foster—to make choices about affiliation. Next, the substance and effect of learning, comprehension, self-transformation and commitment are discussed, but, in contrast to the four previous chapters, the discourses are completely from the viewpoints of the participants. A second part of Chapter 6 conflates and compares the findings and conclusions about the elements of religious engagement during the active appropriation of the meaning-system of each Centre by its affiliates.

Reflexivity exposed: My participatory journey from *seeker* to *sympathizer*

This study was initially conceived as a response to my personal wish to explore Buddhism and pursue my academic interests in religious experience, social constructionist views of experience and its interpretation, and in theories of religious conversion. These interests came together in the aim of exploring the cognitive and non-cognitive ways that individuals structure, maintain, test and transform their personal worldview or reality-perspective in the field of Western Buddhism. Because my knowledge of Buddhism was minimal to begin with, consisting of familiarity with the fundamental doctrines and their import, samsara and nirvana, the Four Noble Truths, the three marks of existence, a very limited knowledge of the five *skandhas*, 'aggregates', and a naïve appreciation of vipassana meditation, when I began as a participant observer I felt, initially, that I was swamped with new information.

Throughout my time as a student of Comparative Religion, I have favoured the interpretive over the explanatory approach within social science,[133] which for me means to learn the language and meaning-constructs of the shared reality of the group in order to understand how these things become meaningful for participants. I noticed that practitioners' experiences began to make more sense to me after I became familiar with the discourse of both Centres. Within several months I found myself participating in the same experimental process that all seekers do: that of learning and testing new concepts and meanings against those acquired during prior spiritual involvements. For me, this reflexive stance included the complexities of resistance to some ideas and observation of ways in which my thinking began to change. This had implications for my own exploration and understanding, and for my empathy with my interview-respondents. The two instances recounted below from my time with BMIMC are but two of the many significant impression points that I experienced.[134] I recount them here to give the reader a sense of my experience of the insider–outsider perspective in the study of religion,[135] which endured for the entire time of my fieldwork.

After I had participated in several vipassana retreats and had begun to experience brief periods of mindfulness, as I discuss in Chapter 2, I began to understand the purpose of its cultivation for both meditation and everyday awareness. I began to form an impression as to how practitioners could both develop the discipline needed for progress in the practice, and hold their minds on an object in the way needed in order to experience the dukkha, 'suffering', and *anicca*, 'impermanence', in the way that they described. My own experiences during two nine-day retreats deepened my understanding of the practice and its meaning-system. During the first, in December 2002, I noticed the tendency of my mind to activate and relive old narratives, past events and their effects, whenever it was 'at a loose end'. On the second, in April 2004, the experience of learning how to identify mental states, to categorize them as one of the five hindrances and to observe their arising and ceasing, especially 'sloth and torpor', gave me an experiential understanding both of the nature of mindfulness and of the way in which mental states could be both investigated and transformed. In turn, this gave me an understanding of mind as the third *satipatthana*, foundation of mindfulness. These were key experiences for me as both seeker and researcher, in that they gave me a sense of faith in the truth of the Buddhist path, which in turn gave me an empathy with the experiences of practitioners who had committed to Buddhism.

My responses to the activities at VI also lacked the experiential focus. Added to that was that I found myself using the Theravadin framework of vipassana meditation as a point of comparison to orient my understanding of the Gelugpa Tibetan framework, which for some time felt overwhelmingly vast and complex. While I looked to both for an understanding of the ethical dimension to Buddhism and its application in my life, initially I looked to the vipassana for my meditative training and to the vajrayana for other elements considered as spiritual: the *bodhisattva* motivation and the emphasis on compassion. Of course these elements exist in both forms of Buddhism: both have analytical practices, concentration practices and lovingkindness and compassion practices. I was simply responding to what *appeared* to be dominant in conceptual and experiential discourse at the two Centres. To this day, I still feel overawed by the depth and complexity of the Buddha's teachings and respectful of those who aim to put them into practice.

Particular aspects of doctrine and thought began to have special import for me, either because they appealed to religious sensibilities that I had gained as part of my own prior experimental history, or because they directly challenged them. Chief among the latter was the doctrine of not-self, *anatta*, sunyata. In my twenties, I had for six years been a committed member of AMORC, the Ancient and Mystical Order of the Rosy Cross, a Twentieth-Century Rosicrucian order which scholars of religion place within the current of Western Esotericism. My strongest memories of the thought expressed in the teachings and rituals of the Order was that mind and being are beginningless and endless. Of Faivre's four distinct usages of the term esotericism: the generalist view of the occult, paranormal and exotic wisdom traditions; the attainment to a centre-of-being by certain procedures; the creation of an esoteric/exoteric dichotomy; and the ensemble of spiritual currents that is the subject matter of formal research,[136] the one that I have always responded to most strongly is *attainment to a centre-of-being*. To me, this expressed the theme of AMORC's ritual and the Order's purpose.[137]

At this point, the reader is referred to the comparative discussion about the way in which the doctrines of anatta and sunyata are approached both conceptually and experientially, by the vipassana and Vajrayana orientations respectively, in Chapter 6. In terms of belief, this view's acceptance is conditional upon other aspects of the belief system's being validated by the practitioner's own experience. In practical and experiential terms, vipassana- and Vajrayana-practitioners alike maintain that they are working their way towards its experiential realization by doing those practices that prepare one's mind for it. My own endeavour to understand the position was almost wholly intellectual. In my exploration of the three views of the self—the absolute, relative and imputed—and their implication for the understanding of self-transformation undergone by practitioners, I began to entertain the possibility that the centre-of-being, so sought-after by many contemporary spiritual practices, may in fact be a reification of the imputed self. There are many possible positions that one could take with respect to this. What I learned from this experience was that the attempt to empathize with the view of another tradition that is radically different from one's own can be truly confronting. The doctrine of *no essentially-existing self* is threatening to a view of the self as having an enduring, unchanging and divine core. I have noticed, however, that I have been more willing, with the passage of time, to see it from the Buddhist perspective. Queen distinguishes three categories of religious researcher: the participant observer, sympathizer and adherent.[138] Although an experimental participator, I also fall into the category of sympathizer. I hold enormous respect for the Buddhist tradition and its practices, and similarly for the views and motivations of its practitioners, but I simply do not have the degree of belief and faith—the necessary conviction—to become an adherent, a self-professed Buddhist.

Chapter 2

Instruction and Practice at the Blue Mountains Insight Meditation Centre

Introduction

The Blue Mountains Insight Meditation Centre (BMIMC), in the tradition of the late Mahasi Sayadaw of Burma, provides facilities for the teaching and practice of vipassana meditation. The majority of the Centre's religious activity takes the form of meditation-retreats, although workshops are held from time to time. The Centre is operated by a management committee, which appoints a Manager, and sometimes an Assistant Manager and other support staff to assist with day-to-day operation. During my fieldwork at the Centre the committee consisted of about eight members at any time. Volunteers help in regular maintenance on community work days, and with administration, shopping, cooking and cleaning during retreats. Certainly the Centre aims to provide a conducive space and atmosphere for the practice of meditation. However, several organizational features limit the amount of social contact possible between participants. First, Noble Silence, meaning no exchange with others, whether in written or spoken form or through body language, is observed in most retreats, and social activity is therefore limited in several necessary ways. Further, the resident community at BMIMC is small and in continual flux. Participants may build Buddhist social networks within the Centre by volunteering, or outside the Centre by attending other centres such as the Buddhist Library in Camperdown, Sydney.

This chapter's exploration of the way in which socialization into the Theravadin worldview takes place through the practice of vipassana meditation must consider how learning takes place in a meditative setting that permits minimal social interaction between participants. Socialization refers to the process by which the roles and norms of a group are learnt.[1] In the context of religious resocialization, the group's worldview becomes a frame of reference for newcomers, within which they potentially re-order their view of the world.[2] Although socialization is held to involve both cognitive and social factors, theoretical approaches differ in the importance attributed to the role of other people in the socialization process.

Two extremes are represented by the views of socialization as the process of accepting the opinions of one's 'significant others',[3] or as an active process of negotiation.[4] Because social interaction at BMIMC is constrained by its retreat-style format, socialization into the practice and its Theravadin worldview depends largely on the instruction about meditation and *dhamma*-talks given by teachers, and on the opportunities taken for practice by a participant, who spends much time effectively isolated in meditation practice.

As this chapter demonstrates, practitioners learn the technique and its interpretive framework by learning and applying conceptual frameworks to their experience. I devote much attention to understanding the relationship between experiential states and their interpretation according to Buddhist doctrine by both practitioners and the researcher. Taking the constructivist view, that all experience is mediated by language,[5] I conceive a meditation practice to be a technology for comprehending experience in terms of the practice's supporting worldview. Arguments opposing the constructivist view, such as Forman's assertion of the existence of a form of pure experience—the pure consciousness event[6]—are outside the concerns of this investigation, which is to establish how meaning is produced by the identification of experiential states according to Buddhist terminology. The Chapter is divided into three sections: the doctrinal foundations and textual sources for the practice; retreats as the context for learning and practice; and the participant's accumulated experience of being on retreat and learning the practice. Much of the Chapter is devoted to the exposition of the nature of beginners' retreats, in terms of the consistency of doctrinal material imparted despite the variation in individual teaching styles. Correspondingly, much space is devoted to the exploration of the conceptual and experiential acquisitions facilitated by participation, practice and learning. While my treatment is unlikely to be exhaustive of the possible range of meditative experience and doctrinal interpretation related to vipassana practice, my participant observation and interview data indicated that these aspects of learning and experiential development were common to practitioners' experiences.

Vipassana Practice at BMIMC: Doctrinal and Practical Foundations

Vipassana is a meditation practice derived from the *Sutta Pitaka* of the *Pali Canon*. It is outlined in two suttas: the *Satipatthana Sutta* from the *Majjhima Nikaya*[7] and the *Mahasatipatthana Sutta* from the *Digha Nikaya*.[8] The major difference between the two is the longer section about the Four Noble Truths in the latter. The homepage of BMIMC's website refers to the practice as 'Satipatthana vipassana in the style of Mahasi Sayadaw', and gives the Centre's inspiration as the Buddhist Theravadin tradition.[9] Data gained from participant observation and interview demonstrate that the instruction given by the Centre's teachers is thoroughly loyal to the method outlined by Mahasi Sayadaw. Similarly, data demonstrated a strong conformity to the meditation technique and its doctrinal position outlined in the Satipatthana Sutta by teachers. For ease of explanation of everything to follow, I first discuss, as the foundation for the practice, the vipassana method of Mahasi Sayadaw and its relationship to the Satipatthana Sutta. This will serve two related purposes. First, it is necessary to understand this connection in order to appreciate the doctrinal and practical uniformity of instruction underlying the apparent diversity of emphasis on points of doctrine and technique demonstrated by individual teachers. Second, a clear outline of the practice and its doctrinal matrix will provide an understanding of what is learnt, practised and tested by practitioners during their socialization into the worldview of Theravada Buddhism.

The vipassana technique of Mahasi Sayadaw

The aim of Mahasi Sayadaw's vipassana method is the attainment of *nibbana* through the cultivation of *sati*, mindfulness,[10] viz. the awareness of immediate experience, which Mahasi Sayadaw defines as concentrated attention.[11] Bhikkhu Bodhi defines it as 'the capacity for attending to the content of our experience as it becomes manifest in the immediate present',[12] and Kornfield as observing 'the natural sequence of changing experience, without judgment.'[13] A popular term for mindfulness among students and teachers is Nyanaponika Thera's *bare attention*, viz. 'the single minded awareness of what happens at the successive moments of perception as presented either through the five physical senses or through the mind'.[14] Development of mindfulness and insight is effected by contemplation of the four *satipatthanas*, 'foundations of mindfulness', and outlined in the Satipatthana Sutta as the body, feeling, mind, and dhammas. *Dhammas*, the Pali term for the fourth *satipatthana*, is sometimes translated into English as 'mind-objects'.[15] Several notable scholars—Nyanaponika Thera, Analayo, and U Silananda who states that no English word covers the full meaning of the Pali word dhammas[16]—advance strong reasons as to why this rendering is unsuitable, and so I leave the term untranslated throughout this book.

That the Satipatthana method is the way to realize nibbana is stated in the second paragraph of the Satipatthana Sutta.[17] Although the precise nature of nibbana is frequently debated, when associated with the goal of vipassana or insight practice it is often described by teachers as 'absence of craving' or as 'liberation from suffering'. Nyanaponika Thera sees the practice as having two goals: the attainment of nibbana and the practical application of mindfulness in everyday life.[18] For either goal, and in both religious and therapeutic contexts, the aim of practice is insight into the nature of psychic functioning,[19] outlined in three objectives by Nyanaponika Thera and Deatherage as to know one's own mental processes, to have the power to shape or control them and to gain freedom from the condition wherein they are unknown and uncontrolled.[20] However, at

BMIMC, where practical instruction is complemented with dhamma-talks that provide schooling in Buddhist philosophy and ethics, these goals are contextualized within the Theravadin doctrinal framework.

A characteristic of the Satipatthana method is the development of mindfulness through vipassana practice alone, without any prior attainment of the *jhanas*, 'meditative absorptions', through *samatha* practice.[21] The differences between the two systems of meditation in the Pali Canon, viz. the development of samatha, serenity or concentration meditation, which aims at *samadhi*, 'concentration' and the attainment of the jhanas, and the development of vipassana which aims at *panna*, 'wisdom', are frequently referred to in meditation instruction and dhamma-talks. Although samatha practice is not taught at the Centre, on beginners' retreats I have heard the difference between concentration and mindfulness—as mental states—expressed as 'concentration is the focus on an object, while mindfulness is being aware of where the mind is focused'. Interview-respondents' comments indicate that concentration and mindfulness are expected to develop concurrently, with the development of mindfulness aided by the mind's ability to remain on an object. This subject is taken up again below in *Learning to distinguish samatha from vipassana practice*.

By directing participants to be aware of whatever mental or bodily experience is predominant in each moment, the immediate aim is to train the mind to observe and note the succession of physical and mental phenomena that appear to it.[22] To this effect, Mahasi Sayadaw's method utilizes two techniques: sitting and walking. The difference between the two lies in the nature of the primary object, the object used to anchor the mind in present experience. Sitting meditation uses the in-and-out movement of the breath as the primary object. Meditators observe the rising and falling of the abdomen while the movement occurs and note the 'rising . . . falling . . . rising . . . falling'. Walking meditation invokes contemplation of the actions of stepping. The recommended noting technique is 'lifting . . . placing', which, with practice, is extended to 'lifting . . . moving . . . placing . . . shifting'. Meditators may note either the movement itself or the resultant sensations at the soles of the feet.

During instruction, the Centre's teachers emphasize some basic principles of the Mahasi method. "Do not think of the processes of rising and falling, and lifting and putting, as words, but be aware of the process of movement. When the mind wanders, it should be noted, for example, 'reaching'. After this, begin noting the rising-falling, lifting-putting again. Make a mental note of each object observed, every item of mental behaviour as it occurs, thoughts and mental functions. After the disappearance of the object, return to the primary object, the abdomen or the walking. Failing to note and dismiss such distinctive objects, such as sounds and sights as they occur, may allow the meditator to fall into reflections about them instead of proceeding with intense attention to the rising and falling, or lifting and putting".[23] Fundamental to the Mahasi practice is the categorization of the range of objects into primary and secondary objects. The primary objects include the rise and fall of the abdomen and the two for walking meditation given above, all of which belong to the contemplation of the body. Secondary objects are any other objects that appear to the mind, such as sense impressions, feelings or thoughts.

Doctrinal texts and teaching resources

The Buddhist worldview is imparted to students and practitioners through a range of reading material. Alongside the Satipatthana and Mahasatipatthana Suttas, from the Nikaya Pitaka of the Pali Canon, are the writings of Mahasi Sayadaw outlining and explaining his approach to the vipassana practice. Reference is sometimes made to the *Anapanasati Sutta*, Mindfulness of Breathing, in Sutta 118 in the *Majjhima Nikaya*.[24] Other sources include writings by Western interpreters, commentators and vipassana teachers, such as those of Joseph Goldstein and Jack Kornfield; writings by Eastern teachers who have popularized Buddhism for the Western mind and writings by teachers associated with the Centre, such as Venerable Pannyavaro, Patrick Kearney and Steve and Rosemary Weissman. Some of the writings in this latter category may be downloaded from the BMIMC website. The Buddhist worldview and the doctrinal foundations of its practice are ever-present in the meditation instruction given at the Centre. During retreat, the participant begins to encounter the fundamentals of the Buddhist worldview almost immediately through spoken instruction and dhamma-talks. This fundamental framework consists of the Four Noble Truths, especially the Noble Eightfold Path in its three aspects of panna, *sila*, samadhi—'wisdom, ethics and meditation'—and the three marks of existence—dukkha, anicca and anatta—'suffering, impermanence and no essentially-existing self'.

Materials from the latter categories of literature above appear to be generally popular with practitioners. However, preference for a type of literature is an individual matter and does not directly correlate with development in the practice. Generally, however, interest in and familiarity with the Pali Canon tends to develop with experience in the practice. Some preferences expressed by practitioners were for the *Abhidhamma*, the *Dhammapada*, and for the study of suttas devoted to a topic of particular interest to the meditator. However, most practitioners express a preference for the Western commentators and interpreters of the vipassana practice and Theravada tradition. Nyanaponika Thera's *Heart of Buddhist Meditation* is very popular among practitioners. Some preferred the writings of the lay Buddhist teachers because such writings were 'easy to read' or 'accessible'. Examples are Joseph Goldstein's *The Experience of Insight* and writings by Jack Kornfield or Sharon Salzburg. These are quite possibly more widely read than Mahasi Sayadaw's writings. Some read the '*satipatthanas* through other literature', such as *The Four Foundations of Mindfulness* by U Silananda. Others are drawn to teachers within the tradition, such as U Pandita. Other Buddhist authors from various schools mentioned were Ajahn Chaa, Tenzin Palmo, Thich Nhat Hanh and Pema Chodrön. Overall, whether practitioners wanted light reading in bed, something inspirational to reflect on, or instruction in the practice for clarification of technique or insight into meditative experience, the general consensus was for material that practitioners could relate to and apply to their daily lives, and which could put their own experience into perspective.

Contexts for Learning and Practice

The Centre does not hold regular Buddhist teachings or philosophy sessions, but doctrinal material, imparted in practical instruction and in dhamma-talks, informs the practice. Activities conducted at the Centre or affiliated with it can all be viewed as learning contexts and fall into three categories. First is the weekly meditation night. Beginning at 7pm, the usual program is for a half-hour's sitting, half-hour's walking, another half-hour's sitting and then a dhamma-talk for about half-an-hour. A roster of four teachers takes turn to lead the night's session. Second, teachers affiliated with the Centre often give one-day meditation workshops or study courses at the Buddhist Library or elsewhere. Examples of such courses are the Sutta Study Weekend held in August 2003, which concentrated on the relationship between samatha and vipassana practice, and the annual series of sutta study classes entitled *Evam Me Suttam*, held at the Buddhist Library, Camperdown, Sydney.[25] All of the learning contexts associated with the Centre include instruction in the practice, and instruction in its doctrinal underpinnings. The third and most significant of these learning contexts is the vipassana retreat.

Retreats

Nearly all of the teaching and practice conducted at BMIMC takes place as a live-in arrangement. Participants remain at the Centre for the duration of the activity, which may be a workshop or a retreat. While a workshop might be for one day or a weekend, retreats are typically from two to four days, nine to ten days or a month long. All activities are highly structured; set periods are scheduled for sitting and walking meditation, dhamma-talks, meal breaks, personal activities such as washing, and chores which are referred to as 'mindfulness jobs'.[26] In general, the one- or two-day workshop or retreat is for beginners, and the four- or nine-day for beginners and advanced meditators. There are also retreats of one month's duration, some of which are self-retreats, meaning that no teacher is present. These are for advanced practitioners only. Despite the variation in length of retreats, the only observable differences between them are in the amount of instruction about meditation and in the time set aside for meditation. From time to time a teacher sets shorter times, e.g. half- or three-quarter-hour periods instead of the typical hour for sitting and walking, during beginners' retreats. Retreat descriptions, outlined in the retreat program or available from the website and the printed newsletter, prescribe the proficiency level at which a retreat is aimed: beginners, beginners and advanced or advanced. Some retreats intended for the last will specify that no meditation instruction will be given.

Sometimes there is an option to take only a portion of a longer retreat, for example, the first weekend of a nine-day retreat, or fifteen days of the thirty-day retreat in January. Participants are encouraged to stay for the length or portion of the retreat that they have chosen, but they they are not prevented from leaving if that is their wish. However, teachers view this as the mind's creation of resistance to the practice. Some teachers discuss this during the course of the retreat. As will be discussed later, recognition of resistance to the practice and the deepening awareness that it fosters can be used as a meditation object. Teachers try, in private interviews, to help practitioners to deal with problems that arise from their participation in a retreat.

Mindfulness-training practices

While vipassana-meditation is taught as the primary practice during retreat, it is supplemented with a range of practices, all with the aim to develop practitioners' mindfulness. These include daily mindfulness jobs, *metta*, lovingkindness meditation and thought reflection. Daily mindfulness jobs are related to the routine operation and maintenance of the Centre, and include such chores as cleaning, washing-up, sweeping and the like, and time for these is included in the daily timetable. Metta practice, as Fronsdal has noted, is promoted by American teachers, a practice that many of BMIMC's teachers also tend to promote.[27] However, his observation that North American teachers tend to teach mindfulness independent of metta, *sila*, 'ethics', and *dana*, 'generosity', is not supported in this setting. Teachers emphasize mindfulness as the foundation of mental transformation. While the inclusion of metta practice is at the teacher's discretion, practitioners in interview expressed strong approval for the development of equanimity and compassion for others that it engenders. Sila, ethical practice, takes two forms: the first, dana, is an Asian-derived practice that involves giving to others,[28] for instance, the voluntary work of the cooks and helpers during a retreat, and the second is the taking of precepts. Thought reflection is introduced by some teachers to complement the vipassana, and uses a chosen principle for reflection during, for example, washing or eating.

Introductory Retreats

Orientation and introduction to the practice

Workshops and retreats at BMIMC commence either on Friday night or Saturday morning. Before the introductory session in the meditation hall, supper (Friday) or breakfast (Saturday) is served in the dining room. This is the only opportunity for participants to talk to each other before the retreat officially begins in the meditation hall, with a welcome and orientation talk by the Centre's Manager. The Manager's talk also outlines the retreat schedule, housekeeping matters such as the selection of mindfulness-jobs, and practical matters such as what to do if there is need to contact someone outside the Centre. If the retreat is to take place in Noble Silence, this is explained. Noble Silence means no written, spoken or body-language exchanges with others, no reading and no listening to music. One teacher explained that silence allows things, including the self, to be confronted moment-by-moment, stating, 'Talk can function to communicate, but it can also allow you to hide from experience'. The Manager then introduces the teacher(s). The retreat typically begins with a short introduction to the practice and instruction for sitting meditation.

The introductory session gives a brief background to Buddhism and vipassana meditation and some information about Mahasi Sayadaw and his popularization of the practice among lay people. The teacher may include some explanation of key Pali terms such as *satipatthana*, 'foundations of mindfulness', vipassana 'insight', and *bhavana*, 'meditation'. Key notions are also explained in more colloquial terms. One teacher defined vipassana as a Pali word that translates as 'seeing clearly', and by extension, 'being honest about what we see'. Teachers then typically draw attention to the emphasis on direct experience in vipassana-meditation. One teacher outlined the Buddha's view that the essence of the practice is experience, not belief. Thus, the purpose of the retreat was to explore, from the perspective of experience, how meditation works. Consequently, 'progress in meditation takes place at the level of direct experience where the conceptual is helpful'.

Another teacher explained that the practice involved praxis, the combination of theory and practice. However, his explanation took a more formal approach, from a doctrinal perspective. He briefly outlined the Noble Eightfold Path by discussing panna, 'wisdom, overcoming defiling mind-states'; sila, 'ethics, moral foundation, being gentle in word, deed, and thought', and samadhi, 'concentration, absorption, and meditation practice'. Another teacher again expressed the same ideas, as 'bring beginner's mind to the practice, also called bare attention, meaning that every moment is unique, a new beginning'. The practice was to 'observe what is happening as it arises and passes away', and to 'observe with mindfulness the physical and mental process; what's happening in the mind and body', adding that 'right effort', mindfulness and concentration (the three samadhi factors of the Noble Eightfold Path) all come into play with practice. During the introductory session, teachers may draw attention to the relationship between the nature of 'suffering' and the goal of Buddhist meditation practice. As a Buddhist form of meditation, the goal of vipassana is to achieve happiness and to overcome sorrow, pain and suffering. Some teachers refer to dukkha, and outline its common translations as suffering or unsatisfactoriness.

Lastly, teachers typically discuss any remaining matters of behaviour during retreat, such as expected behaviours as distinct from those that are left to individual choice as, for instance, bowing to the Buddha-image or the teacher. There may be further instruction in the practice of Noble Silence and an introduction to the five lay precepts: abstention from killing, stealing, false speech, sexual misconduct and taking intoxicants.[29] Although some retreats observe eight precepts, the additional three being abstention also from food after midday, high or luxurious beds and entertainment,[30] introductory retreats limit themselves to the first five. Teachers explain that the precepts are taken to establish participants in sila, 'ethics'. One explained that 'they are not related to Christian notions of sin and redemption', but instead to the principle of right motivation producing correct action.[31] On introductory retreats, observing precepts may be left to individual choice, but most often refuge and precepts are taken formally, at the beginning of the retreat and first thing each morning. Teachers give as much explanation as is necessary to establish the relationship of precepts to the practice, and invariably emphasize that the precepts facilitate a state of mind that is conducive to meditation.

At the end of the introductory session, some instruction to fundamental meditation is given, and followed by a period of sitting practice. Participants are first instructed in the various ways of sitting correctly and comfortably, using meditation cushions, stools or chairs. The purpose of finding a good meditation posture is to be comfortable enough not to be distracted from meditation by discomfort, but, at the same time, not so comfortable as to fall asleep. Initial instruction involves description of the significance of the primary and secondary objects for the practice. Meditators are told to take the abdomen as primary object, and while breathing normally and steadily, to observe and note the rising and falling, or the in-out movement, of the abdomen. The secondary object is anything that appears in the mind, or anything else that the mind wanders to, and this can be noted as 'wandering . . . wandering', or more specifically. For example, in an imagined meeting of someone, note 'meeting . . . meeting', and further, 'bored . . . bored', or 'happy . . . happy', as appropriate. The important consideration is to be aware of everything experienced in the mind and body without entering into internal dialogue about it. In the words of one teacher, 'What matters is to know or perceive the object, not what you say to label it'.

Teachers draw attention to the noting of physical sensations such as stiffness, pain and tiredness. 'If these sensations impel a change of posture, as they often do, instead of moving immediately note the urge as 'wishing to change', 'rising . . . moving . . . touching, &c.' Practitioners are instructed to make the note before the move because that aids development of the patience necessary for the practice. During sitting periods of introductory retreats, teachers often employ statements such as 'just be present with your experience' to keep meditators in the present, and to discourage them gently from allowing discursive thinking or daydreaming to take over. After the introductory sitting session, teachers may give some walking meditation instruction, or leave it until later in the retreat. Alternatively, in beginners' retreats and workshops, some teachers may introduce another form of awareness exercise before the sitting and walking practice.

Beginners' weekend workshop, 29–30 May 2004[32]

After the introductory session on the Saturday morning, the beginners' weekend workshop began with an awareness-exercise, as described in my retreat notes.

> We were directed to go outside for ten minutes, pick three objects, observe them, 'take them in' in detail, and observe our reaction to our observations. On our return to the meditation hall, the teacher commented that from a Buddhist perspective, it is not what we notice, but how we notice things. He offered the following comments on the qualities of such observation. First, we note with precision, 'I'm seeing this, not that'. We saw, observed things outside ourselves, but meditation is largely internal and deals largely with internal things. The second is sharpness, to note with clarity 'the object and things going on around it'. Awareness is necessary for finer levels of observation. Third is movement, 'things shift, they don't stay the same', an observation which is related to 'the recognition of impermanence'. Fourth is insight, 'new ways of seeing', 'I saw some things in my reactions'. The teacher explained that insight is not conceptual, but is 'observing the reaction space'. Five is aesthetics, 'being there with simple things', 'happiness arises in the smaller things', 'the underlying experience of joy'.

The workshop continued with a discussion of concentration and an exercise. Concentration was explained as fixing the mind on an object such as the breath. The teacher said, "You must have good concentration before practising mindfulness. You must be able to hold the mind on one object before turning to place it on a succession of objects." The concentration exercise itself consisted of sitting for twenty minutes, focusing on the breath where it felt clearest, for instance, at the nostrils, throat, chest or abdomen. Then followed a discussion.

During the early afternoon, there was a *meditation and awareness* session, in two parts. The first was walking meditation, which included instructions about what to do, where to place the attention and about noting. For faster walking (at normal pace or slightly less), 'note right . . . left'. At even slower pace, 'note lifting . . . moving . . . placing'. The teacher directed us to register the sensations in the feet, as our practice for the moment. He explained that the slower walking provided the opportunity to register more sensations than the faster walking. Walking meditation was for half an hour, followed by group discussion of our experience with it. The second part was an awareness exercise: we were directed to look at our pen and imagine what it would be like to be that object, in order to 'see what experience would be like from the inside'. The teacher asked each person to report one observation that they had made, observing afterward that some people had 'picked up' on the notion of experience from another perspective. The rest of the day was devoted to alternating sitting and walking meditations.

The dhamma-talk that night was entitled 'The Story of the Buddha and Buddhism'. The talk recounted the well-known facts about the Buddha's birth, family of influence, how the Buddha's father tried to protect him from the real world, and about the four sights the Buddha saw after leaving his family's palace. Further comments concerned the Buddha's renunciation and his finding the Middle Way, the point of reaching enlightenment, and his insight into the nature of existence: impermanence, suffering and no-self. Under the teachings of the Buddha, the teacher outlined the Four Noble Truths. He explained the relationship between the first truth, the truth of suffering and the three poisons, greed, hatred and delusion, and further, our clinging to the 'I'. He then described equanimity as not getting caught up in good or bad things. The second Noble Truth was stated to be craving as the cause of suffering; the third as the cessation of suffering, and the fourth as the Eight-Fold Path. The teacher briefly outlined the eight aspects and their grouping into three: panna, sila and samadhi. It was clear from the brevity that he intended to provide an introduction to the fundamental notions and their import, which could be amplified by the participants for themselves, later.

The second morning typically begins with some further instruction for the practice, and on the second day, we broke Noble Silence, which had been observed from 7pm onward the night before, at 10am with an *awareness* period. The teacher began by asking participants about their experiences of observing Noble Silence. In response to one participant's answer of 'irritation', he explained that the silence makes us more aware of what goes on inside us 'a lot of the time'. He used this response to exemplify how meditation practice can make us aware of mental content without creating 'the story'—the need to attribute cause and meaning to the mental states we experience—in this case irritability. The teacher elaborated by pointing out two aspects of consciousness that apply in meditation: the knowing aspect or being aware, and mind-states such as sleepiness or irritability.

The teacher drew attention to the difference between direct experience through the senses and indirect experience such as labelling. He had made reference to the difference between the conceptual and the experiential earlier when talking about the stories we put around our mind-states. He elaborated on this distinction. External direct experience involved the senses, whereas internal direct experience consisted of bodily sensations and emotions, both of which could be pleasant, unpleasant or neutral. Sensations and emotions are both aspects of, and covered by, feeling. He placed mental states in this category also, explaining that one can have direct experience of thinking, but with the content or story the consciousness or direct experience is lost, and it becomes indirect experience. Similarly with memories: we know that we are having a memory, but it is removed from immediate experience. We were directed to 'get to know the space of mindfulness' for the rest of the day. For the three meditation periods between 11am and 12:30pm, we were instructed to pay particular attention to specific experiences. In the first sitting we were to observe the relationship between the breath and other things going on in the body: the breath as primary object, the other things as secondary objects. During the walking, the aim was to be aware of all sensory information: sight, hearing, smell and touch. In the second sitting, we were directed to focus on the breath while being aware of mind-states such as sleepiness or irritation.

The mid-afternoon talk was a brief look at the historical development of Buddhism. This began with India's change to Buddhism under Asoka's leadership, and continued to the spread of Buddhism throughout Asia, the connection of vipassana with Burma and Thailand and its travel to the West via the influences of Achan Chaa, S. N. Goenka and Mahasi Sayadaw. The teacher finished by recapitulating and elaborating on some points previously made during the retreat: the fact that the weekend had dealt largely with concentration—which was necessary to establish mindfulness and for progression in vipassana—including experience of more of the hindrances. Here, the teacher made reference to the *five hindrances*, the mental states held to be the main inner impediments to the development of concentration and insight, listed as sensual desire, ill-will, sloth and torpor, restless and remorse, and doubt, in the Satipatthana Sutta under dhammas.[33] The manner of identifying and working with the hindrances in practice is discussed below.

In time, the teacher assured us, we would come to notice things such as intention and get a richer sense of things such as impermanence, unsatisfactoriness, not-self, greed, hatred and delusion. Lastly, we received some instruction for the two final periods of the retreat. In the walking meditation we were directed to be aware of the arising of thought and the content of thought; in other words, to distinguish between process and content. In the sitting meditation, we were to be aware of feeling, including emotion, as pleasant, unpleasant or neutral (neither pleasant nor painful). The teacher expanded on this in the final discussion, outlining the way in which thought and emotion arise from feeling, which itself is either pleasant, unpleasant or neutral, a reference to feeling as the second Satipatthana.[34] The retreat ended at about 4pm.

Long-weekend retreat, 12–15 June 2004[35]

This retreat began on a Friday evening. After the Manager's talk and the taking of precepts, preliminary instruction about meditation began with the teacher's direction of our attention to two important aspects of practice. First was concentration, the placement of attention on an object, and second was the fine-tuning of that attention. He then gave some instruction in sitting meditation, beginning with the primary object. 'Keep the back erect, the eyes closed and the hands resting in the lap. Focus on the breath at the abdomen, the in-out movement of the abdomen.' He then went on to explain the nature of, and to direct us toward, secondary objects: sounds, thoughts and the like. Ten minutes were spent under this instruction, and then ten minutes of meditation.

On Saturday, the mid-morning session consisted of a walking session and a question-and-answer session. The instruction given was, for fast walking, 'Note right . . . left', and for slow walking, 'Note raising . . . dropping (the foot)'. When we could register and note the raising and dropping with some mindfulness, we were encouraged to move onto the next level of registering and 'Note lifting . . . moving . . . placing'. During question time, participants discussed their experiences with the practice so far: inability to hold their minds on the primary object, drifting-off and the like. The teacher fleshed out his answers and suggestions with much practical detail, especially about the wandering nature of the mind.

In preparation for the group interview in the afternoon, we had been asked to be aware of how we were observing the primary and secondary objects during meditation. At the beginning of the group interview, each person was asked, in turn, how they observed the primary object. Some responses were: 'Walking is easier because something is happening'; 'Trouble with breathing'; 'Trouble with thought'. At this stage there were some comments on progress with noting. Some people commented about feeling distracted by the cold weather and were instructed to use the sensations of cold and shivering as mindfulness objects. Here the teachers asked, "What sort of noting are you making?" The responses were, 'lifting . . . shifting . . . dropping . . . pressing'. One person answered, 'awareness of birdsong . . . looking . . . freshness on the skin'. We were told, 'You can note it, or just be aware of it', and 'You can bring the mind back to one object'. Other responses included 'tiredness . . . headache . . . emotional stuff'. The teacher's advice was to accept the experience and just to note whatever was happening. The teachers then asked us about our observation and noting of the breath. Were we following the rising and falling? In the feeling of the breath, was there tightness? Were we aware of the length and pressure of the breath? For instance, was there any unevenness within and between breaths? On a related point of practice, in response to a question about why we would discriminate between thinking and remembering, since these were both forms of thinking, we were instructed that each mind-state will arise with different qualities, and to be aware of the differences. The teacher made some concluding remarks about the point of practice: that our minds are quite out of control—being caught between craving and aversion—and that we can live in this way and be in continual suffering or we can choose to do something about it.

The dhamma-talk that night was an introduction to some core Buddhist concepts. Topics included the Buddha as *bodhisattva*, the *Tripitaka* of the Pali Canon (Sutta, Vinaya, and Abhidhamma pitakas), and the systemic and cross-referenced nature of the Canon. The bulk of this dhamma-talk was devoted to an outline of the Four Noble Truths and the Noble Eight-Fold Path as two maps within the Pali Canon that show the way to liberation. These were likened to maps in that they 'indicate a direction to go in', and 'tell us about the environment'. To demonstrate this, the teacher discussed each of the elements of the Eight-Fold Path, showing how they related to the vipassana practice.

Meditation instruction given the next morning expanded on those of the previous day. Returning to the topic of observing the breath, the teacher drew our attention to 'the spaces' which may occur in meditation. He pointed out that in sitting meditation, there will often be a gap at the end of the falling; the mind will 'go', that is, through the seeming loss of the object because of the gap as the movement of the breath is momentarily imperceptible. Then occurs a gap wherein the mind falls into the habit of identifying with its mental contents. The teacher instructed us to return our attention to the sitting and note 'sitting'. There was then some discussion about the path of insight, which is sequential in nature; rates of progress are an individual matter, but each person has to negotiate the same stages.

The evening's dhamma-talk was 'The Place of Faith in Vipassana Practice'. The flow of ideas was: we come to the practice with some faith based on previous experience, or some initial faith engendered by having heard about the benefits of meditation. The faith provokes some effort. The practice is about learning a technique that uses body, mind and mind-states, using trial-and-error. Here we were introduced to the five controlling faculties: faith, effort, mindfulness, concentration and wisdom. The teacher added that sila, 'ethics', is the support for the five faculties, which reduce and remove the impurities. Causes for their development were given as: attention directed to impermanence; a careful and respectful attitude to the practice; continuity of awareness; supportive conditions (such as food, posture, Noble Silence, &c); reapplication of conditions remembered to be supportive; courageous effort; patience and perseverance; and unwavering commitment. It was stated that, given practice, the hindrances sense-desire, aversion, sloth and torpor, restlessness and doubt may start to recede, and the enlightenment factors of mindfulness, tranquillity, investigation, energy, joy, concentration and equanimity may start to arise. The teacher continued, "Mindfulness is the main factor involved in vipassana. Concentration is the focus on the breath. Mindfulness is being aware of what you are doing. Mindfulness stops the hindrances, purifies the mind, and makes it more flexible." There was discussion about the application of effort and concentration. These were seen as opposing factors. Too much concentration can lead to mental laziness. Too much effort without concentration makes the mind restless. The teacher then returned to the subject of faith. It 'clears the mind of doubt and aversion'. Faith needs to be balanced with insight and wisdom. Verified faith brings together the five controlling faculties and clarifies them. Initial energy applied repeatedly is the cause of concentration and mindfulness. Concentration helps the mind adhere to the object, pulling it away from defilements and unwholesome states, but without mindfulness no insight arises. The teacher distinguished between continuous—where concentration is fixed on one object—and momentary concentration, where the attention is fixed on a changing object, as in mindfulness practice. Finally, he commented that concentration, energy, wisdom and faith all work together.

On Monday morning, the last session of the retreat contained a dhamma-talk about metta and a short metta meditation, one of the four Brahmaviharas developed through vipassana practice: compassion, metta, 'lovingkindness', sympathetic joy and equanimity. It was also explained that metta as a concentration practice is complementary to vipassana. The wording for metta meditation was given as (using the first person), 'may I be free from danger', 'may I have mental happiness', 'may I have physical happiness' and 'may I have ease of wellbeing'. Clarification was given for the second phrase, 'may I have mental happiness', as having fewer unwholesome mind-states and more wholesome mind-states. In metta, we first direct these things to ourselves; then second, to a benefactor who is alive, who is not an object of desire, who has helped us and towards whom we feel respect and gratitude; third, we direct these things towards a good friend; fourth, to a neutral person; fifth, to a difficult person and last, towards all beings.

Beginners' retreat, 12–13 February 2005[36]

After the introductory talk by the Manager, the teacher described the role of ethics as foundation for practice, and dana, generosity and the precepts as two supports for the practice. Precepts took the form of a private commitment to a set of rules: to agree to act in a way that was harmless (no killing or hurting); to act with trust and respect toward others; not to steal or take without asking; not to engage in sexual activity or take intoxicants; and not to use false or harsh speech. He directed that most of the retreat should be in silence, and that we were to limit eye-contact with others.

The morning continued with a discussion about our previous meditation experience and an introductory mindfulness meditation. We were split into four groups in order to discuss our previous meditation experience with each other. It seemed that many of the people present had tried other forms of meditation, and the views of several held it to be almost an undirected stream of images, sensations, and thoughts. After some clarification, the teacher suggested that we view this meditation as a way of perceiving and understanding our own experience. Between morning tea and lunch, he led us in an experiential session which consisted of a body scan exercise where we placed our mind on each part of the body in turn, beginning with the feet and working our way up the body. The body scan is a practice that this teacher employs frequently in order to encourage the awareness of the body as the foundation for practice. It consists of sweeping each part of the body with one's awareness, in order to place it on the body as a unitary object. We continued with a short guided metta meditation, which he described as 'not the main practice' but 'used to encourage a sense of acceptance', and a half-hour of sitting, where the primary object is either the breath at the abdomen or the whole body. After this, we were again split into four groups to share our experiences of the half-hour sit, beginning with the question, 'What was the primary object?' This was followed by a short question-and-answer session.

For most of this retreat, participants were largely left to their own practice after exercises described above had ended. During the sitting period at 5.30pm, the teacher remarked that in his experience, this was a difficult time in the retreat, when the mind begins to quieten, and anxieties, tiredness or obsessive thoughts may come to the surface. He told us to be gentle with ourselves and just be with our experience. A dhamma-talk was given later that evening. In the sitting period just before breakfast, there was instruction from the teacher about just being with our experience in whatever is happening, what we were doing, whether it be standing, walking or otherwise. If we found ourselves lost in thought or thinking, we should gently bring ourselves back to the primary object. Overall, there was minimal instruction during this retreat compared with the first two, as much of the time was given to personal practice of sitting and walking.

Weekly evening meditation sessions

Teachers often recommend finding a community with whom to practise regularly. Several teachers from BMIMC take turns in leading the weekly group meditation sessions, held at the Buddhist Library, Camperdown on Monday evenings during the period of my fieldwork, but subsequently moved to other locations on Friday evenings. If there are enough newcomers to warrant an induction to the practice, the teacher takes them into a side-room, where they are given an introductory talk and some meditation instruction during the first sitting or the walking session. For instance, on the several occasions I have sat with one particular teacher, he has taken newcomers apart during the walking meditation period in order to orient them and give them basic instruction. On one occasion when I joined this group, the teacher gave them basic instruction in the practice, after going around the room and getting everyone to introduce themselves and say something about how they went in the previous sitting period. Alternatively, such induction may be achieved by the basic meditation instruction given during the first two sessions, and the opportunity to talk to the teacher at the end of the night.

Instruction given during the first sitting meditation is to keep the mind on the rise and fall of the abdomen. 'When the mind wanders, note the wandering, and bring the mind back to the breath'. After a time, say ten minutes or so, the teacher might tell us to bring our attention back to the mind by, for instance, asking (rhetorically) whether our minds were still on the abdomen. Instruction for the walking meditation is similar to that given at the beginning of retreats. The second sitting session is typically the same as the first, but generally with less instruction from the teacher. The topic for the night's dhamma-talk is left up to the teacher.

A summary of instruction in the practice

This outline of instruction given at introductory retreats is intended to demonstrate several significant features of the learning context and participant-experience at BMIMC. First, all teaching and learning activity falls into three interdependent categories: doctrinal, practical and experiential. The practical dimension, instruction in the technique and its execution, connects the doctrinal and experiential dimensions. It facilitates engagement with immediate subjective experience: bodily and sensory impressions, feelings and mental states, for which the four foundations of mindfulness provide an interpretive framework. All three retreats gave instruction in the foundations of the practice: a definition of mindfulness, a description of the primary and secondary objects and instruction in sitting and walking practice. However, by comparison with the first two, instruction given during Retreat 3 was minimal, allowing more time to be spent in practice. The teacher on Retreat 1 gave significant attention to instruction about how to observe. Much of the instruction during Retreat 2 focused on the practical detail involved in the noting technique, for instance, to note the gaps that occur while watching the breath.

The purpose of instruction in the practice is to engage students with their immediate experience, and to teach them how to observe such experience. On all three retreats, during the introductory instruction and practice period, and for several sessions on the first day, teachers attempted to engage participants with their own immediate experience in various ways. Of these retreats, the second was most typical of retreats generally, in that practical instruction consisted of the standard instruction for sitting and walking meditation. The awareness exercises directed our attention to specific objects: concentration on the breath where it was clearest and on the soles of the feet during walking. During Retreat 3, the teacher emphasized basic body awareness, directing us intermittently throughout the retreat just to *be* with our muscular and joint pain, and to 'be present with our experience'. From these descriptions, it can be seen that teachers explain doctrinal notions and their frameworks in accessible, everyday language, which make it easy to follow for those without prior knowledge of Buddhism. For instance, the teacher on Retreat 1 spoke about suffering, impermanence and no-self, rather than referring to them as the three marks of existence. This can be viewed as directing the beginner's mind to the experiential sense of the object or concept concerned rather than providing a list of terms and ways of categorizing existence that may not meaningfully engage the beginner.

Each retreat also differed in the nature and amount of doctrinal material introduced via meditation instruction and dhamma-talk. Dhamma-talks given during Retreat 1 introduced some key Buddhist frameworks: the three marks of existence; dukkha, anicca and anatta; the Four Noble Truths; and the historical development of Buddhism. Topics introduced during Retreat 2 were the three aspects of the Noble Eight-Fold Path, panna, sila and samadhi; the Pali Canon and its cross-referenced nature; the hindrances and the enlightenment factors. Exposure to core concepts and their meanings during these introductory retreats are both fundamental to understanding the practice and how to effect it, and sufficient for giving the participant an initial orientation to the Buddhist worldview: to provide access to interpretive frameworks that become meaningful through experience with the practice. Interview material indicates that one's first retreat facilitates access to and engagement with the practice, and a sense or feel for the relationship between practice, philosophy and immediate experience. Beyond that, the marrying of concept and experience that is needed to understand the practice is acquired through ongoing practice and study and taking part in more retreats.

The Participant's Perspective: 'Being on Retreat' and Learning the Practice

While the discussion above explored the nature of doctrinal and practical instruction given at BMIMC, here the discussion turns to how the meditator makes progress in the practice, and begins to acquire a set of references for the interpretation of meditative experience. These reference points begin to form an interpretive framework once their interconnections are understood according to Buddhist doctrine. Comprehension of the Buddhist frame of reference occurs by learning to experientially identify, label, and conceptually categorize mental states. Accordingly, an understanding of the processes of apprehension and comprehension that practitioners undergo necessitates an exploration of the experiential states, and their labelling and categorization, according to Buddhist terminology and meaning.

An overview of the experiences with vipassana described in the interview material suggested that experiential development be categorized into three stages. The first stage consists of those experiences especially common to new meditators that are attributed to a lack of mindfulness: poor concentration, a distracted mind and reactivity to pain. The second occurs when the development of some mindfulness allows the meditator to note these mental distractions and label and investigate them as mental states. With this degree of mindfulness and skill with labelling, the meditator begins to notice, explore and attribute meaning to types of meditative experience, which while experientially part of everyday awareness, have special significance within a Buddhist frame of reference. These experiential types are commonly interpreted as *sukkha*, 'pleasure', dukkha, 'suffering' and anicca, 'impermanence'.

The interview transcript excerpts discussed below show that, at this stage, engagement with the practice depends on the combination of developed concentration and mindfulness with the acquisition of conceptual structures to frame their interpretation. The deeper, more intense experiences involve both the prolonged placement of the mind on an object and deeper, sharper observation of objects or phenomena. The capacity to reach this level of mental stability depends both on length of time as a practitioner and on the regularity and intensity of commitment. The remainder of this Chapter outlines these stages in experiential development and conceptual acquisition. These experiences and their classifications are not intended to be exhaustive of the possibilities that present themselves during retreat participation, but are intended to represent the most common and significant sets of meaning-constructs that are acquired during the learning process, and in turn to show how derived meaning is applied to further practice and personal exploration and transformation, the subject of Chapter 3.

Early experiences with vipassana

For their first retreat, participants typically choose a day or weekend workshop, or a weekend, four- or nine-day retreat. For many, a first vipassana retreat is an extension of an experimental journey that may include other forms of meditation, alternative health practices and other forms of Buddhism. Although novices' familiarity with Buddhism and meditation is variable, most attempt to be open to the experience at least for the duration of the retreat. KT expressed her feeling during her first vipassana retreat (a 10-day retreat) thus: the first two to three days had been 'weird', and she was 'not sure', but on the third day she decided to suspend her doubt because the teachers 'seemed to know what they were talking about'. This mixture of resistance and engagement or willingness to 'take it on' appears to be a common response during a first retreat. During the introductory session at the beginning of a retreat, the Manager requests that 'yogis' move slowly, applying mindfulness to all their actions. However, it often takes time for new practitioners to slow their movements down. My notes from several retreats contain comments about some participants having trouble slowing their movements down and being mindful. Their actions—closing doors noisily, fidgeting with personal possessions and making eye-contact—all displayed a palpable agitation. Many people spent considerable time sleeping during meditation and rest periods. One manager told me that, on nine-day retreats, some participants skip meditation periods for the first few days, seeing that as an opportunity to recover from their stressful daily schedule. While it is recommended that the retreat schedule be adhered to, it is not enforced, and people are at liberty to alter it slightly to suit their own needs. Some interview-respondents spoke openly about their favourite avoidance tactics: staying in their room, reading, doing their washing. Most are simply unused to the continual effort to be mindful that is encouraged by the teachers.

As noted above, ideally all retreat activity contributes to the development of mindfulness. The resistance towards being constantly mindful can be used as a meditation object in itself. When one begins to see how all of the expected retreat behaviours and meditation practices relate to the development of mindfulness, the mind begins to slow naturally and one's resistance usually becomes more manageable. There is a visible change in participants' behaviour: they begin to move more slowly, and those who were absent during some meditation periods begin to attend more sessions. In addition, the quality of one's practice changes after the establishment of some mindfulness. While this may not happen on the first retreat or even for several, meditators reach a point whereat the mind feels sharper, there are fewer gaps in noting, objects are clearer and mental states are easier to distinguish and label. Before this point is reached however, many experience inability to focus or concentrate the mind, inability to stop the internal chatter, and constant distraction from physical pain and strong sensations.

Many report that the inability to concentrate and to remember to note the object as it appears to the mind is a difficulty at this stage, and many say that their minds 'wander everywhere'. Learning about the naturally unruly tendencies of the untrained mind often serves as an incentive for the practitioner to keep trying. One said, 'I can chart my progression over the last four years or whatever, and it took probably two years of nothing much happening, not much of a shift or anything, just going and listening and stuff.' This lack of ability to concentrate is usually accompanied by self-annoyance and self-judgement. EC recalled:

> EC: You're told a thousand times, you know, 'Just be in the moment, and whatever's happening, just observe it and don't buy into it', and all this sort of

stuff. But when you're there and experiencing it emotionally, and of course it's a silent retreat so you're not talking, you're dealing with it by yourself. I was beating myself up about it, and so the more I tried to do it properly, the more I wasn't because I was just getting into this vicious circle of 'Oh no. It's not working', and because it wasn't going to work while I was thinking like that, so like I've had very few meditation sessions where it is just calm and blissful. You know my mind is usually racing at a thousand miles an hour, but I just learnt to accept that. I mean gradually, just by doing the meditation I've got better at it, and probably more so in the last year.

A common problem for meditators in this early stage is the accompaniment of the inability to focus by an almost constant self-judgement for one's lack of ability. This reactivity extends into feeling annoyed with objects external to oneself. After persistent effort, one's noting becomes more consistently applied, and one's reactivity subsides. The same practitioner continues:

EC: I got better at accepting what's happening in that sit, that's just what's happening, like I remember when I first went to the Buddhist library, everything used to annoy me, like the urn turning off and the noises because I kept homing in on them and they just became real issues, and I just gradually realized over time that I was letting go of those external things, and it's just been like a process of osmosis, sinking in and being able to practise what you are told all the time.

Another problematic occurrence for meditators, at this stage and for some time after, is distraction by internal experience such as bodily pain and one's internal dialogue. As Nyanaponika Thera's notion of bare attention conveys, mindfulness is ideally an accurate, non-discursive registering of events.[37] Until mindfulness becomes strong, one aims for an object with minimal conceptual elaboration. Recollections and associative thinking are to be avoided, as they deflect the mind from noting the immediate present. One teacher explained to me that minimal internal dialogue is necessary for noting and investigating the object, 'otherwise the meditation just becomes concentration'. The experience of bodily pain from sitting in the same position for up to an hour is possibly the principal hindrance to mindfulness in the initial stage. One is encouraged not to ease the pain by changing posture, but to observe and note the pain as a meditation object. By maintaining one's posture, one takes the opportunity to observe the nature of the pain.[38] The following account is representative of early retreat experiences described by many practitioners.

HD: There was this beginning stage . . . I was the sort of person who had to move every ten minutes. I suffered extreme pain. I could not follow two breaths in a row. I'd go to the teacher and they'd be very encouraging, and I think it was only the fact that I was going along to the American teachers who I could relate to and who talked about pain . . . I gave someone my car keys on my first retreat so I couldn't run away. They had group interviews, and I'd see that everyone was struggling the same as I was, so I kept at it, not very well. I'd skip a lot of the walking sessions and do my laundry, and I'd read, and I'd go and look at the notice board . . . But for some reason I kept going, I don't know why. So every time one of those teachers would come out to Australia, I'd do a ten-day retreat.

The resistance eventually gives way to more mental engagement with the practice. Even before this point, meditators occasionally report the experience of a quiet, calm mind in meditation. At this stage, too, certain experiences are noted and begin to be interpreted according to a Buddhist perspective. Many connect with the notion of suffering through the bodily pain that arises, and when bare attention is successfully applied to the rise and fall of the breath, it may be used to observe impermanence.[39] Becoming aware that one is prepared to work with whatever presents itself, and that the mind is noting objects as opposed to becoming lost in blind reaction, are taken as signs that mindfulness is developing. Gradually, with persistence, one develops a feeling of equanimity toward one's immediate experience. RN, a practitioner of many years, puts it thus:

GE: So your actual approach to do with method is to note it (the object)?

RN: Yeah. Just be aware and see what happens to it. It may stay around for a while, or it might just disappear in a moment or whatever, to just observe with awareness, see what happens to it.

GE: And the trick is, from what I understand, you suddenly become aware that you've let the mind attach to something and so all you can do is just bring it back to the primary object.

RN: Yeah. Just bring it back to whatever you use as your focus of concentration, because it's just a tool to use without clinging onto . . . because if you cling onto the primary object, then it's just a concentration practice.

Learning to distinguish *samatha* from *vipassana* practice

When some equanimity towards one's immediate experience has developed, the mind becomes more conscious of moments when it loses the object and returns to it more easily. With this increased stability the mind can investigate, label and discriminate between mental states without identifying with them. This capacity is greatly aided by learning to distinguish concentration, the ability to hold the mind on an object, from mindfulness, the ability to know where the mind is placed, and is developed through insight practice, which utilizes *momentary* concentration, wherein the object of concentration is constantly changing.[40] Teachers observe that remaining on an object continuously without noting any change turns insight into concentration, and recommend a more vigorous application of the noting technique to counteract this. It is maintained by Engler that from a psychotherapeutic perspective, concentration as withdrawal from sensory input in progressive states induces conflict-free functioning by temporarily suppressing the operation of the drives and the higher perceptual-intellectual functions.[41] Similarly, Bhikkhu Bodhi states that while the attainment of the jhanas silences the defilements, it does not eradicate them.[42] Accordingly, vipassana is dependent on the arising of afflictive mental states, the defilements that one observes as secondary objects. The excerpt from my own retreat notes below describes my own experiential learning to distinguish concentration from mindfulness in the context of vipassana practice.

3:15–4:00pm, Friday 30 April 2004. During the walking meditation period I began with my usual problem of the chattering mind. I decided just to focus on what was immediate to my experience as I walked, which was awareness of the body (mostly my feet and breathing), the sights passing by my eyes as I walked, and the sounds around me such as the wind, and now-and-then a bird. There was minimal thought—possibly some in the background—but these other things were definitely in the foreground. This describes my 'experiential field' of the moment. In truth, my attention was probably shifting very quickly between these things. Each object registered. That is, I was aware of each object as my attention fell on it. I didn't label the objects with words, I was simply 'aware' that my awareness had shifted and was shifting between these objects. I also noticed, and was thinking in words at this point, that in this more aware state, you seem to register the object more fully: colours and shapes seem brighter, more vivid, or 'something'. The dominant sense of the state was 'awareness'.

During the combined sitting and standing meditation period between 4 and 5pm, my mind was again a bit 'all-over-the-place'. At 4:45pm, the teacher indicated that it was time for standing meditation for those who wished to stand. (We had all been sitting.) I got myself into the lying posture instead. I found myself concentrating on the breath at the abdomen, a dominant object for me in this position. In order to calm the mind, I tried focusing on the breath at the nostrils for a while, which seemed to help. I remember shifting focus between the two places (the abdomen and the nostrils), and still having some awareness of my surroundings in the background. As in the walking meditation, I was clearly noting the shift in attention between objects. After a while I noticed that my attention had primarily settled on the abdomen, and my mind had calmed. There were no racing thoughts and no narratives . . . only awareness of what my mind was focused on. I was alert but calm, and had a sense that all other mental states were agitated by comparison. When it was time to get up and go outside for the walking period, I moved my arm and placed my left hand and forearm on the floor in order to help myself back up into the sitting position. This produced a particular feeling in the mind that I labelled as 'agitation'. I was about to get up and go about things at the pace and in the mental state that I normally experience. Instead, I caught this habitual pattern before it manifested, and deliberately kept focusing on the breath while moving very slowly. There was much more of a quality of calm, alertness, awareness, as I got up, walked to the door, opened and closed it, put my shoes on, and began to walk.

My own understanding of the difference between the two meditation periods was that the former was insight, and the latter predominantly concentration, and that each gave rise to its own dominant quality of mind, focused awareness and calmness respectively. The lying position seemed to facilitate an almost exclusive focus on the abdomen, my mind rarely drifted from it, which produced a concentration-type response. The concentrated mind proved to be a good vantage point from which to note the passing stream of objects, and this was the first time that I had experienced both concentration and mindfulness in this close relationship. Two months later, during the June long-weekend retreat, I recorded the following.

> The teacher began with, "Settle into the body. Be aware of the feeling against the cushion. Note the physical sensations." While listening to the meditation instructions I found, at least for a few minutes, that I kept my awareness on my breath, with thoughts, sleepiness and the semi-dream state being caught before they took over. There was the breath-awareness and the secondary-object awareness, but my mind remembered the primary object with more ease and consistency by comparison with previous times. Gaps in mindful attention still occurred, but for shorter periods, and when they did occur and were noted, the mind shifted back to the breath more easily. It seems to me that this quality of remembering the object, this direct awareness of where the mind is placed and of how much of one's attention is placed there, is 'mindfulness'.

Concentration-experiences are those that people generally equate with meditation: states of mind that are peaceful, even blissful, while at the same time clear and focused. People trying meditation for the first time may come with this expectation. Even those with some experience of Buddhism may view, with awe, the possibility of attaining the jhanas that result from concentration practice.

One teacher commented about the expectations that often accompany the subject of samatha practice and the jhanas:

> HU: And you say jhana, and people go, 'Oh! Jhana!' All of the Buddhist stuff is a continuum. It's not like you're in or you're out. It's just this progression of the whole teachings. They weave in with each other, and you just understand at a deeper level, or that your practice becomes at a deeper level. The first jhanic factor is initial application, and the next one is sustained application. And then there comes what they call rapture, and the other one is the one-pointedness. That's it. That's the jhanic factors, and obviously if you practise long enough sitting on the breath and they take on a very different perspective, but they're just normal things that we're all familiar with . . .

Some meditators bring to the practice a previously developed concentration ability and an acquired appreciation of its meditative value. HR first encountered the samatha and vipassana practices, and the difference between them, through reading a book, the technique for the latter being given as to 'fix attention on whatever comes along'. When she tried concentration practice some time later, she found it useful as a support for the vipassana. Her concentration strengthened, her mind was calmer and more centred, and did not wander as much. SI described her prior experience with concentration practice at the Sydney Zen Centre before taking up vipassana.

> SI: The bliss? It was just very deep, and I went into the state of nothingness and timelessness, and I kept on losing the body. That's in my first meditation. When I came out of it I found it didn't really relate to daily life, and that the way you could get the best techniques was in meditation, and then it didn't give you any help to deal with ordinary daily problems or difficulties that arose.

Both practitioners had arrived at their own conclusions about the value of concentration practice before their involvement with BMIMC, but many others learn to attribute value to these two types of experience through practical instruction and dhamma-talks given during retreats and in workshops. With respect to the goal of practice, the experiences arising from the two practices are classed roughly as productive or unproductive, in that experiences of sukkha that arise from concentration are accepted as part of the practice, and as a sign that concentration is developing, but not as ends in themselves.

From theory to practice: an exercise in *right effort*

On occasion, a teacher will facilitate the student's experiential grasp of a concept by means of a short exercise. In one of the Monday night meditation sessions in March 2004, the teacher introduced the concept of right effort, one of the three concentration factors from the Noble Eightfold Path, and its application to meditation practice. During the second sitting, we were instructed to keep the mind on the rise and fall of the abdomen. 'When the mind wanders, note the wandering, and bring the mind back to the breath'. A while later the teacher instructed us to put effort into keeping the mind on the primary object, using as much effort as we needed to, and to note the effort involved. After about five minutes, he asked us to divide into groups of two or three to discuss our experience of using effort in this way. Some comments were 'more awake', 'felt like I was waking up', 'with more effort I was more successful but tired' and 'the effort made me feel tired'. The teacher had us apply effort for a further five minutes and note the effort but with more emphasis on the noting. Noting in this instance meant to be continually aware of how much effort was involved from moment to moment. Discussion followed, with the comment from the teacher that when the effort is noted, less effort becomes needed because the system somehow rights itself. By extending the second sitting into the discussion, the teacher built effectively on the experiential state established in the meditation. Practitioners had identified and established in their minds the factor of right effort.

By learning to work with right effort in this way practitioners could go on to develop an understanding of the relationship between the three concentration factors right effort, right mindfulness and right concentration. In explaining the development of the three concentration factors of the Noble Eight-Fold Path, Ven. U Silananda draws attention to the phrase from the Satipatthana Sutta, 'ardently, clearly comprehending and mindful'. 'Ardently' here refers to investing energy into being mindful and therefore the energy you invest, 'when you have mindfulness combined with energy or effort, the mind can stay on the object for some time, and therefore has concentration'. He adds that the three aspects of the group of concentration must be practised together.[43] This example, like the one before it, has an experiential base which is easy to access and identify with the aid of the labelling technique. The broader conceptual framework takes a period of time to comprehend.

Applied mindfulness: identifying the *hindrances*

The five hindrances to meditation, sense-desire, aversion (usually experienced as anger), sloth and torpor (usually expressed as laziness or tiredness), restlessness (when the mind is distracted) and doubt (about the efficacy of the practice), are listed under dhammas, the fourth satipatthana.[44] The early experiences mentioned above demonstrate the action of the hindrances on the mind before its training to identify them. Inability to hold the mind on the breath is often a result either of sleepiness or restlessness, and one's immediate reaction to physical pain is aversion, wanting to push the pain away. Daydreaming and thinking about a favourite television program can be classed as sense-desire. Teaching addresses these by drawing attention to what goes on in the mind habitually. This was the purpose of observing Noble Silence between 7pm and 10am during Retreat 1, described above. When asked to describe experiences within the period of Noble Silence, one participant's response was 'irritability'. The teacher explained that the purpose was to notice the effect that silence has on our registering and noting of mental states, the rise and ebb of which occur continually in daily life, without our noticing them. We do not need to get annoyed with ourselves for having them, but just to observe their rising and ebbing, their effect on the body, and their quality.[45]

Participants on a four-day retreat ranged from beginners to advanced.[46] To cater for this range of experience, the teacher held a *beginner's mind group* from 5pm to 6pm and scheduled interviews for advanced practitioners in the afternoons on the first three days. The purpose of the group was to discuss problems arising in meditation, how to deal with them, and to clarify points of technique. Among the teacher's responses to the range of questions put to him in the session on the first day of the retreat, the following related to the subject of the hindrances:

1. Where sleepiness is a problem in maintaining a focus on the breath, pay attention to connection between the breath and the sleepiness. Does sleepiness occur on the in-breath or out-breath?
2. When pain comes, focus on it. Do you notice aversion? Then switch your attention to the resistance. Notice the quality of the labelling so as to be more aware of the quality of the resistance—to the sensation, and to being aware—as in, e.g. 'dislike'. Notice the sensation and the relationship to the pain. Try another posture if the pain is really distracting. This is better than fidgeting and losing concentration.
3. In dealing with aversion, e.g. thinking about getting through the next three days of the retreat, 'don't believe the story'. Here the teacher explained that the ideal is not to get involved with the content of the story, or with thinking about the various things and issues that arise in one's mind, such as life's events, or things that need to be done after the retreat. The idea is to note the mental content accurately, then return to the primary object. For example, is the thought of getting through the next three days an aversion?

In the examples above the two teachers used minimal doctrinal categorical terminology, referring to the hindrances as 'mind-states' or distractions, and states that people typically report experiencing and having difficulty with. Learning occurs through noting the different mental states experienced during meditation, with the purpose of training the mind to acknowledge and understand the nature of distraction. From this perspective, aversion and avoidance are seen as a strategy for dealing with existential pain. Another function of training in recognizing the hindrances is to learn to work with them correctly in order to break down our natural resistance to being aware. These were the purposes of a nine-day retreat in April–May 2004.[47]

During this retreat, the five hindrances were treated both as meditation-objects and as a labelling system for the mental states experienced during practice. In this way, a more developed framework was introduced, a typology for noting, identifying and discriminating between mental states. In brief, the method was to note and label the state, and to explore its quality without 'buying into any surrounding story'. The teachers explained that one may find that the story has already begun to unfold as the mental state is noted. This was held to be more likely with sense-desire and aversion, because they are more object-directed than sleepiness or restlessness.[48] The state was to be identified through selection of the hindrance that best described it. During the retreat a small number of talks were devoted specifically to the subject of the hindrances. They were named and described, and how to work with them in meditation was addressed. For instance, on the sixth day, the morning talk described their role in the excuses we make for not being able to meditate properly. These included the like of blaming the schedule or the length of meditation periods or the noise made by other meditators. This method of investigation and recognition for correction was the backbone of the retreat.

The technique was supplemented with two others: application of compassionate understanding and thought-reflection. The teachers explained, "When we think of our own problems and difficulties, we direct feelings of compassion towards ourselves, not least when we develop aversion to our own inability to meditate successfully because we have allowed the hindrances to meditation to dominate." The practice of compassionate understanding was applied to training in the hindrances by labelling them and objectifying their content. This allowed participants to see the process instead of getting caught in the story. By observing the effect of the content on the body, emotions and mind, we directly experienced the suffering caused to ourselves. This demonstrated cause and effect, and also engendered compassion for others because we understood what others experience. I recalled one of my experiences from this retreat in conversation with HU, one of the teachers from the Centre.

> GE: When you were talking about feelings of discomfort, in just letting be, it was interesting because that's one of my own problems. There's that real wanting to get away from unpleasant things. It actually dominates a lot of my meditation.

> HU: That's a realization, that's what's happening. The hard thing is this thing of beating up on yourself, this 'I'm no good, I can't do this', or whatever . . . That's generally what happens next when you have this sort of realization . . . so that's the next thing: 'Ah! I'm judging myself.' So it's kind of like working through all these different strategies we have, that the hindrances

essentially block us from observing what's really happening, and they're just different mental processes, different values or interpretations we put on the experience.

GE: That's actually an area where I had an experience akin to what you're talking about: if you let it be, it changes. I did a nine-day retreat earlier this year, where the teachers were working a lot with the hindrances. They were saying, "Note the mental state, label it, and then go back to the breathing." Well, I was amazed! It took a few goes to do it, but I'd been really, really, sleepy. That was when I'd first noticed it, and instead of just going with it, I noted it and literally, in words, told myself to 'be more mindful'. So I sat there focusing on the breath while I was aware of the sleepiness, and it started to change. And I thought, "Oh. That's how that can be used!" That was my first awareness of that, because before, I was just going with the sleepiness.

My retreat notes about the above experience read

> At one point during the retreat I was having considerable trouble with drowsiness, as I often do. I found that by labelling the mental state 'sleepiness', and further, by sitting with it while focusing on the feel of it, rather than discussing it internally and getting annoyed, I was able to maintain a mindful focus on the state, even while I was experiencing the state at the same time. It seemed that my mind had two states concurrently until a short time had passed, the drowsiness subsided, and the state of mindfulness remained.

This was both my first experience of being able to direct or control my own mental state in meditation, and a striking instance of the direct application of a doctrinal framework to the contents of immediate experience. It may appear that experience is being interpreted in its immediacy, but this learning process has distinct experiential and conceptual components. The bare attention to the state, applying mindfulness to the experience as my example demonstrates, functions to keep internal discourse to a minimum and prevents the mind from identifying with the state itself. After a while, the state itself begins to change and mindfulness remains. This is a clear example of the transformative function of mindfulness at the experiential level where all conceptual activity is about the experience, and internal discourse is minimal. As with learning to distinguish concentration and insight practice, the process has two aspects. The first is learning to identify the hindrances experientially by applying the labelling system to the contents of experience. The second is learning the meaning and value attributed to them by Buddhist doctrine.

In Buddhism, the classification of mental states as wholesome or unwholesome is a consequence of their role in one's progress on the path to enlightenment. This categorization is exemplified by the relationship between the hindrances and the enlightenment factors as negative and positive, unwholesome and wholesome mental states, respectively. This doctrinal stance was explained during one of the dhamma-talks during Retreat 2. It was stated that with practice, the hindrances sense-desire, aversion, sloth and torpor, restlessness and doubt may start to recede, and the enlightenment factors mindfulness, tranquillity, investigation, energy, joy, concentration and equanimity may start to arise. U Silananda makes the statement that the hindrances are removed only when they make room for more wholesome mental states, suggesting that they will not be removed from one's experience before the enlightenment factors themselves are cultivated. He adds that the enlightenment factors are the components of knowledge of the dhammas, which begins with 'discerning the arising and fading away'.[49] Temporary removal of the hindrances occurs in meditation when one is mindful. However, it can be seen that lasting self-transformation involves development of habitual positive mental states. The impetus for sustained application is the experience of the absence of the hindrances in meditation, and how clear the mind itself feels when it is not experiencing one of these mental states, coupled with their designation as unwholesome states.

Insight experiences: pleasure, suffering and impermanence

When mindfulness is developed to a degree whereat the noting technique is rigorously and constantly applied, and the practitioner has learnt to identify and have some direction over the hindrances, the practitioner's mind becomes more stable in meditation. Generally, progress is discerned in the fact that practitioners realize that their minds have lost their tendencies to wander, and they are capable of more prolonged and deeper levels of concentration and mindfulness. They can sustain attention on a single object without slipping into concentration because the technique of constant noting is strong. In the following excerpt, the practitioner, also a teacher, was commenting on his appreciation of the aspect of the practice involving the primary object. However, within his reflection about Mahasi's instructions to do with following the secondary object later in the practice, is a description of how the mind can settle on objects once the hindrances have been dealt with.

> HU: I mean, the whole thing with that—the whole relationship with the primary object—is quite a difficult one to come to terms with because there can often be a sense of pushing this other thing away and coming back to the primary object, and that's not necessarily the skilful way of doing it, either. It's like pushing this thing away. It's like there's an aversion there.

> GE: And that can be the very thing that gives you more understanding of what's going on?

HU: I mean, that's one of the things with the Mahasi system, that it tends to—in my way of thinking—tends to overemphasize the primary object. It's funny because it's presented as a mindfulness practice. If you look at it, it's essentially a concentration practice. If you're continually bringing your attention back to this one object, then it's concentration. But if you actually read the Mahasi stuff, later on after he's gone through all this detailed explanation, 'watch the rising and falling', there'll be a paragraph saying, 'later in the practice, if other things arise you just note them. Don't worry about the rising and falling.' But it's kind of like a little addendum here. But to me, in many ways, that's the practice. My understanding is that at a later point, when a lot of those hindrances and the mental stuff have started to drop away, it's not so much an issue, whether it's the abdomen or some other object, that the mind will naturally rest on a particular single object or process, and concentration will be there naturally without this kind of struggle. To me, mindfulness is in some ways a tool to concentration, a way of dealing with all of this other stuff, you know, the self-judgment, the doubt, the aversions, all the rest of it. It's like these are all the things that are happening, and after a while, after watching all the different things we throw up, they just all start to drop away. And then there's a much clearer object, there's the body or the breath or whatever, and not all this other stuff. But if we just try and go for the object, and all this other stuff's happening, then we don't really know how to deal with it. And then we're in this struggle between 'Oh, come back to the abdomen. Oh, I'm no good at it. Come back to the abdomen.' It's just this constant struggle.

KBN adverts to his ability to select and maintain focus on a specific object:

KBN: . . . Vipassana, which I understand as taking whatever phenomena present themselves as predominant to the attention. So, one brings attention to the primary object. I'll expand on this. The primary object is the breathing for me, like I'll always look at the breathing, but the breathing is never a very dominant object. It's always something else, and in retreats it's often just the sitting. So I've come to slowly realize that the actual sitting, the contemplation of sitting itself, the whole body sitting, is actually an object, the most common object I've used, so the breathing is somewhere within that and I can zoom in onto the kind of smaller phenomena. The sitting as a whole is what I use, being in that sitting, and within that there are objects within that. So that hardness of the cushion or the seat itself which is earth element, that hardness itself can be an object. One can have one's attention on that quite a lot. It gives you a base to look at other things.

This practitioner's reference to the sensation of hardness as the earth element is a reference to the *dhatu,* the elemental aspects of experience. The four elements are a conceptual scheme to map direct experience. In February

2004, instruction about use of the elements in this manner was given during a four-day retreat for beginners and advanced practitioners. Their use as meditation objects is to develop accuracy and precision of awareness. In that they relate to sensory awareness—to movement, tingling, sensation, pressure, heat, light and more—they are related to everyday awareness. Their contemplation aids development of the mindfulness needed for practitioners to observe their experience.

Another aspect of one's practical development at this point concerns the relationship between the experiential state and its labelling. The range of experiences described above, and even their labels in most instances, are common to the realm of everyday experience. This includes the inability to concentrate the mind, the chattering mind and being distracted by physical pain. Even the hindrances, in both effect and terminology, are part of one's everyday reality. However, beginning with the discrimination of concentration and insight, experiences become harder to make sense of without understanding their relevance from a Buddhist perspective, and without reference to the Buddhist frameworks that support the doctrinal constructs. For instance, many people appreciate suffering and impermanence as concepts, the experiences of which do not take much mindfulness to identify in meditation. One can identify them as physical pain and the changing stream of sensations that dominate the mind's attention. However, the deeper experiences relating to these constructs that advanced practitioners describe occurred after many years' experience in the practice. It appears that with the development of mindfulness and access to deeper meditative states comes the need to utilize Buddhist terminology and frameworks in their understanding. The experiential account below illustrates a range of experiences that are often reported by practitioners with considerable experience in the practice.

HD: My experiences so far I sort of put into three stages. There was this beginning stage. I had to move every ten minutes. I suffered extreme pain. I could not follow two breaths in a row . . . A little bit of concentration started to develop. I could use pain as a concentration object. Then I noticed that the pain was not constant—that when I watched it, it would break up—and on one retreat I found I could be mindful all day long. I could feel more sensations than the day before. I had so much energy I didn't need to sleep, and I'd observe many aspects to the rising and falling. I used to do extremely slow walking meditation, like we're talking an hour to do ten metres. I could see all these minute sensations. And yeah, one afternoon I was doing meditation, and suddenly nausea started overwhelming me—it was just extremely unpleasant—and fear as well. I couldn't sleep. I'd turn over and my body was just vibration. In the second period, when everything got more exciting, and interesting and fascinating—and it was really pleasant—the body's really pleasant. Then the dukkha decade followed. That was the third stage, which was basically the 1990s, I suppose. A large part of that was very unpleasant sensations in the body, and I believe that this stage of where you're gaining insight into dukkha very strongly, is very short for some people, and very intense and long for others.

At the time of interview, the practitioner felt that her practice was moving into a new phase, wherein she was experiencing changeability from one sitting to another during intensive practice: from pain in the body to pleasant sensations in the body to equanimity; to frustrating sits where there was little sensation in the body and no discernible object. She had interpreted this as the mind's reviewing mental states such as desire and aversion, with a view to 'giving them up, releasing them'. It must be noted that this practitioner's recall of the changes to the nature of her practice over time is atypical of interview-respondents' experiential descriptions. Instead, when asked about their experience with vipassana, either routine or unusual, they tend to recall either one experience or one kind of experience that occurs regularly. With the development of mindfulness, a practitioner's experiences, means of interpretation and skill in the practice appear to accumulate with time, and specific instances appear to contribute to this sense of overall accumulation, adding to the practitioner's stock of knowledge. Most typically, insight experiences tend to be 'pleasurable', interpreted as sukkha, or of the nature of dukkha and anicca. While the practitioner's experience described above appears dominated by one type of experience—pleasure, suffering or impermanence—at any time, suffering and impermanence tend to dominate, and appear related in practitioners' experiences. Some advanced practitioners recalled experiences of 'deep sukkha'. I instance the following:

> KBN: I was sitting, sitting, sitting, and then I noticed I had built up some saliva. I was swallowing mouthfuls of saliva, and then I had . . . I was like a rocket ship, vapours streaming off me. There was a complete lightness of being, feeling I could just . . . someone said to me it was like a rebirth experience, remembering your mouth being full, so I rushed off to see (the teacher) and he said, "You're just experiencing a deep level of sukkha", but I think, "What was its significance?" It was just extreme comfort, which is probably an effect of deep concentration.

Many advanced practitioners recalled experiences typically associated with vipassana practice, and related to dukkha and anicca, the first two of the three marks of existence: dukkha, anicca and anatta. Those practitioners who reported these experiences had been practising variously between six and thirty years. One practitioner of six years' experience in vipassana, who had developed a strong concentration practice in both Transcendental Meditation and Zen before learning vipassana, found this helpful in developing the momentary concentration needed for insight practice. Some practitioners reported experiencing dukkha in ways that went beyond the registering of the physical pain that occurs from sitting for long periods. The following excerpt, which illustrates the practitioner's development of mindfulness and ability to meditate on pain, also indicates the beginning of what is commonly interpreted as the experience of anicca:

> HD: For some reason I kept going, and then I suppose a little bit of concentration started to develop. I'd do a ten-day [retreat] here and a twenty-day there, and I still thought I was hopeless. But I kept doing it, and then I . . . yeah! I did start to notice that I could use pain. I used to get a sheet of pain in my back. Then I noticed that the pain was not constant; that when I watched it it would break up, and there would be vibration in the pain, and I think I remember telling the teachers that some of the vibrations are painful and some aren't. So that was quite exciting, and I sensed that the teachers . . . they would say, "Oh, keep going."

As indicated, the concepts of suffering and impermanence are easier to identify and interpret in one's experience, and easier to utilize in the construction of one's frame of reference. Some experiences can be interpreted afterwards, as was noted above, and some experiences seem to come as part of an experience-concept package in that they have already been shaped by doctrinal material. During participant observation, in the teachings and instructions from several retreats and Monday night meditation sessions, and from interview material, I observed how certain lists—conceptual maps—are employed to map, out experience, and how the teachers introduce these concepts to aid learning and understanding of the practice.

Mahasi Sayadaw states that the purpose of vipassana practice is to observe and contemplate the swift and successive occurrences of mental phenomena that seem to occur simultaneously, but in fact occur sequentially. With practice comes the ability to observe the arising and vanishing of each process at the very moment of its occurrence.[50] Some practitioners referred to the arising and passing away of phenomena, and some to the breakdown of phenomena, which they took to be experience of impermanence. The experience of arising, and its interpretation as impermanence, formed the basis of reflections and contemplations about dependent origination for one practitioner. When asked about specific meditative experiences, she responded, "I suppose the teaching of dependent origination is something that comes into my mind now, just watching the way things arise, and relate it to other things like the connections between things." Without further description it is hard to tell exactly how the connections are observed, but the meditator's words indicate that she used the basic experience of the arising of phenomena to reflect upon the doctrine of dependent origination. Suffering and impermanence were recalled as dominant in SI's experience of the dukkha *jnanas*, 'insight knowledges of suffering', while on a one-month solitary retreat:

SI: . . . and they took me to depths of concentration that I have never experienced before in my life, nor since, and they took me through. It's still in the dukkha jnanas. You've probably read about them. The dukkha jnanas are the three insight knowledges; you know, when we see impermanence for the first time. You know how we all experience impermanence, but it's quite mental. We're still living in it, you know. They take you to a point where you see mind-moments and nothing else.

GE: So you've actually got to be quite concentrated.

SI: You actually see that there is no mind moment before and there is no mind moment yet to come. There is non-existence except for that one moment, and I'd seen it some time before. They wanted me to get through the dukkha jhanas as soon as possible, and so I still live in the past and future and all of that, but I actually know, I have seen, that they don't exist. It comes instantaneously like a flash, but your behaviour takes years to catch up with your insight, and when they took me through it was like it just happened (inaudible) most horrific experience of your life, and Joseph Goldstein describes it as the time when a yogi picks up their mat and goes home. It's just pain, absolute mental pain. It lasts for about three days—I can't believe it—it's too hard.

From the examples above it can be seen that practitioners' experiences lend themselves to interpretation as suffering and impermanence. Only one interview respondent reported a direct experience of anatta, not-self. Mahasi Sayadaw outlines the goal of practice as the realization 'that the self, the living entity, exists as a continuous process of elements of mind which occur singly at a time and in succession'.[51] The experience of anatta is a stated outcome of the practice. However, comments during interview reflect the practitioner's own contemplations about the notion, as opposed to their direct experience of it. When I commented to one of the teachers that while, in general, practitioners had some understanding of dukkha and anicca, but seemed to have trouble with anatta; that they take it on more as a given, he responded:

EBS: They don't really have any experience of it, because when people come to Buddhism from Christianity, the key representative of the objective space of being is God. The representative in the subjective space of being is *me*. So this relationship between the two is really significant. So I think where this leads people is that there's fear around not-self for a lot of people. People are not fearful of anicca because they can see it, and they have experience of the notion of suffering. They have experiences of not being happy, and the notion of 'just when I think I've got my act together, on some level I don't feel happy'. So they've kind of got it, right? The same with impermanence. It's pretty obvious. You can see things arising and passing away. It's actually not a threat to my existence that things arise and pass away. What is a threat to my existence is that I don't have everyday experiences of this. Everyday experience provides everyday data, and I reckon this is one of the things you only get by intensive meditation.

It appears that the notion of anatta, and its somewhat anticipated experience, serves as an aim and inspiration for continued practice in that it is taken on as a proposition to work with. In this way, it serves the same function as the notion of *sunyata*, emptiness, dominant in the thought and discourse of the vajrayana practitioners discussed in Chapter 4. Two further doctrinal frameworks need mentioning in this respect. The first is Mahasi Sayadaw's *Thirteen Stages of Insight*, which practitioners tend to use as a reference for confirmation of their progress in the practice. The second is the Noble Eight-Fold Path and its eight factors, outlined above. All participant observation and interview data collected from both centres, BMIMC and Vajrayana Institute, indicate that this doctrine plays a sizeable role in the commitment process for both groups of practitioners. Bhikkhu Bodhi's and Keown's comments, that the path is cumulative but non-linear where the eight factors are practised simultaneously,[52] are relevant to a consideration of the learning process for vipassana practitioners. Although the tradition holds samadhi to refer to samatha, concentration-meditation, and panna to wisdom in the sense of insight,[53] and Western practitioners come to this understanding with time, in the early stages of involvement two of the three terms hold slightly different meanings. Samadhi appears to refer to both samatha and vipassana meditations, while panna, 'wisdom', is understood in the sense of knowledge: the application of Buddhist doctrine to experience. Throughout one's engagement with vipassana and Buddhism, the combination of panna, sila and samadhi provides continuous orientation to the practice.

The Four Noble Truths in concept and experience

From this perspective, the doctrine of the Four Noble Truths, which is an overarching framework for the interpretation of experience and existence, is probably the one least able to be experienced directly. People come to an appreciation and acceptance of it through reflection on its import. The following practitioner's experience on his first retreat indicates how the notion of suffering can be grasped experientially, and how it may lead to an acceptance of the Four Noble Truths.

> GE: So, with that first retreat, when you said you were starting to get a sense of the Four Noble Truths and the nature of suffering, how did that apply to your meditation?

EBS: I think it was this realization that there was a way of thinking about my existence that I never thought about before, and that if I applied the scientist approach, to just keep collecting data, that it seemed like it all made sense. Because the way I often describe insight to people is you can kind of do it with those dot drawings that the kids have, that if you join them all up according to one-two-three-four-five, it might turn out like it's a donkey, but if you join them up a different way, it's the same dots, all of a sudden you see an elephant. So it's the same data, but you're seeing things quite differently. So, for me, notions like the Four Noble Truths. So the notion of suffering is the First Truth. I think the first retreat was mainly around that, but the other Noble Truths are quite . . . it takes you a while to really get them, so the notion that the cause of this is craving. So it's like . . . to get that, I think you often need a really good sense of suffering—dukkha just arising—because then you can watch out for the next bit underneath it, which is the craving. So you can't just go straight to craving. I think it does go one-two-three-four. You've gotta get the picture of dukkha in yourself.

GE: In retreats, was that just reflecting on life experience, like watching thoughts and things come up, or was it more to do with physical pain?

EBS: It was more to do with physical, actual experience. So I think in the first retreat, the general notion of dukkha. To get that, I need to have a lot of detail, specifics of dukkha, to get a general sense of dukkha. So I think that Goldstein and Salzburg were very good, the way they were running their retreats, because it's about working at a minute level with pain. So 'Just keep sitting. Just keep watching what the mind does with that pain. Just stay with it a little bit longer. Another ten seconds. Just watch that.' So this notion of working moment-to-moment with what is going on, and seeing moment-to-moment how dukkha arises, and it arises everywhere—in your body, in your mind—and it was a sense of being pointed like a scientist would be to the data. Keep looking at it. And don't just understand it theoretically. Find it in the next moment. You'll find it five seconds later, five seconds later, five seconds later, so it's 'keep bringing it back to what's going on now'. This is the sensation.

Conclusions

Exploration and discussion in this chapter has focused largely on learning as the process of attribution of meaning to experiential states. Familiarity with the practices, experiential states and their interpretive frameworks can be seen to constitute a stock of knowledge that practitioners acquire from their participation,[54] learn to work with individually in the practice, and begin to use reflection upon experience more generally. This stock of knowledge is acquired through two processes: apprehension as the experiential identification, labelling and conceptual categorization of mental states, and comprehension as the acquired understanding of the relationships between these categorizations, within the Buddhist frame of reference, according to Buddhist terminology and meaning. Apprehension was seen to take place in three general stages of experiential development and conceptual acquisition. The first stage consists of those experiences, especially common to new meditators, that are attributed to a lack of mindfulness: poor concentration, a distracted mind and reactivity to pain. The second occurs when the development of some mindfulness allows the meditator to note these mental distractions, and to label and investigate them as mental states. With this degree of mindfulness and skill with labelling established, the meditator begins to notice, explore and attribute meaning to types of meditative experience that, while experientially part of everyday awareness, have special significance within a Buddhist frame of reference. These experiential types are commonly interpreted as sukkha, dukkha and anicca, 'impermanence'. Generally, experiences belonging to the first two stages are easy to recall and articulate. Even the hindrances are within the realm of everyday experience. The later, 'stage-three' experiences become harder to discuss without recourse to Buddhist doctrinal terminology, and without conceptual preparation and mediation beforehand.

From an individual perspective, several factors may affect one's progress in learning the practice. It was shown that learning on a first retreat has two facets. The first is understanding the purpose and structure of the retreat setting and acclimatizing to it, and the second is one's learning and understanding of and development in the practice. With respect to the first, in reality it may take a new practitioner more than one retreat, and usually several, to get used to being 'on retreat', but it does not take more than a few days for even the most agitated participant in the group to begin to settle into the routine. The nature and rate of one's development in the practice can be affected by the number, frequency and length of retreats attended. From the above, it can be seen that shorter retreats give a taste. A novice learns the basal technique, some of the fundamental concepts and their practical applications. Longer retreats give the mind time to settle and to let go of one's everyday life and mental state. When the mind slows things may come to the surface, and this allows for more prolonged observation. The practitioner may gain a clearer picture of what is normally masked by an everyday mental state. For instance, longer retreats allow more time to identify, observe and work with the hindrances. However, the learning process is somewhat different for each practitioner. The acquisition of a stock of knowledge will continue with participation in retreats, workshops and weekly meditation sessions, or by attending Buddhist talks and classes.

The nature of this stock of knowledge will be affected by: the nature of practical instruction and doctrinal tuition given; what is dominant in practitioners' experiences during a given retreat; practitioners' own responses and what supplementary practices and dhamma-talks they encounter. The process of learning vipassana must be understood as more than a matter of learning the outer behaviours of a meditator, and learning the meanings of concepts associated with the practice in the way that one learns a new language.[55] Learning becomes more self-directed by success in accessing states of awareness that are normally obscured in everyday awareness. Beyond the experience of the distracted mind, the meditator accesses mental states that normally have no meaning or existence outside of everyday life. For instance, many have trouble identifying, initially, mindfulness as a quality of mind within their own experience. The effort to do so means that one must learn new concepts, and the experience they designate, which are not part of one's habitual taken-for-granted reality.[56] This also means that, without a concrete model for one's action and experience, role-learning becomes more self-reflexive in the way that Dawson's notion of reflextive role reenactment suggests: that role-taking becomes increasingly about role-making.[57]

Chapter 3

Self-Transformation through *Vipassana* Practice

Introduction

This chapter examines the techniques through which change is produced, experienced, and attributed meaning by practitioners of vipassana meditation through their personal application of the technique. Whereas Chapter 2 explored the learning process as it occurs in the context of the vipassana-retreat, this chapter explores the continuation and extension of learning through personal application. The retreat-setting exposes a practitioner to a specific range of practices, principally vipassana, and to a lesser extent metta, 'lovingkindness', and to a range of doctrinal constructs and their inter-related meanings from the Pali Canon and its commentarial literature. Thus, a practitioner accesses and acquires a new stock of knowledge: that which is held to be true about the physical social world, including sets of meaning-constructs and methods for producing and interpreting experiential states. Acquisition is active in that participants are seen to immerse themselves experimentally in the practice and its meaning-making processes. This chapter's examination of the application of this stock of knowledge to transformation of the self reveals those facets of the new meaning-system that are actively utilized, tested, validated, accepted and accorded value by the practitioners. In so doing, it supports Wentworth's argument for the equation of socialization with active appropriation of the belief system,[1] as discussed in Chapter 1.

As asserted by Stromberg, and Staples and Mauss, religious change may be understood as an act of self-transformation.[2] For the purpose of understanding the nature of the transformative process in context, conceptions of the self, including how its ordinary and transformed states are conceived within the new frame of reference, must represent as accurately as possible those held by the religious actors. The significance that practitioners attach to changes in immediate subjective awareness experienced during practice, and subsequent changes to behaviour and self-appreciation as validation of the truth of the meaning-system, suggests that the conception of the transformed self as identity-change is limited in its capacity to represent the complexity of the transformation process. For this reason, discussion in the latter part of the Chapter, *The Sense of Self and Its Transformations*, considers those conceptions of the self from both Buddhist and academic perspectives, best utilized in the understanding of the self-transformation process in the context of vipassana practice. In accordance with the overall aim of the Chapter, to understand how doctrine is further tested and validated through one's experimental immersion in the practice after some initial socialization has occurred, the current chapter is divided into three sections: *Patterns of Personal Practice, Types of Transformation and Their Interpretive Frameworks*, and *The Sense of Self and Its Transformations*. This Chapter and Chapter 5, which take up the same discussion but for practice at Vajrayana Institute, prepare the ground for Chapter 6, which considers the relationship between meaning derived from the practitioner's exploration of the meaning-system, self-transformation through application, and the practitioner's decision to accept and commit to the new perspective.

Patterns of Personal Practice

Experience has shown the Centre's teachers that many meditators find it difficult to maintain a regular practice once the retreat is over. While retreat experience and learning may induce an immediate resolve in the participant to cultivate mindfulness in daily life, in reality the demands of a busy life mean that time for meditation may be rare, and seem inimical to the maintenance of a calm, clear mind. Therefore, teachers try to help practitioners to put some 'safeguards' in place. Fundamentally, the advice for daily meditation is to abandon the expectation that the retreat milieu can be replicated. Given the shorter periods of time available for daily practice, in periods of half-an-hour or so, more time will be spent on keeping attention on the primary object. Compared with the kind of development that takes place during a retreat, the mind does not achieve the depth of mindfulness or concentration possible on longer retreats, where it has more continuous time in which to settle and focus. One teacher suggested that for progress to occur, a regular time every day should be chosen for at least three months. If daily practice lapses, do not give in to the distraction or resistance, but choose to be attentive as if on retreat and resolve to work with whatever condition you are in. Another 'safeguard' was to be guided by the five precepts in our observations of what conditions our choices in daily life.

All interview-respondents either maintained or attempted to maintain a regular personal practice. Most of them either meditated daily or several times a week, usually for twenty minutes or longer, depending on the inclination of the practitioner and the time available to them. The range is indicated by SI who sits 'two hours a day minimum', and HR, who is not strict about daily practice, and just sits 'as often I can'. In the few weeks preceding the interview, she noted that she had felt the impulse to meditate when she needed to settle internally. The following responses illustrate the range of individual approaches to practice.

HD: I don't have a strong daily practice. I come to the weekly sit here at the Centre. I usually meditate for at least fifteen minutes before I go to bed. I usually do two retreats a year, at least two, so every year I would have done, I suppose, a month of meditation for the last fifteen years.

KT: I meditate regularly; vipassana, *brahmaviharas;* developing the *paramis.*

KN: [I] read books, do meditation. Meditation is semi-regular, a couple of times a week, before bed, weekend afternoons. I do metta on the train.

FV: Vipassana meditation and walking meditation form the main part of my practice. Along with some compassion and lovingkindness practice. If I don't practice daily, then about four to five times per week. On a Sunday I meet with a few other practitioners and we do a group sit.

SI: I wake up in the morning and I do the paramis. Normally I sit two hours a day minimum. If I don't practise daily, I'd probably do a practice about four to five times per week, and I've been doing that for seven years.

BM: *Anapanasati,* or mindfulness of breathing. I study a bit for reflection, then take it into meditation. I try to sit a couple of hours each day. I use mindfulness as an ongoing activity, where meditation strengthens the continuity of mindfulness.

MV: I mostly practise anapanasati, mindfulness of breathing, moving into what we call *shikantaza,* just sitting practice, and metta practice. Maybe six months ago I discontinued that as a regular practice, but I would do metta practice every day. Part of the practice would be metta, then I'd go into mindfulness of breathing-practice.

During interview, many respondents included descriptions of 'everyday' practices: techniques incorporated into everyday activities and contexts outside of the regular sitting or walking practice. Some practitioners also consider regular or quasi-regular reading periods and attendance at workshops and retreats, to be personal practice. Practitioners typically supplement their vipassana practice with metta meditation and other practices that aim to cultivate wholesome mental and emotional states. Throughout the following discussion it will be evident that the changes that individuals report are attributable to success with these practices.

Personal Practice: Techniques to Complement Vipassana

The contribution of samatha practice to vipassana

The experiences recounted as a result of vipassana are predominantly insight-related in that they involve the observation of internal phenomena that are easily categorized according to the four satipatthanas, to be discussed presently. One practitioner reported having unusual bodily sensations and visions, and another described an experience of 'having a sense of energetic connection with everything'. Experiences such as these, when they occur, are typically noted and dismissed by returning to the primary object. Similarly, some practitioners report the occasional experience of bliss states,[3] which they interpret as a byproduct of the development of samadhi, 'concentration', that occurs through vipassana practice, where it functions to support mindfulness for access to more penetrating insight. The differences between the experiential effects of samadhi, 'concentration', and sati, 'mindfulness', their role in learning the vipassana technique, and their role in socialization into the Theravada worldview were considered in Chapter 2. However, of relevance at this point in the discussion is the role of prior experience with samatha in the utilization of vipassana as a transformative technique.

Five interview-respondents had gained experience with concentration practice through their involvement with other meditation groups before their association with BMIMC. Some incorporated it into their vipassana sitting practice in order to settle the mind. The first, KN, had learned concentration practice while in rehabilitation for an alcohol addiction. When asked why she had taken up Buddhist meditation, she explained that during her detoxification a Buddhist nun had taught her samatha as a relaxation technique to induce calm. When she began using the technique she was 'amazed at what she did on her own'. Although instructed to breathe in and out through the nostrils, when she switched attention to the diaphragm instead she felt 'in touch with her feelings', which she had previously experienced as 'frozen', in an experience which she later interpreted as mindfulness of feeling. This triggered the experience of sobbing (and 'put her off' meditating for a while), a therapeutic acknowledgment and release of previously disowned emotion, and revealed what was normally obscured by the practitioner's habitual state of mind.

The second, HR, had been practising with a Zen teacher and found herself 'doing something halfway between the two' (concentration and insight). She connected with the vipassana practice through reading a book wherein the section on vipassana instructed her to fix attention on 'whatever comes along rather than on one fixed object'. When she tried concentration some time later she found it useful for supporting the vipassana in that her mind was 'not wandering as much'. The third, SI, had practised Transcendental Meditation and Zen before learning vipassana. She related:

SI: Depending on the day, I'll do concentration sometimes for a long time. If my concentration's poor, I'll do some fast breathing, [and] focus on that just to get myself settled. That's not a vipassana technique, but something that I've learnt. It helps me get settled really quickly, [and] it really gets me focused.

The fourth and fifth practitioners cited anapanasati, mindfulness of breathing, as their main practice, which they described as a combination of concentration and insight. This practice is based on the Anapanasati Sutta, No 118 in the *Majjhima Nikaya.*[4] Its style, content and aim—the perfection of the four foundations of mindfulness, the seven enlightenment factors, and clear vision and deliverance—liken it to the Satipatthana Sutta. However, by comparison, it places greater emphasis on awareness of the breath.[5] MV described his practice as 'mostly anapanasati in a Zen sense', and related:

MV: Traditionally, in Zen particularly, it's infamous for the Master or the acolyte who's looking after the meditation hall to have said, "There's your cushion. Go and sit on it and work it out for yourself", and you might get a tiny bit more instruction than that, which is basically, 'Watch your breath. Count to ten. Stop, and start again. If you realize that your mind has wandered during that one-to-ten, then go back and start at one'. That's basically all the meditation training you get for quite a while. You struggle with that, and then the Master takes over and says, "Let's fine tune it a bit." So having done lots of that, I think most meditators get to the point where they stop counting the breath, and just let that be after a little practice, and just sit and watch the breath: the differences of in-breath and out-breath. And it starts looking like vipassana anyway, because instead of looking at the breath you're looking at lots of different body parts and doing scanning and stuff.

In each of these cases, the meditator was able to apply samatha technique developed in another contemplative setting to the development of their vipassana technique. Of the three people who had prior experience with Zen, two combined this with their vipassana practice, and felt no conflict between the two. The third, SI, who came to vipassana with prior training in both Zen and Transcendental Meditation, currently practises vipassana only, and has done so for many years. Despite the pleasureable sensations of the bliss-states attained, she felt she needed a practice that was more applicable to everyday life.[6]

Metta, the brahmaviharas and the paramis

From the descriptions in *Patterns of Personal Practice* above, it can be seen that some practitioners incorporate practices other than vipassana into their personal practice. The practices mentioned—metta, the brahmaviharas and the paramis—are all notable for their function in developing a range of positive or wholesome mental states, such as faith, joy, and happiness. The four brahmaviharas, the sublime states of mind, are metta, *karuna,* 'compassion', *mudita,* 'sympathetic joy' and *upekkha,* 'equanimity'.[7] Beginning with oneself as a point of reference for gradual extension, the practice consists of radiating out to people in the immediate environment—neighbourhood, town, country and world—each of the sublime states in turn. Nyanaponika Thera instructs that the extension of these states towards others should be impartial, and in order to achieve this, the four are used as principles of conduct, objects of reflection and subjects of methodical meditation. He also correlates meditative development of the sublime states with the four jhanas where love, compassion and sympathetic joy produce attainment of the first three, and equanimity leads to the fourth, in which it is the most significant factor.[8] This correlation between brahmavihara and the attainment of jhana, where the goal is to produce wholesome mental states and wholesome or right conduct towards others in order to counteract egotism, while not typically included in meditation instruction at the Centre, is more likely to be referred to in a dhamma-talk or in private conversation.

In addition to being the first of the four brahmaviharas, metta is one of the Protective Meditations (Buddha meditations, metta bhavana, contemplation of the loathsomeness of the body, and mindfulness of death) and one of the paramis.[9] Because it is frequently taught on retreats and incorporated into personal practice, its role in self-transformation is considered significant. In metta practice, thoughts of lovingkindness are directed to four people: oneself, someone for whom one has affection, someone for whom one feels indifference, and someone for whom one feels aversion or dislike. Finally, lovingkindness is directed to all of these people equally. The words said to oneself to accompany the contemplation are, for oneself, 'May I be happy and free from suffering', and for another, 'Just as I wish to be happy and free from suffering, may that being be happy and free from suffering'.[10] Nanamoli Thera maintains that it 'gives effect, in some measure, to all members of the Noble Eight-Fold Path but for the first, right view', and therefore its practice alone will not enable one to reach nibbana.[11] As frequently stated by teachers, however, it is practised as a complement to mindfulness meditation, both to stabilize the mind and to foster a spirit of lovingkindness towards others.[12]

Two out of the twenty practitioners interviewed made reference to the paramis as part of their personal practice, a practice that they both learned from the same teachers. In Pali sources, the paramis are the ten virtuous qualities that are said to lead to Buddhahood. They are (in English) generosity, morality, renunciation, insight, energy, patience, truthfulness, resolution, lovingkindness and equanimity.[13] The following excerpts show the application of these practices to self-development, seen in the way in which MV, KT and SI describe their reasons for, and the effects of, balancing vipassana with these practices.

MV: I recognized quite early on that I have this problem with anger . . . and I chose to deliberately do metta practice as a beginning practice. Every day I'd do a certain portion of the meditation, and when I go on large retreats my first meditation in the morning will be just metta, a real solid block of metta meditation, and I've done that for a long time, and I immodestly say that's had a quite good effect.

I asked KT, "What significance does the meditation practice have for you? What role does it play in your day-to-day life?" She responded, "Meditation sets Buddhism apart from from other religions. It helps you to live by the theory." She referred to the practice of brahmavihara as a practical tool. Because of its 'focus on compassion', it 'balances straight vipassana, which can reinforce subtle self-centredness', and 'puts my personal story in a wider context. It helps me to see beyond personal manifestation, how people really are, and puts me in touch with suffering and the Four Noble Truths. In the broader context, especially in my role as Manager (of the Centre, at the time of interview), I see people's problems first-hand'. She added that she does a lot of contemplation practice, and was currently developing the paramis as part of her practice. SI had incorporated the paramis into her daily practice.

SI: I wake up in the morning and I do the paramis [quoting the text used]. I say it slowly and quietly, and I really listen to what I'm saying, and then I run through the paramis according to the last 24 hours, and say with generosity . . . I might pick someone. How could I have been more generous with them? Or I might pick someone I was too generous with. I go through the people in those 24 hours, always with my family, and then with anyone else who has come into my life, and I find that the same people come up all the time.

GE: So you find that you do watch your natural responses to people?

SI: Yes, I do. I'm getting better at putting them [my responses] on hold, and I try to deal with them with wisdom, and aversion's my big thing.

The purpose of these practices is to generate wholesome mental states and right action, and to maintain these in the face of hostility from others. They are also practised to counteract the impulses of clinging and attachment to oneself. The fact that practitioners deliberately choose to incorporate these practices into their regular sitting practice and into their daily activities (see below) highlights the importance for these practitioners of developing a nonself-centred approach to relationships. Metta in particular appears to have value as an ethically transformative practice, in much the same way as the practices for generating *bodhicitta,* the 'mind of enlightenment', are valued by affiliates of Vajrayana Institute, and are explored in Chapters 4 and 5.[14] Both kinds of practitioners appear to value the transformative connection between the development of concentration and the development of compassion towards others that come about through practice of these techniques. That the choice of practice expresses their need for an ethically-based spiritual practice—one that facilitates the development of a practitioner's inner subjective life in harmony with an ethical foundation for living—is given more attention in Chapter 6.

Everyday practices

Everyday practice refers to the application of mindfulness during the execution of tasks carried out in everyday life. Practitioners expect that mindfulness in everyday practice will not be as concentrated as in formal sitting and walking, where physical and sensory distractions are minimized, thereby allowing the mind to focus exclusively on inner phenomena with greater attention to detail. Whilst practitioners distinguish between these and their sitting practice, they maintain that the effects of formal mindfulness practice, doctrinal study and 'everyday' practices, are not easily separated in that 'the practice doesn't end when one gets up from the meditation-cushion'. Everyday practice is a continuation of the meditation session. RN responded thus when asked how she integrated meditation practice into her daily life:

> RN: I suppose on one level there's no distinction between formal practice. I mean practice is practice. It's not 'this is the practice and this is daily life over here'. The practice is being mindful. Vipassana is awareness, and it's mindfulness practice. So it's just about wherever you are, and whatever your circumstances you can practise. For me, that's what I like about the practice. It's not something I go off and do. It's not separate from my daily life, but there's opportunities to intensify the experiences of awareness and deepen the practice by taking those formal opportunities to work with the mind. So, integrating those formal experiences into daily life is not an issue, in a sense, because there's no real black-and-white distinction. It's more just using those skills or the opportunity in the more intense practice, [and] developing those skills that are then applied in other experiences out of the more intense situations. Yes, it feels that the practice is just life.

DN demonstrated how situations in daily life are seen as opportunities for practice.

> DN: That's what I'm trying to put now into daily practice. When there's a particular thing that's come up, I go 'How am I relating to this?', and it's usually an anger thing. I actually do a lot of formal practice during the day. Say something comes up, I try to deal with it then, so to me that's formal practice even though it's daily life, and it's remembering to do it. It's like when we

focus on the rise and fall of the abdomen, and suddenly we're thinking we've forgotten to remember to do it. I try to use things to bring me back to the practice.

BM, who spent eight years in a Theravadin monastery as a fully-ordained monk, learnt to integrate teachings and practice into his daily monastic life. While not bound by the training monastic rules at the time of interview, he reported that he still integrated these things into daily life. The examples he gave were the integration of mindfulness and meditation into daily life and activities, and particularly a level of calm that can direct perception and behaviour. He also found that keeping the lay precepts helps the mind to be calm and to refrain from unwholesome activity.

The two following excerpts also show how practitioners may employ different techniques for different purposes. KN's application of techniques consists of concentration for dealing with anxiety; vipassana for the goal of enlightenment, and for dealing with people and 'day-to-day stuff'; and metta for problems with hatred and anger, and for developing the wisdom to change negative views. She had also found that keeping the Five Lay Precepts (see *Glossary*) helps her to maintain an awareness of the consequences of her actions, which in turn helps her to avoid 'making unwholesome choices'. In answer to the question 'What role does the meditation practice play in your day-to-day life?', she said that the awareness and the slowing down of the mind carries over into general day-to-day experience, and further, in slowing down the mind, insight meditation creates a distinction between the watcher and what's happening in the mind. Similarly, SI, a practitioner of many years' experience, demonstrated her use of different practices in different situations.

SI: For the mindfulness I use doorhandles and water . . . I devote a minimum of three hours a day to formal practice, and then the other things like standing in a queue, getting into the car, door handles, they're just reminders to come back to the present moment, to pay attention. Then I read things that are for something different from just meditation, say, looking at discontinuity and watching change, and seeing what happens: what mind-states come out of the change. That's not what I do when I'm standing in the line at Coles. Then I'm looking at patience and tolerance and that sort of stuff.

GE: From what you're saying, in the way you see it, there are two distinct practices for two distinct purposes. But would you say that your mindfulness practice informs your practice of the paramis; that being aware of your feelings towards people gives you that . . .

SI: They are distinct in one way, but it's a bit like saying whether I do concentration or wisdom practice. They both blend together all the time. I think you need the formal practice, to be sitting when things are easy or not easy just as a daily thing, and that just flows into your normal daily life. I just think it's important to have both, and I find, when I'm not sitting, I don't have as good clarity in daily life, and I have never ever found any big insights in daily life that I have not had the opportunity to see in formal sitting.

As noted above, everyday practices are seen fundamentally as opportunities to work with mindfulness, and its relationship to formal sitting is in the application of mindfulness continued from one context to the other. As the comments by KN and SI indicate, the extension of the technique into 'everyday' practice allows the meditator to bring the concentrated mind into everyday awareness, although not to the degree possible on a retreat.[15] Practitioners also treat it as a reinforcement of the sentiments embodied in metta practice. As noted earlier, the capacity to practice in an 'everyday' setting becomes important for those whose lifestyle limits the amount of time available for regular meditation, because practitioners can feel the need for formal practice and daily life to be more integrated.

Types of Transformation and Their Interpretive Frameworks

The satipatthanas as categories of change

Chapter 2 outlined the role in socialization of learning to classify all phenomena as one of the four satipatthanas: body, feelings, mind and dhammas.[16] Here, the satipatthanas are treated as categories of transformative experience in order to understand both the nature of transformation *per se*, and how it is interpreted doctrinally. I begin the discussion with the consideration of the primary role of the body in both sitting and walking practice. As 'body' the *Satipatthana Sutta* lists mindfulness of breathing, the four postures (walking, standing, sitting, and lying), foulness in the body parts, the elements, and the nine charnel-ground contemplations.[17] Objects used are in accordance with Shaw's list of basic phenomena employed in training in the practice: the contact of the feet on the ground, the movement of the breath in and out of the body, and sensory impressions.[18] Meditation on the foulness of the body is occasionally referred to in conversations between meditators, but typical objects are those relating to immediately body-based experience. KBN's description of his personal practice demonstrates the contemplation of the whole body as an object *per se* and as a site of sensory awareness.

> KBN: [In vipassana] one brings attention to the primary object. The primary object is the breathing for me. I'll always look at the breathing, but the breathing is never a very dominant object. It's always something else, and in

retreats it's often just the sitting. So I've come to slowly realize that the actual sitting, the contemplation of sitting itself, the whole body sitting, is actually an object, the most common object I've used. So the breathing is somewhere within that and I can zoom in onto the smaller phenomena. The sitting as a whole is what I use, being in that sitting, and within that there are objects within that, so that hardness of the cushion or the seat itself which is earth element, that hardness itself can be an object. One can have one's attention on that quite a lot. It gives you a base to look at other things . . . So it's the base, the primary object, but in a wider sense, the primary object is the body, not that it's a unified thing.

As a result of close attention to the body as an object and to the sensory phenomena that take place within it, several meditators report a deepening awareness of bodily processes and a deeper appreciation of the interrelatedness of mind and body. This developed awareness can produce a number of effects, as shown in Chapter 2. Practitioners may connect with the principles of bodily pleasure in meditation, but more noticeably with the principle of dukkha, suffering, through bodily discomfort and pain. BM noticed a calming of the body–mind experience resulting from his anapanasati practice, but also registered a sense of suffering arising in the body.

Elements of this improved body–mind connection resulted in attitude-changes for some. HR connected with vipassana initially as a body-based therapy, and then developed a more holistic appreciation of the practice and its supporting tradition. She told me that she had paid more attention to the mind–body connection as an effect of practice, and noted feeling calmer and more centred in everyday life, which she took to be a 'flow-on' effect. Her interest in vipassana had been precipitated by a sense of frustration with her personal situation at the time. She had felt under stress at work, and had been feeling tired, lonely and over-extended while suffering from a back injury. Feeling that she had lost connection with her centre, she found that she wanted to connect with words such as 'stillness, centre', and identified a 'need for connection with nature in a spiritual way'. She found herself saying, "If I could just get back to yoga and meditation." Yoga had been her only exercise for some time, and she enjoyed the enhanced sense of physical well-being she gained from 'doing the postures better' and 'getting more flexible'. She had liked vipassana because it did not contain any ritual, and seemed cerebral at first, but after doing mindfulness practice over several years and seeing a psychotherapist for about two years, it forced her to examine her relationship with her body. In addition to her vipassana practice she was currently sitting with a Zen teacher who teaches a form of mindfulness practice. In this practice, noting or labelling is more specific. For instance, in labelling a feeling, it is not simply labelled as 'feeling' or 'anger', but as feeling anger with 'so-and-so' over 'such-and-such', while checking the body for tension and reaction.

The Western concerns mentioned are about the connection between alternative Western spiritualities and alternative therapies. HR's language echoes some of the thought associated with the current Western interest in and adaptation of indigenous spiritualites and health practices, especially in the way these practices and their salvational goals can offer solutions for the existential anxieties of some Westerners. This is expressed in sentiments such as enhanced physical well-being being associated with 'self' and 'centre'. Significantly, for some individuals these experiences of deeper connection with the body and their apprehension of Buddhist ideas such as dukkha, suffering, and sukkha, pleasure, and their interpretation according to Buddhist frames of reference, form the basis for the individual's deeper exploration of the Buddhist worldview and eventual commitment as an adherent.

According to Nyanaponika Thera, the Pali term *vedana*, 'feeling', signifies, in Buddhist psychology, pleasant, unpleasant or indifferent sensations of physical or mental origin. He distinguishes feeling in this sense as the first reaction to any sense-impression, from the English sense of 'emotion', which he describes as a mental factor of a more complex nature.[19] This immediate reaction is contemplated as pleasant, unpleasant or neutral, and its significance is expressed by Analayo as 'to know how one feels'. This reveals the degree to which attitudes and reactions are based on initial affective input.[20] Vedana occurs in the Satipatthana Sutta as the second satipatthana, and in the doctrine of the five *khandhas*, 'aggregates', as the second in the sequence: *rupa*, 'body', *vedana*, 'feeling' *sanna*, 'apperception and conception', *samkhara*, 'volitional activities', and *vinnana*, 'awareness or consciousness'.[21] In a one-day vipassana-workshop, held in early 2005 at the Buddhist Library in Camperdown, Sydney, theoretical attention was given to the commonalities between the two doctrines. The teacher outlined the body-feeling progression common to both doctrines, followed by the comparatively more mentally-oriented factors in both cases: by mind and dhammas in the former, and by perception, formations and consciousness in the latter. Following from this, the bulk of discussion related to the way in which our basic responses to the objects of the senses and internal sensations, mostly pleasant or unpleasant, formed the basis for the more complex constructing activities and processes of the mind. From this perspective, the distinction between vedana and the Western appreciation of 'emotion' is an important one. The strictly Buddhist purpose of the contemplation of vedana is to bring awareness to the hedonistic quality of one's immediate response to any phenomenon.

For many practitioners, mindfully observing the arising and passing of all emotional states[22] allows them to process a range of experiences and responses. This can be seen in the experiences of several whose material has already been presented. HR's description of her Zen practice shows its basic applicability as a mindfulness and clarification practice: to label the feeling as feeling (having specific content) with 'so-and-so' over 'such-and-such', and to check the body for its reaction. KN's success with vipassana, first learnt in a therapeutic context and continued as a spiritual practice, included the experience of reconnection with feelings which were 'frozen' previously. She was exposed to vipassana originally as part of counselling for addiction-management. She understood the statement 'suffering is caused by craving' through her own meditative experience of bare attention to feeling, and through making the personal effort to break the addiction-cycle. This practitioner experienced profound change in being able to see beyond the immediate goal of getting over the addiction, and through understanding how the Four Noble Truths frame life experience in such a way so as to provide an effective way of dealing with the suffering it produces. In the following excerpt KBN describes his personal orientation to the practice as a technique for dealing with repressed emotion.

> KBN: That's why I'm at the point in my practice now, if in a sense my life project's to undo this fearfulness and defensiveness, and don't forget at eleven years of age I was torn out of my family, which had broken up, so I had abandonment experiences. Well. It's all embodied in your body, so in a sense you are learning to love. It is putting aside fear and learning to love; it's unlocking the body in order to be able to do that, so that you get a new relationship to the mind–body process, but the other beautiful thing is, as one breaks down these old fears, one can relate more fully to one's partner, one's mother who abandoned one at ten. To be able to open that stuff up, it's not that one takes an attitude of being compassionate, it's there, and you're able to communicate out of it. So that's the life thing. It's not a compartment at all, the actual focus is living. It's kind of opening up to feeling, and you've got to remember how intellectual my life's been in a sense, and that difficulty that got me into the practice—about relating to others—so it's probably an opening up. It's arriving at compassionate love. You're able to love other people without any fear. It's a long road back to that initial impulse, so it's giving away fear and defensiveness, but at the same time, the practice is about experiencing those things.

KBN's use of the word 'feeling' to denote his emotions is significant because of his implied equation of the two. His use of phrases such as 'opening up to feeling', and 'embodied in your body', illustrates the therapeutic function that mindfulness of the body and feelings have for him. Throughout my contact with vipassana practitioners I observed that individuals held one of two views of their emotional experience. Some noted their states of feeling or emotion and then let the experience go, with a view to developing equanimity. Others, such as KN and KBN, undertook an extra step of reifying the emotion that arose in meditation, especially afflictive emotion, for the purpose of processing and accepting it before moving beyond it. Rubin observes that Buddhist meditation is on occasion therapeutically ineffective and attributes this to the Buddhist view of afflictive emotions as defilements needing purification, a view which establishes an aversive relationship to experience, and an ambivalent relationship to emotional life generally.[23] The experiences of KN and KBN appear to demonstrate the converse. Both accepted the emotional content of their experience, both pleasant and painful, and learned to relate to it in a new way. This both enhanced their self-esteem and validated their faith in the practice.

The third foundation is called 'mind' in the Satipatthana Sutta,[24] although it is referred to as 'consciousness' in some texts.[25] Bikkhu Bodhi states that 'mind' as an object of contemplation refers to the general state and level of awareness.[26] Many related changes they experienced to both the slowing down of the mind in meditation, and becoming more mindful in general. EC's response to my statement, "What would be useful for me is if you could describe what you think the point of the mindfulness practice is", was the following:

> EC: Well. I think that, as they say, the concentration meditation makes you feel great, but I don't feel in the long run it's terribly beneficial, because you're just blotting everything out, and it's almost like escapism, whereas the mindfulness meditation I think, for me it's really helped me be more understanding and compassionate about things because it's looking at things in a different way. You're not fighting, as I said before. When I first started I was fighting with things, whereas now I've learned to accept things more, and I'm sure it's through the meditation, through, like those noises, just accepting that they're there, and they're part of it, and I'm not just buying into it. And I'm sure that's carried through into how I relate to people, and things like that.

Just before this response, EC had stated that, when she first began meditating, she could not tolerate any distraction such as noise, and had difficulty being mindful. As is evident from what she says, the mindfulness practice has helped her to develop patience and tolerance in and out of meditation.

In the fourth satipatthana, the contemplation of dhammas, are the five hindrances, the five aggregates, the six sense-bases, the seven enlightenment-factors and the Four Noble Truths.[27] The dhammas are frequently the subjects of dhamma-talks, and, as categories of phenomena, may be used as objects for investigation in vipassana. Bikkhu Bodhi refers to the Pali term dhammas as 'comprising all phenomena classified by way of the categories of the dhamma, the Buddha's teaching of actuality', and further notes that as categories of meaning they are specific to Buddhism.[28] The transformative role of contemplation of dhammas is in understanding the relationships between them as frameworks of meaning for further contemplation. Such meaning-making is aided by the experience of them as phenomena belonging to one of the first three satipatthanas. This is exemplified by the five hindrances, the first category of dhammas. In vipassana one learns to observe all unmindful mental states and label them as one of the hindrances, as discussed in Chapter 2. In this way, one learns to objectify them instead of *identifying* with them. Referring to Nyanaponika Thera's description of the hindrances and the enlightenment factors as the qualities to be abandoned and acquired respectively,[29] learning to understand their meaning as dhammas involves understanding them in relation to the seven enlightenment factors. Learning to discriminate between unwholesome and wholesome mental states according to Buddhist doctrine involves objectifying these states before they can be conceptualized as classes of object by the meditator, who then learns how the members of each class are related internally, and how classes relate to each other. When such learning begins to occur, the meditator can be said to have entered the stage of comprehension.

While the five aggregates are referred to in dhamma-talks, they are seldom used as objects for meditation or as the subject of study. Throughout my period of fieldwork, the most concentrated attention given to this doctrine occurred during a one-day vipassana workshop given in early 2005 at the Buddhist Library, Camperdown, Sydney. Here, the teacher drew comparisons between the sequences of the aggregates and the four satipatthanas as classes of contemplation-object. However, throughout my period of fieldwork at BMIMC, I noticed that the four satipatthanas, and not the aggregates, were consistently utilized as meditation objects in themselves and as a phenomenological classification-system relating to the experience of personhood. Conversely, The Four Noble Truths as a core Buddhist doctrine is frequently discussed in dhamma-talks, and several respondents discussed the way in which they come to realize its import, as the Buddhist view of conditioned existence and the path to liberation from it, by acquiring an experiential understanding of dukkha, suffering. This may occur through the contemplation of bodily pain, and/or the identification and contemplation of *tanha*, craving, and its role in our habitual mental activity, as exemplified in several places in the current study.

Experienced practitioners often referred to insights into aspects of doctrine that come as one becomes experienced in the practice. From the perspective of the researcher, these insights require prior acquisition of interpretive skills to understand. While talking to RN about her practice I said, "What I'm looking for are links between your experience in vipassana and how you interpret it, and how it gets carried into your daily life". She responded:

RN: It's about purifying the mind, so I suppose, sitting in a formal way and observing the mind, and seeing, I suppose, the teaching of dependent origination is something that comes into my mind now, just watching the way things arise and relate to connections between things, the understanding of that and the ability in the more intensive practice to develop equanimity with regard to whatever arises, and detaching and developing that sense of non-self which is a major teaching of the Buddha. I suppose that's a way, the intensive practice, the opportunity to do that in daily life, bringing it into daily life, just seeing whatever arises in day-to-day life as well as in intensive practice, as being empty of self, and developing more skill in doing that, and developing an equanimity, you know, mind states that are able to observe that without being so influenced by it and reacting to them and attaching to whatever, so for me that's what the practice is about and purifying the mind so the mind's not being drawn into anger or greed or being caught so much in the delusion of the self. So it's about developing more ability to work with equanimity in whatever arises.

While setting out to illustrate the importance of generating the correct mental states with which to work in meditation for her practice, RN also demonstrated how she generated the appropriate view to be used in meditation before the meditative state itself, evident in her use of the phrase 'detaching and developing that sense of non-self which is a major teaching of the Buddha'. This is also illustrated by the way in which she worked with doctrinal principles in meditation to develop equanimity, one of the seven enlightenment factors.

A three-fold categorization of transformations

Many conversion studies theorize the conversion process as change to one's worldview and sense-of-self. As shown above, practitioners experienced a range of changes resulting from practice. Answers to the question, 'How has your meditative experience affected your outlook on life?' illustrated changes to both the habitual functioning of one's internal states and to one's sense-of-self. BM reported that meditation brings the clarity needed to deal with and contain upsetting emotions, and he responds to these by 'finding how big you need to be, rather than just reacting'. Meditation cuts down the potential of unwholesome activity, and because of this, he does not get so caught-up in anger 'coming up in himself'. Instead, he acknowledges it, but then lets it go. KT responded, "I don't take life as seriously. I'm able to move through mind-states and emotions much more quickly." She found that she was much more content in herself, had a broader ability to relate to people, and was less judgemental towards others. These answers are typical of the responses to this question. The utilization of accepted sociological notions of self as self-concept and notions of religious change as identity-change limit appreciation of the complexity of personal changes that occur as a result of Buddhist practice.

The collection of interview data shows that Buddhist practice leads to changes in subjective and objective levels of self-perception and understanding. In all, these changes can be grouped into five types, involving change to body-awareness; feeling and emotion—especially habitual responses—and success in dealing more effectively with unwholesome feelings; the mind and habitual mental states; the sense-of-self, including self-image and self-esteem; and in worldview. That this five-fold categorization reflects Western rather than Buddhist concerns can be seen from what follows. The second category contains feeling and emotion, reflecting the way in which affective response is appreciated and labelled by Westerners generally. Similarly, the third category consists of the mind and mental content such as thought, to represent the more-Western divide between thought and feeling. The fourth category, the sense-of-self, relates to the object that is to be refuted in Buddhist doctrine, the *atman* in Sanskrit, and as such, is the object of deconstruction processes facilitated by Buddhist analytical techniques. The last category, changes to worldview, involves changes that occur to one's outlook on reality as a result of the acceptance of the new religious perspective and its interpretive framework.

It can be seen that the changes belonging to the first three categories: body, feelings and mind, fit into the categories outlined in the satipatthana system of body, feelings, mind and dhammas as discussed above, describing the self in its sense of subjective immediacy. Accordingly, the range of changes can be condensed into three categories: changes within one's immediate subjective field of experience; changes to one's sense-of-self and changes to one's worldview as one's internal frame of reference. These categories of change are interdependent and mutually reinforcing. For instance, while first-category changes are effected by bare attention to immediate experience such as feeling or emotion, other changes involving one's sense-of-self are flow-on effects from these subjective changes. Certain changes, for example, 'becoming more compassionate and less judgemental', which lead to 'better relationships with others' and 'the sense of having more control over one's life', and further, 'various aspects of one's life becoming more integrated' seem to result from a sense of more direction over one's immediate responses to everyday occurrences. These facets of change involve the self as a social being: a self in relation to other selves. This category, which is shown to be a consequence of complex interactions between two aspects of self: the field of immediate subjective experience, and the self-concept, the self-as-object, is examined in more detail further down. For the present, discussion moves to a consideration of the correspondence between the fourth Satipatthana, dhammas, and the third category of change, viz. changes to one's internal frame of reference.

Interpretive frameworks for change and progress

As noted above, meanings corresponding to the categories of phenomena listed under dhammas are specific to Buddhism. Of the four Satipatthanas, the first three, body, feelings and mind, concern phenomena identifiable within common experience, and some that are particular to and attributed meaning according to Buddhist thought. Analayo, perceiving the sequence of contemplations as one of increasing sensitivity, arranges the sequence within each Satipatthana into a progressive pattern, from coarse to subtle objects of awareness.[30] Generally, the coarser objects are those identifiable in immediate experience, and the more subtle are those that require definition and understanding according to their Buddhist frame of reference. For instance, feelings are divided according to affective and ethical quality: pleasant, unpleasant and neutral, and worldly and unworldly respectively. Bikkhu Bodhi gives as the basis for this worldly–unworldly distinction the experience of joy, grief and equanimity according to the experience of the householder and the renunciate.[31] Similarly, mind is divided into ordinary and higher states of mind.[32] The purpose of this exercise was to identify the nature of objects utilized in transformation-practice, as distinct from the frameworks that facilitate their reinterpretation. In the following, the aim is to explore the process by which change is articulated through Buddhist frameworks of meaning.

The establishment of a relationship between one's experiential development and the increasing reliance on Buddhist doctrine for its articulation may explain the apparent correspondence between two of the categories of change and the frameworks used to articulate them. In category one is subjective self-transformation involving the first three Satipatthanas, and in category three, changes to one's internal frame of reference, analogous to, but not to be directly equated with the dhammas. For these practitioners, the experimental immersion process was seen to involve the validation of the new religion's frames of reference by applying them as interpretive frameworks for their own transformative experience. However, while some can be seen to place in an interpretive context the immediate subjective effects of practice, others are utilized to inform and orient thinking more generally.

Often, when asked which Buddhist teachings and practices were significant to them, interview-respondents explained how Buddhist concepts, doctrinal frameworks and practices supported each other in bringing about changes in their awareness and thought. Consider the way in which BM answered the question, 'What Buddhist teachings are you drawn to, and what significance do they have for you?' His reply consisted of anapanasati, his main practice, in which his 'body–mind experience was calmed', allowing him to 'see through habitual patterning' and to feel 'connected to all four foundations of mindfulness'. He also cited the Noble Eight-Fold Path—the aspects of which he applies in daily life—and its connection to the Four Noble Truths. He found the suttas relevant for 'checking one's practice' and for 'creating ways of perceiving the world'. He saw his Buddhism as grounded in the practice, but used doctrine to orient his practice. His reference to the practice of anapanasati and the Noble Eight-Fold Path, and the connection between the latter and its broader context of the Four Noble Truths, was indicative of the doctrine-practice relationships that were dominant in his experience and its interpretation, and implied a reflexivity between the two.

Similarly, when asked about the significance of meditation for her, HR reflected upon the way in which she came to understand the Four Noble Truths. She explained that when she first heard of them, the logic underpinning them was not obvious, but it became clearer to her at a later stage. She reached a point in her meditation practice wherein 'all of the distractions could be sorted into the five hindrances', and with this came the realization that behind them all was either desire or aversion. This she related to the Second Noble Truth, which identifies the origin of suffering as craving.[33] She also learned to categorize mental states into wholesome and unwholesome, and to further define unwholesome states as one of the five hindrances. Here, we find the same reflexivity between experience and its Buddhist interpretation as noted in BM's experience. Understanding of the second Noble Truth as the cause of suffering, craving, helped her to understand the doctrine of the Four Noble Truths. Doctrine also enabled her to interpret her experience of the five hindrances and to further clarify their nature as desire or aversion. Reflexively, experience leads to understanding the rationale behind the doctrine, and the doctrine helps practitioners to frame their experience in a new way.

Those in the second category, such as Mahasi's Stages of Insight Knowledge, to be discussed below, and the three factors of the Noble Eight-Fold Path, are used to orient practitioners' engagement with Buddhist practice more generally. These tend to bring about, or operate as interpretive templates for, change in worldview, the third category of change. These perceptual changes may come about through contemplation of one's experience in two interrelated ways. The first is as a result of learning to interpret experience through Buddhist categories of thought and their interpretive frameworks, and in this sense, the framework is both the mechanism and the end-result. The second is as a result of applying the meditative techniques and noticing the changes to oneself and one's thinking, and finding incentive to take Buddhism more seriously and explore its belief system in more depth. The following accounts by three practitioners, presented in order of years of experience in the practice, describe a variety of changes that may occur to one's reality-perspective. Some of these concern the way in which individuals may undergo a change in some aspect of their outlook without involving a major reorientation, while others involve a more definite perceptual shift towards Buddhist ways of thinking. In the first example, EC's personal reflections on a teaching she had attended helped her to deal with some anxiety about death. She was able to benefit from a shift in mental orientation to the reality of the inevitability of death and her fear of it, although still entertaining doubts about the doctrine of reincarnation.

EC: But I remember someone asked at a Buddhist talk, "Can you be a Buddhist and not believe in reincarnation?" And the monk said in a word, "No." I always had real trouble with that, but since going to talks again, and hearing this concept that it's just like a stream of consciousness or something that goes on, I still don't know what I believe in, but the funny thing is, I think that's what's happened to me is that a fear of dying has sort of gone . . . that somehow that's shifted. You know, maybe if I was in that situation where I thought I was going to die it might be different, but just before all this talk about reincarnation and spirituality was going on, I guess there were times when . . . but now I don't think like that. There's a shift there somehow, and I don't know where that's going. But that's why I can't say I'm a Buddhist because I can't say, "Well, yes. I do believe in reincarnation."

This kind of shift in orientation of a view of reality is also exemplified by the experience of HR, who 'was for a long time a committed materialist'. She found that she currently had 'more of an open mind to seeing other ways rather than a material view of the world', and was now open to reports of mystical experience. In addition, her experience related above concerning her classification of the five hindrances as either desire or aversion, and her relating this to the origin of suffering as craving, became more salient for her when large changes seemed imminent. In her own words, rather than 'just rushing around doing what has to be done', she was 'not focused so much in the activity', but was more aware of her own internal state. This is an example of the apprehension and employment of a Buddhist doctrine or part thereof, the second of the Four Noble Truths, as a framework for the reinterpretation of experience. Understanding craving in terms of desire and aversion employed another experiential framework, that of the five hindrances, illustrating the way in which aspects of the doctrinal framework become meaningfully related for the practitioner. Although not directly stated, it was suggested that the identification process made facing her own reality more comprehensible and manageable.

Similarly, one of HD's answers to my asking how she incorporated Buddhist thought into her life concerned her appreciation of both attachment and aversion as the source of the three poisons, greed, hatred and delusion, themselves understood as a source of suffering in the world.

HD: It's so ingrained in my life that I hardly know how to answer it. When you view the seven o'clock news on television, you're seeing it from the view of greed, hate and delusion. A lot of worldly stuff you do automatically view it as greed, hate and delusion, and you do get less het up about it. It's a source of—because we're not enlightened beings—it's a source of sorrow, perhaps, and that's how you see it and so a lot of the questions people ask and the things that people discuss just seem totally irrelevant to me. You see how deluded people are, and when you say deluded, it sounds very critical or disrespectful or whatever, but it's the Buddhist idea of delusion, of not understanding attachment and aversion, and that everything's impermanent.

In another part of the interview, she explained how she had come to see the world in terms of samsara:

HD: I suppose I see the world now as samsara, and as I practise more and more it seems less and less real, but I'm still functioning in it at a certain level. And beings are trapped in it, samsara, through delusion, this idea of separation that's developed, and I know that the Buddha talked about the arising and waning of world systems and that sort of thing, and I can relate to that, and the fact that it's so hard to say what you believe in when you're a Buddhist.

GE: The Buddhist worldview that you hold, would you say that that's your entire picture of reality, or do you use it as an adjunct to other things? Do you still use bits of your Christian worldview or do you hold a more scientific outlook on the world? Can you get a sense of how they go together, or whether you're purely Buddhist from that perspective?

HD: I'm a dentist, so I've got an interest in science and medicine, so I can definitely suspend Buddhist beliefs and just talk about the body as something solid, in study and in talking to other people and whatever, I can get right back into the conceptual world. But I suppose my view of reality is that everything is arising and passing away according to causes and conditions, and really that's the basis of it.

The above examples all illustrate the way in which a practitioner had gained insight into an aspect of reality from the Buddhist perspective. In the example from EC, and in the first from HR, there was a softening, a loosening, of previous thought to do with a facet of human existence, as if initiated by reflection upon and acceptance of other ways of seeing reality. By comparison, from HR's second example, to do with the Four Noble Truths, and in HD's to do with samsara, there is a definite shift towards interpreting reality in terms of Buddhist doctrine. A way of expressing the difference between these two is suggested by Bedford, who distinguishes between two uses of worldview: an experiential feel for what reality is versus a comprehensive system of beliefs.[34] It may be that there are several ways in which perceptual shifts can occur. What I suggest here is an initial shift in one's experiential feel for reality, followed by the articulation of this shift in terms of the new belief system. In this way, the final result may involve the imposition of formal categorical terminology onto a framework that has already begun to shift. Interview data suggest this process to be slow and complex, and variable among individuals in terms of the beliefs and meditative effects involved.

Progress on the path to enlightenment in Buddhism is assured by developing the qualities or precepts of the Noble Eight-Fold Path and its three aspects of panna, 'insight' or 'wisdom', sila, 'ethics' and samadhi, 'concentration'. Both Nyanaponika Thera and Griffiths see panna as the result of the internalization of Buddhist categories of thought. According to Nyanaponika Thera, by constant practice of satipatthana, 'the contents of thought will gradually assume the thought-forms of the dhamma in the sense of the Buddha's teaching of actuality and liberation'.[35] Griffiths, taking vipassana and panna as equivalent terms, perceives vipassana practice as an effective method for 'training the awareness to perceive the universe in accordance with the categories of the Abhidhamma', and for making 'those categories coextensive with the way one perceives the world'.[36] This suggests that the Buddhist path to liberation is a process of internalization of the content of the Abhidhamma, through the reinterpretation of experience according to its framework and categories.

Both de Wit and Griffiths allude to the intellectual and discursive nature of panna. De Wit describes it as a discriminating awareness of the contribution of our mental sense-faculty from the contributions of our external sense-faculties to our experience of reality. The mental purification process is a cultivation of this awareness. He maintains that our thoughts about experience need not be discarded in the purifying process. Instead, 'through meditation we begin to see that the qualities of phenomenal reality are not contained within the concepts we have about them'.[37] Similarly, Griffiths maintains that wisdom involves a discursive and intellectual understanding of how things exist, to the point that 'the ultimate development of wisdom in the state of nibbana is also discursive'. He describes two elements of wisdom as 'seeing as' and 'knowing that', and expresses their intimate relationship as 'concept and reality become fused in the highest development of panna', and maintains that 'the element of knowing is never completely transcended in the vipassana-panna complex of ideas'. In summary, Griffiths sees wisdom as a 'discursive knowledge and vision' culminating in nibbana, which he defines as a 'continuous dispassionate cognitive or intellectual vision of the universe as a causally conditioned flux of point-instants in which there is no continuing principle of individuality'.[38] This definition takes account of doctrinal perspectives that one must comprehend in order to see reality from the Buddhist perspective, specifically, the three marks of existence and dependent origination.

Mahasi's *Thirteen Stages of Insight Knowledge*

For the practitioner of the vipassana method of Mahasi Sayadaw, conceptual mapping of the development of panna, the process of shaping experience in terms of the Buddhist worldview, would culminate in its placement according to Mahasi Sayadaw's Thirteen Stages of Insight Knowledge. This can be seen as a significant interpretive framework, as it provides the meditator with a guide to the range of experiences encountered in vipassana practice, and their interpretation in terms of progress on the path. This framework has been referred to variously as Mahasi's 'stages of insight', 'stages of insight knowledge', and the dukkha jnanas, the 'insight knowledges of suffering'. When practitioners make reference to it, it is in the sense of an overall guiding and validating framework for vipassana-generated experience. The stages themselves are not elucidated in interview nor seen as personal attainments. In this way, use of the thirteen stages as a guide serves to keep practitioners focused on the goal of practice, enlightenment.

These stages are outlined in the second part of Mahasi Sayadaw's *Practical Insight Meditation: Basic and Progressive Stages*,[39] and in a talk given by U Janaka, a teacher in the tradition, at BMIMC in 1998.[40] The Thirteen Stages, consisting of nine mundane and four supramundane stages, are knowledge about: discerning mental and physical phenomena; causal relations or conditionality; comprehension of all three characteristics of phenomena; corruption of insight (attachment to pleasant experiences, sometimes mistaken for nibbana); dissolution; fearfulness; misery; desire for deliverance; re-observation, or review of the three marks experienced at Stage 3; *comprehension;* equanimity; adaptation; maturity; and the Path. While both Mahasi Sayadaw and U Janaka describe the earlier stages in some detail, the extent of detail falls away in Mahasi Sayadaw's writing at Stage 5 *dissolution,* and more sharply at Stage 4 *corruption of insight* in U Janaka's writing. U Janaka describes the first two stages in considerable detail, and the next two in slightly less, possibly because, in U Janaka's experience, this may represent the point at which most meditators' development ends.

Some reports of experience do, however, lend themselves to placement according to these stages. For instance, KN refers to the slowing down of the mind in vipassana to create 'a distinction between the watcher and what's happening in the mind', which may correspond to Stage 1, *discerning mental and physical phenomena.* According to both teachers, at this stage the meditator can differentiate between two types of *nama:* the noting mind and the noted object. The experiences of other practitioners such as HD, KBN and SI bear some similarity to Stage 2, *knowledge of causal relations or conditionality,* and Stage 3, *comprehending the three characteristics of phenomena,* in that they report observing the arising and passing away of phenomena. However, on observing that their experience can be classified according to these stages, these meditators simply take it as a sign that 'practice is progressing'. KBN commented on the stages as a restrictive framework for charting progress, contrasting their guidance with the Zen view of enlightenment. The observations below were made following on from a point about Zen and the non-rational mind.

KBN: It's like a counterpoint to the Mahasi, the Theravadin orthodoxy. It's like this . . . bang . . . thirteen stages . . . bang-bang-bang . . . where are you? . . . Keep striving. So it's very oppressive to take on that whole apparatus of the Mahasi tradition and its Thirteen Stages of Insight Knowledge, because it discounts the kinds of experiences you might have in everyday life, which are valuable for working with your experience [and] is what the Buddha in my understanding is teaching us: work with your experience.

GE: And so it's not necessarily in a deeply meditative state, but it's how you respond to things?

KBN: No. I'm very convinced that whatever life throws up is grist for the mill, for the practice, and this just isn't in the sitting, because it's awareness of whatever you bring your attention to.

GE: But you look for certain maps within the teachings to give you certain clarity, by the sound of it.

KBN: Oh yeah, the conceptual scheme of the Thirteen Stages of Insight Knowledge I would say is my map as it would be for anybody, but that's on a level of generality.

As Griffiths suggests, treating changes to worldview as the progressive internalization of Buddhist categories of thought, as the process of coming to see an aspect of reality in Buddhist terms—and even placing them according to stages of progress—does not exclude the application of non-Buddhist frameworks to the same experience. However, with one exception, no other interpretations were offered by practitioners.

KBN recounted his experience of chest pain during a long retreat at the Centre, an incident he referred to at least twice during interview. He also explained how he interpreted the pain in terms of 'heart chakra stuff', the pain of opening up to his own emotions for others. His use of a Hindu-derived framework to interpret the function of physical sensations in a way that made sense to his own personal goal of emotional growth shows how practices and frameworks may be adapted for personal enhancement, and raises the need to explore how personal goals affect one's use of frameworks. RN remarked on the fact that people reach for other frameworks when existing frameworks inadequately articulate experience:

RN: We don't verbalize and use words that we know within a framework that exists out of the Buddhist philosophical understanding to explain something that doesn't really fit into our use of words. So on one level that's the difficulty, to be eloquent enough to speak with the words you've got in your vocabulary anyway, and just using any framework to interpret experiences that don't fit into existing frameworks. Sometimes people develop their own understandings because they have trouble understanding it [experience] through existing frameworks.

According to Griffiths, modern Theravadins regard vipassana as the way *par excellence* to nibbana.[41] However, Nyanaponika Thera sees the practice as having two goals: nibbana, and mindfulness in everyday life.[42] All Buddhist doctrine is written from the perspective of attaining enlightenment and liberation from samsara. With time, and in the service of more religiously oriented goals, one's thinking tends to become more oriented to the categories of Buddhist doctrine. In order to attain nibbana, there may be more mental and emotional investment in Buddhist interpretive frameworks. With respect to either goal, and practitioners generally aim for both, the important factor is clarity of awareness and its noting. One category of change remaing to be explored is the second according to the three-fold categorization of change: the sense-of-self. The theoretical considerations of this Chapter necessitate examination of the models of the self, from Buddhist and social-scientific perspectives, in more detail.

The Sense-of-Self and Its Transformations

Accordingly, discussion here deals with both the changes to the sense-of-self undergone by practitioners, and the necessary interpretive frameworks that they employ to understand this change. As stated above, two of the three categories of change involve the self: the self in its subjective immediacy, and one's sense-of-self or self-concept. In the following account, EC describes a set of changes she underwent as a result of applying some of the Buddhist principles to her everyday habitual thinking. Her view of herself as being more tolerant and less judgemental than previously she attributes to developing mindfulness in everyday life and responding to teachings about compassion. Harvey notes that the final goal of Buddhism is achieved by cultivating wisdom through meditation, but such wisdom can be initiated by reflection on teachings,[43] and it is reinforcement of principles through study and meditation that, with time, often leads to these changes. EC's account is representative of many who report constructive changes that have occurred to them, or to *me*, as a result of study and practice. In her case, this was the cumulative result of four years' activity.

GE: Are there any significant concepts within Buddhism that appeal to you?

EC: The compassion side of it is really big for me, and has really helped me, being compassionate and generous I think, having compassion for people. Because I was raised by a very critical mother, and I know I have a critical part of me that is still there, but I find that I'm much more understanding with people than I used to be, and I know for a fact that it's because . . . well it's not even the meditation, it's going to the teachings more than the meditation. I know the meditation helps me, but I think getting out there putting these things into practice from what I've heard and just thinking about the concepts, and thinking about how my actions affect other people and being able to see that, and also not being as dogmatic about things. I mean it is hard to explain, but I would say that I've changed a lot in the last few years, and it's probably all due to going these retreats and Buddhist talks and things. And I would say that the talks are probably more important than the meditation . . . Another thing I've just thought about is being mindful in everyday life—not that I do it all the time—but that thing of noting what's happening, and not buying into it, just noting. And I have always been quite a critical person and get annoyed easily with people doing things, and I don't find that that happens nearly as much any more, because I'm able to look at it, and think 'Mmm, yeah, I'm being impatient again', but not thinking, 'Now stop being impatient. Stop being judgmental and critical. You've got to stop being like this'. I used to give myself a hard time and never got any better. It only got worse. So now I will say things like 'Mmm . . . being judgmental. Oh, all right', and I just find increasingly that it's dropping away, that judgment of things and people. So as far as that mindfulness like in everyday life—as I said I don't do it all the time—but I particularly relate it to being judgmental because that is one big issue I've had. And so when I find that I am being judgmental, you know whether it's just walking down the street and thinking, 'Oh my God look at that person's hair!' or something, I'll say 'Mmm. Being judgmental again', and I just find that by doing that, less and less am I noticing these things. I'm just not doing it as much.

This account is representative of many in the literature about religious change, including that brought about by meditation, involving changes to one's sense-of-self. For instance, Bedford reports a series of changes to members of the *i and I Art of Living Foundation* as a result of their meditative experiences: their worldview was charged with less negative emotion than previously. They experienced changes in lived reality, and the view of the self became more positive. In sum, the changes indicated a positive relationship with self and reality.[44] Although MacPhillamy expresses concern for harm done by long-term monastic training,[45] Burns and Ohayv noted the ocurrence of positive changes in Western monks engaged in long-term vipassana meditation in Thailand, who reported an increase in personal happiness, self-control and self-confidence, and a decrease in depression and defensiveness.[46] The account is also representative of those by the practitioners at both BMIMC and Vajrayana Institute. However, as discussion below shows, these changes are the end-product of more complex changes involving both the self in its subjective immediacy and the sense-of-self as a socially objectified being. The appropriate explanatory models of the self in its subjective immediacy and in its socially constituted objectivity are outlined below.

A Buddhist view of the self: absolute, relative and ordinary

In Buddhism, both reality and the self are spoken about in terms of absolute and relative view. From the Theravadin perspective, absolute reality, the absolute view, is described by the doctrine of the three marks of existence, and according to De Wit, relative reality is samsara.[47] The ordinary view, the view of the self as solid and unchanging, keeps the individual in samsara. The difference between the absolute and ordinary views, according to De Wit, is how the person is perceived. He refers to these as the enlightened, ego-less mode of experience and the egocentric mode of experience, respectively. In the experience of absolute reality, the concept of ego is exposed as having no substance or existence of its own. The key to transforming the ordinary into the enlightened view is in understanding what I have chosen to call the 'relative self', the Buddhist understanding of the person as a set of interrelationships, as outlined in the doctrines of dependent origination, the aggregates, and the satipatthanas.

The dominant model for the relative self, the model for the self to be transformed, is the notion of person inherent in the satipatthanas, the objects of which according to Nyanaponika Thera comprise the entire person and that person's whole field of experience.[48] As discussed above, transformation through vipassana practice involves change in one's relationship with the body, feelings and emotions, and the mind's state and cognitive content, through the application of mindfulness, the moment-to-moment awareness of the phenomena of immediate experience, to see behind the veil of our everyday awareness. To understand the value of such deconstructive practice for the Western vipassana practitioner, one must appreciate the Buddhist view of the sense-of-self, of the 'I', the object imputed onto the relative self. From the Buddhist perspective, the transformative process is aimed at realizing the lack of inherent existence in this I imputed onto the relative self, which Buddhist scholars often describe in terms of the five aggregates.

This imputed sense-of-self may be equated with what is designated in Western thought by the ego as the representational aspect of the self.[49] Both Buddhism and contemporary Western psychology see the self as a construction of the mind.[50] Writers such as Epstein and Watson stress that Buddhist practice aims to deconstruct the representational component of the ego, the internal experience of one's self, and not to destroy the ego as mediator of the organism's processes in the Freudian understanding.[51] In this sense, Buddhism aims to transform the view of self as a reified object into a composite of interrelated parts.

A contemporary Western view of the self

As stated in Chapter 1, in order to explain the nature of self-transformation effected by the use of Buddhist doctrinal frameworks and practices, a clear distinction must be made between the self-as-subject, and the self-as-object, a basic distinction made by William James.[52] James's divisions of self into subject and object, *I the knower* and *me the known*, Watson labels as *self* and *self-concept*. This self-concept can be divided into material, social and spiritual aspects, which, as Leary emphasizes, are not ontologically distinctive dimensions of the self, but *owned* aspects,[53] and a *pure ego*, which provides the core sense of continuity in the individual. Watson believes that, from all contemporary Western perspectives, models of the self have two levels. The first includes the self-image as process, and contains a simple and implicit notion of self. Possessing inner coherence, it is a rough summary of the self, and is open to the environment. The second is the self-concept as representation, bolstered by language and culture, and both adhered to and affected by emotional components. Here the self becomes increasingly reified, and is considered autonomous.[54] It can be seen that James's self-as-subject, the level of immediate subjective experience, belongs in Watson's first level.

Referring to the Buddhist three-fold categorization of change outlined above, the three types of change are: changes within one's immediate subjective field of experience; changes to one's sense-of-self; and changes to one's outlook on reality, or worldview. I the knower, the self as subject, the immediate field of subjective experience equates with the relative self as it is conceived in Buddhism, and to the first category of change. James's self-as-object, the self-concept and corresponding to Watson's second level, relates to the imputed I, and to the second category of change. To rephrase the statement above, the satipatthanas describe the field of phenomena within the person's experience in subjective immediacy. Further, it is suggested that this self-image as process is the target of the deconstructive function of mindfulness as it operates in meditation. The objective of any Buddhist analytical technique is to deconstruct ordinary experience, especially of the sense of a permanent, solid self, into its component interrelated processes. This is the ultimate process aimed for in terms of the changes belonging to the first of the three categories of change outlined above.

The sense-of-self and its transformations through vipassana practice

The second category, changes to the self-concept, are the result of deconditioning processes effected by meditation techniques. In terms of theoretical understanding, the task here is to show how changes to the subjective and objective selves relate to and reinforce each other. The following excerpt from the interview with EBS is relevant to the self-transformative dimension of the practice because it deals with how the self is understood in this context. We were discussing the importance of developing mindfulness in vipassana meditation with respect to my own experiential understanding of its relation to the sense-of-self. In my experience and interpretation up to that point, my experience of mindfulness had been linked to a strong sense of *I*.

> GE: . . . but what I'm confused about is in that knowing [where your mind is placed] is still a sense of I, and it might be just me, but I relate to a sense of *I* very strongly.

> EBS: I think the sense of I is really important, the way you describe that, because I think . . . because I was just reading Freud, *Civilization and Its*

Discontents, and in the translator's introduction he says, 'There are a few words that don't translate properly from German into English', and he says 'whatever the word is for self, actually the translation is not self, but *sense-of-self*'. This is really big news, because when you think about Jung, the way the English-speaking people . . . you know, Jung's notion of the self, but actually that word is the sense-of-self, that's quite different, and that's not a noun anymore. It's almost like a verb. It's kind of a dynamic, the sense-of-self, and I reckon that's the same with Buddhism. What people fight with is this notion of 'is there a me or not-me?' But people don't get it. They go 'There's an I there', but if you kind of go, 'There is nothing you can call an I, but the sense you have of that is really strong, and that's fine, that sense of it. It's OK to have that sense-of-self.

GE: It's the *attachment* that they're trying to break.

EBS: Yeah, and once you have that notion that 'I have a strong sense-of-self', and so the issue is to be OK about that, that I have a sense-of-self, and in some ways, that enables me to get through life, my everyday life, and it creates coherence in the way I think about whatever this thing is that's me, my relationship to other things and so on, but in time what happens is that sense-of-self dissipates with meditation. That's one of the things that happen.

GE: But it has to be established first. I mean, it's through that sense of I, that I know what mindfulness is. I wouldn't know it otherwise.

EBS: I think you're right. There's something about the development of human beings from late childhood into early adolescence, there's something where this sense-of-self seems to be really important, so this notion that a child could be born, bypass the sense-of-self and be fully enlightened, I don't believe that. Because again, thinking about the relationship in psychology, the development of the human being, what we know about that, and what this whole Buddhist story is about, strikes me that people need to have a reasonably strongly developed sense-of-self in their childhood, adolescence, and perhaps in the early part of their twenties, to then be able to go on to journey, starting to break down this sense-of-self.

This sense-of-self, the sense of personal continuity that arises from the interplay of the aggregates, is the self to be deconstructed and the one that meditators attempt to hold onto. Walsh's descriptions of his experiences in vipassana meditation include those often equated with the slowing down of the mind: the quietening of internal dialogue and hypersensitivity to stimuli. He also draws attention to others that contradict the image of the peaceful meditator, for instance, fear of losing control.[55] Remarks made on retreat by one teacher of many years' teaching experience addressed the resistance to change and the desire to cling to forms of self-identification that he had observed in practitioners' self-reports. Walsh's description of material that erupts into awareness during vipassana: fantasies, thoughts and ideas, and of his attachment to it,[56] is reminiscent of my respondents' experiences and my own. RN comments on the clinging nature of self: about the desire to hold onto mental states, including mindfulness:

> RN: In vipassana, that mindfulness, that's just another object in itself too, so it's not even being attached to that, being attached to your mindfulness, or not even being attached to your mind. That's when it gets quite challenging for me, because the desire is to hold onto that sense-of-self, and that sense-of-self is often associated with the mind, because there's nowhere else it could be. If that's not the self and all these bits of the body, then it must be the mind, even though it can be on quite subtle levels. You think you're just observing, and then there's the other part of you that's observing the observing, and thinks it's the self.

Another description of Walsh's experience also conveys the subtlety of the shifts, in both perception and one's clinging to it, that may occur. He became aware of his identification with *I* thoughts that occur in meditation, those thoughts that are concerned with *I*. After some time, he observed the *I* thoughts following rapidly one after the other, to a point where there was some distance from the *I* thoughts *which still occur* (italics mine.).[57] During a teacher–student interview, one teacher, in the attempt to convey an understanding of the experiential shift in perception that occurs, explained that instead of the sense of 'I am seeing', one has the sense of 'just seeing'.

The following exemplifies how one may see behind the self-images that make up one's social self. Although the meditative process, and the subjective responses—such as basic feelings and the labelling underlying the identification of them—are not clearly articulated, it still gives a sense of the practitioner's deconstructive process applied to her self-concept. When I asked HR if her vipassana practice had resulted in any changes to her worldview, she illustrated instead the changes she had experienced to her 'notion of self', one of the results of which was not taking herself so seriously. On reflection about the notion of no-self, she said that in meditation she had seen things that she does to construct her self-image. When she sees these things, she 'sees that it is only a construction, not a reality', and she referred to moments when these are seen, 'rather than cogitated about'. An example of this was seeing 'mother' as one of the functions she performs, and seeing herself constructing an image of herself as a maternal person. Another example was as a 'great intellectual'. The more she meditates she said, 'the harder it is to sustain these views and the attachment to them. They begin to jostle each other'. Acknowledging these constructions has enabled her to 'let go of what we construct around persons and relationships'. HR's example illustrates the way in which change may occur to one's social self-image by the examination of one's self-concept more generally. By comparison, KN's example demonstrates how changes are made to the self-image, in this case the establishment of a stronger and more positive sense-of-self, by employing vipassana techniques to observe, identify and modify subjective impulses of craving.

KN was a recovering alcoholic, 'in rehab.' when she was first exposed to vipassana practice. She found that Buddhism refines the skill of watching the mind, a skill she had already learned in rehabilitation. Because of the effect of childhood experiences, she had been diagnosed as *disassociative*, with a poor sense-of-self from a psychotherapeutic perspective. In her understanding, dissociation occurs when 'something becomes so painful that you switch out', and 'there is no watcher and no nothing'. She said that mindfulness practice helped her to deal with both dissociation and her alcohol addiction. In the latter case, it was by teaching her to label, observe, and to let go of the addictive desire, and by giving her a sense of not having to identify with the desire through the understanding that 'thought, emotion, desire, is not the self'. Indicative of the way she had seen herself was, 'I am a recovering alcoholic'. She said that the practice helped her to move beyond this self-image. In the discussion of mindfulness of feeling above, KN described how, while focusing on her breath at the abdomen she became aware of feelings that were previously 'frozen', and was able to release them. Taken together, these changes suggest that the negative self-image as an addict was deconstructed and replaced with a positive one, that of someone who was able to identify with her feelings and work with her own inner capabilities and skills, made all the more potent because of her newfound capacity to accept and manage their intensity and emotional charge.

Another aspect of KN's experience is noteworthy because it indicates both how various elements of Buddhist practice work together to reinforce a constructive sense-of-self, based on the changes at the subjective and objective levels above, and also how the three factors panna, sila, and samadhi of the Noble Eight-Fold Path function in unison as an appealing spiritual discipline for Westerners. This is illustrative of the way in which the ethical dimension to practice enhances the quality of sense-of-self as an integrated being. In response to the question 'What Buddhist meditation techniques do you practise, and what significance do they have for you?', she replied that she kept the five lay precepts, which helped her to avoid 'unwholesome choices' and to avoid those actions that were 'another form of wanting to get away'. In her experience, slander (of others) results in feeling 'unhappy with yourself'; 'intoxication takes you away from what you should be doing'; 'being wholesome is staying with what is real', and 'telling the truth is real'. When it is remembered that this practitioner had been diagnosed as dissociative, it follows that 'feeling real' is important to her. This example shows how keeping the precepts reinforces a set of values for constructive self-definition at the level of self-concept. Added to this, the mindfulness developed in meditation, the overall level of awareness developed by noting and exploring the objects of practitioners' awareness, can enhance their sense of self-esteem by giving them more sense of self-containment and self-direction, internally and externally. KN remarked several times during the interview, 'awareness allows you to be aware *in* what you're doing'.

KN's approach illustrates how meditation and ethical practice, and the growing understanding of *wisdom*, combine to form a transformative strategy for managing inner and outer life. Many interviews indicated that the opportunity to engage with these aspects of the Noble Eight-Fold Path, and to experience their combined effects, results in deeper long-term commitment to the Buddhist path, a subject for exploration in Chapter 6. In contrast with KN's personal situation and experience of self are those of KBN, who can be seen to have had a strong sense-of-self to begin with, and to be one who was possessed of a value-system that includes seeing himself as a 'nice person'. In his account of how he began meditation as a way of dealing with a personal crisis, the crisis itself did not make him question his values or his identity; he simply responded to its effect by seeking techniques to give him peace of mind. In his account of his application of those, and the effects of meditative experience in his situation, it can be seen that his self-image as a reasonable person formed the basis for the deeper subjective adjustments to his coping mechanisms that took place.

GE: Can you tell me what meditation did for you?

KBN: I think it gave me a base for relating to other people. It gave me a way, it was a coping mechanism to begin with, I think. I've got to think back to those experiences, probably more calm, calming type thing, just giving me a way. I think I have to say in retrospect, because many other things have happened since these early experiences, it gave me some armour-plating, really. It's probably a bit paradoxical, a base from which I could deal with these difficulties. And it was obviously . . . in retrospect it was about life's adequacies. It's like one's relationship with the world, it can be predicated on a premise that one day gets attacked, and you realize that it's no longer an adequate premise, and I think in this case my premise was that, being relatively friendly with people, being a nice person . . . I'm sure it's quite common, and suddenly you run into people who actually mean you harm, and how do you deal with that? I suppose at school I had to deal with the odd bit of bullying. I didn't have well developed defence mechanisms, so I had to find a way of dealing with these people. So the meditation practice helped me, not by giving me a particular way, so much as by giving me some resources, or maybe even buying me time, but certainly delivering me a bit of calm . . . One of these people in particular, I think, was the sort of person that would drive people mad, a really nasty piece of work. In retrospect it raised this problem of how do you deal with others who mean you harm? But that's the critical problem for

Buddhists, and historically it was. How did monks deal with violence in a way that was consistent with the first precept? So I see this is one of the big problems of living. Buddhism and this problem of others meaning you harm, and then also your anger, things like anger towards others, really negative states. To summarize it really, it was a relating-to-others problem . . . In fact, later in teaching I had similar occurrences, and of course I was doing the meditation practice. As a teacher, I didn't have those resources before I was a meditator.

The full account suggests that throughout this period of public bullying, KBN did not consider direct retaliation a viable response, in keeping with his self-image as one who is friendly, accommodating, and somewhat defenceless in the face of aggression. The change that occurred was not directly to the self-image, but to the way in which KBN mediated his internal responses to aggression. He used vipassana to calm the mind, to give it a sense of space, of freedom from the stress induced by the bullying. It seems that the experience of a gap between the mind and the specific mental content lessened the mind's identification with this content enough for the respondent to be open to other ways of responding to the problem. Later in the interview KBN recalled how being mindful of the doctrine of anatta in effect reinforced this newfound distance between the observer, the ego and the feelings. How changes are made in this way by fostering a new impersonal relationship between the ego and the feelings is also illustrated in other excerpts from the same interview with KBN. In the first, he discusses his experience of the relationship between the ego and the feeling of fear.

> GE: . . . something that was talked about at Vajrayana Institute recently was the fact that we are so conditioned to have a defensive ego that you're supposed to take things personally, and get in there and show people what's what if they offend you.

> KBN: That's what the ego is, it's a defensive construct. That's the understanding I've arrived at, anyway. Why are we so afraid to open up, it's fear, sometimes dreadfully limiting fears, but that's just something to work with. It's like what is the nature of that fear that won't allow me to say whatever, it's like the investigation of reality, so even though that's an enlightenment factor, it doesn't mean it's just in the practice, in the sitting, it's in life.

In this second excerpt he distinguishes between the ego and seeing the feelings that arise as impersonal.

> KBN: Actually we haven't talked much about the three characteristics of experience, because the Buddha's theory, the way it is a general theory of experience which says that experience is constituted by these aspects of suffering,

impermanence and not-self. The not-self thing, I remember once talking about this once in a discussion group that we had. It's like if you're doing the washing up and you're getting angry with your step-son about something, you see the anger arise, and the fact that you see it arise, it passes away. The fact that you brought attention to it, you've recognized, and you cut it off. That's not-self, that's sati, 'mindfulness'.

Conclusions

The examples presented above illustrate how self-transformation may involve the sense-of-self in both its subjective and objectified aspects, to wit, how changes to one's self-concept may be supported by more subjective transformations underneath. Many practitioners like the combination of vipassana and metta, and the way in which the effects of practice harmonize with their values validates their sense of engagement with and commitment to practice of the Buddhist path. Practitioners expressed strong appreciation for the inclusion of metta on retreats as a compassion practice, but as a concentration practice it also functions to stabilize and quieten the mind. From their vipassana practice meditators gain more insight into their internal states and feelings, and learn to modify the expression of their impulses. Many responded to the labelling of pain on physical, emotional and mental levels as dukkha. The combination of practices and their effects can be seen to effect change on both subjective and objective levels. In vipassana, internal phenomena such as the experience of anger or irritability are treated as impermanent mental states to be observed in terms of arising and ceasing. Practitioners are directed to note and therefore frame it in this way, exploring the phenomenon in terms of quality and its effect on the body and mind, without 'buying into the story' or the context of the phenomenon's arising, such as an argument or other occurrence. The 'bare attention', the non-judgmental awareness brought to bear on the phenomenon, effectively isolates it—whether it be an impulse, feeling or mental state—from its existential context so it can be objectified and seen as impersonal.

In terms of describing the transformation that results from the interaction of the relative self and the imputed self, the ego—the self to be denied in Buddhist thought, between the field of immediate subjective experience in constant flux and the sense-of-self as a solid sense of I—they appear to depend on ultimately redefining the latter in terms of the former. This occurs as a result of meditative insight into the nature of one's experience, which functions to deconstruct the sense-of-self as a solid and permanent core. This process may be concurrent with others that strengthen the self-image, including its sense of self-worth. All of this suggests the ways in which transformation may occur, and how it ultimately affects the total sense-of-self. In order to explain the manner of change to identity in terms of the roles that Buddhist doctrine and practice play in effecting these changes, a theory must account for the mechanisms of change underlying the two types of change perceived in sum. It was seen how the changes experienced by practitioners could be categorized into three types: changes in immediate subjectivity, changes to one's self-concept, and changes to one's internal frame of reference, or worldview. Because of the importance of the first type of change for one's overall sense of well-being and connection with the practice, any theory of religious change needs to be capable of accounting for this aspect of this sense-of-self.

Chapter 4

Participation and Exploration
at Vajrayana Institute

Introduction

Vajrayana Institute (VI) is a Gelugpa Tibetan Buddhist Centre in Ashfield, an inner-western suburb of Sydney. The Centre is part of the *Foundation for the Preservation of the Mahayana Tradition* (FPMT), a worldwide network of 144 Buddhist centres, study groups, and projects in 31 countries.[1] It was founded by Lamas Thubten Yeshe and Thubten Zopa Rinpoche, the latter of whom is the current head of the organization. VI has a Director, a Board or Executive Committee, a Centre Manager, an Office Manager and a small number of paid administrative staff. Since VI's beginning, in 1991, there has been a succession of Tibetan teachers-in-residence, the first of whom, from 1991 to 1999, was Geshe Thubten Dawa, who remains affiliated with VI and is much loved and respected by both older and newer students. The current teacher-in-residence, since August 2003, is Geshe Ngawang Samten.

There are also other resident SANGHA members and practitioners. Primarily a teaching centre, VI provides tuition in the *dharma* and space for people to learn and practise the dharma, which includes opportunities to perform service. The Centre offers courses in meditation, a weekly program of teachings by Geshe Samten and other Sangha members, and *pujas* or devotional celebrations of chanting and visualization. With the exception of tantric initiations and practices, any member of the public is welcome to take part in VI's activities. Participants are also welcome to become members of VI by paying an annual fee, and those who wish to become Buddhist may do so by taking part in a formal refuge ceremony.

In this Chapter, I explore the ways in which students and practitioners come to acquire a sense of reality from the perspective of the FPMT. I describe what they may encounter, the available teaching and ritual activities, and what they learn about the teachings and meditation practices in order to illustrate how the shared reality of the group may be accessed. I then discuss students' journeys: how they begin to form their own appreciation of this worldview through participation in these activities. Towards the end of the chapter, I present a set of interrelated foundational, doctrinal beliefs in order to illustrate what knowledge is needed for comprehension of the FPMT's worldview. In so doing, I attempt to convey the nascent sense of the fundamentals of the worldview as an interpretive framework, without intending that this illustration be thought of as universally representative.

In this Chapter I do not treat tantric initiation and practice as part of the experimental process. Tantric initiation is not open, except as a blessing, to those who have not taken refuge. Therefore the subject is largely outside the bounds of this Chapter, which has to do with the two stages, apprehension and comprehension, *before* commitment. Tantric practice is discussed as comprehensively as possible in Chapter 5 in terms of its self-transformative function, with due consideration for the respect and privacy with which it is meant to be treated by practitioners. It is relevant to the discussion in this chapter insofar as participants may hear certain references to it, which become part of their stock of knowledge, in classes and in private conversations. Accordingly, discussion of deity yoga practice is limited to its performance as a *sutra* practice. I explore the way in which practitioners engage with the Buddhist path, through their own practice, in Chapter 5. It is recorded how their own transformative experience contributes to their comprehension of the worldview, and thence, for many, their decision to commit to the Buddhist path by taking refuge. I emphasize that the stages of the experimental model—apprehension, comprehension and commitment—may not always be discrete and sequential steps within a longer process, but they are outlined this way for ease of explanation. Individual experiences may differ in their manner of assimilating the information, for instance, learning about one aspect of doctrine before moving onto another by attending the relevant teachings, or by simply assimilating information as it is encountered. What is a commonality between individual experiences of socialization is that, for those who commit to the Buddhist path, the stages are mutually reinforcing.

The FPMT's Religious Foundations and Scriptural Authority

The FPMT views itself as part of the Gelugpa school founded by Lama Tsong-kha-pa. While it holds the teachings of Sakyamuni Buddha as its ultimate source of religious authority, in common with the other Tibetan Buddhist schools, it adheres to the philosophical view of the Middle Way School of Nagarjuna, practises the bodhisattva path, and includes the sutra and tantra systems in its teaching and practice. It is noteworthy that while the Gelugpa system of tantric theory is based on the Guhyasamaja, Cakrasamvara and Kalacakra tantras,[2] during my fieldwork at VI I did not hear reference to the first two, and the Kalacakra was referred to only as an initiation. Generally, reference is made to specific tantric practices rather than to root texts. Within the FPMT, scriptural authority also rests with the teachers and writings of the Gelugpa school, and especially those of its founders' two seminal treatises, *The Great Exposition of the Stages of the Path*, referred to simply as the *Lam Rim* at VI, and *The Great Exposition of Secret Mantra*.[3] The teachings and practices at VI are manifestly based on the former treatise. Tsong-kha-pa's Lam Rim outlines the characteristic Gelugpa presentation of the path to enlightenment and its stages. It is based on the earlier work, *A Lamp for the Path to Enlightenment*, by Atisha Dipamkarashrijnana, who is simply referred to as Lama Atisha.[4] According to Cutler, all the books on the stages of the path from the Gelugpa perspective 'published until now' are derived from Tsong-kha-pa's *The Great Treatise on the Stages of the Path to Enlightenment*.[5] Several Lam Rim publications are used by teachers and students and are kept in stock in VI's bookshop. These are Tsong-kha-pa's work (cited above), published in three volumes by the Lam Rim Chen Mo Translation Committee,[6] *Path to Enlightenment in Tibetan Buddhism* by Geshe Acarya Thubten Loden, and *Lam Rim Outlines* by Karin Valham, which the author describes as a meditation manual. This book renders the Lam Rim practices quite accessible for new practitioners. In addition, the fourteenth Dalai Lama's *Illuminating the Path to Enlightenment* (his commentary on Atisha's Lamp for the Path) and Tsong-kha-pa's *Lines of Experience* are available by donation.

The *Lam Rim Chen Mo* of Lama Tsong-kha-pa

Valham describes the *Lam Rim* as a set of practices outlining the sutric path. Lam Rim texts divide the path to enlightenment into three scopes. The small scope is for those who wish to avoid a lower, suffering rebirth in a future life and gain a happy rebirth by learning to live in harmony with the law of karma. The medium scope is for those who desire to be free from samsara by becoming familiar with the path to liberation and being liberated from ignorance. From the Mahayana perspective, the Theravada tradition is concerned with these first two scopes only. The great scope is for those who adhere to the Mahayana motivation, also referred to as the bodhicitta motivation: the motivation of the enlightened mind to attain the state of enlightenment to free all sentient beings from suffering.[7] This progression is mirrored in the three volumes of the Lam Rim edited by Cutler. The first volume deals with the concerns of the first two scopes, and prepares the practitioner for Mahayana practice by setting out the preliminary practices for the development of bodhicitta. The second volume is devoted to the motivation and practice of the bodhisattva, which Cutler considers to be the heart of the treatise. The third volume deals with the theory and practice of calm-abiding and analytical meditation, equivalent, respectively, to the *samatha*, concentration and *vipassana*, insight practices outlined in the previous two chapters.[8] Teachings and practices at VI emphasize the concerns and goals of the great scope: the development of compassion and equanimity, the generation of bodhicitta and the development of wisdom-realizing emptiness.

Other texts and study material

Next to the *Lam Rim*, the most significant text is the *Heart of the Perfection of Wisdom Sutra*. Referred to simply as the Heart Sutra, it is part of the *Prajnaparamita*, the *Perfection of Wisdom* literature, whose principal concern is the wisdom generated by perception of the nature of the dharmas as emptiness. This view is in opposition to the Mahayana view of the *Abhidharma's* analysis of reality: that dharmas are final realities out of which we construct the world.[9] The body of the sutra outlines the correct view from the Mahayana perspective, expressed by Avalokiteshvara's response to Shariputra's question, 'How should any noble son or noble daughter, who wishes to engage in the practice of the profound perfection of wisdom, train?' The response is that 'they should see perfectly that even the five aggregates are empty of intrinsic existence'.[10] This sutra is frequently referred to in teachings. It is also recited by students at the beginning of many teachings at VI to reaffirm this correct view as the goal of practice. All study, ritual, meditation and activity is directed ultimately to this end. Other textual sources of religious authority, cited as recommended reading in many teachings, are writings by the Dalai Lama, Lama Thubten Yeshe and Lama Zopa Rinpoche.[11] Throughout their involvement with VI, students are encouraged to engage in a balanced programme of study, reflection and meditation. While it is stressed that meditation plays a vital role in one's development on the path to enlightenment, study and intellectual development is a strong aspect of the Gelugpa lineage and training system. There is a long list of recommended reference material obtainable from VI's bookshop or available in its library. Prepared course notes and handouts are made available to students in class. Most teachings, workshops and seminars are taped, and made available on CD to students shortly after the relevant event.

Religious Activity at VI: Teachings, Ritual and Meditation

This section describes the initial phase of socialization into the FPMT's religious reality: the ways in which participants learn about its belief system and to attribute meaning to its doctrine and practice. Role theorists assert that socialization occurs through acting the role of the adherent, outwardly conforming to a narrowly prescribed set of role expectations.[12] However, research suggests that learning in contemplation-based religious groups occurs in three interrelated ways: as learning a new role, as learning a new symbolic universe and as apprehending the nonverbal consequences of ritual and meditation.[13] What follows will demonstrate the learning process at VI to combine all three; the roleplay facilitates the learning that occurs through conceptual and experiential means. It is expected that the following exploration of the range of religious activity on offer, and how participants explore and make sense of it, demonstrates how doctrinal, practical and experiential factors combine to facilitate the learning of a new religious reality.

For ease of discussion I have grouped all religious activity at VI into three categories: teaching, ritual and meditation. Included in the category of ritual activities to be discussed here are pujas, sutra recitations and those ritual elements that accompany teachings at VI. According to the belief system itself, the course content and the ritual structure are meant to initiate and perpetuate mental transformation in the participant, as are the reading and practice to be done privately as 'homework'. Seen from the perspective of the organization, the benefit of learning to utilize these teachings is that, whether individuals become committed Buddhists and members of VI's community or not, they will be better equipped to live their lives with less 'suffering'. From the researcher's perspective, the participant-explorer ideally derives an understanding of the worldview and the practical application of its principles, which results in their socialization into the shared reality of the FPMT. The rest of this Chapter addresses the learning aspect of socialization in terms of the way that students acquire a working knowledge of this shared reality through their involvement in VI's activities.

Teachings and Courses

All teachings delivered at VI fall within the great scope of the Lam Rim. In terms of delivery, VI uses a variety of teaching formats: classes, retreats, workshops and discussion groups. By far the most dominant form is the class format. Classes, generally referred to as 'teachings', may be one-offs devoted to a particular topic, and may run for an evening, a half-day, day or even a weekend. Longer courses may be of five or six weeks' duration, and these in turn may be part of a much longer program of as much as eighteen months' duration, requiring attendances on one night a week for one-and-a-half hours. All teachings fall into two distinct styles: the Western, classroom style and the more traditional Tibetan style. Although these two terms are generally not used in VI's discourse as it appears in announcements and newsletters, some practitioners have used them in interviews to distinguish between the two formats. Both involve receiving teachings from a teacher, and are ideally supplemented by private reading, study, contemplation and meditation. In other words, the principles taught in formal classes are to be understood more deeply through application in private reflection and meditation.

There are three fundamental differences between the two types of teaching: the level of interaction between the teacher and the student during teachings, the inclusion of meditation practice in Western-style teachings, and the amount of prior knowledge required for understanding by each. The Western-style facilitates more interaction between the teacher and the student, and is reminiscent of a classroom where the teacher delivers a lesson that may include exercises, questions from students and opportunities to clarify points of doctrine. These courses are interactive, engaging, and often fun. Traditional-style teachings run for the same lengths of time as the Western-style teachings, and are given by a lama or geshe in Tibetan and translated into English by a translator who is familiar with the teacher's style and the teaching itself, quite often a root text. Here the atmosphere is more sober and quieter. While a lama or geshe may set time aside for questions and answers, generally there are no spontaneous questions or comments from students. This is offset by providing discussion groups for the larger courses such as Atisha's Lamp for the Path to Enlightenment, in which students are free to raise topics and questions, clarify points and definitions, discuss the content of their own experience, and share their own understandings and meanings with other participants.

The second difference has to do with the inclusion of meditation in the Western teachings. The traditional teachings do not contain meditation; with the exception of prayer, the entire time is devoted to teaching and listening. In Western teachings a short meditation is included, often after the preliminary prayers, and again before the concluding prayers and dedication of merit. Sometimes these meditations consist of focusing on the sensation of the breath at the nostrils for a few moments. At other times, after several minutes of watching the breath in order to quieten and concentrate the mind, the teacher reads a short passage or a short visualization. One teacher told me that when we listen in this way, we absorb the meaning of the teaching more deeply. When a meditation is used during a teaching, it is to illustrate a point or principle, and the type of meditation used depends on the topic being considered.

The third difference has to do with the level of prior knowledge or understanding needed by the student. In the Western-style teachings there is little assumed knowledge. Principles are elaborated in detail with more introductory explanation, and illustrated with examples from everyday life. Also, references for further reading are given, and use is made of teaching aids such as notes and handouts. The traditional-style teachings typically consist of the study of a root text over a considerable period of time, for instance, the Wednesday night teachings in 2004 for *Atisha's Lamp* (above) and their accompanying Friday morning discussion groups, or similarly intensive study of an aspect of doctrine such as the *Three Principals of the Path*. Points are often elaborated by discussing doctrinal and symbolic associations of aspects of the teaching. Compared to the first way, this may come across as a condensed shorthand of sets of meanings, but for a student with existing knowledge it reinforces meaningful connections between different aspects of the teachings, and may provide moments of deeper insight through the way in which something is expressed. While all are welcome and encouraged to attend these teachings, some prior basic knowledge of Buddhism helps one to follow the flow of ideas more effectively.

In addition to one-day seminars and workshops, and the weekly meditation sessions, VI offers many courses taught in the Western style, which allow newcomers to explore the foundations of Buddhism. *Introduction to Buddhism*, a short evening course, is designed for newcomers, and presents an overview of Buddhist philosophy and Tibetan Buddhist practices. It usually runs for four to five weeks throughout the year. Other short courses of five-or-so weeks' duration present certain aspects of the Buddhist teachings, or focus on specific topics of interest. For instance, *Buddhism and Western Psychology*, which I attended twice during my period of participant observation, compared and contrasted the approaches to specific topics, for instance, the nature of mind, from within Buddhist philosophy and Western Psychology.

Popular among students is the eighteen-month foundational course *Discovering Buddhism*, which allows students to acquire a foundation in all aspects of the Buddhist path, by spending several weeks focusing on one topic at a time. I have selected this course as an example of how one appropriates the meaning-system for oneself by attending teachings and doing the associated practices. The *Basic Program*, an international FPMT course, commenced at VI on Thursday evenings in 2004 during the period of my fieldwork. This course, as part of a comprehensive study of Buddhist philosophy, focuses on nine classic Indian or Tibetan Buddhist texts, and is meant to give an overview of the entire Gelugpa system, but in more detail than the Discovering Buddhism course. The discussion group for this course is held just prior to the teachings on Thursday nights. This is largely revision of theory in the form of a clarification of meanings of key terms and ideas, and is not intended for the discussion of personal experience.

Western-style introductory teachings: *Discovering Buddhism*

The Discovering Buddhism course, affectionately known as DB, consists of fourteen subject areas or modules, each of five to six weeks' duration.[14] Listed in general order of presentation, they are Mind and Its Potential; How to Meditate; Presenting the Path; The Spiritual Teacher; Death and Rebirth; All About Karma; Refuge in the Three Jewels; Establishing a Daily Practice; Samsara and Nirvana; How to Develop Bodhicitta; Transforming Problems; Wisdom of Emptiness; Introduction to Tantra and Special Integration Experiences. As written in the introductory booklet for the course and expressed by the teachers, the course is meant to be an introduction to Buddhism, and participants do not need to be Buddhist in order to benefit from the course.[15] According to the course teachers it is also designed to be practical, and meant to be applicable to everyday life. Each module lasts for five to six weeks of about one-and-a-half hours on one night a week. The following is an outline of such a night in a Discovering Buddhism module.

Students assemble in the *gompa*. They stand and bow as the teacher enters. After teachers finish their prostrations and sit down, those students who wish to prostrate do so. Prayers are recited and the motivation is set, typically in the manner outlined above but occasionally with a variation, such as a reflection about fitting personal motivation into the larger motivation of seeking enlightenment for the sake of all sentient beings. Minds are settled by meditating for a few minutes. The bulk of the class time is spent in teaching and discussion, with exercises and further meditations depending on the class's topic. Many comments and anecdotes related during discussion are about how to deal with difficult people and situations, and about management of anger and other strong feelings. Many of the answers and suggested strategies concern the practice of patience, compassion, and a view of emptiness in the sense of there being no self to hurt or to take offence. During my participation in these modules, I observed a similarity of responses in class, the reason for which, I suggest, lies in what students may consider appropriate material for discussion in class. After the setting of homework for the next week—usually reading and meditation exercises—there may be a prayer, but the merit gained by attendance at the teachings is dedicated to the benefit of all sentient beings. This always completes the class and precedes the departure of the teacher.

The last night of the module consists either of an examination or the giving of personal points of view (PPV), and usually both. The PPVs are reports about what students derived from the module, in the form either of essays or of statements about their gains from the course, and what they have liked and disliked. The teachers' purpose in this is to see how participants are reacting to the course and to gauge how they have understood the course content. Generally, people report how they have attempted to apply the principles in their daily lives and what changes they have noticed in their own thinking, behaviour and responses to living. This is often focused on control or direction of their own impulsive responses—such as anger, and its expression or control—and their resulting actions. Throughout the course that I attended it seemed that students were directed in their questions and responses by what they considered appropriate to the context, and interview material was helpful for illuminating responses to the course material. Usually, a week or so after a module has finished, there is a day or weekend non-residential retreat held at VI, consisting of meditations related to the course content.

Ritual activity accompanying teachings

All teachings at VI are accompanied by traditional ritual activity, the elements of which consist of bowing as the teacher enters the gompa; prostrations, prayers and setting the motivation before the teachings; and prayers, dedication of merit and bowing as the teacher leaves the gompa after teachings. The correct execution and purpose of these behaviours is explained in teachings. For instance, prostrations were taught during *Discovering Buddhism* module 12, and in *Practice and Ritual Teachings* in June 2005.[16] There are three kinds of prostration: the hands placed at the heart in a prayer position while the person bows slightly; the half-prostration, which consists of touching the forehead to the ground; and the full-length, full-body stretch. In the half- and the full-prostration the hands are cupped with the thumbs inside and bent at the knuckle to represent the form bodies of the Buddha and the precious jewel. Held thus the hands then touch in succession the crown, throat and heart to represent the body, speech, and mind. Some touch the forehead as well. In the full-length prostration one crouches after touching the forehead, throat and heart, and then extends the hands forward on the floor to support the body before stretching the body's length on the floor, face-down. One then touches the crown with the hands in the prayer position before also stretching the arms forward on the floor. Finally, the arms arc outwards and down to the waist, making a large circle on the floor, before one gets to one's feet. It is stressed to try not to drop to the knees first, but to drop to the hands.

During Practice and Ritual Teachings in June 2005, a handout about full-length prostrations was given to students, and the three forms of prostration were demonstrated. During discussion about the meaning and purpose of prostrations, it was explained that in prostrating one is paying respect to the triple gem, i.e. the Buddha, the dharma and the sangha. One teacher also stated that it is important to do what you feel comfortable with and what you understand. From a theoretical perspective I found this significant. Because students are free to choose their own form of prostration according to their own level of understanding and acceptance, it means that they are also free to express their own level of acceptance of the ritual dimension. Unless one attends teachings that include explanations of specific practices, the nature of the role expectations with respect to ritual in this setting can be unclear to a novice practitioner. As I looked around the gompa on many an occasion, I noticed that students had preferences for styles of prostration. Some students, whom I knew to be Buddhist adherents of many years' practice, would somehow manage to do their full-length prostrations in the tiniest of spaces. I was happy to place my hands at the heart and bow whenever a teacher entered the gompa, and touch my crown, throat and heart three times after the teacher had prostrated and sat down. This symbolized my respect for the teacher as a symbol of religious authority, and my respect for the teachings that meant so much to the students with whom I was studying and developing friendship.

In addition to the Heart Sutra, several preliminary prayers are recited before teachings. These are typically the Seven Limb Prayer, the Outer Mandala, the Mandala Offering and the Refuge and Bodhicitta Prayer. Teachings conclude with the dedication of merit, and usually the Long Life Prayer for His Holiness and Lama Zopa. During Practice and Ritual Teachings in June 2005 the teacher explained that prayers are said to 'set the mind in the right direction', as 'motivation is important in Tibetan Buddhism', and 'it turns everything into dharma'.[17] For instance, according to McDonald, the *Seven-Limb Prayer* encapsulates a method for mental purification and accumulation of wisdom.[18] The seven limbs are prostration, offering, confession, rejoicing (in the virtues of all beings), requesting the Buddhas not to pass away, requesting the Buddhas to turn the wheel of dharma, and dedication at the end to 'put positive imprints in the right direction'. There is a benefit associated with the practice of each limb, which remedies a negative mental state or feeling. In order, these are: prostration is the remedy to pride, offering to miserliness, confession to negative karma and disturbing thoughts, rejoicing to jealousy, requesting the Buddhas not to pass away is the remedy to obscurations that prevent one from meeting the Buddha (perceiving the Buddha's true nature), requesting the Buddhas to turn the wheel of dharma is the remedy to ignorance, and last, dedication is the remedy to heresy (losing faith in or turning away from the path).

Following this is the recitation of the Outer Mandala and Mandala Offering (Inner Mandala). Taken together they function as a way of accumulating merit through the act of sincere offering. The Outer Mandala is recited while making the hand mandala, which was demonstrated in several teachings that I attended. The symbolic significance of erecting the middle and ring fingers from the base made of the upturned palms and interlaced thumbs, index and little fingers is that they represent Mount Meru. Then the offering is visualized as having dissolved and gone to the Triple Gem to the accompaniment of *Idam guru ratnam mandalakam niratayami*, translated as 'I send forth this jewelled mandala to you, precious wisdom guru'.[19] McDonald notes that the Outer Mandala, performed with the intention of mentally transforming the entire universe into a pure realm and offering it to the objects of refuge, is held to accumulate much merit, and that the immediate benefit of offering from the heart is alleviation of attachment and miserliness.[20] While performing the Inner Mandala, the practitioner brings to mind those objects for which one can feel attachment, aversion or indifference: people, belongings, one's own body and other objects, and then visualizes them as having been transformed into pure objects and offered to the buddhas.[21] An examination of the texts of the two prayers suggests a symbolic macrocosmic and microcosmic correspondence between them.[22] While through the Outer Mandala the universe is offered as a pure realm, the substance of the Inner Mandala brings one's attention back to the personal sphere of specific mental states to be transformed. This suggests that, in the symbolic association of the pure realm with one's mental states, the latter are transformed.

These are followed by the *Refuge and Bodhicitta Prayer*, recited sometimes in Tibetan and sometimes in English. It is said three times to signify body, speech and mind. Reciting this can be seen as a reaffirmation of any private or formal intentions and vows. After preliminary prayers, the motivation is set by the teacher. The wording is not always the same, but what is said always conveys the same meaning, viz. that any merit earned by listening to the teachings will be dedicated to the benefit of all sentient beings, as in 'May the merit I gain by listening to these teachings lead to my enlightenment for the benefit of others'. This motivation defines these teachings as Mahayana practice. Teachings are concluded with the dedication of merit and the Bodhicitta Prayer, which, in reminding practitioners of their bodhicitta motivation,[23] are largely self-explanatory.

From the tradition's perspective these practices orient the mind towards the dharma; affirm one's refuge-commitment as a prior undertaking of commitment or as commitment for the duration of the teaching; accumulate merit and aid the mental purification process. An experienced practitioner would be conscious of these functions by being familiar with the notions and their embodiment in the texts and symbolic gestures. Their performance can also play a role in teaching, transmitting and reinforcing some core doctrinal notions and key values. With some of these the meaning is obvious and self-explanatory, such as setting the motivation and the dedication of merit. With respect to the prostrations and prayers, their meaning is generally not obvious through practice alone, but needs to be acquired through explanation in teachings or in conversation, or through reading. For the newcomer to Tibetan Buddhism, they could be mystifying. However, these preparatory practices can be seen to serve two collective functions. First, they prepare the mind to be receptive, even if this is just a settling and slowing-down effect. Second, these actions can also be seen to delineate and define the ritual space in which teachings and religious activity take place. They give a sense of structure to the day or night's teaching in that they divide ordinary social space from the ritual space of learning and transformation.

Meditation practice at VI

A large range of meditation practices is included in the FPMT teachings and literature, and practised at the Centre. Meditation practice *per se* takes place in specific teachings where those are relevant, and in designated meditation sessions. There are several ways of classifying the types of meditation practised. Valham divides them into the three scopes according to purpose. Seen in this way, it is clear that the bulk of practices performed in teachings and meditation sessions are related to the great scope, under which Valham places meditations for developing equanimity, generating bodhicitta, calm-abiding and emptiness practices.[24] McDonald's book *How to Meditate*, used as a meditation text at VI, divides the meditations into four sections: meditations on the mind, analytical meditations, visualization meditations and devotional practices.[25] While both classifications follow the purposes to which the meditations are put, McDonald maintains that all meditation techniques can be included under two headings, stabilizing meditation and analytical meditation,[26] in line with the accepted

Buddhist classification. Taking the nature of the meditations typically taught and practised at VI into consideration results in the following three-fold list: concentration practice, analytical meditation and purification practices, all of which are discussed below. It is clear from an examination of the practices taught that most of these are a mixture of three meditative techniques: concentration, analysis, and symbolic manipulation or visualization, working with images of a desired state of affairs,[27] although some concentration and analytical practices involve visualization.

At its simplest, concentration meditation is the act of focusing exclusively on the sensation of the breath at the nostrils or the abdomen, to bring the mind to a state of single-pointed awareness. During the short course *Single-Pointed Concentration*, held on three consecutive Wednesday nights in May 2004, this term was defined as 'the ability to keep the mind focused on one thing', and similiarly, calm-abiding as the ability to 'keep our minds focussed on the object, for however long we like, with physical and mental pliancy'. These were distinguished from mindfulness, which is 'knowing that we are keeping the mind on the object'. Calm-abiding is practised to develop control over the mind, so that it is stable, that is, not distracted by external objects.[28] This concentrated mind provides the basis for cultivating *special insight*[29] and achieving subtle understandings of emptiness. In teachings and meditation sessions, calm-abiding meditation is taught and practised in two forms: as breath concentration and deity visualization. As the former, it takes the form of focusing the attention at the opening of one of the nostrils and just being aware of the sensation of the breath at this point. It is performed this way for several minutes at the beginning of some teachings to allow the mind to settle.

The purpose of analytical meditation is to develop special insight, leading to wisdom. According to Lama Tsong-kha-pa, insight is the capacity to distinguish an ultimate or a conventional object, while serenity involves one-pointedness on an object. He states that 'an undistracted mind is mental one-pointedness, the serenity aspect, while accurate reflection on facts and meanings refers to discerning wisdom, the insight aspect'.[30] In order to develop special insight, and wisdom, the mind must be first stabilized by using the above techniques. The analytical practices of this tradition involve placing awareness on objects and examining some characteristic or quality, and may involve the use of imagination or visualization. While their object is either the self or another phenomenon, they may be meditations on the mind categorized as: analysis of perceptions or assumptions about existence, e.g. life, suffering, death, human relationships, our cognitive process and meditations on emptiness.[31] While these categories represent the range of analytical practices typically taught at VI, their practice in teachings is determined by the point of doctrine or practice they are illustrating.

The first category, meditations on the mind, such as meditation on the continuity of the mind, meditation on *mind as knower* and *meditation on the spacious clarity of the mind,* do as their titles suggest. They bring the analytical function of the mind to bear on some aspect of itself. For instance, an exercise given in class during the 2003 five-week *Buddhism and Western Psychology* course involved focusing on sounds in the environment, without labelling them but to be aware of the sound (generated by a noisy overhead fan) without any verbal or conceptual elaboration. The point of the exercise was to draw our attention to how we perceive and conceive objects, and how much we depend on labels to order our perception of phenomena, so as to understand the mind's constructing activities.[32] Several people found it difficult to observe the sound without having a label or the concept for the sound beforehand, as if they needed to impose the concept onto the sound in order to make sense of their experience. Because of this we were directed to focus on our breathing, and then transfer this awareness to the ears and focus on the sounds in the same way as before. Some people found this slightly easier. Wortz discusses the therapeutic use of these two techniques, viz. focusing on the breath and on sounds in the environment, in a clinical context for the alleviation of anxiety,[33] a known use of concentration meditation. The technique had the effect of focusing the mind and enabling the participants to attend to their bare experience.

Meditations on emptiness are of two types: on the emptiness of the person and on the emptiness of phenomena.[34] Meditations such as these are designed to deconstruct our ordinary, conventional view of objects acquired through investing the label itself with a sense of inherent existence.[35] A significant example of a meditation on the emptiness of the self is the four-point analysis of *Ascertaining the Non-Existence of a Personal Self.* The four-point analysis consists of identifying the I as the object to be refuted, determining that it has to be either identical with or separate from the aggregates; considering its existence as one of the aggregates; and considering its possible existence as separate from the aggregates.[36] This meditation was done in class and during the retreat for module 14 of Discovering Buddhism: *The Wisdom of Emptiness.*

In both concentration and analytical practice visualization is employed, the purpose of which is held to be purification of the mindstream by working with images of desired outcomes such as the deities as aspects of our own enlightened nature. While deity visualization can be either sutra- or tantra-practice, in teachings and meditation sessions it is done as a sutra-practice. During his commentary on the Guru Yoga of Lama Tsong-kha-pa on 12 July 2003 at the Buddhist Library in Camperdown, Sydney, Geshe Dawa explained that some classes of tantra involve generating oneself as the deity, for which one must have the tantric initiation, or empowerment, to do so. Therefore, the deity visualizations are done in class as if the deity were external to the practitioner.[37] As a sutra practice, deity visualization can be considered either a concentration or a purification practice. As the former, it is done with the purpose of making the visualization as clear and vivid as possible, and then holding this image for some time. In this way the image becomes the meditation object in place of the breath. The visualization as a purification practice utilizes the image held in concentration for the purpose of planting suggestions or imprints into the mind.

The visualization is seen as made of pure light, luminescent and transparent. The deity is at the height of the forehead, as large as possible and facing the practitioner at a distance of a body-length. First the throne is visualized with details specific to the deity, followed by cushions or suitable ornaments. Then the deity is visualized, transparent and made of light, followed by the robes one inch from the body. Next the specific hand gestures are added, followed by implements such as bowls or bells. Finally, personal details such as hair, jewels and facial expressions complete the image. Prayers are recited while holding this image. Following this, the deity's mantra is recited during the active part of the visualization, such as visualizing light (of the appropriate colour) and nectar flowing from the deity's heart to the practitioners, entering and purifying their bodies, speech and mind, and purifying illness, negative karma and obscurations. The deity melts into light and is absorbed into the practitioner. That image may be held for some time. The practitioner may then make a short dedication. This is the basic outline of the deity visualization as it is practised at VI as a sutra or action tantra practice. By far the most prevalent deity visualization used for teaching purposes is Sakyamuni Buddha,[38] but Vajrasattva, because of his relationship with the function of mental purification, is used frequently. VI's bookshop sells small booklets which contain preliminary prayers and practices, and visualizations for certain deities, to be performed as either sutra or *kriya* (action) tantra practices.

The weekly meditation sessions provide new students with an opportunity to try the various techniques, and to sample the practical and experiential dimensions to VI's religious activity. They also provide regular practitioners with the opportunity to develop their practice. The typical session takes about an hour, and includes three different meditations. The first is usually a concentration practice, focusing on the breath for about 10–15 minutes. The two following meditations are left to the teacher's discretion. These are often visualizations, for instance the nine-round breathing purification, and a guided deity visualization such as Sakyamuni Buddha or Tara. While there is minimal doctrinal material presented in these sessions, I suspect that many newcomers, depending on their prior exposure to any form of Buddhism, would be struck by the detail and symbolic elaborateness in some of the visualizations and the purpose of such practices. This was my experience on the first few occasions I attended the meditation sessions, which were my introduction to Tibetan Buddhist meditation.

VI runs several kinds of retreat, although when and how often depends on the teachers concerned. A *Lam Rim* and *Chenrezig* retreat was organized by Tashi Choling Buddhist Institute and members of VI in January 2003 and 2004. On both occasions the teacher was Geshe Dawa. In each case the ten-day retreat comprised two parts. The first was a three-day Lam Rim retreat to introduce newer students to the fundamentals of Tibetan Buddhism and to allow advanced students to deepen their understanding. The second part consisted of a four-armed Chenrezig initiation, followed by a seven-day Chenrezig retreat involving daily sessions of visualizations and recitation of the mantra *om mani padme hung,* and commentaries by Geshe Dawa. Participants were permitted to attend either or both parts of the retreat. The retreat held from 4 to 14 January 2003 (which I did not attend) included an initiation of *Amithaba,* the *Buddha of Infinite Light. Nyung Nae* retreats, held periodically for several days, include a period of fasting in which no food or water is taken, and contain practices such as recitations and prostrations for accumulating merit and purifying obscurations. There are also retreats devoted to a specific meditation practice, such as nine-day vipassana retreats and the two-day Mindfulness retreat in December 2005 led by Venerable Antonio Satta. In November 2006, a week-long samatha retreat was led by B. Alan Wallace. This explored methods for developing calm-abiding, and included instruction in the practice of the four immeasurables: lovingkindness, compassion, empathetic joy and equanimity.

Sutra-recitation, *Guru Puja* and *Tsog*

The organization and facilitation of group rituals are by practitioners with several years' acquaintance with VI and its activity. In the main, attendance numbers are small, and new participants are rarely seen to take part. For this reason it can be said that, apart from the ritual aspects of classes and retreats, ritual does not play a part in one's initial participation and experimental learning, although this may change as one progresses through the initial stages of familiarization with the worldview and its meditation practices. Accordingly, these practices are not treated here in any detail, but are mentioned briefly in order to provide a complete picture of what is available in terms of religious activity. Apart from recitation of the Heart Sutra at the beginning of teachings, sutras are recited occasionally to aid the accomplishment of special tasks or projects. One which I became familiar with over the few years of my involvement was the *Sanghata Sutra.* In an email from the Centre on 1 December 2004 it was written:

> 'Lama Zopa Rinpoche has recently suggested that all FPMT Centres recite the Sanghata Sutra 20 times. The recitation of this sutra yields enormous benefits for all those who hear or recite it. It is a direct record of a teaching that was given by Buddha Shakyamuni on Vulture's Peak in Rajagriha, and is one of a special set of sutras called *dharma-paryayas,* or transformative teachings, transforming those who hear or recite them. Wherever the Sanghata Sutra is established the Buddhas are always present. As such, the recitation can bestow a powerful blessing on the place where it is recited.'

On 4 December 2004, it was recited by a group of practitioners with the specific purpose of clearing obstacles to the building approval by Ashfield Council for the new premises at 9 Victoria Square, Ashfield. The text of the sutra was divided into as many sections as there were people to recite it. On this occasion, this meant that ten people had eleven pages each to read through three times. In the following few months there was an effort to read the sutra as many times as possible before the Council's meeting on 28 June 2005, which was to consider approval for the building renovations. Examples of Guru Puja and Tsog Offerings performed at the Centre are those for 'all sentient beings affected by the tsunami disaster' on 5 January 2005, and for the 70th Birthday of His Holiness the Dalai Lama on 6 July 2005.

The Participant's Journey Begins: Learning and Experimentation at VI

Understanding the learning-phase of socialization involves understanding the students' means of access to and comprehension of the perspective. As discussed, people are welcome to attend whichever activity they wish. Generally though, people new to the Centre will choose a meditation session or a teaching rather than a puja or a sutra recitation. Many attend Discovering Buddhism early on, and sometimes one of the resident Geshe's teachings. Whichever teaching is tried first, experimental participation begins by assuming the role of student, whose purpose is to learn about the Tibetan Buddhist path as presented by the FPMT. This entails participation in teachings, exercises, discussion groups and private study and practice, or effectively everything outlined above. A participant first encounters the ritual elements that accompany teachings. They see others bow as the teacher enters the gompa, and regardless of how they feel about it, they follow suit. Then they see others prostrating and praying. During the teaching or meditation session they encounter Buddhist ideas that may be familiar or unfamiliar. Understanding of the material is supplemented and reinforced by discussions and meditation exercises, wherein the student both reflects on and applies the Buddhist principles to the task of dealing with and transforming problems. With time and exposure to doctrine and practice, a student begins to acquire a structure of assumptions about the nature of reality and the self from an FPMT perspective. However, the doctrinal material takes time to acquire, absorb and understand, and this process of acquisition and comprehension is affected by a number of factors.

The first consideration is how learning is affected by the choice of courses to attend, or how the range of teachings and activities to choose from facilitates exposure to the meaning-system. In courses such as Discovering Buddhism students are free to attend the modules of their choice, although a particular level of interaction with the material is expected. A related consideration is that of how well one relates to the various notions and frameworks of meaning. Do specific ideas 'feel right' or 'gel with' an individual? As we shall see, some concepts are found to be confusing. In the same way, we must consider students' responses to the practical or ritual elements of the shared reality. Compared with the sparse ritual dimension to the activities of Blue Mountains Insight Meditation Centre (BMIMC), the ritual activity of VI appears much more complex and esoteric. A student attends a teaching and encounters an array of prayers in Tibetan or English or both languages, and while the prayer sheets have the prayers in both languages so that the English translations can be followed, it must take some time before the prayers begin to feel familiar, or indeed, to mean anything. A student attends a meditation class (as I did), where the instructions are clear enough, but come the visualization of a deity, it is full of previously unencountered symbolism. This raises the question of how people begin to relate to the ritualistic elements of the Tibetan Buddhist worldview, including the recitation of sutras for specific purposes. Some explanations of ritual practice struck me initially as appealing to magical reinterpretations of cause and effect, especially the idea of accruing merit (to be discussed). Generally, people acquire the meanings of ritual actions and symbolism as they interact with older students, and are given the chance to ask questions. They clarify their understanding at the dedicated classes and short courses on ritual and practice, as exemplified by the above discussion of learning to prostrate.

Comprehending the shared reality and its framework of concepts

After some period of involvement with VI and engagement with the teachings, it becomes apparent that the teachings and practices contain a congruence of doctrinal stance and meaning. This congruence is not apparent at first. It takes some time to gather enough of a framework of ideas and their meanings through classwork, practice sessions, question-and-answer sessions and the like for that to become so. Social constructionists argue that an individual encounters a culture's or a group's shared reality as a taken-for-granted reality, a self-evident fact. One's acceptance of and engagement with this reality-view perpetuates its seeming self-evidence.[39] It follows that the shared reality of the FPMT and VI is perpetuated through the continual teaching, apprehension, internalization and embodiment, in thought and action, of the Gelugpa Tibetan worldview as outlined in the Lam Rim. Apprehension of this taken-for-granted reality by a student-practitioner is as a coherent and self-supporting interpretive framework for experience. We shall see that—as students begin to test the doctrinal precepts against their experience, and find them to be useful interpretive tools for thought and action—their faith in the validity of the framework, the shared reality, is strengthened. This in turn strengthens the intention to take the Buddhist worldview and path more seriously, and to explore it more thoroughly.

In order to see how the student begins to explore the teachings and to perceive elements of doctrine as a coherent interpretive framework for experience, it is necessary to understand how students build and organize their stock of knowledge, and why. The meaning and significance that they attribute to specific topics, concepts and doctrines accords with their understanding of them, and meditation practice and experience is material to their learning, apprehension and comprehension of the teachings. For this reason, what I have referred to as a basic framework of doctrinal notions is outlined and discussed at the end of this chapter to define the basal premises that a student must begin to understand in order to make sense of the Vajrayana path and its practices. This framework is meant to be illustrative, rather than representative, of the participant-experience.

Beginning to acquire a framework of ideas

The participant-student is free to choose which courses and teachings to attend. There is no fixed order or curriculum to follow. Typically, the students and practitioners that I interviewed had attended some Western-style and traditional-style teachings. Most had done some of the Discovering Buddhism course. Those who had been involved with VI since before 2002, when Discovering Buddhism began, had taken other beginners' courses, and moved on to some of the more advanced courses. Some students had attended the regular meditation classes for a time. In the main, however, students and practitioners tend to go to 'teachings' rather than the weekly meditation sessions or the infrequent courses on meditation (not including the specialized meditation retreats held every so often). AN, who had been coming to VI regularly for about six months at the time of interview, had attended the ten-day Introduction to Buddhism course at Kopan Monastery during his travel through Asia. Since his return to Australia and becoming involved with the Centre, he had attended a few of the weekend classes, four of the Discovering Buddhism modules: Karma, Samsara and Nirvana, How to Develop Bodhicitta, and Transforming Problems, and taken part in some traditional-style teachings: Atisha's Lamp for the Path, and the Thirty Seven Practices of the Bodhisattva. Such patterns of attendance demonstrate that people try, as part of their exploration of the belief system, a variety of the teachings offered at VI.

'Repetition, reinforcement, response'

Learning can be facilitated by repetition: hearing the same information expressed in different ways during continual attendance at teachings until a sense of familiarity with the concepts and their interconnections begins to grow. Some students refer to 'levels' of understanding, for instance, CR:

GE: It's really interesting that you've drawn the distinction between the more traditional and the more Western-focused teachings.

CR: Yeah, they're both fantastic; they both support each other. In the end it's the more traditional teachings that are the real essence of it, once you get into more serious study.

GE: That's interesting. Can I ask you a question, and you tell me if I'm on the right track? Is it fair to say that the Western style allowed you deeper access so that you could appreciate the more Tibetan style of teaching?

CR: I wouldn't necessarily say it was that, because I think with the Tibetan one, it was just attending those again and again and again, and doing reading, that I got used to the style. I started to understand the terminology, and I started to realize that every time I heard a teaching, it was presented in a slightly different way, and I always got something from it. I would understand something each time that I mightn't have understood before. I also started to understand the role of imprints, and so I would go to teachings, even though I felt like I wouldn't be able to understand it, for the imprint, so the next time I'd understand a bit more, and the next time a bit more, and some of the quite difficult teachings I've been able to get a bit of an understanding of through that, just going back and listening again and again. So it just kind of goes along on its own, and it does talk about the practical as well. Because Buddhism is very practical, but it's like they go hand-in-hand. The Western teachings are particularly good for when you are a beginner though. But I went to both hand-in-hand. I didn't feel like I needed to go to one and not the other, although there were times when Geshe-la might have been teaching on something. I do remember times when I went and thought, 'I haven't got a clue what this is about', and so I might not go back on that night. They might have offered an introductory course, and then I would have done that. I did some of the introductory courses a couple of times. It was good having teachings on different levels on offer, and it's such a completely different style you can't really compare them.

This excerpt exemplifies the way in which students choose courses in order to flesh out their own understanding, and therefore negotiate or direct their own learning. They are prepared to keep attending teachings and courses in the faith that they, by understanding a little at a time, eventually arrive at a clearer understanding of the whole teaching. The excerpt also shows how the notion of karmic imprints may be employed as a mental strategy to cope with the *feeling* of not understanding a teaching.[40] They maintain that listening to a teaching will benefit them on some level even if they do not understand what they are hearing at the time. MM offers an appraisal of her own learning process.

MM: The first course I did was on thought-transformation, the seven-point mind-training, you know, all sentient beings have been my mother,[41] the equalizing self with others. So I did that and at least I got an intellectual understanding of it because the way it seems to work for me is, because I've got a strong intellectual study background, I seem to need to get an intellectual handle on things first, see how it works and then it will percolate down to the heartfelt level, that seems useful for me. Sometimes I'll get realizations through somebody saying something out of the sutras, and I'll think, 'Oh yeah. Wow'. Often I need this kind of intellectual overview, and then it will percolate down to something that can become a heartfelt practice.

NJ relates that her initial response to teachings at VI had intellectual, intuitive and strong emotional dimensions. She had been discussing, with a friend, the possibility of taking refuge.

NJ: I remember him saying to me the day after September 11, there was going to be a refuge ceremony at VI, and he said, 'You need to take refuge', and I thought, 'Yep. That's the right thing to do', and so I did.

GE: How much did you understand of the Buddhist teachings at that stage?

NJ: I'd done the introductory Lam Rim course.

GE: Can you remember what it covered?

NJ: Yeah. Things like, um, the Four Noble Truths, teachings about death, [and] there was a short thing about Tantric practice. There's karma and rebirth—it was Lam Rim—so it covers the basics, renunciation and bodhicitta and wisdom, yeah, and I had a basic idea.

GE: So it tends to give you the basics.

NJ: Yeah the foundation, the structure, but, it just seemed to me, actually I'd never actually connected to something that made as much sense. It really made lots of sense to me, and it made sense with a lot of things I'd thought previously, and I had read about Tibetan Buddhism before all of these things happened, years ago. I went to Tibet about seven or eight years ago, and before I went, I read some stuff about Tibetan culture, and I'd read the Tibetan Book of Living and Dying, and I'd read a few other books about Tibetan Buddhism, so I'd had a little bit of an idea, but it was more like a . . . this was the first thing I'd come across that had made sense to decide that you fitted into it. I don't know how to put that, really.

GE: So if I understand what you're saying, you got a certain sense of what it was about from the Lam Rim teachings?

NJ: Look I don't know. The word intuition isn't a great word, but I think it was much more of an intuitive thing that an intellectual thing. I trust it, the Lam Rim made sense, it just made sense, the Buddha, these teachings make sense, they are very practical and useful.

As the three examples above demonstrate, participation in activities and exploration of the material is not directed by mere curiosity. For many, the impetus for further exploration of the teachings is provided by the strong response they had to their first teaching. This teaching provided a solution to a problem they were experiencing, even if awareness of the problem itself, or the extent to which they wanted help with it, emerged only while they listened to the teaching. The following examples illustrate how instrumental, because of the intensity of the effect it has on the individual, a first teaching can be in a decision to explore Buddhism. CR recalls her first teaching, the *Eight Verses of Thought Transformation*:

CR: Anyway, we came and there was a monk teaching, a Western monk, and he was teaching on the Eight Verses of Thought Transformation. It was fantastic. The whole concept was to cherish and to hold most dear the person who has harmed you, you know, the person you've been really kind to who's then harmed you in turn. They're the most precious treasure to be able to see them like this. And I just had this feeling of relief. I thought 'Oh! This is the place. This is what I need to hear'. I love those Eight Verses of Thought Transformation.

GE: It's really significant, because the impression I'm getting is that you knew how you wanted to deal with it, but you needed validation in some way?

CR: I needed to know how. I knew I didn't want to hate him (an ex-partner), but I didn't know how not to be caught up in anger. You know . . . how exactly to deal with it, and then I walked in and here's this person talking exactly about that thing, coming to this state of equanimity, and I wanted that with everything, not just with this, but with anything that comes your way in life, whether it's good or bad. To be in this place, not where you're indifferent, but where you're not going up and down like a roller coaster. You're able to just enjoy things that are there to be enjoyed, but not in a way that makes you attaching and grasping at them, and then ends up causing you more suffering.

And similarly, another respondent recounted:

RI: The first time I went to VI it was with Geshe Dawa teaching. But I remember clearly, when something popped, feeling very uncomfortable . . . this guy talking in Tibetan. I didn't like being there, felt very embarrassed. So I listened, and tried to listen patiently. Don't know what the subject was. Actually the topic was anger. Seemed like he was looking at me. Geshe Dawa was basically saying . . . it was like he was talking to me and saying . . . but the real thing that blew my mind was when he was talking about anger and antidotes, and I had no idea that there were antidotes to anger, various ways to get rid of anger, use antidotes, patience. Wow. Of course patience is the antidote to anger. Impatience is a lack of patience. I just have to be more patient, and I went away thinking, 'Wow. A lot of that stuff's really weird, but that guy really knows what he's talking about'.

These excerpts illustrate how the individuals concerned responded to teachings that showed them how to deal with difficult emotions. That below outlines AN's response to the ten-day introductory course at Kopan monastery, to discovering the philosophical and ethical frameworks supporting Buddhist meditation practice. His prior exposure to meditation, by his own admission, had been superficial and limited.

AN: But once I went to Kopan I got a bit of exposure, she (the teacher) just basically ran through a lot of different teachings about bodhicitta. That was the first time I'd heard about that, and the concept of exchanging self for others and the concept of thinking of others as your mother. And we went into reincarnation, which before that I thought was just a cool idea but didn't realize there was a whole system of logic behind it and that it really is an argument and not just a New-Age catch cry. And so I really got wind of the fact that there is real substance to the study behind it, and it's not as airy-fairy as images I'd had of it before, and so that sparked off the intellectual side of me that thought, 'Oh. I want to learn more, and it's not all just waffle. There's serious stuff here'.

The experiences recounted above, and others recounted in interview, all indicate that the student's perception of an underlying depth and structure to the belief system, and an underlying truth demonstrated by their own experience of its applicability to their situation, is instrumental in their desire to explore further. For all practitioners, it seems that information is taken-in conditionally: conditional upon being shown to be of value, and to be effective in terms of dealing with experience. From here, certain core doctrinal concepts are explored, and incorporated into a stock of knowledge through the process of applying it to a life-problem. It is when people hear a teaching, and realize that it applies to some issue or problem in their lives, that the internalization process, the process of making *the* information *their* information, is begun. These are the concepts that are mentioned as either significant for them, or the exploration and understanding of which has been integral in their initial socialization, and later, commitment processes. When participants have seen both how a teaching or principle can be applied to a problem and be shown to frame experience in a constructive way, they then wish to understand the Buddhist teachings in a more holistic way.

After a time, when some confidence in the belief system has been acquired, it seems that the experiential testing may not be so intense, and students tend to look for coherence between aspects of the belief system as an interpretive framework. At this stage, the various ideas must have some meaningful connection between them. Despite the fact that many do not recall their own exploration process in this way, that is, when they began to perceive doctrine as an integrated whole, the content of people's conversations within the Centre shows that this happens. In interview, I asked questions about students' encounters with Buddhism and VI, what courses they had done, which they responded to, and how they related to the Buddhist concepts and ideas. Respondents typically found these questions easy to answer. The answers were typically about concepts encountered early, concepts that are either easy or hard to understand, and especially about those that were remembered as being significant because of their practical value, as related above. For instance, MM's answers included finding the teachings about karma 'hard' because 'I have no concrete or tangible proof of it' (referring to rebirth), but, because of the way that her reasoning led her to this conclusion, she had no doubt that karma exists in this lifetime. Other important concepts were the six perfections, especially patience, and bodhicitta motivation.

While not all practitioners demonstrated clear recall of the order of courses they attended, or how their knowledge was acquired, and therefore how concepts began to form a framework, all of the responses discussed above highlight the importance of the way in which concepts were most relevant to dealing with, understanding and framing their life experience, both immediately and in the long term. So the researcher's question as to how and why students have accumulated a stock of knowledge, how concepts and frameworks are acquired and built on, is answered in terms of problem-solving at first and then in terms of more general meaning-seeking.

An example of how such recall may exist for a practitioner, of how they may build a working understanding of the path, and of how their choice of courses and reading material enables them to build on acquired knowledge is provided by NC. He recalls his early involvement with the Centre's teachings, and the way in which he began to explore and assimilate elements of the doctrinal framework. In 2003 he began attending the Centre, and took the six-week course on Buddhism and Psychology. He then began Discovering Buddhism, and completed the modules Introduction to Tantra, Emptiness, Mind and Its Potential, How to Meditate and Presenting the Path. Before and during this time, he had read the Dalai Lama's book on the Lam Rim, *The Path of Bliss*, more than once, and had used Kathleen McDonald's book *How To Meditate* intensively for three months. He said to me that ideas about tantra had suggested the importance of revising renunciation and bodhicitta, doctrinal elements he had become familiar with from reading the Path of Bliss. He said, "Introduction to Tantra made me want to go back and get a closer look at Renunciation and Bodhicitta", and further, "Tantra is a really powerful tool to use, but to use it properly, it is important to have these basics of renunciation, bodhicitta and emptiness sorted out at least to some degree." Teachings from the Introduction to Tantra module, and the traditional teachings he was concurrently attending on Saturday afternoons,[42] were raising questions for him around the correct view of desire, including the use of sexual energy.

An essential framework and its components

By taking part in teachings and activities, students begin to acquire the stock of knowledge with which to form an interpretive framework for further teachings, for more complex Buddhist philosophy and for life experience. Throughout my participant observation I noticed that certain principles and concepts were dominant and most meaningful in formal discourse, conversation and interview. They were repeated often in class, and appeared to give most meaning to the material presented in teachings by supporting other points of doctrine and the reasoning behind VI's ritual activity. The ideas outlined below are proper to Mahayana thought as it is understood within that system. I have not discussed basic Buddhist doctrine such as the Four Noble Truths, but only the notions that are crucial to an understanding of the perspective of the FPMT as a taken-for-granted meaning-system. All of the notions below fall under one or other of three headings: The Three Principals of the Path, the Nature of Mind and Mental Purification and the Role of the Teacher.[43] The layout and explanation of the core notions not only reflect what I believe that students need to comprehend as a minimum in order to make sense of doctrine and practice, but also reflect what I needed to clarify for myself before I felt that I could grasp the FPMT curriculum.

The Three Principals of the Path are renunciation, bodhicitta and correct view or wisdom-realizing emptiness. They are three qualities or attributes of the Mahayana practitioner that need to be developed in order to reach enlightenment. A cornerstone of Buddhist thought is that samsaric life is characterized by suffering. The basis for the motivation to develop these principles is in understanding the nature of suffering. Renunciation and bodhicitta are defined by Powers as the definite intention to leave cyclic existence, and generating the intention to attain enlightenment for the sake of all sentient beings, respectively.[44]

Part of the commentary to the Medicine Buddha Initiation conferred by Geshe Dawa in 2005 addressed the principle and practice of developing renunciation from the experience and understanding of the suffering nature of samsara.[45] The Geshe's translator began by stating that the sutric or tantric practitioner should have three qualities: renunciation, bodhicitta and right view. Renunciation should be a definite conviction: 'When one thinks about the suffering nature of samsara, one develops renunciation', and 'It is hard to develop renunciation if you do not see the suffering nature of samsara'. IIe went on to say that when one experiences difficulty and hard situations, one wants to get out of them. The Mahayana teaching maintains that when one can see similar situations in others, this transforms slowly into bodhicitta. Bodhicitta is developed with the method of lovingkindness and compassion. In the same way that one's understanding of renunciation is the path to liberation, one's development of bodhicitta is the 'path to the perfect state of enlightenment'. Throughout my involvement with VI, I found that students understood these two concepts easily enough—and were willing to accept them as motivations for practice quite quickly—because they related to the doctrine of the suffering nature of samsara, which made sense in terms of their own life experiences.

Emptiness and compassion are the two characteristics of the enlightened mind of the Buddha. Powers relates that, in Tsong-kha-pa's view, training in wisdom and the cultivation of compassion are associated,[46] and indeed this is constantly reinforced as a fundamental principle in teachings. Although the term emptiness refers to the lack of inherent existence of all dependently originated phenomena, the term is most commonly used in discourse to signify the emptiness of self of any inherent existence. The Gelugpa refer to emptiness and dependent origination as the absolute and relative view of phenomena generally, including the self. In Discovering Buddhism, students were encouraged to think of a phenomenon in terms of dependent origination, expressed as 'View it as a dependent origination, dependently arisen through causes and conditions'. Similarly, with the self, the absolute view is emptiness. The relative view, the self as dependently originated, is represented doctrinally by the aggregates and dependent origination. The 'I' that appears as permanent and self-existent in one's ordinary experience, labelled the ego in Western psychology, is imputed onto the aggregates. The enlightened view is seeing this 'I' as a construction, as being empty of inherent existence, and as the product of the interdependent interaction of the aggregates.

Meditations on emptiness are outlined in the literature, and sometimes taught and practised in teachings. However, little reference was made to them in interview. When practitioners were asked about which Buddhist concepts they responded to, or that had significance for them, a notable absence was the concept of emptiness. Instead, they spoke of karma and reincarnation, thought transformation and bodhicitta. The answer to this may lie in the fact that people try to work with the notion of emptiness conceptually, and this is hard to do when one does not have a clear sense of the term. When discussion has focused on the notion of emptiness in teachings, students typically refer to the emptiness of self, and the way in which this idea of no permanent or essentially existing self may be used as a mental strategy for stopping one's 'self-cherishing' and defensiveness in relationships with others, especially during conflict. This strategy suggests that doctrinal notions need to be applicable to one's circumstances. Students appear to relate more easily to terms such as karma, and spiritual aspirations such as thought transformation and bodhicitta, that are more applicable to the interpretation of their immediate experience. In addition, as the section on meditations taught and practised at VI indicated, analytical meditation tends to be overshadowed by concentration and visualization practices, which may be perceived as being more directly applicable to managing one's mental and emotional life. According to Gilgen and Cho, reasonable agreement exists among scholars that the Eastern system is monistic or non-dualistic in nature, and the Western outlook is primarily dualistic.[47] In the West there is a tendency to think in terms of a Creator and a created,[48] and almost without exception, the students and practitioners that I interviewed came from Christian backgrounds. The notion of emptiness is conceptually abstract, and according to doctrine, not amenable to immediate meditative exploration.

In many of the teachings I have attended the nature of mind is defined as clear and knowing, where clarity means the mind's capacity to perceive the emptiness of existence.[49] The teachings hold that to come to know one's own mind as clear and knowing, one must purify one's mindstream and accumulate merit.[50] Several sources cite Manjushri's advice to Lama Tsong-kha-pa: 'To attain spiritual realizations one must combine meditation on the path to enlightenment with purification, accumulation of merit, and praying to one's guru as a Buddha'.[51] The accepted wisdom of practitioners is that the attainment of enlightenment does not occur by study and meditation alone, but must be accompanied by actions that result in mental purification and merit-accumulation. Terms such as these: karmic imprints, karmic seeds and the conditions for their ripening, creating merit, removing obscurations, purifying, and the mindstream or mental continuum are heard frequently in teachings and in conversations at VI, and form part of its discourse. As both participant observer and religious seeker, I was frequently struck by the interchangeability with which these terms were often used. It became evident that in order to understand the reasoning behind the idea of mental purification that is embodied in many of the practices, one must understand its relationship the notion of karma.

The doctrine of karma and rebirth, and its relationship to the nature of cyclic existence and its six realms was referred to frequently in teachings. However, the notion implicit in the use of terms such as creating karmic imprints, accruing merit and removing obscurations to omniscience is that of the mindstream or mental continuum, which is the agent which carries karma from one life to the next, and therefore creates the conditions for future lives. This continuum is affected by karma, and while it is clear and knowing this nature is obscured by karmic imprints caused by unwholesome actions of body, speech, and mind. In order to reveal this clear and knowing nature of mind, the mental continuum must be purified of obscurations or karmic imprints. Before this process is described it must be pointed out that, in this Western Buddhist context, there is a way in which the notions of karma and reincarnation may be isolated from each other. Some of my respondents stated that they 'have trouble with rebirth', although they appear to accept the notion of karma. The following shows how some students may accept the notion of karma without necessarily accepting the notion of rebirth.

MM: The ones I find hard are the teachings on karma, and yet at the same time, strangely, I find it difficult because I have no concrete or tangible proof of it, beyond what I've already told you. And I'm at the point, like a lot of the teachers say, 'You may as well behave as if karma exists, because if at the end of your life you've done that, you've lived an ethical life. If it did exist, and you got to the end of your life and you'd behaved as if it didn't, then you'd be in a lot of suffering'. That's something I could get my head around. But I have no doubt in my mind that karma exists in this lifetime. I've got to the point, particularly with anger—I think this is very much a stage of my own practice—that if I let fly with my partner, I think I suffer more than he does. And it motivates me to do something about it.

GE: So, it's not karma you have an issue with so much as reincarnation?

MM: Yes, that's right. I think a lot of Westerners would be similar to me. If I've come to appreciate other things as being true for myself through experience, probably further down the track, and I suspect you need to be a long-term practitioner before you can do that, that will reveal itself to me too, and it will reveal itself in a way that's appropriate. So I'm willing to say that I've got an open mind on reincarnation, but certainly that in this lifetime, yes, I can see karma happening. The part I find consoling about karma, I mean I find I go through things now where I still get into 'poor me' victim stuff when something gross happens to me, but now at least further down the track maybe at two or three weeks distance I think but actually karma does give me succour about this.

Another practitioner said, "Well, to be a Buddhist, you have to believe in reincarnation. It makes the whole thing work." The terms karma and reincarnation have become virtually part of the language. While Westerners in general have become familiar with them, and many may even entertain a belief in them as Campbell suggests,[52] the transcript excerpt above illustrates that students question concepts and doctrines that they encounter, and do not accept them blindly. It also shows that they are capable of discriminating between notions that appeal directly to their experience and reasoning, and those that they find unsupportable, at least initially. The way that karma may be conceptually isolated from reincarnation, from a Western practitioner's perspective, is understandable in terms of the narrative of purification—or revealing an essential nature within oneself—which underpins much Western alternative spirituality. While there may be a seeming contradiction between a conditional acceptance of the emptiness of self and the purification of something pure that has become defiled, this in itself indicates the way in which the mind will attempt to make sense of new material according to existing understandings. For many with a Christian background it makes sense to leave reincarnation out of the picture initially, and come to terms with a purification process in the context of one lifetime.

Many of the practices are for the purpose of accumulating merit. During *Practice and Ritual Teachings*, on Monday 20 June 2005, the teacher explained that while the idea of merit was 'complex', simply expressed, 'It puts positive tendencies on the mind'. In teachings and in casual conversations it is expressed that just hearing a teaching accrues merit, purifies negative karma, and 'gives you the imprint' so that one can have deeper realizations. One may generate merit through all good action and receive it through past good actions. I have felt on occasion that the two notions, accumulation of merit and mental purification, are used somewhat interchangeably in a form of mental shorthand to express the idea that progress on the path involves some positive and committed action on the part of the aspirant. While one may get the impression that the understanding of merit and its accumulation is akin to the idea of a 'piggybank', where merit from wholesome action is accumulated to offset negative karma accumulated by unwholesome action, I suspect that practitioners' understandings come to be more in terms of the effect of actions on one's mindstream or mental continuum. Although the notion of accumulating merit and the ways of doing this are referred to frequently, the notion and process of purification is given much more formal treatment in doctrine and teachings.

Whenever I have heard the notion of purification being spoken about at the Centre I have tended to think of transforming mental tendencies, our habitual responses to things. I asked CR, "If I said two words to you, (attaining) enlightenment, or purification? Are they the same thing, or are they different?" She responded:

CR: Ah, I haven't really talked about purification. Actually, they're different. Purification is one of the things on the way to enlightenment. So on the one hand you are . . . I've been talking about developing qualities. But the other thing you're doing is purifying negativities, so, the less room there is for negativities the more room for positive qualities, and that is something that is really important to me because there are things that I've done in my past. And one of the things that's really great about Buddhism is this idea that there's no karma that's too heavy that it can't be purified. But it's also an idea that's different to Catholicism. Whereas in Catholicism you were going to someone and confessing your sins, but you were asking for forgiveness from an outside God, and then boomf! The forgiveness would come down on you or whatever. Now, sometimes with Buddhist purification practices it might look to an outsider that it's the same thing. You know, say, you're doing your Vajrasattva purification practice and you're visualizing the deity on the crown of your head and raining down nectar and purifying. In fact all of the visualizations that you do of a deity do involve that aspect of being purified of negativities.

With respect to the process of purification, in teachings reference is often made to the Four Opponent Powers: the power of dependence or reliance; the power of regret or release; the power of the remedy and the power of restraint. The power of reliance is going for refuge and generating bodhicitta. In this way, the object of refuge, the three jewels, becomes the object of non-generation of non-virtuous karma, and refuge becomes a foundation of purification. The idea behind the power of regret is that the nature of regretting non-virtuous action is virtuous. The power of application of the antidote involves dedicating one's virtue, obtained by performing practices—ideally several practised simultaneously—towards purifying non-virtuous karma. These practices include meditating on bodhicitta or emptiness, reciting sutras or mantras, making prostrations and building stupas. The power of the promise means to promise to oneself not to engage in the negative action again.[53]

From this it can be seen that all of the meditations and ritual practices described above are purificatory actions. What determines their efficacy from the Mahayana perspective is the motivation with which they are done. Any action may be considered a small, medium or large-scope practice, depending as one's motivation is for a better rebirth, liberation from samsara, or attainment of enlightenment to alleviate the suffering of all sentient beings. Another doctrinal aspect that needs to be considered here is how the three aspects of the Noble Eightfold Path: wisdom, ethics and concentration—known as the three higher trainings in this system—are applied in practice. The ethical dimension is implicit in all action performed with the Mahayana motivation to attain enlightenment for the sake of others. The point of taking vows, and making refuge and initiation commitments, is to reinforce one's motivation continually, and therefore to ensure that every action becomes a way of accumulating merit and purifying the mental continuum.

Conclusions

This Chapter has explored how the student begins to engage with the shared reality at VI through attending teachings and other activities, and how they begin to acquire the meaning of core terms and concepts that begin to form an interpretive framework. It was found that students initially begin to explore and test concepts applicable to their own life experience and perceived problems. Once a small set of ideas is validated as viable and useful in this way, the student begins to explore the doctrinal architecture more widely in order to see how different parts of the framework fit together. How doctrine and practice is applied to the goal of self-transformation is explored in Chapter 5. It was found that acceptance of the framework as one's own view occurs when students begin to test their responses to doctrine through its practical application to their own lives. An important factor in an individual's learning process is evaluation of newly-apprehended material in the light of previously-explored religious frameworks and practices. This is treated, in the light of an individual's entire religious biography, in Chapter 6. From the foregoing it is suggested that, while practitioners will come to understand the same basic doctrinal notions and their meanings, not everyone embraces the perspective entirely in the same way. For instance, all seem to accept the doctrine of karma, including the idea of accruing merit, but some do not accept the idea of rebirth. The liking for compassion practices, coupled with the attempt to act from an understanding of emptiness, which is expressed in the acceptance of the notion of bodhicitta, appears to orient these practitioners in their engagement with Buddhism generally.

Chapter 5

The Practice of Self-Transformation at Vajrayana Institute

Introduction

This Chapter examines the techniques through which change is produced, experienced and attributed meaning by practitioners at VI. Whereas Chapter 4 explored the learning process, this Chapter explores the extension of learning through personal application of principles and practices designed to effect self-transformation and validate the meaning-system for oneself. From the Mahayana Buddhist view, self-transformation takes place within the context of the path to enlightenment, where the mind gradually comes to see reality from the view of emptiness. The distinction between traditionalist and modernist forms of Buddhism made by their orientation to the doctrine of karma and rebirth highlights a difference between BMIMC and VI. Traditionalist forms of Buddhism emphasize the accrual of merit, while modernist forms focus on the development of wisdom leading to enlightenment by textual study and meditation.[1] BMIMC's modernist orientation emphasizes meditation and doctrinal study, whereas within the Foundation for the Preservation of the Mahayana Tradition (FPMT) traditionalist and modernist trends co-exist, as I noted in Chapter 1. The combination of traditional ritual and textual study and meditation reflects the intimate relationship between merit-making activity and the development of wisdom through personal application. Practice in this view is anything that creates merit and 'puts positive tendencies on the mind', and all of these forms of activity are seen as merit-making, and therefore as transformative activities.

I include an exploration of tantric thought and practice in this Chapter because a study of self-transformative practice at VI would be incomplete without it.[2] If I were to follow a strictly chronological, stepwise description of one's engagement with and progress in the practice, the subject of tantric initiation and practice would follow Chapter 6, as one is expected to take refuge—to become Buddhist—before engaging in tantric activity. It is considered here because information about its doctrinal and ethical underpinnings, and certain facts about its practice not guarded by secrecy are part of the discourse of enlightenment and its means of attainment at VI. This information is accessible through formal and informal conversation. While the section below examines those practical activities that belong to the category of sutric practice as distinct from tantric practice, the aims are the same for both. I have deferred discussion of their differences until the latter half of the Chapter.

Aims, Techniques and Outcomes of Sutra-Practice

According to the Buddhist worldview of the FPMT, all actions and mental states are categorized as virtuous or non-virtuous, wholesome or unwholesome, and create positive or negative karma accordingly.[3] The existence of a third category, neutral, where because of the passivity of the mind during neutral actions (for instance, sneezing and fainting), neither positive nor negative karma is created, does not appear to be relevant to practitioners' concerns of self-transformation and spiritual progress. The process of mental purification is meant to reverse the effect of prior negative action, and to replace tendencies in that direction with positive ones. All virtuous action, e.g. performing pujas, reciting the refuge prayer, study, meditation practice and virtuous action in daily life, is thought to result in the accumulation of merit, which is the first of two collections—merit and wisdom—to be amassed by the practitioner when they enter this path.[4] The comment:

> CR: Really, for me the whole reason I'm doing those practices is to give my mind some sort of imprints that are going to help me in various situations in my life, and help me to be a better person.

Illustrates the purpose of mental purification for success on the path to enlightenment, and (my inference) the importance of the Bodhisattva motivation for the aspiring practitioner.

During my period of fieldwork at VI it was clear that participants felt the desire to establish a daily practice. While some were successful at setting the time aside to maintain a regular practice, others stressed that sometimes 'life got in the way', and they ended by not meditating as much as they would have liked. Many interview-respondents emphasized that the descriptions of their daily practice routine reflected what they did under ideal conditions. Typically, practitioners who maintain a regular practice spend up to an hour a day in quiet reflection, meditation practice, tantric commitments or reciting the refuge prayer and vows, as illustrated by the following examples.

> NJ: I've taken Kalachakra Tantra initiation. Traditionally, the practice is done three times during the day and three times during the night, and that's a lifetime commitment. I do mantras, not because of my commitments but because they are beneficial tools we have been given. At the moment I'm

doing a Sakyamuni Buddha visualization to develop my concentration. I do half-an-hour at minimum. I read the King of Prayers every night.

CR: I now have a set practice that takes me about an hour a day, but it's not a sitting down and meditating-on-the-breath practice. So it's like Medicine Buddha and White Tara and Green Tara, Kalachakra initiation, Cittamani Tara, which is a higher yoga tantra of Green Tara.

AN: I start usually with the breathing to focus, and usually it's a breathing-out all the mess, the impurities and the obstructions and stuff and breathing in calm,[5] just as a centring thing, and yeah, I usually do the exchanging self for others or a compassion one.

These examples illustrate the emphasis placed on visualization for the purpose of mental purification that was present in many descriptions of daily practice. This emphasis on purification (in contrast to bare attention, for instance) within this form of Buddhism appears to have produced two interesting effects. First, the concentration and purification practices, especially the deity visualizations, tend to dominate practice in teachings and meditation classes at VI. It appears that, for some students, the path is more easily approached in terms of the purifying action of one's visualization of a deity, wherein the role of concentration for focusing the mind is easily understood. Analytical meditation, while taught, is under-represented in individual preferences, although Tsong-kha-pa's Lam Rim teaches that practice in stabilizing and analytical meditation must be balanced in order to attain enlightenment.[6] It appears to be thought by some that the analytical meditations on *emptiness* can be postponed until enough mental purification has taken place for realizations of emptiness to occur more easily. NJ expressed the view that 'You have to work your way to particular levels of realization' in order to have a realization of emptiness. When asked about her impressions of the analytical meditation we were guided through in one class,[7] she responded, "Well, you have to have a good degree of concentration to do those meditations. I am building up my concentration."

Second, when students and practitioners do not find adequate time to meditate, their desire for practice may be satisfied by the performance of meritorious works with the view that the same merit will be accumulated by virtuous action. This can be seen to act as a psychological safety-net for assuaging the guilt that arises, for some, from failing to meditate. In cases where lay vows are broken or commitments are not kept, adherents are told that they can 'purify their vows' by using the *four opponent powers*.[8] Practitioners feel that it is important to keep their commitments, which may consist of prayers, mantra recitations and deity visualizations, ideally treated as forms of meditation. By their own admissions, however, these may be done in a rush, and from their perspective it is better to keep their commitments with a distracted mind than not at all. The reasoning employed here has appeal for practitioners who attempt to maintain a commitment to the path while accommodating the demands of a busy life. Several practitioners described how they create opportunities in spare moments throughout the day for practice. CR expressed these sentiments in her description of her attempts to keep her regular tantric commitments.

> CR: But it's really good not to not do the commitments. I've spoken to people. Everyone has said, 'This is from Geshe Logoan Rinpoche, to everybody'. If you've made the commitment it's very important to keep it. It's not something to lightly not do.' And I know that sometimes when I haven't done them, it's because I've chosen to watch television or read, or do something else instead first, and I've left it until 11 o'clock at night when I'm exhausted, and then I've fallen asleep doing them. Because I worried about . . . you know, I've got a busy life. And Lama Zopa said the same thing. You can say the Sadhanas, if you know them off by heart. You can say them walking along to the bus stop. You can say them on the train. I do my practice on the train coming up here because it's over an hour, the train trip, and so I just sit there. I get my mala out, and do it. It's not as ideal as sitting in my gompa, obviously. I'm not concentrating as well, but that's the way I can do it. At least, the good thing about having commitments is I'm doing something. If I didn't have those commitments I'd do nothing. There'd be days I'd do nothing, and sometimes, there have been times when I feel the commitments—which I freely made myself— were like a burden. I've had that, sort of, like, 'Oh no. I've got to get through this. I haven't done my practice yet'.

Similar sentiments were expressed by another practitioner. In describing his approach to and experience with performing his daily refuge commitments, AN related candidly how considerations of motivation and discipline relate to the meditative aspect of the practice.

> AN: That's what I really welcomed about the refuge undertaking is that you bow to the Buddha, you do the prostrations and do the refuge prayer three times in the morning and at night, and I thought, 'Oh that's great because I'll meditate', but what I end up doing is just doing that and thinking, 'Oh well. That's enough. I don't have to sit and meditate', so in a way it's been very good because I've done it every single day, and it takes a minute or so. I've got a little altar at home, which is good in terms of focusing for the day, so that's been really useful because I start and end the day with that, but in a way it's substituted whatever practice I would have done, so I don't end up sitting very much.

> GE: OK. So that obviously sets you for the day, as you said, so how do you feel when you're doing it? What kind of state are you in?

> AN: I'm getting more strict with myself because a lot of the time I'm finding . . . because, especially in the morning, I'll just be doing it and thinking

about other stuff. I'll find I've done two, but not mindfully at all, so I'll make myself do it again and say it properly to make sure the motivation's there and it's not just . . . because I remember that I did that with all the Christian prayers. Just recited them, so it's good. It is a way of making myself, especially on certain mornings when you realize that your head is just running everywhere else but there, so in a way it's a bit of a centring, and a testing of how centred I am that morning, because sometimes I am focused automatically without effort.

GE: You've obviously reached a point where you're making yourself do it properly, so do you feel better for it? Are you feeling any particular benefits?

AN: I like the continuity and commitment, because there'll be times when I've jumped into bed, and forgotten, and each time I've made myself get up and do it. So yeah, that fact that it gives a bit of structure to the day, so at night I find it's helpful because it makes me, when I'm saying 'to act for the liberation of all sentient beings', I'm actually at the same time trying to dedicate all the merits of that day, of how I tried to act for the benefit of others. It kind of does make me do a stock take, whereas in the morning it's setting the motivation for the day 'cause I'm really cloudy in the morning and I would probably go through to ten or eleven without even thinking, whereas this does make me think about how I'm going to act during the day, because unless I did that, I would just act without being really mindful or thinking.

GE: Your commitment to this particular practice, you're basically renewing your refuge twice a day, why are you doing it?

AN: There are reasons on both sides of that. One is that I said I would in a special ceremony, and that has to do with my guru-devotion, so I guess that's more the schoolchild in me, because no one actually asks, but I would always think if they did, these are people I wouldn't want to lie to. I would want to be able to say 'yes' because I said I would. In terms of willpower I usually let myself off the hook, so I'm enjoying the benefits of not letting myself off, so there are disciplinary benefits, and all the mental benefits which I hadn't really thought about much. I hadn't really thought about whether it makes me calmer or the mental space. I don't think I've ever gone 'I'll feel better after I do this' or 'I'll feel calmer'. They're definitely the products of it. So it would be more the motivation and the discipline and the content. Yeah, I guess it could be peace of mind, because I realize I don't have peace of mind until I do it. I don't entertain the possibility of not doing it.

In AN's view, the commitment will keep him motivated because he has given his word to keep it. In this sense the motivation, as opposed to the meditation, becomes the focus of practice. This is similar to other responses about personal practice, and given that Westerners are attempting to develop a practice in the midst of leading busy lives, AN's response is understandable. By contrast, NC's approach to and experience of the refuge-commitment is based in its performance as a meditation and not as an obligation. As illustrated in the discussion below about Samatha, 'single-pointed concentration', his practice produces a sense of spaciousness, of opening up, which gives him 'a deepening sense of refuge'. These two accounts indicate how practitioners may value different aspects of a practice. The former approach has more to do with keeping the commitment. AN allows his relationship to his practice to become fused with the feeling of simply needing to keep his commitments. The latter values the practice for its meditative effect. NC's motivation is a result of his experiential engagement with the practice itself. Both understand the purpose of the refuge commitment, and both value the positive effects of meditation. Before his involvement with VI, NC had already developed a rudimentary Buddhist frame of reference for the interpretation of meditative experience through involvement with other groups and Buddhist material. Another factor to consider is the effect of variation in individual response to religious authority, and one's understanding of the Centre's teachers as the voices of such religious authority. Such variation is indicated by the way in which some simply pay respect to the person who occupies the position, and a small number who seemingly assign the teacher a parental role. Heelas's notion of detraditionalization involves a displacement of the voice of authority from established sources to the self, with a corresponding decline of belief in the pre-given or natural order of things. However, this same voice, he maintains, is originally acquired in terms of established values and practices.[9] Considering that deference to authority is prescribed by the Gelugpa lineage as that a practitioner needs to have a teacher or guru in order to practise successfully, I suggest that one's existing approach to religious authority is, at least initially, carried into the process of one's active appropriation of the meaning-system. Several writers allude to Tsong-kha-pa's statement that one must purify, accrue merit and pray to one's guru as a Buddha in order to reach enlightenment.[10] The nature of individual variation in the view of the guru may be a question of whether one responds to the suggestions of an external figure or expresses the promptings of an internalized voice.

Teachings from the Discovering Buddhism module *The Spiritual Teacher* outline the nature of the teacher-student relationship required for successful Buddhist practice, including the qualities that a student should look for in a spiritual teacher.[11] Respondents have indicated their acceptance of a teacher's authority if the teacher appears to embody the religious ideals of the FPMT, and practitioners accept the lineage leaders and teachers as representatives of religious authority.[12] The FPMT provides many role-models of authority to guide motivation and attainment: buddhas, bodhisattvas, lineage founders and leaders, lamas and their disciples and teachers at FPMT Centres. While buddhas and bodhisattvas can be seen as models of the enlightened being, local lamas, geshes, sangha members and lay teachers can all be seen as authority figures in a more immediate sense. If the decision is made to take refuge and later, tantric initiation, the decision to accept the guru's authority is formalized. From my own observations, the lama or geshe becomes a strong influence. As a representation of the enlightened mind they are strong symbols of religious authority.

Samatha, single-pointed concentration

According to Gelugpa doctrine the primary aim of cultivating samatha is the attainment of liberation and full awakening or buddhahood so as to be of service to others. Gen Lamrimpa and Geshe Tashi Tsering both outline three levels of motivation: a fortunate rebirth, to attain liberation or nirvana and to attain full awakening.[13] These correspond to the three scopes of the Lam Rim. The two writers also draw attention to subsidiary effects and benefits of samatha practice: the development of psychic powers and other forms of heightened awareness,[14] and control of mind and body.[15] Anecdotes about feats performed by highly developed lamas are part of the shared reality of the FPMT, to the point whereat some practitioners' perceptions of their extraordinary abilities have been instrumental in those practitioners' decisions to become Buddhist. However, while the cultivation of psychic abilities is accepted and spoken about freely at Vajrayana Institute, such cultivation is not seen as the goal of practice. All doctrine about samatha-cultivation taught at VI is either directed toward training the mind in the practice of calm-abiding, or towards providing students with a conceptual understanding of the stages of progress in development. The relevant aspects of doctrine include the absorptions: the levels and states of meditative stabilization, the faults, and their antidotes.

In their personal practices, practitioners employ samatha for the same purposes and uses as it is put to in teachings: to settle the mind initially and to develop the ability to keep a focused mind on the object of attention. This is to ensure greater success with other meditation techniques such as visualization or purification practices, or analytical meditation, as explained in Chapter 4. Here, concentrating on the breath is used to focus the mind so that one's visualizations—usually deity visualizations—will be clearer and more sustained. It is understood that the image of the deity or meditation-object must be clear and relatively stable for effective use in purification exercises. CR discussed her approach to deity visualization.

> CR: I'm at the stage of trying to get my visualizations to be clearer. So, when I said before that I didn't meditate on the breath, that would be a good thing for me to do because it would help me to be able to keep my . . . my single-pointed concentration that I'm practising usually involves the visualization of a deity and saying your mantra, so I might do a sadhana and the visualization of a deity. While I'm visualizing the deity I'm saying the mantra, and at the same time I'll be visualizing something like sending out light to all sentient

beings. The rays of light might have the particular deity on it so it goes to the crown of all sentient beings' head, and white nectar or something comes down into them, purifying them of all negativity, bringing them every happiness. So, you know, the visualizations . . . it's always related to the world. It's not somebody sitting on a cloud being happy. The deity's always emanating out, and it might be bringing people in . . . Some people prefer just doing the breathing, but meditating on the breath is nothing. The only purpose of meditating on the breath is to be able to stabilize your mind so that you can meditate on something like a deity or something. But ultimately what you're trying to have this single-pointed concentration for is the understanding of reality, which is emptiness. This is the whole purpose of it, so you can single-pointedly concentrate on your understanding of that and then have a direct realization of reality.

GE: You need to be able to hold your mind on it.

CR: Yes. So my understanding is that a lot of this, all of this visualization ends up . . . that's the ultimate goal.

GE: So you are not interested in bliss states just for themselves?

CR: Um . . . no, it's a bit pointless. It's *completely* pointless.

The same practitioner experienced the effects of concentration practice while doing a sadhana. I had asked her whether any of her experiences in meditation had been striking in some way.

CR: During the sessions where it comes to the point, like you've done this whole sadhana which includes various bits and pieces, then your visualizing, which is meditating. You're visualizing the deity and saying the mantra. We might be saying that, we might be doing that for half an hour or longer. The sessions were quite long when we'd be going through that section, and just that really intense feeling of actually becoming one with the deity, of actually being the deity, and being able to send out rays of love to other beings, to all other beings, to the entire universe.

GE: What did the state feel like? Can you describe it?

CR: It was just, it just felt, um, you just kind of totally . . . it's like when you, well for me, I really love drawing for instance, and when I get caught up in . . . I went to life drawing classes for a while, and when I was caught up in that it was like nothing else existed. It was like, you know, the whole, the rest of the world just disappears, you're just caught up in the thing. It was like that, just being there, one with this experience and not, not aware of noises or of anything going on outside or discomfort or anything. Just, you know in this moment, like being in, completely in the present moment. I was thinking too at Kopan monastery we used to do a meditation on the breath, it was on the different channels and that one with Geshe Dawa that also involved visualizing various energy channels, going through the different *chakras*, so that was Cittamani Tara. So at Kopan again, that visualizing the energy channels by breathing in through one channel and then breathing out through the other, and then through the central channel, you can just . . . become sort of one with the moment, and also get quite an expansive feeling of the mind. It's not like you are restricted within this skull. We did meditations on the mind where you are imagining the nature of the mind and the mind just goes out, you know, it's just a very expansive and open kind of feeling, and it's sort of about making that connection, too, like even though you're there, one with the moment, but it's like this incredible connectedness . . .

NC's experience of a mental opening-up, a sense of spaciousness while doing his refuge commitments, demonstrates how the daily performance of the refuge-commitment can be seen as a transformative practice.

NC: And I think, since taking refuge, the thing that changed over the last couple of months is a real deepening of that sense of refuge. One of the things that really changed . . . like in the morning I'll do prostrations and a refuge prayer . . . I'll spend a few minutes without doing a formal prayer, just thinking about the Buddha, dharma and sangha, and what opens up in my mind now when I do that is very different. There's a real spacious . . . like when I'm focusing on the Buddha, dharma, sangha, there's a real spacious lightness that opens up. So there's this actual sense that happens now of that in the refuge. So since taking refuge the thing that changed most is my faith that those things offer refuge has become internalized. So if you talk about conversion, that's probably happened since the refuge ceremony about two months ago. But it's probably really only in the last four weeks that that thing has changed.

GE: So that sense of spaciousness . . . you used that word before.

NC: Yeah, that sense of spaciousness and lightness and all the sort of qualities I'll get on a good day if I'm doing a meditation on emptiness. In my mind when I'm doing it, 'cause I'm thinking 'OK, Buddha, dharma, sangha', in my mind that's what appears around them. My previous going for refuge prayer was fairly . . . it was heartfelt and sincere, but it didn't have the same effect on my mind. When it happened, I wondered whether it was an impact of the formal ceremony, or was the impact of the continued practice. I don't know. I'm sure making the commitment makes it easier for my mind to settle down. It's funny, I'm quite practical and I'm much more likely to explain things in psychological terms than in religious terms, but because it was quite a significant difference, there was obviously something. My mind decided it was ready to view things differently or . . . I can't quite put my finger on it.

Although the first example is a deity visualization and the second involves the performance of refuge commitments, both respondents describe concentration-type experience, effected by the slowing down of the mind when the momentary processing of mental content is restricted by the concentration on the breath or the visualization.[16] CR refers to an expansive feeling of the mind while NC describes an internal spaciousness. The way in which the two practitioners attribute a transformative function and meaning to the experience is significant, and suggests that the attribution of meaning to concentration-type experience has a transformative function in this meditative setting. CR's was to do with the way the experience took her outside the sense of being 'restricted within this skull', and while her own evaluation does not appear to reach beyond this sense, it is conceivable that repetitions of this type of experience over a period of time might affect the way one habitually relates to one's sense-of-self. NC, on the other hand, connects the sense of spaciousness to his deepening sense of faith in refuge, which he connects in turn to the growing ease with which his mind settles down.

Analytical meditation

Emptiness is the central doctrine of Mahayana Buddhism. While it is but one of The Three Principals of the (Mahayana) Path to enlightenment, it is the core notion supporting the whole framework of meaning. According to Hopkins, 'Phenomena are empty of a mode of being called inherent, objective, or natural existence'. The 'concept refers to our ordinary sense of the way things exist'. He refers to the Middle Way, the refutation of both inherent existence and total non-existence, and states that 'It is possible to realize a sense of valid, nominal existence through gaining the understanding that emptiness is an elimination only of inherent existence'.[17] VI's teachings stress that the emptiness referred to is the lack of inherent existence of a phenomenon from its own side, and that all phenomena are subject to causes and conditions, and do not inherently or unchangeingly exist. It is also stressed that this does not mean that we do not actually exist; we merely do not exist in the way that we seem to. Teachers stress this in the hope that students get the right understanding.

Hopkins' statement, that 'emptiness becomes the context within which a yogi purifies his perception' is useful for understanding the approach taken to emptiness meditations. One is given a conceptual description or definition of what is to be realized in meditation before one has the realization. The meditation outlined in Hopkins' *Meditations on Emptiness,* and referred to in other texts, is used in teachings at VI, although infrequently.[18] During my time of participant observation this meditation was led twice: in *Mind and Mental Events* in 2003 and in the Discovering Buddhism module *Wisdom of Emptiness* in 2004. The purpose of the meditation is to create a shift in the meditator's perception of self. NC was one practitioner who found the analytical meditations interesting and useful. I asked him:

GE: When you're talking about doing the meditations on emptiness, which ones are they?

NC: I do the one where you go through trying to locate the self physically, and then mentally, and then there's another one that I read in a book where you're trying to look back at the meditator, look back at myself, look back and try to locate the meditator, and then just visualizing all of the body parts and all the mental faculties spreading out and then just reside in that emptiness. The thing is going through trying to locate it and then looking back at the self who is thinking, and that's when I get a sense of there isn't anything. So the other one, I do this when I'm running, saying, well, 'If there was an existent self, permanent, who was running, if it was a part of the body, then it would be always running, the whole thing about it can either be part of the body or separate from the body, it can't be both'. So I do that when I'm running, look back at the aggregates moving.

GE: So, it's trying to give yourself a particular perspective.

NC: You're going through all those logical reasons about why, how, and where the self doesn't exist, and so just going through those logical steps of, 'Well I can't locate it. It's not there. It's not in my thoughts, and then, looking back at me who's thinking all those things . . . '

NC was the only respondent to offer me a description of an emptiness meditation. Ray's observation that most Westerners have trouble understanding the connection between emptiness teachings and the practical spiritual life is supported by my findings, from interview data, that people relate more easily to those concepts to do with the phenomenal world and one's ethical orientation towards it, such as the bodhisattva motivation and the development of bodhicitta. Ray explains how the teachings on emptiness make the bodhisattva path possible. The bodhisattva's understanding that all phenomena are inherently empty makes their exposure to so much suffering in samsara bearable.[19] By reflecting upon the sentiments such as these, students notionally accept and attempt to work with the concept of emptiness as a strategy for living. The Discovering Buddhism students gave me the sense that they think that if they are to understand emptiness at all, it is likely to be some time after they have acquired more knowledge and skill in meditation. They do not appear to entertain the idea that they could grasp it at this point in their exposure to the teachings.

Transformative activity outside the meditation-setting

In common with my interview-respondents from BMIMC, many VI affiliates see their Buddhist practice as extending beyond their participation in retreats or maintaining a practice-period each day. The study of Buddhist texts and reading material, including quiet reflection on the teachings, results in the acquisition of Buddhist interpretive frameworks which are then applied to the interpretation and understanding of life situations according to the Buddhist outlook. As outlined in Chapter 4, VI stocks a wide range of relevant reading material, including several versions of the Lam Rim by lineage founders and members, and meditation manuals and prayer books. Textual study is encouraged as a support for learning and practice, and reading is set as *homework* in the Discovering Buddhism course and as preparation for other courses. It is considered here as a transformative practice because it seems to reflect a preferred and deliberate orientation to practice by a handful of adherents whose orientation to the practice appears to be through textual study.[20] Two in particular told me in interview that they do not meditate, despite that one of them was a tantric-initiate. In addition, many practitioners report the derivation of benefit from such study. Regardless of the depth of reading and textual study, attempting to see a personal problem and its solution from a Buddhist perspective is part of the experimental process. It allows students to try out the framework or meaning-system for themselves. From the view of a self-transformation technique, applying a Buddhist interpretation to a problem is an effective way of trying and testing Buddhist doctrine and its practical application. Many observe changes resulting from reading and personal reflection in the way that DE relates:

> DE: I've just been getting more and more out of listening and thinking, and it's beginning to change my thoughts. When I have derogatory thoughts about somebody, now I notice and think 'You don't actually have to say that'. You treat somebody in a particular way and they respond.

Tantric Activity at Vajrayana Institute

Orientation to tantra

Tantric Buddhism is held within the Mahayana view to be a method for attaining enlightenment. In the introductory section of the Lam Rim, Tsong-kha-pa outlines his division of the Mahayana into two: the Prajnaparamita, Perfection of Wisdom method which is sutric, and the mantra method which is strictly tantric.[21] Teachers and practitioners hold to the view that tantra is another path to enlightenment within the Mahayana orientation.[22] Ideally, all Mahayana Buddhists practise the bodhisattva motivation, the greater scope according to the Lam Rim, which is to attain enlightenment for the sake of relieving the suffering of all sentient beings. According to Kelsang Gyatso, the Lam Rim instructions enable one to engage in a meditation practice with any one of the three levels of motivation, but the three are progressive: each one lays foundations for the next.[23] Tantric practice proceeds from the assumption that the practitioner operates from the bodhisattva motivation: the intention to attain full Buddhahood in order to help to end the suffering of all sentient beings.[24]

It is expressed in teachings and in conversations that one must be ethically prepared for tantric practice. Received wisdom holds tantra to be the quick way to enlightenment, but one must have the Mahayana motivation and be committed to the bodhisattva path. It is also emphasized that one must not 'get carried away with tantra' and that sutric study and practice continue to serve as a foundation for progress on the path when one becomes a tantric practitioner. It is important to note that tantra without proper ethical training and without the correct motivation is considered dangerous. As expressed by the teacher of the Discovering Buddhism module Introduction to Tantra in January 2004, 'You are stirring up energies that you can't control'. Tulku Thondup explains the expected ethical orientation in terms of simultaneous practice of the three vehicles: living physically according to the moral codes embodied in the *pratimoksa* disciplines, mentally maintaining bodhisattva aspirations and practices, and beyond that taking the tantric view of everything as the path of pure nature.[25]

Within the FPMT, in order to take tantric initiation practitioners are expected to have taken refuge, signalling their commitment to the Mahayana Buddhist path. During *Introduction to Tantra* the teacher stated, "Taking an initiation implies that one is taking vows, and is therefore a Buddhist." The refuge commitment is sealed by the new adherent's taking as many of the five pratimoksa vows as they feel able to keep, but it was explained during a teaching that, ideally, Buddhists are expected to undertake to refrain from killing as a minimum. This refuge commitment means that some ethical discipline is put into place before tantric practice is undertaken. Within the Mahayana vehicle, tantric practice is founded on The Three Principals of the Path: renunciation, bodhicitta and wisdom-realizing emptiness. In teachings from *Introduction to Tantra* and in the commentary to the Medicine Buddha initiation in May 2005 (which I attended as a blessing), both teachers highlighted the need to develop bodhicitta. In the former, the teacher stated that the first gate to tantra is 'absolutely flawless bodhicitta motivation'. Similarly, the Vajra master of the Medicine Buddha initiation stated that one must 'have a good crop of bodhicitta'. In the commentary after the initiation he elaborated on the three qualities necessary in a tantric practitioner. Renunciation must be a definite conviction; when one thinks about the suffering nature of samsara, one develops renunciation and seeks the path to liberation. It is hard to develop renunciation if the suffering nature of samsara is not seen and accepted.

In difficult and onerous situations, one wishes to get out of them, and one can see the same needs and desires in others. This transforms slowly into bodhicitta, which is developed with the method of lovingkindness and compassion. On my asking one tantric-initiate, "What is your personal belief system?", she responded:

> CR: Well, I suppose I just believe. It's believing that the purpose of life is to develop your qualities, to help all beings; that there is a reason for being here which I used to be not sure of, and that reason is to be of service or help to others. And that the way to do that is to . . . you do have to develop your own quality, because I can't help others the way I am, not properly. I can try but I don't really know how, and quite often I get it wrong. I get angry, I have all those things happen, so, but also I don't think that everybody has to be a Buddhist, to reach, um, to reach a state of, you know, of enlightenment. I'm sure you do need to be towards the end, but I'm not sure . . . but I think, to develop qualities anyway, and to be of benefit in the world, and to be a good and loving person. There are many paths to that.

> GE: And so your purpose in being a Buddhist is for those things you just stated. It sounds to me like you're working towards enlightenment, but these other qualities . . .

> CR: That's the only reason for reaching enlightenment . . . is to be like a Buddha and to come back and to teach and to help.

Another factor important for understanding practitioners' orientations to tantra is the way in which it is routinely spoken about and regarded. In conversation, while it may be discussed as something extra to sutra practice, it is not promoted as something to be held in awe. Those students who show an interest in tantra want to know how it relates to Buddhism more broadly, and do not set out to find easy access to its secrets out of idle curiosity. This point is worth emphasizing in the light of criticism of the way in which tantra has been appropriated by contemporary Western culture. While Urban suggests that this is largely as a form of spiritual hedonism, his comment appears to relate to Hindu tantra. Guenther believes that the word Tantrism has become almost synonymous with Hindu tantra, and more is known about it than Buddhist tantra.[26] Tantra as a Buddhist practice has the same ethical foundations as all Buddhist practice, as discussion here will demonstrate. According to Ray, tantra has its own way of articulating Mahayana philosophy in the context of tantric meditation.[27] Wayman believes that the terminology in the Buddhist tantras makes sense if one sees them as reflecting Buddhist tenets from the Abhidharma, or from the Mahayana presentation in the Madhyamika and Yogacara schools.[28]

Among the participants at VI the tantric practitioners are not obvious, and their tantric involvement was disclosed in interview rather than in ordinary conversation. This approach is demonstrated in the orientation to tantra displayed by two committed practitioners before and after they were initiated. NJ and MM had very strong experiences in meditation, coincidentally both in Theravadin Buddhist settings, which are reminiscent of tantric experience. In both cases these experiences were at odds with the meditative settings in which they occurred, and prompted the two seekers to find satisfactory explanations for their experience. After finding FPMT Centres, the Root Institute in India and Vajrayana Institute respectively, and beginning to investigate the Gelugpa Tibetan system, both became involved with Vajrayana Institute and took on voluntary administration duties. They also settled into a routine of sutric study and practice in order to broaden their understanding of Buddhism. Given this and the fact that they do not consider their levels of practice special or advanced, it can be accepted that these practitioners work within the doctrinal and ethical frameworks of Mahayana Buddhism.

For practical purposes, two differences appear to exist between sutra and tantra practice. The first is the tantric emphasis on working with desire. In the Discovering Buddhism module Introduction to Tantra I attended between January and February 2004, it was explained that while sutra uses the energy of lovingkindness and compassion, tantra uses the energy of desire and craving or attachment. Tantra is not in itself virtuous, nor essentially pure, but it becomes pure with the right motivation, which means utilizing the desire for enlightenment in order to attain it. More specifically, for higher tantric practice it refers to transforming the energy of the desire for the partner into other emotional qualities such as the desire for enlightenment and compassion. In this way a selfish desire based on craving is transformed into a selfless desire. The second difference has to do with the nature of the deity visualization employed for ritual purposes. In the commentary to the Medicine Buddha initiation conferred on 30 April 2006, Geshe Dawa explained that in sutra practice the practitioner remains an ordinary being, but in tantra the practitioner arises as the deity, and the place or setting becomes the pure realm. The outcome is bringing on the path, and enlightenment is involved in the moment of sitting. Similarly it was explained in Introduction to Tantra that sutra is the causal vehicle. It creates the causes for enlightenment, and tantra is the resultant vehicle wherewith the result is taken into the path.

The nature of tantric initiation and commitment

Elsewhere I have explained that one is expected to take refuge before one takes tantric initiation, ensuring that both an ethical orientation and a bodhicitta motivation are in place before engagement in tantric activity.[29] The Sanskrit term *abhiseka* means empowerment or conferral of power. Tantric initiation empowers one to do the tantric practices of a specific deity, for instance, taking a Vajrasattva initiation empowers one to do the practices of Vajrasattva at the appropriate level. It is understood within the tradition that an initiation may be taken as an empowerment that comes with commitments, or as a blessing. In the latter case, one accumulates merit by attending the initiation and listening to the commentary given by the Vajra master, but does not become empowered to do the tantric practice. The practitioner decides which of the two options they choose by either reciting or not reciting the vows at a certain point in the initiation. Some practitioners have related to me how they took initiation accidentally by inadvertently repeating the vows along with other initiands. This can result in practitioners' being initiated into tantric practices that they feel they are not duly prepared for, or being given commitments that they know they cannot keep. Aspects of discourse surrounding tantric initiation illustrate the way in which safeguards may be built into the system. RI told me that you have to have very good visualization, 'otherwise it's just like a blessing'. This was meant in the sense that if you do not have success with visualization during the initiation, then you have not been initiated. Further to this was the question whether one is really initiated by going through the motions without feeling connected to the proceedings. RI also volunteered that what you hear and understand during the ritual determines the effect that the practice has on you and on what you should do, especially in the way you interpret the commitment instructions given.

When one takes initiation, instruction about practice comes in the form of imposed commitments. At interview, those respondents who indicated that they were tantric-initiates also explained that they took their commitments seriously, even though they often found them hard to keep. Occasionally, they would indicate the strategies they put in place in order to keep themselves motivated. For instance, CR explained:

> CR: At least, the good thing about having commitments is I'm doing something. If I didn't have those commitments I'd do nothing, there'd be days I'd do nothing . . . But it's really good not to not do the commitments. I've spoken to people, everyone has said, this is from Geshe, from Logoan Rinpoche, to everybody, if you've made the commitment, it's very important to keep it, it's not something to lightly not do.

One of the significant aspects of tantric practice spoken about, in the Introduction to Tantra and in conversation, is that the initiand is not told before the initiation is taken what the commitment will be. To my knowledge the commitment is determined by the Vajra master, and anecdotal evidence suggests that it may be unexpectedly light, as, 'Try to say the deity's mantra as many times as you can during the week', or very heavy, by comparison. A commitment may be as finite as, 'Do one thousand mantras', or seemingly infinite, as in 'Do (a specified number) every day for the rest of your life'. This can be seen as a psychological safeguard in two ways. First, it has the effect of warning off the idly curious.

Second, the fact that practitioners are given commitments and are expected to keep them maintains an approach of seriousness toward tantra, and helps committed practitioners to maintain their motivation to practice.[30] However, if they fail to keep their commitments they can purify, using the Four Opponent Powers, or renew their vows by taking another initiation.

The Discovering Buddhism module Introduction to Tantra is designed to impart an awareness of the basics of tantric practice and to convey the seriousness with which it is to be undertaken. The four classes of tantra: action, performance, yoga and highest yoga were described very briefly to outline how each class builds on the skills and knowledge acquired through practice of the preceding. Action tantras involve the use of *mudras*, 'hand gestures', and recitation of mantras. One is helped in the practice of this lowest class of tantra by being connected with external things. The teacher compared the energy used with the energy we use when smiling and laughing. In action tantra, when we meditate on the deity we do not arise as the deity.

Compared with the focus on external things in action tantra, performance tantra concentrates more on mental activity, and begins to use the energy of desire.[31] Comments by the teacher indicated this class of tantra to be concerned with visualizing the consort deity with desire, and arising as the deity, even if that is of the opposite sex. The third class, yoga tantra, uses visualization of the purification of body, speech and mind. The meditation practice concerns visualization of the self as the deity informing all our acts. In this way it is a purifying, de-coarsifying practice. Highest yoga tantra was described as the system of highest possible development, wherein each deity has a subtle specialty. This class makes use of the system of chakras, 'the winds' and the three wind-channels (central and two side-channels).[32]

For reasons of secrecy, the teacher did not elaborate on the practical aspects of highest yoga tantra beyond this point. She gave additional theoretical information about the interlinking of generation and completion stages with the grounds and paths, and about the correspondence of stages in the death-process in the meditation with the Buddha bodies that the fully enlightened being assumes at entry to Buddhahood.[33] Enough information was given to gain an intellectual grasp of significant aspects of practical developments throughout the sequence of the four tantra classes—as instance the progressive intimacy between practitioner and deity—but without being able to derive appreciation of the experiential states involved.

The maintenance of secrecy

From this it can be seen that Vajrayana Institute's teachings maintain and propagate an attitude of seriousness and respect toward tantra. In the manner of its self-representation, it attempts neither to conceal deliberately nor to reveal anything more than practitioners need to know in order to understand the relationship between the sutric and tantric paths. Thus, the subject does not attract idle curiosity from newer participants. Initiations, when they occur, are advertised in the newsletter and by email. During the time of my involvement with VI, a handful of initiations involving Medicine Buddha, Chenrezig, Tara and Vajrasattva were held. I believe that these were all action tantras. From time to time, the Vajrayogini self-initiation, a highest yoga tantra, is advertised in the newsletter, but I have neither seen nor heard any other reference to this deity at VI. Because only action tantra initiations are visible, one has to think that higher tantric activity is successfully kept private between the guru and student, and, I suspect, between a small group of older, more experienced students. Accordingly, tantric practitioners do not discuss their tantric involvement. In interview some were willing to reveal which initiations they had taken, but very little else. They successfully keep much of what they do secret. When I asked them about their daily practice and meditative experience, they told me as much as they felt that I needed to know, and they related this within the context of their commitment to Buddhism generally. As BP commented, "When I first started coming I didn't realize that you're not meant to blah on about what initiations you've taken. You're meant to just go along . . . I mean it is meant to be a private thing, but because it's for your project, I'll discuss it."

Another aspect of the secrecy surrounding Buddhist Tantra is perpetuated by its own experiential emphasis. As indicated by the descriptions of the four classes of tantra above, it is by nature an experiential practice, and understanding of its meaning is derived from its performance.[34] This suggests that there is no intentionally concealed secret. This idea is supported by other characteristics of the practice. Ray notes that one must receive initiation before being given permission, texts, and practice instructions.[35] However, as Wayman notes, sadhanas contain the bare description of the deity; their texts do not contain enough practical detail for informed practice. That some of these practices are available in booklets on sale in the bookshop[36] indicates that the texts have the secrecy of obscurity, and the guru is meant to supply the missing detail. Wayman's point supports my own discovery during initiations held at VI that the sadhanas outline what to say and visualize, but nothing else.[37]

Whenever the Buddhas, Buddha families, bodhisattvas and deities were discussed at VI, I noted a lack of systematization or categorization of these beings and their qualities. The Buddha families and their sets of correspondences were sometimes briefly referred to in teachings, but not studied in any systematic way. In interview I was puzzled at first when respondents were not forthcoming with this kind of information about the deities' symbolic associations. After they had told me what practices they did, I would ask them about the meanings of the deities, and they knew that Chenrezig is compassion, Tara is compassionate action, and Vajrasattva is mental purification.[38] According to Wayman, although Westerners want to know the meaning of the deities and their mantras, the deities do not have meanings in the Western sense of intellectual understanding. Such meanings arise through the regular practice and service of the deity.[39] This is exemplified by some of the instruction given during a Medicine Buddha Practice day held on 28 May 2005.[40] The convenor stated at one point that the Medicine Buddha is the archetypal healing energy in all of us. Sometimes, in the visualizations, she would give some direction, for instance, to 'try to feel the presence of the Medicine Buddhas', and mentioned that throughout the literature their names and colours are not always consistent.

The lack of public visibility of initiations of higher status than action tantra is congruent with informal discourse among practitioners themselves. One never hears discussion of the nature of visualizations, or experiences that practitioners may have of the three higher classes of tantra. Two connected issues, the existence of such secrecy and the public nature of those initiations that are visible, may reveal the intent of the Vajra master with respect to the capacities of practitioners. Ray comments that lamas will sometimes give public initiations, even to those with no preparation, thinking of them as ceremonial blessings sowing positive karmic seeds which will ripen in the future. He contrasts these with the private initiations between teacher and student, wherein the commitments are held to be different.[41] Added to that is the current fashion for serial initiation. Several of my respondents were 'serial initiates' as seen from the list of initiations that they had taken and had attempted to keep commitments for, for example, 'Kalachakra and two Vajrasattvas', 'One Thousand-arm Chenrezig, Four-arm Chenrezig and Green Tara'. CR reported that her daily practice, consisting of 'Medicine Buddha' and 'White Tara' and 'Green Tara', 'Kalachakra' initation and 'Cittamani Tara', which is a higher yoga tantra of 'Green Tara', took her about an hour. From the religious perspective, multiple initiations may be seen to allow the practitioner to accumulate merit by attending blessings periodically. Pragmatically, it is conceivable that serial initiation allows Western practitioners the opportunity to renew vows on occasion, and to restate their commitment to the path.

Understanding the nature of deity and deity yoga

During Introduction to Tantra the teacher explained that the basis of tantra is to access the pure Buddha mind; that 'the idea behind visualizing the deities is that you are getting in touch with what's already there'. She said:

CR: All these deities are just emanations; different emanations of the Buddha. It might seem like to people that there are all these weird goddesses and gods or something that you're paying homage to, but it's all just different emanations of the Buddha and that's really different aspects of your own buddha-nature. One might be enlightened action; one might be ultimate compassion. They're just different aspects of the qualities that you want to develop.

It is held that visualization of deities stimulates the growth of corresponding potencies already latent in the practitioner's own mind,[42] which, according to Lama Yeshe, has the underlying nature of essential clarity and purity.[43] Practitioners typically both relate to deity visualization and practise it as a concentration practice. Ideally, tantric-practitioners are meant to have achieved some success with both concentration and analytical meditation before they enter tantric practice. According to Wayman, 'Contemplation of the yoga of the deity is meant to bring about the complete characteristics of calming, and one is meant to have the voidness contemplation'.[44] The Dalai Lama holds the view that Action and Performance Tantra are practical for many people because 'although they involve meditation on emptiness and on a deity, they are yogas in which the mind's realizing emptiness does not manifest as a deity. The meditator is mainly concerned with achieving clarity of appearance of a divine body, mantra letters and so forth, and thus cannot mainly meditate on emptiness'.[45]

It is evident from conversations and interviews with practitioners that many have not attained this meditative stability, although they strive for it and work to strengthen it using deity visualizations as a concentration exercise. This is exemplified in CR's description (above) of her use of concentration in order to make her deity visualizations clearer. By keeping commitments and doing the sadhana of a deity, intention toward enlightenment is expressed and reinforced. In practical terms, these tantric practitioners have a fundamental understanding of the path and its grounding in the bodhisattva motivation. This excerpt illustrates the approach to practice and self-development held by those who practise deity yoga:

> CR: One of the things I like is that when you've taken a highest yoga initiation you can then imagine yourself as the deity. You can arise as the deity, and so it's this whole idea of doing that because you're imagining what you will become in the future, and bringing that result into the present, and the purpose of that is to try and remind yourself in your day-to-day life of who you actually are, and who you actually can become, not puffing yourself up and being proud or whatever, and a lot of the time I don't remember it at all, to be honest. I think just by familiarizing my mind with it again and again, by doing this daily practice, then hopefully, I'll be more likely when I'm in a situation where I could yell at someone or get upset or angry or whatever, that I'll have a bit more to draw on, to pull me back from that, so I can deal with things more compassionately.

It is significant that CR articulates the connection between her habitual states of mind and the purpose behind her practice of deity yoga. She is honest about her tendency to express anger and her forgetfulness in employing techniques for managing it at the time. However, her expressed intention, that she remind herself of her true nature as distinct from its habitual outer manifestation, is representative of the way in which the deities are meant to be understood and practised. Harvey notes that unwholesome mental states, such as anger, are seen as distortions of the mind's underlying intrinsic purity. The deities symbolize the positive energies that the impurities may be transmuted into.[46]

One important consideration for understanding practitioners' existential reality involves the way that they view the dualistic notion of purity–impurity in relation to the nature of deity. According to Harvey, the Dalai Lama maintains that in all four *tantras* the body is divine, and even in Action tantra 'one must be able to maintain the view of being a deity and having a divine body, while remaining free from conceptions of ordinariness and of inherent existence'. The Dalai Lama also draws attention to the emphasis placed on physical cleanliness and the external activities in action tantras.[47] At the beginning of the Medicine Buddha initiation, which I attended three times as a blessing, participants—regardless of whether they intended to take initiation as a blessing or as an empowerment—washed their mouths with saffron water before they entered the room. Ideally one must be able to see oneself as a divine, and hence purified, being. Practically speaking, one must believe in one's ability to realize one's own buddha-nature and its inherent emptiness. While practitioners can see their buddha-nature as a model of the transformed self and as their own development potential, as has already been demonstrated, realizing emptiness—conceptually or experientially—is difficult here. Perceiving the desire energy itself as pure may present difficulties for some Westerners.

There appear to be two interrelated problems concerning the correct way to view desire for tantra practice. The first is in seeing it as essentially pure, and the second is in engaging with it without becoming lost in its energy. Here there is a seeming contradiction between the 'Hinayana view' and the tantric view. Tulku Thondup outlines the essential differences between the Hinayana, Mahayana and Vajrayana views. Hinayana practitioners avoid encounter with the sources of negative mentalities and emotions. Mahayana practitioners apply the right antidotes to negative concepts and emotions and their sources. Vajrayana practitioners accept and transmute negative concepts, emotions and their sources into enlightened wisdom.[48] Despite the Mahayana bias in this statement, it conveys the sense that one must be able to identify, accept and manage one's habitual mental and emotional impulses in day-to-day existence before utilizing them effectively for higher training. Although it is clear how prior sutra training establishes the right mental orientation to tantric practice, students sometimes express both ambiguous and ambivalent approaches to the nature of desire and its treatment. Some of this vacillation is suggested by Buddhist doctrine itself. It may be confusing for some practitioners, especially if they are relatively new to Buddhism, to hear desire spoken about alongside the three poisons of greed, hatred and delusion, sometimes also expressed as desire, aversion and ignorance.

Such people may find it difficult to discriminate repression from the suppression—to check and contain the impulse—needed as a precursory step for the kind of transformation in which one expresses an instinctual energy such as desire with the appropriate motivation in a specific ritual context. It may be difficult to conceive of using the basic energy of desire without labelling it as unwholesome. In addition, as Guenther notes, in the tantric view body and mind are seen as interdependent and interpenetrating. The whole person is given equal value, as opposed to the higher value placed on the mind in Western thought generally. In his view the extreme dualism of body and mind has led to the body's being treated with aversion.[49] These concerns are echoed in the following conversation that I had with NC, who had expressed an interest in tantra, about the way to view and deal with desire. He was recounting the answer to a question he had asked the resident Geshe about the nature of desire and attachment.

NC: What I understand now as true, complete renunciation is a very profound position, a profound understanding that everything in our existence is a form of suffering, and Geshe Samten said that when you have true renunciation, your desire for liberation . . . it won't be intellectual, it will be an urge.

GE: It will just be an urge that will consume you?

NC: Yes. It's not something that you'll have to think about. It'll just be there. I'd been having trouble with the whole. It's a pretty enormous way to be thinking, to get to the point that you can accept that even, because I always go back to the point of 'Oh. Look at the sunset, it's beautiful', and I know it's not going to last, but ten minutes is lovely and, you know, even that pleasure . . . Say an enlightened being was there, they would take pleasure, because they're not in samsara once they're enlightened. But, it's a hard concept to, um . . .

GE: So, did he actually say things like it doesn't mean that you can't enjoy pleasurable things, but you just don't get attached to them?

NC: Not on that night particularly. He did say that it doesn't mean that you give everything up, because if you say that everything's suffering, you can understand where people go off on that tangent, this extreme of giving everything up, you can understand where they get that from. If they know that you're still able to do things without attachment, it's a tricky one to get. The example I use with myself, I used to be quite overweight and I used to eat a lot, and now when I look back at my relationship with food, it was greedy, attachment, it was not really satisfying. I'd eat but it wouldn't really satisfy me. I was eating for the wrong reasons, and it was a real grasping relationship with food, whereas now I love to cook, and I love food, and I prepare food for people, I get a real enjoyment out of it, but there isn't this greedy grasping thing. So I'd sort of used that as an example with myself, like a renouncing of food as a source of pleasure and satisfaction, by grasping at it but now that I've given it up, I now enjoy it more than I used to.

GE: It seems to be something about the nature of that extreme grasping that pushes the pleasure away. It's an odd one.

NC: Exactly, it pushes the pleasure away. You see that clearly. It's when we grasp at things, there's that addictive quality of wanting it . . . it pushes the pleasure out. And then there's that other fear in your head, but if I give up the grasping will I lose it? How can I give up the grasping? There's one thing that I always want to ask about, but I'm too embarrassed to ask about, is sex, you know, because it's got to be one of the biggest grasping things. But I think that renunciation is getting to the point where you can . . . The idea in tantra of using desire, I've never really understood in tantra how that works. The one thing that has become clear to me is that if you can enjoy things without grasping at them, and you are really freeing up your attitude towards them, then there's enjoyment. But where's the desire? If you free up your grasping, isn't your desire dropping away? That's how I feel about it. When I think about it with all sorts of desires, I try to recognize it for what it is, and I suppose if you can use the desire and recognize what it is, and mentally say 'I want to bring this desire into the path and dedicate it toward the path', that's given me something to think about.

These comments reflect NC's understanding of desire and its renunciation, after considerable reflection on his prior approaches and behaviours related to desire and craving. His new understanding was a result of incorporating, after the recognition that the impulses were capable of modification, the Buddhist position into his own thought. Bodily and mental impulses, the sources of attachment and aversion, need to be seen simultaneously as pure and as things to be renounced. The ideal state of preparation for tantric practice—being accomplished in concentration and insight, and having a view of one's body and mind as pure and divine—is an aspirational attainment rather than a reality. It must be considered that the bodhisattva path, as a prerequisite to tantric practice, orients the mind towards attainment of the appropriate view of self within a framework of compassionate and ideally selfless motivation. This ensures the practitioner's self-discipline with respect to influence—of the internal field of bodily, emotional, and mental energy—on the reification and inflation of the ego.

As one would expect in the case of a practice that is meant to be secret, no-one really spoke about tantric experiences. Two practitioners reported striking experiences that occurred to them in Theravadin Buddhist settings before they had made contact with Tibetan Buddhism. They are significant because the experiences themselves, though very different, lend themselves to a tantric interpretation because of the imagery used to describe the experience, and the intensity of the experience conveyed by the two individuals. The individual context for both was one of extreme emotion in that both had been dealing with highly emotionally-charged situations before the experience occurred during meditation.

The Sense-of-Self and Its Transformations

The transformative techniques and their effects

For many the Mahayana motivation to attain enlightenment for the sake of all sentient beings expresses the goal of practice. Often the more short-term goal is the improvement of one's mental and emotional life. Practitioners have often expressed the sentiment that by working on themselves they improve their relationships with others, and in this way they are working toward alleviating suffering. From this, more immediate personal goals can be seen to support the ultimate goal expressed by the Mahayana motivation. One experienced practitioner, CR, said of her commitment:

> CR: It's believing that the purpose of life is to develop your qualities, to help all beings, that there is a reason for being here, which I used to be not sure of, and that reason is to be of service, of help to others, and that the way to do that is to. . . you do have to develop your own quality because I can't help others the way I am, not properly. I can try but I don't really know how, and quite often I get it wrong.

According to the outlook of the FPMT, all practice done with a Mahayana motivation can be seen to be transformative in some way. Although McDonald's book divides the meditations into four sections, viz. meditations on the mind, analytical meditations, visualization meditations and devotional practices, she maintains that all meditation techniques are either single-pointed concentration or analytical meditation,[50] in the same way as the vipassana practitioners do. However, while concentration and analytical meditations are prescribed as greater scope practices in the Lam Rim,[51] the commonality between virtually all of the practices employed by Vajrayana students to effect transformation is the use of visualization, and this as a concentration practice. Most practitioners reported incorporating deity visualization into their personal practice, the general effect of which was reported as a calming influence on the mind, which improves the individual's focus and sense of mental well-being.

Those concentration-type experiences that were reported by practitioners, namely NC's experience of spaciousness contributing to a deeper sense of refuge, and CR's expansive feeling of the mind during a sadhana and while doing a channel-clearing, were notable for their transformative effects. Csikszentmihalyi and Bedford comment on the positive psychological changes, complex in nature, that result from these types of experience.[52] In particular, CR's experiential account echoes Csikszentmihalyi's description of flow experience. The purely psychological benefit of concentration experience can be seen alongside another aspect of this experience. The sense of self depicted in these experiences seems to be one of enhanced interiority rather than sacrality; it does not have the overlay of sacrality that many New Age or Western alternative practices assume. This interiority is not rarefied or essentialized. It is more a case of the mind's relaxing, loosening up, letting go of content, emptying, not of disengaging from its concerns. It is more an extension of one's sense-of-self than a rarefication.

The devotional practices, which include the refuge prayer,[53] seem to function principally to reaffirm one's outlook and to reinforce one's motivation for self-transformation. Much of the discussion in this and the preceding chapter emphasizes the significance of the Mahayana emphasis on correct motivation for religious practice, and for some the maintenance of correct motivation appears more highly regarded than meditative attainment. In interview, some conveyed a sense of achievement in maintaining an attitude of altruistic motivation despite not having meditated as much as one might. The fact that many practitioners report personal change as an effect of their Buddhist involvement generally—study and reflection on specific situations—without describing any substantial meditative input suggests that the majority of changes occur as a result of strategies employed in everyday awareness rather than as a consequence of an altered awareness generated in meditation.

Many of the changes reported by practitioners concern the use of mental strategies for managing their feelings, especially anger and defensiveness, and for managing their habitual mental states. They report feeling generally calmer and more content in themselves. For many practitioners, the ability to deal with negative feelings was an important achievement for them, but in comparison to the changes achieved by the practice of bare attention to one's immediate experience in order to note the impulse to action before it manifests, the Vajrayana practitioners achieve similar results by the use of suggestion, by holding images of the desired result. Using images of the self much change can be seen to occur by direct reflection on and modification to the self-concept. Before these processes are discussed, the relevant models of the self from the Gelugpa Tibetan Buddhist and Western academic perspectives are outlined, in order to establish what is meant to be transformed through practice, how this transformation occurs, and how change and its mechanisms may be treated theoretically in the context of socialization research.

Theorizing the *self-in-transformation*

Understanding the self and its transformations from the Buddhist perspective in terms of three aspects: the ordinary, relative and absolute, is discussed in Chapter 3 with respect to its explanatory power for the kinds of self-transformation effected by vipassana practice. These aspects are, respectively: the solid and continuous sense of I equated with the Western ego, the relative self as depicted by the principle of dependent origination, and the self in the absolute sense, viz. anatta in Theravadin thought and sunyata, 'emptiness' in Mahayana thought. At VI the terms 'absolute', 'relative' and 'imputed' are used frequently in courses such as Discovering Buddhism and Buddhism and Western Psychology. Conversation, class discussions and interview material demonstrate that students do not naturally think in terms of the threefold model of the self. As previously related, the notion of emptiness appears to be held as a conditional belief, held to be true on the condition that individuals will one day have a direct realization of it, and therefore validate it for themselves. The notion of a changeable mindstream able to be affected by thought and action appears to operate as a conception of the subject of transformation. In this way the views of the ultimate and relative selves are accommodated conceptually. Generally, the concept of buddha-nature appears to function as a commonsense view.

In the Gelugpa system there are two ways of perceiving and working with the absolute view: emptiness as the impersonal absolute, and the Buddha as a model of the enlightened being who has realized emptiness. The buddha-nature is said to be of the nature of emptiness. The use of the term buddha-nature may give the impression of something capable of reification, and it is possible that being unfamiliar with the notion of emptiness that deity images are meant to embody might lead some students to think in terms of an essentialized, holy being, at least initially. The use of buddha, bodhisattva, deity-images and images of one's guru are meant to remind oneself about inherently empty aspects of one's own buddha-nature. However, cognitively speaking, one must first be able to see buddha-nature as a quality or set of qualities belonging to a buddha, more specifically, the fully-enlightened Sakyamuni Buddha, in order to see the model of the enlightened being as representing oneself. This involves reification to the degree necessary to objectify the image, or to see it as a discrete object.

Teachings often make the distinction between the ultimate and relative views. The former is seeing the self as inherently empty. The latter is seeing it in terms of a dependent arising—this term was used frequently in Discovering Buddhism teachings during my period of fieldwork—that is, as a set of interdependent causes and conditions. Watson notes that the Gelugpa distinguish between the essential self which is to be denied and the transactional self: the sense-of-self as we experience it, which is produced by the interplay of the aggregates.[54] This relative or transactional self is frequently understood and expressed in terms of the aggregates and dependent origination in the literature. In Discovering Buddhism module 9, Samsara and nirvana, the twelve-step formula of dependent origination was presented as describing the nature of cyclic existence, samsara, and explaining how the person may both remain in and be liberated from samsara. It is significant that teaching and instruction in both centres, VI and BMIMC, rarely discuss the doctrine of the aggregates beyond a brief mention. The notion of the person employed in vipassana practice is framed by the four satipatthanas, and other notions are dominant in FPMT discourse: the principle of dependent origination, and mind and body to signify the aggregates. This is significant because of the reference to the five aggregates, in the Heart Sutra, used to explain the emptiness of phenomena. The doctrine of dependent origination is used in its more general sense that phenomena are impermanent and subject to causes and conditions. Similarly, nama and rupa, mind and body, appear to be used to signify the subjective field of mental and bodily phenomena that give rise to the sense of I.

The sense of self or I, our own sense-of-self, the object designated by I which feels solid and continuous, is imputed onto the relative view. Geshe Acharya Thubten Loden further divides this imputed sense of I into two. The first is the I imputed onto its base, the five aggregates, and exists conventionally as a dependent arising. The second type of I arises from the superposition of inherent existence onto the first type. It is the second type that is inherently empty. Geshe Acharya Thubten Loden states that the first type exists relatively. To refute this I is to take the nihilist position.[55] Watson's generalized two-level model of the self,[56] discussed in relation to transformation through vipassana practice in Chapter 3, may be applied here to equal effect. Two aspects of her model relate to the sense-of-self. The first, in her Level 1 and corresponding to James' self-as-subject, deals with self-image as process. It consists of a simple but coherent notion of self, open to the environment. This aspect appears to correspond to the I imputed onto the aggregates that Geshe Acharya Thubten Loden describes,[57] the I that when refuted leads to nihilism. This I is ultimately meant to be seen as a dependent arising, but the Gelugpa view holds it to be real, nonetheless.

Aspects of the Vajrayana practices involve the field of immediate subjective experience. At least two already considered can be seen to involve this subjective field: the four-point analysis of the emptiness of self meditation and the deity yoga of the three higher tantras. Discussion above has already alluded to how mental and bodily energy may be directed, depending on the kinds of concepts embodied in the images. One can only assume that in higher tantric practice practitioners are meant to focus directly on their experience of particular feelings and mental states while they make the visualizations. Watson's second level is the self-concept as representation, which is bolstered by language and culture, and becomes increasingly reified. It is considered autonomous, but is adhered to and affected by emotional components. It also includes James's pure egoic component of the objective self, which he considers to provide the core sense of continuity in the individual.[58] Buddhist doctrine and contemporary Western thought both see this core sense of continuity as a construct of the mind. This is the I that is imputed onto the I arising from the interplay of the aggregates, as Geshe Acharya Thubten Loden stresses.

This distinction between the two imputed senses of I from the Gelugpa perspective and the two sites of self-awareness as understood by Watson clarifies misapprehensions about the different aims of Buddhism and psychotherapy that sometimes occur in the literature. Concern has been expressed about the misunderstood differences between the aims of Western psychotherapy and Buddhist meditation by Western practitioners, claiming that it might lead to perception that the notion of emptiness means non-existence. Comparing the two approaches, many scholars agree that Buddhism assumes a strong and healthy ego-structure to begin with, whereas much Western psychology aims to strengthen it. Although some have seen the two goals as incompatible, several researchers, including Epstein and Watson, maintain that this view is reversible when the terminology has been clarified. Engler observes that meditation requires a mature level of ego-organization,[59] something that Watson believes is necessary before this ego-organization, the sense-of-self, can be safely seen as a construct, and adding that without a firm basis of mental health it is possible to confuse pre- and trans-egoic states in meditation.[60] The aim of Buddhist insight is to deconstruct the self-representation, the autonomous and reified way in which we see and treat ourselves, and not to destroy it.[61]

Berger and Luckmann, in their treatment of socialization refer to aspects of the person or self, such as immediate body experience, which are never completely socialized in the sense that their experience is somehow outside of what can be socially constituted through the use of language.[62] As outlined in Chapter 1, social constructionist approaches such as socialization theory and symbolic interaction, which focus on the formation of the self-concept or representation through socialization, have difficulty in successfully accommodating the subjective field of experience and its role in personal change. It seems that the changes commonly reported by practitioners, such as more effective management of negative feelings, are effected in the subjective field in terms of internal recognition and checking of the impulse, but managed more broadly and in a continuing manner by the way in which people wish to see themselves objectively. In contrast with the purely analytical approach to meditation taken in vipassana, primarily dealing with the self-as-subject, the practitioner at Vajrayana Institute is given role-models with which to work, in the form of Sakyamuni Buddha, and the families of buddhas, bodhisattvas, and tantric deities. In purification practice involving visualization they use the imagination to suggest a desired state of affairs, and here negative feeling is regarded as unwholesome. The deities used for practice embody symbolic representations of qualities belonging to enlightened, undefiled beings who serve as role-models for the practitioner's desired state of mind. As explained in Chapter 4, by this stage the practitioner has acquired a structure of understandings about the path to enlightenment, and therefore is familiar with the ideas symbolized by the buddha and deity images. This demonstrates how changes implicating the self as both subject and object can occur.

During the Buddhism and Western Psychology course held between July and August 2003, the teacher applied Horney's psychoanalytic perspective to the understanding of the relative and imputed selves, with the aim of clarifying the nature of self-attachment and self-cherishing. The relative and imputed selves correspond to Horney's real and idealized selves respectively. The teacher explained that an aim of psychotherapy was to develop the relative or real self,[63] and to lessen identification with and attachment to the idealized self: the image of our ideal self. Although Horney's clinical view differs marginally from the view asserted here, the teacher was making use of the concept of the idealized self to illustrate the way in which we develop an over-attachment to this sense-of-self, resulting in 'neurotic egocentricity' or 'neurotic pride'.[64] The aim of Buddhist practice is to deconstruct the imputed self, that is, the sense of permanence created by the interplay of the aggregates comprising the relative self.

Conclusions

In the same way that the vipassana practitioners were seen to undergo concurrent processes of strengthening the sense-of-self while deconstructing it as a solid and permanent core, similar effects can be observed to occur for the Vajrayana practitioners, but as a result of engagement with a different set of techniques. These are primarily in the use of suggestion through imagining a desired state-to-be, and prime among these is deity visualization to stimulate growth of desirable qualities that are considered to be latent in the practitioner's mind.[65] The practitioners of this school have a strong inclination toward concentration and purification, in line with the emphasis on balancing meditation with virtuous action aimed at purification of the mindstream. Compared to the vipassana practitioners, whose training is specifically in the analytical method of observing the arising and ceasing of the first three satipatthanas—sensations, feelings and mental states delineating the field of immediate subjectivity—it seems that, in general, Vajrayana practitioners may achieve outwardly similar modifications by concentrative visualization of deities as models of the perfected personality. Almost all meditative experience discussed throughout this chapter is related to the aims, techniques, and outcomes of concentration practice.

This last point is important to bear in mind when one considers the purpose of practice within the FPMT: to attain enlightenment for the sake of all sentient beings. While not all interview-respondents from Vajrayana Institute explicitly stated their commitment to the cultivation of bodhicitta or to the bodhisattva motivation, this motivation is continually expressed in instances of collective activity such as reciting the refuge prayer at the beginning of teachings, and personally by keeping commitments. For all adherents this involves reciting the refuge prayer daily, and for tantric-practitioners, keeping the commitments given in initiation. In addition, practitioners privately engage with those practices and virtuous actions that they know will facilitate their eventual attainment of the goal of enlightenment.

For the practitioner, transformation and progress on the path is reflexively monitored through changes to the imputed self or self-concept. From the Buddhist perspective the practitioner aims to see the imputed and relative selves as inherently empty, but from a social-scientific perspective visible change is equated with transformations of the self-concept, which can be seen to occur as result of the interplay of deconstructive and reconstructive processes. As discussed above, many of the changes reported by practitioners concern the use of mental strategies for managing feelings, especially anger and defensiveness, and for managing habitual mental states more generally. These transformations take place within the personal field of immediate subjectivity, the relative self, and their objectification is felt as change to their sense-of-self, their self-concept. For the practitioners concerned these are tangible results, and therefore signify that progress is being made. In this way a practitioner's sense-of-self, including concerns for the quality of one's mental life and personal relationships, is his or her testing ground. Concomitant with practice of the path to enlightenment—informed by one's continuous learning and increasing comprehension of the Buddhist path—is the continual testing of the information contained in teachings and texts against one's own life experience. The way in which this learning, testing and change affects one's decision to commit to the Vajrayana Buddhist path and to the FPMT is the subject of Chapter 6.

Chapter 6

An Overview of the Experimental Journey: Vipassana- and Vajrayana-Insights

Introduction

This book set out to examine the natures of engagement in religious activity, of experience and of religious change for the students, practitioners and adherents at two Western Buddhist Centres in Sydney, NSW, Australia. This final chapter explores the entire socialization and commitment process as it is experienced by affiliates of both Centres. As foreshadowed in Chapter 1, data obtained through participant observation and interview support the view of the process as an outcome of the experimental approach to involvement that Buddhism in its Western forms permits. Taking Lofland and Skonovd's description of a *motif experience* as 'those aspects of a conversion which are most memorable and orienting to the person *undergoing* personal transform-ation', and of the experimental motif as 'a pragmatic, *show-me* attitude', learn-ing to act like a convert, withholding judgment for a considerable length of time after taking up the lifestyle of the fully committed participant,[1] it can be seen that participants' experiences support the application of the motif to this religious context.

All of the students, practitioners and adherents were active agents in their own processual advancement. Participants in the activities of both Centres allowed themselves time for exploration, testing and validation of the Buddhist worldview. There was no evidence to support the view, in earlier conversion research, of the convert as a passive receptacle for information.[2]

At the time of interview, respondents had either committed to Buddhism, i.e. actively chosen to take on the Buddhist perspective of a Centre, or had decided to remain a student committed to ongoing participation in a Centre's activities, and to the study and application of teachings or practices. Commitment was understood by vipassana practitioners as the recognition that at some point a change in orientation had occurred; that at some point they had accepted the Buddhist principles as true for them. Conversely, the decision to commit for Vajrayana practitioners was marked by the taking of refuge. In both cases, com-mitment is the result of an active process of exploration and decision-making, based on the capacity of the Buddhist worldview and its practices to map personal experience, and to aid in its interpretation and negotiation by providing lived experience with meaning.

Chapters 2 to 5 explored the nature of engagement with the religious and social activities of a Buddhist centre: how one begins to comprehend and test its worldview for oneself through study and practice. In so doing, those chapters focused entirely on one of two overarching concerns of the book: what is actively appropriated by the practitioner through the process of experimental immersion and what is its manner of appropriation. The model of commitment proposed in Chapter 1 consists of three stages: apprehension, comprehension and commitment. Whereas Chapters 2 to 5 considered the first two stages—apprehension and comprehension—Part 1 of this last chapter considers not only the third stage—commitment—but also the second concern of this book: the role of socialization in the path to commitment. This latter consideration embraces the way in which individuals reach this stage as a result of engagement with the meaning-system in the preceding two stages. This bears on some concerns that are central to theories of religious conversion: the relationship between religious background, prior religious history and the new affiliation; the temporal sequence of responses to the new religious group; and the implication of these in the decision to convert. The discussion in Part 2 of this chapter synthesizes the conclusions reached in Chapters 2 to 5, in order to compare the nature of the meaning-system acquired and the manner of its acquisition by participants at either Centre.

Part 1: The Commitment Process: The Experimental Model and Its Stages

Complementary to the consideration of what is actively appropriated during the socialization process above, this section presents the socialization process as a staged model with commitment as the end-point. The model of commitment proposed in Chapter 1 consists of three stages: apprehension, comprehension and commitment. The first stage, apprehension, corresponds to the process of hearing and responding to teachings, and the decision to learn and understand more of the system of knowledge and practice. The second stage, comprehension, is a natural consequence of the learning that takes place through religious involvement when a student begins to organize apprehended elements of doctrine into a comprehended framework. Comprehension is also aided by the practical application of doctrine to lived experience, thereby testing and validating the practitioner's acquired stock of knowledge.

In the attempt to understand the phenomenon of religious seekerhood in the West, in the alternative religious context generally and the Western Buddhist context specifically, this section also considers how individuals' experimentation may predispose them to a Buddhist outlook. It explores individuals' primary religious socialization and experimental participation in other spiritualities before their Buddhist involvement. This latter examination addresses questions about the nature of determining factors in movements between groups, the depth of involvement in each case, and how structures of beliefs or assumptions are tested and tried during the experimental process. Accordingly, this section takes into account the religious biographies of respondents from early childhood to the time of interview.

The Blue Mountains Insight Meditation Centre

Religious backgrounds of respondents

All but three respondents came from Christian backgrounds. One of the three, EJ, was a native Buddhist from Sri Lanka. She was interviewed because she had re-established her connection with Buddhism through this Western form. Of the two others who were not from Christian backgrounds, KN was raised agnostic and SI answered 'none' to religious background. Despite their lack of religious education, both of them reported having been attracted to religion in some form in early life. While still a child, KN asked a neighbour to take her to Sunday school. SI had wanted to become a Catholic nun at fifteen and remembered developing an interest in Religion and Philosophy while still in her adolescence. The other eighteen respondents were raised in Christian environments, which for some included attending church and a Christian school. The patterns of religious involvement among these individuals had varied in intensity and in nature. Several denominations were represented. The majority were Anglican, and the others included Catholic, Uniting Church, Presbyterian and Methodist.

Responses to the question, 'How did you relate to your religious background?' entailed three considerations: the amount and nature of recall of events, the strength and nature of belief, and affective response. There was variation among respondents in their ability to recall their religious upbringing. Some answered with a brief statement and offered a small number of brief memories. Others gave more elaborate descriptions of those circumstances and events that had affected them. With respect to the strength and nature of religious belief held by respondents, and to the strength of feeling for one's religion as a child, a wide range of responses was expressed, from total belief and commitment to total uninterest, and from feeling totally involved to being 'left cold'. EBS's experiences were of the former kind.

> EBS: I always had a positive relationship to being Catholic, I really enjoyed the ritual, I really liked being an altar boy. I had a strong sense of the spiritual from an early age, and in some ways felt it was a haven for me, given that

my family life was a bit disrupted, and I was a fairly sensitive kid. So I had a positive relationship with that. And then at about twelve or thirteen I had a strong sense that the Catholic way of approaching religion as I understood it, which was through my experience of the church and so on, was wrong. I just had a strong inner sense of that, a feeling that . . . it was the experience that this was not right. What has always fascinated me in retrospect was that I had a sense at that same time that it didn't mean that the whole area of spirituality was wrong . . . it was just that that approach was wrong.

GE: Can you remember anything specific about it that you felt was wrong?

EBS: I think it was to do with issues of just believing, the whole notion in Catholicism of the priest knowing what was going on. I think I was starting to have an appreciation that some of the people who were in positions of power, I really didn't have a lot of respect for.

Other comments of EBS's indicate that he had a sense for the experiential that he felt the church did not embody despite its ritual. His sundering with his childhood affiliation appears to be a common experience. Many respondents left their Christianity and began to explore other options in their late adolescence and early adulthood. The biography of one practitioner had a pronounced experiential element, which can be seen to have influenced his exploration of Buddhism after leaving Christianity. RL reported having, within a Marist Brothers Catholic setting, a type of spontaneous experience of no-self at sixteen. He described it as the ground's falling from under his sense-of-self. The significance of this experience is its spontaneity and its lack of prior conditioning within RL's Catholic setting, wherein there was no prior contact with Buddhism. Pilarzyk refers to experiences of this type as 'shock experiences', as 'ruptures in the natural taken-for-granted reality', and understands them to be part of religious change for some individuals.[3] The memory of this experience became a strong reference point for RL's questioning of the Christian faith and his subsequent Buddhist involvement.

In sum, one's childhood Christianity can be seen to have three influences on later approaches to spiritual involvement and self-discovery: a taste for the experiential in some cases, a preference for what Lofland and Stark called a religious problem-solving perspective;[4] and a respect for an ethical approach to living. The data strongly support the view that the ethical teaching and training provided by a Christian upbringing emerges and becomes more significant as one engages with Buddhism in adulthood. It is suggested that Christian behavioural ideals are internalized strongly as part of early religious socialization. These ideals find expression through Buddhist practices and doctrinal frameworks in adulthood, especially through compassion-practices; through ethical elements of meditation practice, such as the five lay precepts taken before and during vipassana retreats; and through the focus on the three aspects of the Noble Eight-Fold Path: panna, sila and samadhi. One element of several biographies was a description of the way in which the practical application of the ethical dimension in Buddhism enabled individuals to circumvent the authority structure of Christianity that they encountered in their childhood. As HR said, 'In Buddhism, it's what you do. The belief-authority structure is different compared to the Judaeo-Christian system'.

Experimental histories and personal journeys

The purpose of surveying the previous areas of exploration and involvement by practitioners was to derive an understanding of what leads people to try Buddhism and Buddhist meditation. This section follows the types of affiliations formed by seekers and the types of belief and practice responsible for predisposition to and engagement with Buddhism. The principal explorations were other forms of Buddhism, including Zen, Friends of the Western Buddhist Order, different Theravadin centres and different teachers, such as Achaan Cha; Eastern-derived meditative and mental hygiene techniques such as Transcendental Meditation, forms of Yoga and Tai Chi; and some minor involvement with Western Esotericism in that two respondents had been affiliated with local Gurdjieff groups. It appeared that the majority of sampling and exploration had taken place within Western alternative spirituality rather than within mainstream religion. After leaving their childhood Christianity, practitioners followed one of two lines of exploration and involvement.

The first was moving from Christianity straight to an exploration of some form of Buddhism, as seven of the twenty had done. Two of them had strong secular influences in between: KN in rehabilitation and KBT in the form of education in the hard sciences, which he saw as having a strong effect on his view of reality. Another one, artist MV, had travelled in Asia during his adolescence, and there he developed 'a visual taste about Buddhist, Hindu and Confucian culture'. He had developed a vipassana practice alongside his Zen Buddhism, and undertaken sutra studies with local teachers. His description of his personal practice showed it to contain both influences. He was one of two practitioners to do so.

The second was moving from Christianity into an involvement with some form of alternative spirituality before moving on to Buddhism. Twelve of the twenty moved from their childhood Christianity into these practices, predominantly into the meditation-mental hygiene movement as opposed to Western Esotericism. Some examples of their choices for engagement were Yoga, Zen, Vipassana; Transcendental Meditation, Zen, Vipassana; and Yoga, Self Transformation (a self-growth movement), Tai Chi and Vipassana. In several cases, vipassana involvement consisted of exploration with the Wat Buddha Dharma and the Dhamma Bhumi Centre before coming to BMIMC. KM and EBS had been involved with local Gurdjieff groups. EJ, an indigenous Buddhist from

Sri Lanka, had read Krishna Murti and had explored both Siddha Yoga meditation and Western vipassana with the Goenka method and BMIMC. Many practitioners from both paths had encountered alternative ideas in some form from their reading before their contact with Buddhism, without engaging in other practices or belief systems. DN had read Krishna Murti, Theosophy, Suzuki, some popular Japanese Zen writers and writings by the Dalai Lama. Although having practised Yoga, RN had read in other religious traditions, viz. Judaism, Sufism and Hinduism, at university-level.

The progression of involvements or affiliations with spiritualities and groups, as exhibited by the biographies of these practitioners, illustrates some strong characteristics of the testing process. The first of these involves the aspects of religious activity in terms of the groups and practices explored. The second is to do with the emergence and clarification of one's needs, values and sentiments with ongoing participation. Individuals' decisions with respect to selection and testing of a practice or affiliation with a group, and the decision to terminate the contact and move to something else, are based on a criterion or set of criteria that are identified during the trying-out of a practice or a spiritual group. While the language used by some respondents occasionally gave the impression of 'just trying to get a feel for something', the reasons for their decisions became clear on explanation. A dominant facet of exploration in experimental journeys was involvement with various forms of meditation. These investigations took place largely in spiritually oriented contexts, such as Transcendental Meditation and various forms of Yoga.

Each of those practitioners who explored some form of meditation before their exploration of vipassana expressed their desire for meditation to be practical or applicable in daily life in some way. This is a criterion that seems to have gained increasing clarity in their thinking throughout the progression of their exploration process. While some seekers were simply 'trying things out', others by contrast, were initially motivated by a need for a better sense of well-being. As the following narratives will demonstrate, this need for a better sense of well-being may have arisen as a result of physical and mental illness or from a more general feeling of just needing to find oneself and the answer to life's problems. However, these narratives show serious engagement with vipassana to have arisen in connection with the identification of the need for a practice applicable to daily life. From this has arisen the identification of further criteria: to provide techniques with which to enhance direction over one's mental and emotional life, and to provide a sense of meaning to experience and self-growth.

It is not entirely clear at which point these criteria emerged as important to the individuals concerned. It is 'the nature of the beast' that respondents speak with the wisdom of hindsight, and that their articulation of their previous experiences takes place through a Buddhist lens. However, often their perceptions appeared to have formed during their prior exploration, and became more clearly articulated through access to Buddhist ways of thinking. An example is HD, who commented, "I was into Siddha Yoga, and I think it lacks. The meditation is very much concentration, which, of course, does suppress the hindrances and you do feel good but the insight doesn't arise." Although employing Buddhist terminology, HD's remarks indicate that some discrimination has taken place with respect to identifying her desire for a technique which facilitates the development of wisdom. An instance of an individual 'just trying things out' is EC, who expressed the recognition of a growing interest in meditation.

> EC: I actually found the relaxation-slash-meditation part of it [yoga classes] the best part, and after I left that class, I did several others over the years, but I never found one where they emphasized the meditation part of it before, I mean it was called relaxation, but when I look back on it, it was sort of meditation, and it went for quite a while at the beginning and end, so that was a big part of the yoga class, and I had never found that again in a yoga class. It was more for that aspect of it than the postures.

EC's interest can be seen to change focus with her progression through various involvements. First, the yoga exposed her to meditation and aroused her interest, after which the vipassana awakened her to the more religious aspects of Buddhism. Conversely, HR originally 'did meditation because it was with the yoga'. She had been a Hatha Yoga practitioner and had cultivated an interest in the mind–body complex. She 'liked working with the body' and 'paying attention to the body'. Yoga, being her only exercise, had enhanced a sense of physical well-being, gained through a feeling of improved flexibility, and the sense of achievement gained from postural improvement. After a twenty-year gap, she was feeling the effect of job stress and personal issues, and feeling tired, overextended and suffering from a back injury, she felt as though she had lost connection with her centre and wanted to connect with words such as *stillness* and *centre*. She found herself saying, "If I could just get back to yoga and meditation."

After some exploration with Zen and Vipassana at the time of interview, she was committed to the ongoing exploration and application of both practices, being drawn to vipassana and to the insight aspect of Zen practice equally. HR reported that, some time after beginning Zen, she tried some concentration practice and found it useful for supporting the insight practice. With her concentration strengthened, she found that 'her mind did not wander so much'. Another significant aspect to her involvement with vipassana practice is shown by the fact that although originally drawn to the practice because of her interest in the mind–body complex, and because it 'didn't contain any ritual' and 'seemed cerebral', with time and acclimatization it awakened a respect for the more religious elements of Theravada Buddhism.

As related in Chapter 5, some practitioners had achieved success with concentration practice before trying vipassana. SI had practised both Transcendental Meditation and Zen. She relates, "I was having trouble with anxiety and depression, and that's what really got me into meditating. I sat at the Zen Centre for three and a half years, and absolutely no change in my life at all, neither in meditation nor in daily living." She tried vipassana because she found the concentration practice that she had successfully developed to be inapplicable to life's problems. Several practitioners expressed a strong preference for the insight practice with the aim of developing wisdom, as opposed to a concentration technique—facilitating pleasurable feelings and blissful states—that produced no lasting change. It appears that practitioners were motivated by a sense of the potential for practical application of principles and techniques in everyday life. Significantly, only one practitioner, KM, identified an affinity with concentration practice as opposed to insight, and reported success with integrating the concentration into her daily life, both in terms of achieving a regular practice time and in terms of feeling its effects.

One practitioner, KN, had learnt insight techniques in a therapeutic setting, as part of an alchohol rehabilitation program. The changes that she described as resulting from her application of mindfulness can be seen to have had a profound effect on her day-to-day functioning and on her self-esteem. Her involvement with BMIMC gave her access to the Buddhist framework to which she had been preconditioned through her meditative experience in rehabilitation. Two practitioners, KM and EBS, had been involved in local Gurdjieff groups. They both likened aspects of Gurdjieff's approach to aspects of vipassana meditation.[5] KM likened the approach to mindfulness, and EBS responded to the notion of 'being awake'. Significantly, neither respondent would offer any more comment than this, because of the pledge of secrecy that they had undertaken.

The journey from engagement to commitment

In making the decision to try vipassana, participants share the common perception that meditation is beneficial physically, mentally and spiritually. The following excerpt from an interview with HU, a vipassana teacher in his early fifties, suggests that while changes have occurred during the recent few decades in the specific reasons as to why people initially try meditation, it is generally not out of idle curiosity[6]:

> HU: I guess then I was looking at it as a cosmic consciousness kind of thing, and then over time it had a greater depth than that. But that was the hook for me. Interestingly when I look at people who come now, mostly it's not that that's bringing them in, it's suffering that's bringing them in. I think that there are just people that have crises in their life, whether it's alcoholism

or the death of somebody, or their own mental turmoil, that they come to
meditation looking for relief. There is someone who comes to the Monday
nights, and she'll often talk afterwards. She has trouble sleeping, often has
panic attacks and you know she's looking for the meditation to help her with
this, and it seems to be to some extent. But it's not the same cure as taking a
pill. And so a number of . . . it's more the older people who are coming for
those reasons, but occasionally some of the younger people will come up
and talk, and the way they're talking, it's not suffering that's bringing them.
There's a real curiosity.

Virtually all of the respondents had explored some other form of meditation,
including Buddhist forms, before trying vipassana meditation in another Theravadin setting or at BMIMC. All had begun exploring the alternative spiritual
scene in some way, and were motivated to find out more. For some, it is a chance
meeting with someone who introduces them to the practice. DN recounts this
kind of experience.

GE: What drew you to vipassana?

DN: Accident, I suppose. That was what presented itself to me. It's like I said
earlier, it is people in your life. It's often just individuals who you meet that
you make some connection . . . I met someone whose mother lived next door
to me and he came home from travelling after being a monk while he was
overseas, and we met and became friends, and he said 'sit down there and
watch your breath, I'll show you how to meditate'. Up to that point I'd been
reading and having an interest in different kinds of philosophies, particularly
Krishna Murti, and my friend came along and said, 'Here's a Mahasi vipassana practice'. So call it fate or karma or whatever. And why did I take up
Buddhist study? [in response to my question] Well I think that Buddhist study
was a natural extrapolation of the practice. The more I practised, the more
I was interested in this and that, and that still happens. I've just come back
from six months' practice in Nepal, and re-inspired to study the sutras, and
just get involved at that level. I've done thirty years of practice, but not a lot
of that time being a formal book-reading, word-reading student, just dipping
in occasionally, that's all I've ever done. But more and more I appreciate the
value in the Buddha's actual words, and some of the old commentaries on the
teachings are quite profound.

As this example shows, many people try a vipassana retreat as an extension of
their own explorative process, which includes other forms of Buddhism, other
forms of meditation and alternative health practices. In this instance, DN's
prior reading had already awakened a curiosity about meditation. Many respondents recall with enthusiasm their positive response to their first retreat experience. This was a result of the ability of the teacher or teachers to give clear

instruction and explanation in the practice, and also to give dhamma-talks about subjects of relevance to students' lived experience. In the following examples, it is also clear that participants' perceptions of these teachers as being genuinely practised in meditation and in ethical application of the principles were instrumental in their continued involvement in the practice. KT explained how she 'spent about a year toe-dipping'. Having tried Friends of the Western Buddhist Order and feeling unsure how well aligned it was with Buddhism generally, she decided that she wanted more experience with Buddhism and did not want to rely on Sangharakshita's view alone. After trying Zen, and finding that 'nothing really jelled with these places', although 'something was getting through', she tried a ten-day vipassana retreat. She recalls that she found the first two to three days 'weird', and she felt unsure about the experience. On the third day she decided to suspend her doubt because the teachers appeared 'to know what they are talking about', and decided to follow their instruction for the extent of the retreat. After the retreat KT began to explore the practice in earnest. She had been impressed by the way in which they grounded their practice in daily life: the techniques and explanations, and the emphasis on compassion and understanding. This blend of wisdom and compassion appealed to her. Similarly, EBS and HU recalled:

EBS: A friend of mine did a retreat with Goldstein—must have been in 1984—and he gave me *The Experience of Insight*,[7] and he was going to this retreat. And I went to this retreat, and it completely blew my mind apart. And it just felt like all this searching that I'd been doing was manifest in this interesting experience. I had a lot of confidence in Goldstein, I thought he was a character who as a human being, I hadn't come across someone like that. He seemed like he had incredible integrity. And Sharon Salzburg was very genuine, I really liked that. So I think because of this situation I saw in Salzburg and Goldstein, they were brilliant, the way they lived their own lives. So I was very impressed by that and basically I just had an incredible experience meditating. I just felt like the structure that was given about the Four Noble Truths, and the nature of suffering, and impermanence, the exploration of self, and the notion of greed, hatred and delusion, and then, the way they can get you to methodically keep looking at this, and see that that's what's going on, and relate that to all these experiences. It was one of the most amazing experiences I've ever had.

HU: I saw an advertisement for a retreat at Wat Buddha Dharma, and there were two things I was interested in, the retreat and the existence of Wat Buddha Dharma, and so I went out there and did a weekend with Phra Khantipalo. This would have been in the '80s I guess, around '81. And that was kind of a bit of a 'check it out to see what it's like' place, and then there was a ten-day retreat that was advertised with Joseph Goldstein. I must have known about him, I must have read one of his books or something, because I was quite keen to do that. I went and did that retreat, and that put a lot of stuff . . . I really connected with him and the practice.

The examples above are from practitioners who came to vipassana after having done some previous exploration of other philosophies and practices, either from within Buddhism, for instance KT and HU, or within another Western alternative area, for instance DN largely through reading and EBS through prior involvements with Kriya Yoga (Ananda Marga) and a local Gurdjieff group. In each case the respondent found something of philosophical and practical value that became a foundation for further exploration. As Volinn suggests, involvement in meditation-based groups can be seen as movement towards an experience, or a sense for the experiential, instead of fleeing from personal unhappiness.[8] The concerns of vipassana practitioners were not limited to interest in the experiential for itself, but were with the utilization of meditative experience for dealing with the generality of life experience. This is an aspiration that some begin to recognize quickly, but that all develop in time. However, some encounter vipassana and its philosophy in the midst of personal unhappiness. This is illustrated by SI's story.

> SI: I was having trouble with anxiety and depression, and that's what really got me into meditating. I sat at the Zen Centre for three and a half years, and noticed absolutely no change in my life at all, neither in meditation nor in daily living. And I went to the Buddhist library and I thought 'I'll just see who else is teaching and what's available', and I ran into Patrick, and I didn't know he was a teacher, and he talked about the Blue Mountains Insight Meditation Centre, and not long after there was a dana day up there and my girlfriend asked me if I wanted to go up, and I walked into the place, and I thought 'this is for me'.

HD exemplifies the kind of initial response that participants may have on hearing a teaching on a topic that is relevant to their life experiences.

> HD: We were going through marriage-problems, and we went to a counsellor . . . [who] referred my husband to a physiotherapist who ran relaxation-classes, but who was actually a Tibetan Buddhist. So we started going along to these, and I found him a most admirable person. He recommended that my husband do a meditation retreat with Phra Khantipalo who was visiting Bendigo where we lived, and I went to the Centre to pick my husband up on the last day, and was invited in by the teacher to hear the last bit of the talk. And it was quietly revolutionary to me, and I turned onto it immediately. He was talking about dukkha, which is that bit of unsatisfactoriness and I had recently had a baby, and I don't know why, but I really thought that all my

troubles would disappear when I had a baby, and to be confronted with the fact that it didn't happen, in fact, things got sort of more complicated even though she was wonderful and we loved her, was . . . was dukkha, and here was a man who was laying that out to me. So on the basis of that we were prepared to visit Wat Buddha Dharma where he was from, and eighteen months later sold up and moved there.

In contradiction of potential perceptions of meditation retreats as facilitating flight from personal unhappiness, the experiences of these respondents show how learning to identify the mental states and habitual thinking that cause personal unhappiness leads to an intensifying of this movement towards both the experiential and the philosophical dimensions of Buddhist activity. More than this, personal unhappiness and its causes are encapsulated by the Buddhist doctrines of the Three Marks of Existence and the Four Noble Truths. Being able to relate one's own experience to Buddhist doctrine is a factor in the movement from comprehension of doctrine in the abstract to its internalization as accepted truth.

The function of specific meditative experiences, and their interpretation in learning the practice and comprehending the fundamentals of its supporting doctrine was outlined in Chapter 2. If one perseveres in the face of the initial inability to concentrate the mind, and with the initial aversion to pain, and learns to use these phenomena as meditation objects, one begins to develop mindfulness to the point where different afflictive mental states can be distinguished. At this stage one still has periods of distraction and the mind still loses the object but, through noting and accepting the dominant mental state of the moment, there is a smoother resumption of mindful attention to the primary and secondary objects. With commitment to the practice the point is reached whereat the mind can stay with an object and continue to note its qualities, such as its arising and ceasing, without slipping into concentration. This development gives access to specific insight experiences. Typically, one has already identified oneself as a Buddhist before this capacity for experiential insight has been fully realized.

Of more relevance to the act of commitment is the realization that self-transformation has occurred. In Chapter 3, three types of change are outlined as changes within one's immediate subjective field of experience, those to one's sense-of-self and those to one's outlook on reality, or worldview. Although these transformations are mutually reinforcing in terms of continued learning and internalization, and respondents' reasons for seeing themselves as committed Buddhists reflect all three types of change, their verbalized responses foreground the changes to do with sense-of-self, particularly in their management of their mental and emotional life in relation to others. Participants may recognize that they have changed, and adopted the Buddhist meaning-system and path as their own. Processually, however, they may not be able to define whether it was their internalization or their adoption of a new universe of discourse with primary authority for them that either predominated or came first. What is clear is that both involve the comprehension and application of principle and practice to the understanding and negotiation of life experience.

Discussion until now has defined the process in terms of duration: the process is gradual, involving subtle change over a period of time. Traditionally, researchers who have applied the essentialist definition of religious change as the 'radical reorganization of identity, meaning, and life', have further described the conversion process in terms of the completeness of the personal change (see Chapter 1), itself identified by the place occupied in the person's belief system by the new worldview: at the centre or the periphery. Nock's distinction between conversion and adhesion, respectively a reorientation of the soul and the acceptance of new religions as useful supplements rather than substitutes,[9] has been usually applied as a two-fold categorization. Typically, the meditation practices and their interpretive frameworks are not mixed with other perspectives. Of the twenty practitioners interviewed, only one mixed vipassana and metta practice with others; in this instance with *shikantaza* from the Zen tradition,[10] although his comments suggested that he had moved away from the Zen practice in recent times. Two of the teachers interviewed practise yoga as a health technique, but both consider themselves to be Buddhist.

While many of the practitioners described themselves as Buddhist, the Buddhist worldview cannot be assumed to provide an exclusive framework for their sense of root reality. Their day-to-day lives required them to interact with and negotiate Western styles of thought. Many practitioners were members of the scientific and medical professions, e.g. HD as a dentist, SI a health professional, KBT a geologist and JD a biologist, and therefore schooled in the Western scientific paradigm. The several who were working or had worked as psychologists: DN, EBS, LP and others would have been educated in the Western Social Scientific paradigm. These included HR and KBN, university academics in the discipline of Education before their retirement; RN an adult educator; KT an architect; HU a solicitor; and RL a full-time dhamma teacher who had studied Law in his early adulthood. While these practitioners saw no conflict between Buddhist and scientific thought, it may be that no direct paradigmatic conflict had occurred to challenge their view. Other practitioners: administrators KN, EJ and EC, and an aged-care worker KM, would have received more than basic education. It appears that the question of how exclusively Buddhism provides their sense of root reality is irrelevant to them. Buddhism appears to map their sense of engagement with the world adequately in terms of first-person concerns.

This view describes the sense in which Buddhism appears to be adopted by all of my respondents, i.e. that it should map experience generally rather than provide the adherent with a meaning-system of absolute truth.[11] The physical world as an objective reality is part of everyday taken-for-granted reality that does not affect their engagement with Buddhism as a map, a guide to the interpretation of first-person experience. Elsewhere I have explained that Buddhism needs to provide valid interpretive frameworks and strategies for living in order for commitment to be sustained. According to a definition of commitment based on total or radical change, it can never be complete. The process is open-ended and continual and conditional upon continued relevance for the individual's worldview through its validation of experience.

The nature of Buddhist affiliation and religious identity

In order to understand the nature of socialization into and commitment to the Theravadin worldview underpinning vipassana practice, a set of questions was asked of interview-respondents to ascertain its characteristics. The question, 'Do you consider yourself Buddhist, and if so, why?' was used to establish what being Buddhist meant to the adherents. Many answered 'yes' to the question and gave their reasons. For instance, HD stated:

> HD: Yes, there was a point where I found that I could sincerely prostrate, and say 'I take refuge in the Buddha, dharma, and sangha', and really mean it, and I thought 'I've got some faith now. I'm Buddhist'. And faith is one of those factors that you need for your practice, and so, yeah, I'm a Buddhist.

HD and many others described their commitments as being based on faith or belief in the teachings, and on the value of the practices in their daily lives. HD's use of the term 'faith' may be understood in the specifically Buddhist sense of having faith in awakening to the dharma.[12] Faith is one of the five spiritual faculties held to be necessary to attain nibbana in Theravada Buddhism.[13] The same sentiments were expressed by others. KN reported that her self-identification as a Buddhist was based on a set of beliefs, viz. in rebirth; that enlightenment is possible; that the Buddha existed and achieved enlightenment; in the Four Noble Truths because they are validated in her experience; and because she has experienced the claimed benefits of the practices. Most of those who answered 'no' to the question indicated that they did not wish to accept the label of Buddhist. For instance, FV said, "I think I'm reluctant to identify myself as anything in particular. If I were to, it would be Buddhist." Later she said that she had begun to consider herself Buddhist 'in a quiet kind-of way, just to myself', during the previous six to eight months. Three adherents, KT, HR and HU, said that the social context they found themselves in would determine whether they would outwardly call themselves Buddhist. Significantly, HR was the only respondent of the twenty to have taken refuge formally, which included taking the five lay precepts because she had wanted to make a commitment. Because no refuge ceremony is performed at BMIMC, she found a Theravadin nun to give her refuge. Some found the label to be inadequate in some way. For instance, RN described herself as a seeker for truth.

> RN: Oh no. I sort of regard myself as a Buddhist, but I suppose I regard myself more as a searcher for the truth, and I see Buddhism as the means to discover that, through the Buddhist teachings. You know I think perhaps that for me that's the Buddhist principles of living, the basic teachings as far as taking refuge in Buddhism. So in that sense I'm a Buddhist and that's how I usually explain myself to people because it's sort of simpler in a way just to say I'm Buddhist.

Even though RN's statement may appear contradictory in that she sees herself as a seeker for truth rather than a Buddhist, she also sees Buddhism as the means for discovering the truth. Statements such as these encapsulate the view of commitment that practitioners appear to hold; that it is conditionally based on the capacity of the Buddhist principles to provide a viable interpretive framework for the understanding and negotiation of experience. This is best expressed by EBS:

> EBS: You know, I'm so inspired by the Buddha's story, because it's a story of him following his own instincts. That's really big for me. So I'll often say to people, if something came along that gave a better exposition of my own experience, I'd actually swap to that. I'm not attached to Buddhism for Buddhism's sake. I'm attached to the notion of going with my own experience, trying to make sense of what my life's about.

This sentiment was expressed by other respondents. EC, while having devoted considerable energy to her practice over the previous four years, was unsure at the time of interview of how she felt about being Buddhist. She simply 'didn't know', although other comments made during the interview showed her commitment to the teachings and practice to have deepened over the four years of her involvement. She commented:

> EC: Well, I just think that it's a good way to live your life. This is why I don't call myself a Buddhist. I'm not reading the scriptures and finding out about everything that went on in the Buddha's life, not really into studying it in that way and getting some knowledge. I just look upon it as a really good way to live your life. I find most other religions are quite dogmatic, whereas I don't find that Buddhism is . . . It's not the scriptures that I read. I'm a practical person rather than a theoretical person.

EC's response demonstrates the way in which the label *Buddhist* may conceal the more relevant aspects of an individual's engagement with Buddhism. Her approach is practical, but her understanding of *being Buddhist* includes scriptural study, which she does not engage with by her own admission. It is also conceivable that many are uncomfortable with the label for the reason suggested by Fronsdal. He observed that early American vipassana students, many of whom were part of the counter-culture movement of the '60s and '70s, described their involvement with Buddhist practice as spiritual rather than as religious, to distance themselves from mainstream religion.[14] The acceptance or rejection of the label Buddhist does not reliably indicate why a commitment is made. Practitioners committed considerable personal time and mental energy to the endeavour of learning to apply the teachings and vipassana technique in their daily lives. In addition, the approaches of EC and RN are possibly representative of different stages of progress in the movement from the experimental participant to the committed practitioner. Both felt that their experience was validated through a Buddhist interpretation, but RN, with more experience, is more prepared to take on Theravada Buddhism's doctrinal and hierarchical authority.

Respondents were asked three questions related to their own experience of the commitment process. Was their adoption of Buddhism a process or a specific event? Was the adoption a sudden or a gradual process? Was there an identifiable turning point? In response to the first two questions, all respondents saw their participation as mainly a process, and all but one saw the process as gradual. BM described his adoption of Buddhism as sudden, being within four months after his visiting a monastery. He was twenty-one when he entered the monastery. Two practitioners saw their adoption of Buddhism as a process, but marked by events. In answer to the question, 'Was the adoption of Buddhism a process or a specific event?', HD answered:

> HD: Both. Because there was that immediate hearing about dukkha [a reference to the first teaching she attended] . . . It's like a veil lifted from the eyes, from the mind, but there was also that more gradual faith-process happening.

HD had in fact identified two turning points throughout the course of the interview: the realization about dukkha, and that whereat she realized that she was able to prostrate and know that she meant it. Both of these events had struck her as being significant points of decision. Similarly, HU recalled:

> HU: I went to a nearby monastery where there was a Western monk, an American monk, and did a meditation course there. And that was for about eight or nine days, and that was kind of it. I had an experience as if the whole of my body just kind of melted, I guess a powerful experience that was kind of like the hook. It was still in terms of this cosmic consciousness and experiences and things [a reference to an earlier answer], and so I guess that was

kind of why I really wanted to keep doing this, to recreate that and to kind of understand it. So, I can't remember any particular point where I embraced the teachings, it was more just a gradual over a period of time becoming more familiar, and I guess just seeing the truth in them.

While some people did identify one or more events or turning points, these were seen as part of an extended process of understanding and acceptance of the Buddhist tenets. It is significant that time, duration, or in some cases order of events, does not seem to have been important. Instead, the emphasis was on what was experienced or learnt. Engagement was viewed as a cumulative process of exploration: learning, testing and validating doctrine, practice and experiential norms against their own reasoning and experience. This is evident in the approaches of DN and EC, of thirty and four years' experience, respectively:

DN: Certainly when I started I was just a meditator, and I was looking for a meditation practice, and I wasn't a Buddhist. It took a number of years and interactions with monks and personal practice and a number of retreats. At first I was doing at least one ten-day retreat each year, and as time went on I'd do longer and longer retreats. So, in the process of doing annual ten-day retreats, after a number of years I just found myself looking at myself as a Buddhist. At first I was obviously not a Buddhist and I wouldn't allow myself just to say I'm a Buddhist because I was sitting down and doing some chanting and meditation, and taking the precepts. It wasn't enough for me to identify, so I deliberately didn't identify, so it took a few years. But that's been a long time now that I've regarded my self as a Buddhist, and sometimes I still challenge that and say 'what's that mean?'

EC: I can chart my progression over the last four years or whatever, and it took probably two years of nothing much happening, not much of a shift or anything, just going and listening and stuff. I'd say the last year has been the biggest thing, but I suppose that's the way with a lot of things, it's *cumulative* [italics mine] and the longer you go, the more benefit you get from it.

Other excerpts from EC's interview transcript indicate that, in the four years of her engagement with vipassana, she has devoted considerable time and effort into attending retreats and teachings, and into developing a personal practice. Although she does not consider herself Buddhist, she clearly believes that Buddhism provides 'a good way to live your life'. The results of her efforts are of two types. The first is experiential: the development of mindfulness after two years' effort of seemingly not progressing. The second has to do with changes to her beliefs, attitudes and habitual responses, arising from the combination of the interpretation of experiential states and changes, and reflection on

Buddhist principles during dhamma-talks and daily activity. EC's approach to her practice is illustrative of the approach generally taken when a student or practitioner has some knowledge and experience on which to reflect, in that the mechanics of the process, whether seen as one seamless accumulation of knowledge and experience or as sequences of discrete events, or as both, were insignificant in comparison to the substance of learning, experience, and self-transformation.

Because BMIMC does not offer a formal refuge ceremony there is no overt sign of commitment to Buddhism, and the existence of a point of commitment must be identified by the participants themselves. The nature of responses indicates that in the period from encounter to commitment to Buddhism, their interest, sense of engagement and commitment to its doctrinal and practical aspects all deepen with exposure. For many of the respondents this was a process that was visible in hindsight in that, looking back, they could see changes to their thinking, emotional states and behaviour accompanied by a shift toward acceptance of the Buddhist view. While some respondents' experiences suggested that the commitment process consisted of two or three stages of increasing intensity of interaction, the bulk of the data support the view that a gradual process of intensifying engagement culminates in any one of the decision to commit, the recognition that one *is* committed, or continuing unsurety.

Vajrayana Institute and the Perspective of the FPMT

Religious backgrounds of respondents

All but one of the respondents from the FPMT had a Christian background. The majority had been either Catholic (eight of eighteen) or Anglican (four). Other denominations of Christianity represented were Orthodox (one Ukrainian and one Serbian), and Protestantism. The one respondent who answered 'none' to religious background also reported that as a child of about seven, after being exposed to the Anglican faith taught in the English public school system, she sought religious education in Catholicism at the local presbytery. Her Catholic affiliation lasted into her early adulthood. For all of those raised as Catholics, except for one, KI, Catholicism remained the dominant if not only religious influence throughout their childhood and early adolescence. EF recounted:

> EF: . . . It was the only thing we knew. It wasn't just a Sunday thing. It was in your whole life, really . . . It was just part of our growing up. I mean, it was totally part of our life, in that we had prayers in the house. In my house, my mother was very religious, so we said the Rosary every evening, and every time you went out the door you were sort of sprinkled with holy water. And Sunday, as a young person, was very much involved in the church.

Although nearly all those of Catholic upbringing went to church and received a Catholic education, the intensity of personal involvement varied. For instance, NJ said, "Now I can see how much Christian ideas influenced me because I'm part of this culture, but growing up, I didn't feel a strong connection to it at all", whereas AN said, "I don't have any bitter rejections of it." Those who came from a Protestant denomination were, in general, exposed to more variability in religious influence. Sometimes this was occasioned by attending a church or school from another denomination, owing to its availability and location. MVR was 'brought up Presbyterian', but 'went to Anglican schools'. Sometimes this was because of the differing outlooks of parents. RI's religious affiliation was Presbyterian, but he felt more drawn to his intuitive mother's and grandmother's view of the world, which was to 'believe in a lot of things that I can't see, can't hear, can't touch'. In short, he 'preferred their tealeaves to God'. MW, from the Orthodox Church, recalled going to the Ukrainian Orthodox Church with her father, but also described her mother as a religious seeker who explored both Baptist and Christadelphian forms of Christianity. Often the content of respondents' recollections reflected most strongly their parents' dominant concerns. WR, from a Serbian Orthodox background, could remember going to religious rituals, being impressed by the liturgy, helping her grandmother prepare the food for special feast days, and listening to the discussions of politics and ethics in the house, but not hearing any discussion of scripture.

Although some recalled enjoying the social part of religious life more vividly than the scriptures, several adherents told of the constancy with which the ethical aspect of Christianity seemed to surround them. MC recalled memories from his adolescence, and MN described the nature of the Christian beliefs that she held into her early adulthood, up to the time that she was married, with two small children.

> MC: Yeah, I started going to the Uniting Church. I had a girlfriend that went to the same group. It was a far more social environment and experience. I met an awful lot of people outside of school, that would have been Year Eight. We used to go on trips everywhere, so I was actually going to a different church to the one my family went to. That was the year that the three churches . . . all joined together, within a year of that. But then again, I didn't go to the services, I just went to the study groups and things like that.
>
> GE: And when you went to the study groups, was it for social interaction?
>
> MC: Almost totally social interaction, but it was still with . . . I mean there's got to have been an awful lot of . . . ethics that was going on, morality and practice. I mean it's always there. It's just a part of the way they all interacted with each other, even in a social environment, because there were a lot of older people who were driving people around and doing other things, so you basicly, difficult to remember exactly how much . . .

MN: I believed in Christianity, and definitely in the Ten Commandments, and that children needed some sort of religious upbringing . . .

GE: So, you believed in God and Jesus?

MN: No, I didn't believe there was a Creator. I did not believe in Adam and Eve. However, I did feel that there was some sort of spiritual being that we could pray to in a time of need, but I didn't worry whether he answered my prayers or not. Now of course, being a Buddhist, you're actually making life positive for yourself . . . 'Obey your parents' was very important to me. Stealing, killing, the Ten Commandments were very, very important. I think they were more important to me as a way of life than as a religious concept. I don't believe in Moses or the Bible, but I think the Ten Commandments . . . they were ideals that I wanted to follow my life through, just another thing, like parent–children discipline would rub off onto your children.

Experimental histories and personal journeys

Apart from the feel for moral or ethical training that appears to have stayed with them since their original Christian socialization, respondents' approach to Buddhism was influenced by aspects of philosophy and practice acquired from previous experimental affiliations before their involvement with Buddhism. Most had explored one or another spiritual group or practice from the contemporary Western alternative milieu. These included other forms of Western Buddhism such as Queer Dharma, Goenka Vipassana and Zen; forms of Eastern-derived meditation and mental-health practice such as Transcendental Meditation, Yoga and Tai Chi; Western Esotericism and its off-shoots, such as Theosophy, Spiritualism and Occultism; and courses given by self-growth organizations such as Landmark Forum (est). The meditative mental-hygiene category is under-represented, and the self-growth and New Age category is the most-represented.

The same two kinds of path from childhood Christianity to Buddhism taken by the vipassana practitioners were also taken by the Vajrayana practitioners. Nine of the Vajrayana practitioners interviewed: NJ, AN, RI, MVR, MW, EF, MF, KD and ER, had passed straight from Christianity into Buddhism. Four of these (NJ, AN, RI and EF) had met other religious ideas in their travels, but had no other religious affiliations. Two (RI and MVR) had read about Western Esotericism without affiliating with a group. The second route, from Christianity to Buddhism by way of some form of alternative spirituality, had been taken by seven: CR, LL, LLM, VP, MB, BC and LB. Of these, one had been involved in meditation mental-hygiene (Transcendental Meditation) and, with five others: BP, MM, MN, NC and DE, had been actively exploring in groups and organizations in the self-growth and New Age category. Two (WR and MC) were loosely connected to Western Esotericism or Occultism by their interests, reading habits and contacts. As a generality, it appeared that these Vajrayana practitioners had moved within the Western Alternative Reality tradition either by means of a fluid association with esoteric influences having no stated organizational affiliation (with Western Esotericism and Occultism) or as active participants in self-growth and New Age groups.

Examination of the explorative journeys of these seekers shows them to involve both social participation and exploration of ideas through reading material. Some practitioners appear not to have actively participated in a group or organization, but to have confined their interest to reading. This is most noticeable for those whose explorations involved areas of Western Esotericism. Because of the manner of reporting, in some cases it was difficult to determine the number of affiliations an individual had had, but it is evident that practitioners had been exposed to many spiritual ideas through their reading and travel. This latter is a significant exposure. Some (NJ, AN, MM, MVR and DE) had visited meditation centres and/or gone on retreats during travel overseas, and some (RI, EF and WR) had been influenced by Eastern religious ideas during visits to Asian countries on business.

The explorational path of some shows a prior orientation toward alternative-reality tradition in some observable form. Two practitioners (MVR and WR) had explored some facet of Western Esotericism beforehand. For MVR, from a Protestant Christian background and with an interest in mysticism, religion and psychology, this was through reading. She did not mention any prior group affiliations. She was drawn to the symbolic systems of Tarot and of Jungian psychology. She was drawn to what she perceived as being the philosophical wisdom contained in the symbol system of the Tarot. Despite that, she reported that she felt as though this did not contain the depth of wisdom she wanted, describing that as 'a ground of being'—a term she borrowed from Paul Tillich—for which she had sought deliberately. What appeared to have attracted her to Gelugpa Tibetan Buddhism was the way in which its particular understanding of ground of being, that is emptiness and dependent origination as ultimate and relative selves, works with other aspects of the perspective.

WR was one of two practitioners attracted to various forms of the metaphysical subculture that have their origins in late Nineteenth-Century occultism and spiritualism. Her interests included healing, reincarnation, psychics such as Edgar Cayce, Tarot, colours, auras and a variety of psychic phenomena and abilities. Both practitioners appeared to have been drawn to a local FPMT centre initially by their perception of the healing abilities of a local geshe. As they became more familiar with Mahayana Buddhism their orientation shifted to include appreciation of its ethical approach and its focus on compassion, which then could harness and use their interest in healing. Both have taken refuge and call themselves Buddhist. In conversation, both give the impression that their entry into Buddhism was facilitated by similarities between notions of healing using colours in occultism and the Gelugpa systems of colour correspondences for the deities. Several of the Vajrayana practitioners had explored self-growth organizations, but these appeared not to have had any lasting effect. Two had explored Landmark Forum or '*est*' (Erhard Seminar Training) and reported having a virtually-identical response to it. Both recognized in hindsight that it contained ideas that were akin to emptiness, but both were put off by the selfish emphasis it placed on 'I' or 'me'. CR and NC offered these comments about their experiences.

> CR: I did a whole lot of courses at Landmark Education, you know, Forum. They were fantastic for me at the time, and a lot of it I've discovered since, was borrowed from Buddhism. Concepts akin to the idea of emptiness, and this idea that things don't exist in this concrete way, but in the end it just seemed empty, because it didn't have thousands of years of wisdom, didn't have a Buddha. It came out of America, it came out of Werner Erhardt who had read a lot of books. When I was doing these personal development courses, after a while I started to get really sick of them, because it just seemed to be focused on me, me, me, even though they were talking about being of service in the world, there was that, but it still seemed to be very I-centred.

> NC: A lot of what it talks about is really about emptiness. The final thing they say is that you and your life is empty and meaningless. They've got a slightly different slant on it, but the effect of it, when they do it in the course is that you're left there with a hollow blank feeling, the same sort of feeling that [inaudible] when you're doing meditations on emptiness. I think within about a year, the whole New Age thing, the thing it lacked to me . . . it all seemed quite selfish, you know. How can I be happier . . . How can I be richer. It was all very self-centred. To me that seemed a bit hollow.

The expressed dislike for the emphasis on oneself suggests that this aspect of est's philosophy prompted the two seekers to leave. The identification of both characteristics by CR and NC can be seen as the expression of preconditions for their future involvement with Mahayana Buddhism. The aspect of est discourse that they likened to emptiness (but did not describe in detail) struck a positive note with both, while the emphasis on *me* was the opposite. Insofar as they both went on to explore and commit to a tradition that accommodates both of these conditions, it can be seen that their involvement with est supplied the opportunity for them to explore their own ideological and religious needs. Though both CR's and NC's manner of expression suggests that the identification of both personal needs and desirable qualities of a spiritual discipline is retrospective, the explorative histories of these seekers show how a set of needs, identified during the passage of time, act as a set of prerequisites or preconditions for the next, in this case Buddhist, involvement. NC said that he learned from est to accept that everything in his life was his responsibility, but felt that the shortcoming was that 'it brings you up to this point where you're feeling great, but doesn't give a lot of skills to make changes happen in your mind that stay and last'. After exploring Life Skills, his dissatisfaction with the self-centred approach of these kinds of organization led him to read Khalil Gibran, the Lebanese Christian mystic, because, in NC's words, 'he talks about focusing on other people rather than focusing on yourself'. Moments later in the interview he said that he wanted Tibetan Buddhism because he had heard it was intellectual and complex, and he desires the analysis and use of intellect.

NC's statements revealed that his interaction with these groups and ideas had defined a set of conditions that he needed to satisfy. First, he wanted a discipline that gave him techniques to effect enduring personal transformation. Second, he seems to have accepted the notion that life is inherently empty and meaningless, although not in terms of the Buddhist meaning of emptiness or sunyata. Third, he accepted responsibility for his own life. Fourth, he realized that he was not happy with a selfish approach, and fifth, he wanted something that engaged his intellect. All of these issues pre-existed his encounter with Gelugpa Tibetan Buddhism, which can be seen to facilitate satisfaction of these wants. First, as outlined elsewhere, all of the meditative and contemplative exercises within Buddhism are techniques for effecting enduring self-transformation, and they work as part of an integrated and coherent religious system with a clearly articulated philosophy. Second, at the centre of this system is the notion of emptiness, the view that all phenomena are empty of inherent, unchanging existence, and exist according to causes and conditions. Third, in the Buddhist view—Theravada and Mahayana alike—one is ultimately responsible for one's own mental purification and attainment of enlightenment. Fourth, the Mahayana perspective highlights compassionate action towards others, and fifth, the Gelugpa lineage is distinguished from other Tibetan Buddhist lineages because of its emphasis on intellectual understanding and debate as a necessary mental training.

The journey from engagement to commitment

Before their contact with VI, several respondents had explored another Buddhist group, or were familiar with some Buddhist literature. MB had attended teachings for sixteen months before taking refuge, but he had been reading Gelugpa Tibetan Buddhist material, including material by the Dalai Lama and Kathleen McDonald's *How to Meditate*,[15] before that, and he therefore had some familiarity with the meditations and key Gelugpa concepts and practices.[16] For some respondents, contact with VI was precipitated by dissatisfaction with another form of Buddhism. For others, the FPMT was their first experience of Buddhism. The manner of contact with VI varied between respondents: through a friend or acquaintance; seeing the newsletter Vajrayana News;

attending the Buddhist Library in Camperdown, Sydney; travel to another FPMT centre; seeing a brochure in a cafe; attending an art or cultural exhibition; or through attending a public talk by a popular lineage member such as the Dalai Lama or Venerable Robina Courtin.

After first contact, individuals had usually attended a teaching, course or a workshop. Participants are initially engaged by a teaching through its relevance to their own life circumstances, rather than a meditation session or a social activity. Such teachings as the Eight Verses of Thought Transformation and the antidotes to negative mental states have at once practical applicability in ethical appeal; value in terms of learning outcomes in that their practice results in both non-harm towards others and mental transformation for the student; and also provide a philosophy or broader rationale for action. I suggest that the responses to these early experiences should be seen as positive responses to experimental learning situations, as distinct from pre-conversion reactions to crises where in the religious seeker is merely seeking a solution to the crisis.[17] The recognition of practical life-enhancing strategies within the Buddhist teachings is the quality that creates initial interest in Buddhist philosophy for participants. When this happens, seekers are impressed both by the interpretation of the problem and its solution according to Buddhist principles.

AN had been curious about meditation in his early adulthood. Before he went to Asia he saw Buddhism as being 'New Age, with not much depth'. While travelling in Nepal he did the intensive ten-day *Introduction to Buddhism* course at Kopan Monastery. Those teachings and practices gave him a sense of depth, history, logic; and things' being well-studied, reasoned and worked out. Added to those were the qualities that he perceived in the monks and nuns whom he met there. He felt proud that he could sit meditating for an hour, an improvement on his previous fifteen-minute meditations. The course teacher explained 'a lot of different teachings about bodhicitta, and the concept of exchanging self for others, and went into reincarnation', which he then understood to be supported by 'a whole system of logic', and he appreciated it as 'an argument, and not just a New Age catchcry'.

The capacity of these teachings to engage students also functions to provide the foundation for comprehension of more complex points of doctrine further on. In AN's case, the same core doctrines of bodhicitta and karma were still significant to him after his exploration in Nepal. His discussion about karma with a then resident nun at VI, in which she explained that it was 'not punitive, not a punishment, not retribution', was significant for him in deepening his understanding of the Buddhist perspective. As illustrated in Chapters 4 and 5, the concepts of karma, renunciation and bodhicitta are integral to an understanding of the FPMT's Gelugpa worldview. The topics of many first teachings that respondents cite as being influential are those common to human experience: how to manage one's mental states such as desire, attachment, and especially, anger. The Buddhist view is that these are the mental states that keep sentient beings in samsara, the 'three poisons' of greed, hatred and delusion, or differently expressed, desire, anger and ignorance. It is significant that these foundational topics are given considerable attention in teachings, public talks and the FPMT literature. With time, as students come to appreciate more of the doctrinal framework, they build on their initial appreciation of the practical applicability of teachings and practices.

For a small number of practitioners, encounter with Buddhism and the FPMT has a strong emotional component consisting of intense emotional reactions to various aspects of Buddhist culture and symbolism, the descriptions of which are reminiscent of encounters with the numinous. MW recalls three specific events or encounters that ignited her interest in Buddhism. She went to the Art Gallery of NSW to see a Buddhism exhibition, and several events occurred quite quickly:

MW: . . . and I was really struck by the beautiful pageantry, especially the Vajrasattva statue. I had one of those things, you know one of those 'Oh my God' moments. The chant master from the Gyuto monks gave a presentation on what Buddhism was about, a very simple presentation, and I almost cried because you know I was going through a divorce and life was not going to plan. I was just hanging on every word, and then I heard Robina Courtin. So I had about three moments. I saw the statue, and it had been quite dehumanizing working in the corporate world. I had to put on the persona . . . and then to hear this guy talking about love and loving yourself. I went along to Robina's weekend seminar, and started doing Discovering Buddhism in June or July.

At the time of interview, MW had not taken refuge and was still exploring. She was one of a small number to accord aesthetic elements an influence in their decisions to explore Buddhism. The aesthetic dimension—apart from practitioners' aesthetic appreciation of the deity iconography used in ritual—as it is encompassed by the chanting, in the imagery within decorations and in the sutras, appears to have been incidental to the process in almost all other Vajrayana biographies.

The tantric-type experiences of two practitioners, NJ and MM (discussed in Chapter 5), before their involvement with the FPMT and VI, need to be considered in terms of their effect on the course of exploration and future practical orientation of the two individuals. Both had begun exploring Buddhism in its Theravadin form. Both had their experiences in a Theravadin monastery while they were learning meditation: breath concentration and vipassana respectively. In both cases, the nature of the experience is unusual for a Theravadin setting, and describes body-based experience that one would normally associate with tantric practice. For NJ, the experience at Bundanoon, near Sydney, and again at the Root Institute in Bodghaya, India, did not recur. However, her other experiences from around that time show similarities to MW's responses to Buddhist iconography and symbolism discussed above, but that hers were much more intense. NJ recalled that, while still in India:

> NJ: I was reading Lama Yeshe's book *Introduction to Tantra* while sitting in this cafe, and I turned the book over and saw his face [in the dustjacket photo], and I just started to sob in the cafe. These things kept happening. Someone started reading the King of Prayers, and I just lost it, I became so emotional. It was a really powerful experience, but I didn't understand why . . .

These experiences did not automatically lead the respondents to take refuge. They spent time in learning and familiarization with the teachings and practices before they made the decision to take refuge. For both, however, this exploratory period was a relatively short several months. After returning from India and attending the introductory Lam Rim course at Vajrayana Institute, NJ took refuge. Similarly, after her experience, MM began to explore Tibetan Buddhism, and after feeling dissatisfied with the approach at one centre (which she did not name), she tried and committed to the Discovering Buddhism course at VI. As noted above, these experiences are atypical. The more usual, which are less emotionally charged and more cognitive in nature, are akin to that described by CR:

> CR: In January there was a Western monk teaching on the Eight Verses of Thought Transformation. It was fantastic. The whole concept was to cherish and to hold most dear the person who has harmed you, you know, the person you've been really kind to who's then harmed you in turn, they're the most precious treasure to be able to see them like this. And I just had this feeling of relief, I thought 'Oh, this is the place, this is what I need to hear' . . . And I kept coming back. In the Easter of that year I went on a retreat with Geshe Dawa, up in the mountains, and he was talking about emptiness and things that were a lot more advanced. Even though I couldn't quite get it all I could certainly get enough to make it such a worthwhile experience, and I was starting to get more of an understanding of where Buddhism was coming from.

The effect, for CR, was of hearing and relating to the teaching on thought transformation, as outlined in Chapter 4, with evident application to her life, in this instance to the task of transforming strong negative emotions. This is one of several significant events or moments for CR. Another event involved stories she had heard about the psychic abilities of the lamas. Several respondents reported occurrences in which a lama had looked straight at them during a class about a subject with direct application to the respondent's state of mind at the time. Such stories are regarded as 'proof' of the lama's ability to see one's internal state, and therefore as evidence of the efficacy of the techniques of mental purification. Another event for CR was the taking of refuge and vows, which for her involved an examination of her responses to the Buddhist belief system, especially the doctrinal framework of karma and reincarnation, as related above. CR's experience echoes the experiences of many who report two or three moments or points of significance. However, invariably, the initial feeling of connection with a teaching does not precipitate commitment. There was no report of a sudden decision. For all, the process of active appropriation of the meaning-system happens gradually, and practitioners do not expect to become experts quickly.

While allowing for individual variation, two factors are observed to influence the decision to commit. First, students reach a point whereat they begin to see how significant ideas fit together. Following this is a growing appreciation of the consistency of thought behind the teachings. NC had read some Buddhist literature after some unsatisfactory involvement with est and Life Skills, and then decided to search out a centre. He sought out Queer Dharma, but after a brief period decided not to become involved because he considered that it was not well-run. He wanted to investigate Tibetan Buddhism because he had heard that it was 'intellectual and complex', and looked forward to the challenge of using his intellect and analytical skills. The first course he attended at VI was Buddhism and Western Psychology in mid-2003. He recalls, "Because I'd read those books, things just started dropping into place straight away." He reread the Dalai Lama's book containing a short series of discourses on the Lam Rim, and remembers being engaged by the concept of renunciation. During a business trip to Malaysia for several months, he read Kathleen McDonald's How To Meditate, and said that "For three months those meditations were my practice." On returning to Australia he began Discovering Buddhism. He recalled that the module about tantra made him 'want to go back and get a closer look at Renunciation and Bodhicitta'. He also expressed appreciation of the notions of emptiness and compassion, and how all of these notions interconnected. He attended the Discovering Buddhism modules Emptiness, Mind and Its Potential, How to Meditate, Presenting the Path and 'the Saturday teachings by Geshe Samten'. His recall of the significant points of these teachings for him indicates that he had been attempting to flesh out his understanding of core Mahayana ideas and the interconnections between them.

Second, after a period of synthesis of information, and the observation that constructive changes have taken place within one's sense-of-self, seekers reach a moment of self-reflection when they review the outcomes of their experimentation such that a conscious decision is made, either to keep exploring with more intensity or to take refuge if this intensification point has already been reached. In either case, this moment of self-reflection marks a definite decision.

Taking refuge: the formalization of commitment

By contrast with the private nature of one's sense of commitment to the Buddhist path for vipassana practitioners affiliated with BMIMC, the FPMT's refuge ceremony is public in that it is open to anyone who wishes to witness it. The taking of refuge marks one as a Buddhist, as practitioners are told during the ceremony. When one feels ready, one takes refuge. The purpose and significance of the refuge ceremony can be seen in Appendix 7: Refuge Teachings, Sunday 19 June 2005. Essentially, one takes refuge in the dharma. One also takes as many of the five lay precepts as one feels able to keep. At the time of interview, almost all respondents had taken refuge. A small number had not for the reason that they did not feel ready. When asked 'Do you consider yourself a Buddhist?' DE responded, "At the moment I don't think so, I'm studying Buddhism. There may be a point where I will say "I'm a Buddhist." Similarly, MW responded, "I believe that when the time is right, because of what it's all based on, it's a bit silly to take refuge if you don't feel ready."

Typically, one spends a period of time before the ceremony deciding whether one is ready to take refuge. For instance, CR related, "It was a gradual process that involved checking things out for yourself." At the time of interview she recalled that she had been involved with Vajrayana Institute for six years, and had taken refuge three-and-a-half years earlier, leaving a period of two-and-a-half years in between first coming to Vajrayana Institute and taking refuge. She explains:

> CR: That was after I decided, because when I first came I was just . . . immediately I could tell it was something that was going to be useful to me in my life. So I kept coming, but I was coming on and off, and I didn't believe in all the things like karma and rebirth, those sort of things. I wasn't quite sure about those, I was just listening. So it took me a couple of years before I decided that I wanted to take refuge.

This approach and that of NC below are typical experiences for the reasons discussed above. Up to this point, refuge has been seen as the outcome of socialization and self-transformation. However, a consideration of the refuge ceremony (and the ordination ceremony as an extension of this) beyond that as a processual endpoint lends itself to interpretation in two ways: as an external sign of internal commitment or as an anticipated rite of transformation. Staples and Mauss view the use of certain kinds of language and rhetoric as a means to achieve a transformation of self, as opposed to Snow and Machalek who hold that the conversion rhetoric reflects underlying change that has already occurred.[18] While respondents' narratives tend to support the latter view, aspects of NC's experience can be seen to support both of these views. At the time of interview he had taken refuge because of the self-transformation that had already occurred, and reported that he also felt ongoing effects from his having done so.

> NC: . . . the decision to take refuge was because I think I'd seen enough practical impact on my life, over the last year particularly, to develop the confidence that there was good practical application, and I'm a practical person. To me, the value is in seeing tangible differences . . . I got the point where I thought, 'Well. This is well worth me committing to more, and I'll get more benefit by committing more', so that's what got me to decide, and I think since taking refuge, the thing that changed over the last couple of months is a real deepening of that sense of refuge. So if you talk about conversion, that's probably happened I'd say, around taking refuge, since the refuge ceremony about two months ago.[19]

In harmony with the view of Staples and Mauss of conversion rhetoric as a means to achieve a transformation of self, Wilson maintains that an experimental approach to ritual provides opportunities to take part in activities inconsistent with participants' established self-images, in the hope of bringing about personal change.[20] In the ritual context of the refuge ceremony the anticipated change is to do with the intensification of one's commitment through one's new role of being Buddhist. The strongest support for the view of Wilson and of Staples and Mauss is provided by the narrative of MN, which differs markedly from those of others. MN had been suffering from anxiety and depression, and after a period of searching she began to feel determined to become ordained as a nun. In her own words, she felt desperate. On encountering VI and its religious program, and receiving instruction from sangha members, she realized that she had held an idealized picture of spending her time as a nun in a serene environment. Having become ordained she faced the challenge of undertaking religious practices that she felt little affinity with at first. However, in her capacity as nun she began teaching meditation in the community, and visiting terminally ill patients in hospices. During our interview, she spoke openly about her identification of her need to be needed and useful, which being unfulfilled for some time previously, she believed had caused her illness. She found that her role as a nun both fulfilled and legitimated her desire to help others. While this narrative is atypical, it illustrates the way in which a role- or status–change may effect a positive transformation in this context.

Part 2: From Experimental Immersion to Commitment: Comparisons and Conclusions

While Part 1 of this Chapter explored and described the journey for adherents of each of the two Centres, BMIMC and Vajrayana Institute, what remains is to give attention, by way of salient comparisons, to the conclusions that this study may allow to be drawn. Although I have used the term 'meaning-system' to emphasize the meaning-construction activities that take place during socialization, throughout I have accepted Berger and Luckman's view of a shared reality as one that is maintained by a group consensus, and embodied in collective and private discourse and practice.[21] Despite doctrinal, practical and organizational differences between the two Centres, they are both Buddhist. As such, their teachings are founded on the same core Buddhist doctrines, central among which are the Four Noble Truths and the Noble Eightfold Path. This, in addition to consistencies in approach to engagement with and appropriation of the meaning-system, and in the change produced by such activity exhibited by the practitioners within each Centre, allows the two sets of data to be compared. This final section of the work highlights the nature of strong themes to emerge from the data.

A Comparison of Religious Backgrounds

Virtually all of the respondents from both Centres were from a Christian background. While most backgrounds were Anglican or Catholic, other denominations were represented. The dominance of Christian upbringing in the lives of these practitioners is understandable when it is considered that modern Australia, while a secular society, is still a predominantly Christian country, religiously speaking. The three who had no exposure to religion in their family environment, KN, SI and ML, were curious enough to instigate their own religious exploration before reaching adulthood, at the ages of about nine, fifteen and seven respectively. Their accounts indicate that they acquired a religious perspective from their wider social environments such as school and circles of acquaintances, which were Christian. I deduce that the curiosity was with their positive interpretations of other people's actions—going to church and to Sunday school—rather than with Christianity *per se*. Significantly, in each case these individuals became actively involved in religious exploration and activity. The fact—that two out of the twenty vipassana practitioners and the one Vajrayana practitioner who reported having no familial religious influence, developed an interest in religion at an early age—suggests that the exposure to and affinity with religious ideas generally, rather than any specific ideology or tradition, may be a causative factor for seekerhood. It is conceivable that seekers' early religious socialization conditioned them to a style of perception and deliberation founded in a transcendent frame of reference, akin to Lofland and Stark's notion of a religious problem-solving perspective,[22] in that exploration was ideologically or experientially motivated. The ideologies explored were religious or spiritual, not political or to do with purely secular, pragmatic, this-worldly concerns.

The notion that these individuals were predisposed to interpret reality and experience according to a transcendent frame of reference is supported by a number of considerations. Practitioners' experimental journeys consisted of movement between organizations with transcendent worldviews. Seekers moved on from their childhood Christianity to explore other worldviews: those of Buddhism, spiritual traditions and practices or self-growth organizations. Those who tried the self-growth area likened it to New Age thought, and went on to explore other spiritual practices. Even one, RN, who saw herself as a seeker for truth rather than as a Buddhist, chose a religious perspective as her primary view and means of ongoing seekership.

A Comparison of Personal Journeys

The explorative journeys of respondents were seen to take one of two paths to reach Buddhism. The first, with the exception of one who spent time in rehabilitation, moved from Christianity straight into a form of Buddhism, albeit that most of these individuals explored at least one other form of Buddhism before settling into a pattern of study and practice with either BMIMC or VI. The second route was from Christianity through various forms of alternative spirituality into Buddhism. In both cases, prior exploration of other areas of Buddhism included some well-known traditions and organizations, and some well-known teachers. Exploration also included crossing the Theravada–Mahayana divide. Explorative histories and decisions did not indicate a direct link between any one's original Christian denomination and the forms of Buddhism explored and eventually adopted. Choices of groups and practices were determined by access to other groups through prior knowledge and contacts. One obvious difference between the two paths is the stance taken toward authority. Many forms of the self-growth movement and alternative spirituality have been labelled self-religions by Heelas because of their apparent reliance on inner guidance rather than on external religious authority.[23] Similarly, Sutcliffe and Bowman define the common feature of alternative spirituality in comparison with official religion to be a preference for the ideals of self-determination and -agency over institutional membership and ideological boundary.[24] Conversely, those who take the first route may be expressing a preference for a clearly defined authority-structure and a textual basis for study and practice.

It is conceivable that the needs for defined authority and textual foundation are recognized by the seekers of both routes. They are offered by both forms of Buddhism in the form of refuge in the Buddha, dharma and sangha. According to Sharf, historical and ethnographic evidence places the privileging of experience with certain Twentieth-Century Asian reform movements, and especially those urging a return to Zazen or Vipassana. While he does not dispute the possible experience of altered states, he suggests instead that such discourse functions ideologically and performatively 'in the interests of legitimation and institutional authority'.[25] This can be seen to operate within the FPMT and VI, where the emphasis appears to be on motivation and faith rather than on meditative prowess.

An overview of the experimental affiliations of vipassana and Vajrayana practitioners highlights some difference in preference between the two categories of practitioner. Before their vipassana exploration they tended towards the Eastern meditative techniques such as Transcendental Meditation, Yoga and Tai Chi. Experience before Vajrayana tended rather towards self-growth movements and Western Esotericism. While both paths involved the exploration of ideas, vipassana practitioners had expressed more inclination towards involvement with practices facilitating the development of concentration-type techniques and experiences. The Vajrayana practitioners who showed an interest in Western Occultism or Esotericism exhibited an affinity for the kind of associational or symbolic thought that occurs in Western Esoteric belief-systems such as Astrology, Magic and Alchemy, althought as noted in Chapter 5, teaching at VI does not emphasize the conceptual aspect of knowledge but the direct experience of the deity through practice. Although it is a minor trend, it may be one way in which the passage from Western Esotericism into Vajrayana Buddhism facilitates the transition from conceptual learning to a more experiential orientation.

Ellwood maintains that membership in groups that facilitate the phenomenon of seekership, allowing people to 'try' before they commit, simply reaffirms the seekerhood status of participants without leading to radical change.[26] Western Buddhism also facilitates this experimental approach. Gaining access to information about the activities of Western Buddhist groups is easy, and therefore what is on offer is easily assessed. Buddhist centres in Sydney and its surrounds, such as BMIMC and VI, present themselves as options within the alternative religious supermarket, have the same advertising means and methods, may have their own websites, are listed on Buddhanet, in the phonebook and in the Buddhist library newsletter, and advertise using pamphlets and posters. However, it is noteworthy that the prior samplings and affiliations of individuals who chose a prolonged exploration of Buddhism as described above were largely limited to one or two, without the continual movement between and simultaneous or serial involvement in related groups that seems characteristic of some practitioners of alternative spirituality.[27] This may be a matter of the temperament of those concerned. It must be remembered that the phenomenon of seekerhood itself is not native to Buddhist thought, and both Centres promote the view that mental transformation does not result from casual or infrequent effort.

Other characteristics of the nature of seekership as it is manifest in these Buddhist settings are worthy of mention. The substance of practitioners' reasons for the choices they make in terms of experimental participation and later commitment shows that they do not blindly accept the truth-claims of organizations and their authorities. However, many demonstrated their willingness to accept the authority of the dharma, almost in contradiction to the current of alternative self-religion, which places the source of authority within the individual, and values 'lived experience' above 'dogma'.[28] One final quality is indicated by Sutcliffe's contrast between two views of the seeker: Lofland and Stark's emphasis on the seeker's difficulties and discontent, and Straus's focus on the seeker as active creator of life-change.[29] The project for these practitioners is to be willing to explore, to be shown and to be guided, *without* becoming enmeshed in religiously authoritative and hierarchical structures before they are sure that what is on offer is both efficacious and ethically satisfactory.

The Acquisition of the Meaning-System: The Role of Doctrine, Practice and Experience

The manner of doctrinal instruction and acquisition

Both Centres recognize a textual source as their basis of religious authority: the writings of Mahasi Sayadaw and the Satipatthana Sutta from the MajjhimaNikaya at BMIMC, and the writings of Lama Tsong-kha-pa in the FPMT. At each Centre participants are exposed to a consistent perspective transmitted through oral and written instruction, and practitioners aim to understand and accept it. People are free to choose what they accept, initially and for some time to come, as illustrated by the small number of respondents from Vajrayana Institute who demonstrated a resistance to the teaching of rebirth in the apprehension stage. However, as demonstrated in Chapter 4, once the doctrine of rebirth is understood in relation to others, for instance the nature of samsara and the path to nirvana, practitioners are more willing to accept it as part of their valid stock of knowledge. When the interrelationships between aspects of doctrine become apparent, practitioners are more willing to accept doctrinal positions incapable of direct experiential validation on the strength of their relation to another that they believe to be true.

The most significant difference between BMIMC and Vajrayana Institute is in their style of instruction. BMIMC, operating primarily as a vipassana meditation Centre, teaches predominantly one practice and its doctrinal foundations in a retreat setting, and engenders a practical and experiential emphasis to learning. Buddhist concepts and frameworks are used to interpret immediate experience accessed in vipassana practice. The frameworks themselves are learned through attending dhamma-talks given on retreats, participating in private and group student–teacher interviews, attending other courses, and private study and reading. The style of instruction at BMIMC facilitates the practitioners' engagement with their immediate subjective field of experience: bodily and sensory impressions, feelings and mental states, all doctrinally framed by the four satipatthanas. Here the function of doctrine is to attribute frameworks of meaning to experience. The consistency of approach among vipassana teachers was evident despite individual differences in the explanation and demonstration of the fundamental principles of observing one's experience. All meditation instruction had the aim of keeping students engaged as much as possible with their immediate experience, and of teaching them how to observe their own experiences.

Conversely, VI facilitates a range of teaching formats which students are free to choose from, and learning occurs largely as a result of attending teachings and engaging in social discourse. Teachings appeared to be more effective in socialization than either the ritual performances or meditation sessions. While the purposes of the practices are explained in some teachings, it is held that students' understanding of their purpose and symbolic significance will ripen with experience. Although the division of VI's teachings into Western- and traditional-style creates a somewhat artificial distinction, interview material indicated that students benefitted initially by executing a strategic approach to their attendance. Several differences between them, namely the level of teacher–student interaction, the inclusion of meditation to illustrate principles in Western teachings, and the seeming amount of assumed prior knowledge required in some traditional teachings, make the Western teachings appear more accessible initially. Traditional teachings often consist of commentary on a root text and amplification of specific topics or points of doctrine. The Western teachings appear to progress more slowly, give more detailed definitions of concepts, draw illustrations and examples from daily life and involve more interpersonal interaction. After acquiring some familiarization with doctrine, students' knowledge and appreciation of its consistency as an integrated meaning-system is consolidated through attending several courses of each type over a period of time, usually one or two years.

The topics that initially engaged participants were those both fundamental to the Buddhist perspective and common in everyday experience: the nature of mind, suffering, attachment and the three poisons, especially anger. Vipassana practitioners typically engage initially on hearing a teaching on one of the topics outlined above, or on attending a vipassana retreat and responding to the quality of instruction given by the teacher, which give the new student an appreciation of the combination of ethics, meditation and wisdom supporting the Buddhist framework. With the development of some mindfulness, practitioners begin to identify, distinguish and direct their mental states. Vajrayana students typically respond to teachings on thought transformation, anger and the nature of mind, or to practices such as exchanging self-for-others, which reflect their everyday experiential and behavioural concerns in relating to the wider world in an ethically viable manner. Motivated by this initial response, students attend other teachings and begin to acquire more conceptual and experiential understanding of the Buddhist perspective of the FPMT. Study, reflection, meditation and testing of the ideas in everyday life allow students to evaluate the validity of teachings and practices. With time, students begin to accept the concepts and their interrelationships as a frame of reference for their own thought and behaviour. This needs an understanding of some core ideas: karma and reincarnation, the mindstream and its purification and the bodhisattva path and its Three Principals and six perfections. While VI's teaching curriculum covers an extensive range, those having a profound effect on the individual are the aspects of doctrine that encapsulate one's innate desire for mental transformation within a frame of reference with a more altruistic outlook. These are typically to do with the bodhisattva motivation and the development of bodhicitta. More-abstract topics are investigated either after refuge has been taken or after one has a sufficient grounding in the basics to have already acquired a frame of reference for the information. This orientation is also aided by the student's appreciation of the effects of meditation practice.

Most-influential doctrines

Hearkening back to the characteristics of Western Buddhism outlined in Chapter 1, it can be seen that the doctrinal, practical and experiential focus identified by American researchers in the field holds for the affiliates of both BMIMC and VI. American scholars note that Western Buddhism draws upon the common foundations of all Buddhist schools: the Four Noble Truths and the Noble Eight-Fold Path and the meditative practices of mindfulness, concentration and lovingkindness.[30] In my view, the most influential doctrinal outlook appeared to be the Noble Eight-Fold Path in its three-fold aspects of wisdom, ethical thought and practice, and meditation. In the Gelugpa system of the FPMT, these aspects are called the three higher trainings.[31] They are rarely referred to directly in teachings at VI, but their function is seen through their place as three of the six perfections of the bodhisattva.[32] The doctrine with equivalent import, and one that is continually referred to in teachings, is The Three Principals of the Path: renunciation, bodhicitta and wisdom-realizing emptiness. However, the three aspects: meditation, ethics and wisdom, as they are encountered by novices provide an initial orientation to the aims and practices of Buddhism.

When individuals are new to either Centre they encounter a belief system in which meditation has a clearly defined purpose: the experiential understanding of wisdom as it is defined by doctrine. In all forms of Buddhism, commitment to ethical thought and behaviour is central.[33] Novices begin to learn about Buddhist ethics as a foundation for the practice and as an aid to developing wisdom. People's interest in Buddhism may have a meditative focus at first, but this appreciation grows to include all three aspects. The meditation techniques specific to the particular Buddhist orientation can be seen as a method for applying doctrinal principles to transformation. Central to one's engagement with Buddhism of both forms is the way in which one develops an appreciation for sila, ethics. Practices that encourage feelings of compassion and lovingkindness are appreciated for the values they embody and the effects they produce. Practitioners find that, in time, their habitual responses toward others change. They experience less reactiveness, behave less judgementally towards others and have more patience with themselves and others, not out of patronage or tolerance but from a recognition of the commonality of human experience. Ethical practice comes to be valued more and more by the practitioners as a foundation for engagement with others through the practice of compassion, attention to right speech and action, devotion to the development of equanimity, and particularly for Vajrayana practitioners, through fostering the bodhisattva motivation.

Ethical practices are completely integrated with other practical techniques aimed at attaining enlightenment, in the views of both Centres, and many Westerners find the Buddhist combination of ethics and meditation appealing, coming to value the meditation–ethics relationship as a strategy for living.[34] The respect for an ethically motivated life and the desire for an ethically grounded framework for thought and behaviour appears to have been engendered by practitioners' Christian upbringing, and continues to provide an orientation to the world and a rationale for putting personal beliefs and values into practice. Many agreed with the ethical sentiments of Christianity, but remembered having a negative reaction when those around them espoused moral values they did not practise. Many felt that Christianity did not provide a method for ethical practice, in contrast to Buddhism, where the practice of ethics is inextricably bound to the practice of meditation and the development of insight.

For the vipassana practitioners there is a difference between the way the three aspects work when someone first begins to explore Buddhism and the way they begin to function when understood from the doctrinal perspective. The relationship between wisdom, ethics and concentration, in terms of wisdom produced by insight, ethics as the foundation for the practice, and concentration as an aid to the effectiveness of these remains central to the practice indefinitely. For the committed practitioners of both Centres, meditation and ethics work together to give a morally viable, practical and satisfying means of engaging with the world. The doctrine of the Three Marks of Existence is found to orient participants in the practice conceptually and experientially. Impermanence and suffering are easily conceptually grasped and, for the vipassana practitioners, experientially accessible. However, realization in meditation of the emptiness of self, anatta for vipassana practitioners and sunyata for Vajrayana practitioners (see below in *The Self and Its Transformations*), is understood to require persistence in the practice. The attempt to integrate a conceptual understanding of this doctrine into everyday life takes practitioners beyond attachment to the self towards a more Buddhist understanding of self as a construct.

The doctrine of the Four Noble Truths serves as a guide for thought and contemplation until some of its import and conceptual significance as a reality-view begins to be understood by evaluation against experience. Generally, this evaluation occurs through growing appreciation of the samsaric world as characterized by the three marks of existence, and a growing appreciation of the way wisdom, ethics and meditation orient one to the practice as discussed above.

Practice and the role of the experiential

While participants' initial motivations for religious experimentation *may* have embodied a desire for the experiential in terms of experiencing 'that elusive altered state', or for self-growth devoid of any deep religious conviction, they go on to develop an appreciation and respect for the more religious elements of the Buddhist worldview through experimental participation. Individual appreciation of practice is almost solely meditation-based initially, and any appreciation of the exterior ritual elements tends to develop after one has some feel for the relationship between doctrine and practice. At BMIMC this ritual consists of taking refuge and precepts on retreats, whereas VI maintains a much richer ritualistic focus, comprising prayer and sutra recitation, pujas of various types—guru, deity, healing—the refuge ceremony and tantric initiation. Still, for the practitioners with whom I was most involved, a feeling for this ritual took some time to develop, and more immediate interest was for the meditations encountered in teachings.

For both types of practitioner, practice-periods range from half-an-hour upwards, with some vipassana practitioners spending longer than an hour a day on practice. Many of these incorporate metta and related techniques into their routine. Vajrayana practitioners almost invariably practise concentration, and usually in the form of deity visualization. Those who have refuge commitments and tantric commitments beyond that attempt to keep them as much as possible. Both types of practitioner spoke of the practice inside and outside of the formal meditation, referring to the fact that opportunities arise in daily life for practice in terms of being aware of one's attitudes and mental states. Because of the focus on bare attention to one's experience fostered by vipassana practice, practitioners had created their own experientially structured approach to everyday practice.[35] Certain everyday events consisting of routine and repetitive actions were used as mindfulness practices, and the monitoring of one's responses often led to instant metta practice. By contrast, Vajrayana practitioners responded to similar emotional situations by being aware of their own responses, and bringing to mind principles held to be applicable to the situation, for instance reminding themselves that there is 'no essential self to protect from insult'.

For both types of practitioner, the intended outcome of practice is two-fold. The traditional textual sources and doctrinal and practical instruction at

BMIMC and VI advise that the goal of Theravadin vipassana meditation practice is nibbana, and the goal of practice from the Mahayana view is the realization of the inherent emptiness of all phenomena, respectively. Some respondents stated this as their goal explicitly and some did not. The second is the enhancement of quality of life in this life, in samsara, on mental, emotional and physical levels. While Western Buddhists may appear to focus on the latter goal at the expense of the former, practitioners' own accounts suggest that the two are mutually reinforcing in their capacity to provide a strong and sustainable motivation for practice. Observation of improvement in the quality of mental and emotional life validates for practitioners the efficacy and worth of the teachings and practices, and in turn, reinforces their faith in the worldview of their organization. Both perspectives, the vipassana and the Vajrayana, emphasize the practice of mental purification for the production of wholesome mental states. While the relationship between meditative experience and the personal transformation it produces is heavily implicated in practitioners' decisions to commit to the Buddhist path, I must stress that for respondents, commitment is the beginning of the path to enlightenment rather than the end-point of experimentation.

It is difficult to state with certainty whether practitioners' enthusiasm for personal transformation and the techniques utilized to achieve it overshadow considerations of longer-term goals. While the two goals appear related for practitioners, variations may exist among individuals as to the relative importance of each. Some practices could be seen to be efficacious in that their effects could be felt within a reasonable time from immediately to several days or months. Others were valued for other reasons. For instance, practitioners expected that some effects of practice, such as attaining nibbana or realizing sunyata, would become evident in the long term, and accordingly, did not see these as realistic short-term attainments. Instead they viewed them as worthwhile ambitions because of the orientation these postulated attainments maintained toward ongoing commitment. It is this combination of efficacy and sentiment that can be viewed as a significant driving force in the lives of these practitioners. These sentiments themselves reflect the way in which the Buddhist principles relate to one's own values. In this sense, one's values are articulated by Buddhist doctrine, and given practical expression through its meditation and ritual techniques as much as they are shaped by it.

The Commitment Process

For both types of practitioner the commitment process begins with a period of intensifying involvement, from months to years, with the principles and practices. It is marked by a series of events or decision-points, as opposed to one turning point. Self-transformation is observed to be more-or-less incremental during the period. There were no reports of sudden, dramatic change in self-concept or identity, but rather an awareness that a more subtle type of change had occurred to habitual mental and emotional states. The experience of both types of practitioner demonstrated a strong relationship between recognition that self-transformation had occurred—that one had already accepted the Buddhist outlook to some degree—and that one was either committed to it or wished to commit because of it. The realization or decision itself is a conscious product of reflection on principles and the results of practice. While these responses vary in intensity, the experiences related by respondents, with a few notable exceptions, have the quality of quiet illumination as opposed to the intense emotion that is traditionally held to accompany conversions. Individual variations occur in terms of duration, intensity, and in the particular doctrinal meanings and practices involved in individual commitment processes, but virtually all respondents described their process as gradual and cumulative, with the majority seeing it as marked by two or three points of change.

Some of these points have the quality expressed by Stromberg's notion of impression point in their almost instantaneous perception of self, symbol and commitment. However, others instead are better described by Pilarzyk's notion of shock experiences.[36] Pilarzyk refers to emotionally-charged experiences possessing intrinsic spiritual or existential significance for the convert quite separate from group constraints. To him, they are natural products of movement between logically contradictory meaning-systems that, as Berger notes, are radical attempts to reorganize everyday life. However, in antithesis to Berger's emphasis of the individual's need for a cognitive redefinition of reality in order to justify a new worldview,[37] the more striking experiences reported by respondents suggest that these shock experiences provide impetus for meaning-seeking activity and change as opposed to justification of change that has already occurred. The three experiences that fit this description, the experience of no-self and the two that I designate as pre-tantric experience, all occurred before the respondents' contact with the Buddhist framework of ideas that best explains them. In all three cases this explanatory framework, when it is comprehended, provides the necessary plausibility-structure for the individual's self-understanding and change. VI can be seen to provide the required plausibility-structure for the tantric-like experiences of NJ and MM, and similarly, the Theravadin worldview of vipassana meditation for RL's spontaneous experience of no-self.

It must be stressed that while individual experiences vary according to the preponderance of intellectual or experiential quality, the majority are described as being predominantly intellectual or cognitive in character. Some individuals responded to visual images and cultural symbolism they encountered, but they did not have the shock-quality of those outlined above. Early experiences in both vipassana and Vajrayana settings consisted of strong responses to the content of a teaching or a meditation that appealed to intellect and feeling.

Numerous descriptions above illustrate the way in which these responses lead to mental and emotional receptivity to more of the surrounding framework of ideas, a receptivity that leads to the later acceptance of Buddhism.[38]

Distinguishing between points that either lead to commitment or symbolize the commitment itself, and those that occur around the time of encounter with Buddhism highlights an otherwise hidden aspect of socialization into Western Buddhism. While these radical experiential events remain in the minority, their occurrence may be obscured by accounts of Buddhist religious change that describe its nature as a quiet transition. These events—especially the two tantric-oriented experiences, the experience of intense emotional and bodily responses that lend themselves to a tantric explanation—occurred in contexts of emotional intensity the existence of which can be interpreted as both a precipitant and an effect of the event. It is conceivable that these shock experiences seldom occur. The majority of engagement experiences consist of the strong but serene response described as 'quiet illumination' to the presentation of fundamental Buddhist ideas. In many of these cases the participant does not become aware of, nor actively problematize their question or circumstance until they hear it expressed in the framework of ideas presented in the teachings.[39] However, as asserted above, these experiences become encapsulated in a plausibility structure that contains the original rupture in taken-for-granted reality, validates the initial occurrence, and encourages practitioners' subsequent interpretation and acceptance as experientially normal for that perspective. With respect to this last, both Buddhist perspectives discourage their use as sources of attachment and pride.

The nature of self-transformation, religious identity and biography

Traditionally, studies of religious conversion have taken the notion of radical personal change and its implication of suddenness as the indicator of conversion's having occurred. Aside from the difficulty of identifying the occurrence of a complete transformation of the individual's worldview and sense-of-self, I suggest that sustained belief remains conditional on the intactness of the plausibility structure for the adherent. In addition, qualities that Pilarzyk attributes to alternation—taken to denote partial as opposed to complete adoption of a new worldview and its prescription of identity, as defined by Berger and Luckmann,[40] Travisano[41] and Pilarzyk[42]—are typical of adherents' experiences. First, there is a milder cognitive transformation than implied by *radical personal change* accompanied by gradual and easy changes in lifestyle, meaning and identity.[43] In their attempt to isolate the true convert, Snow and Machalek postulated four rhetorical indicators—four properties of speech and reasoning—of conversion status: biographical reconstruction; adoption of a master attribution scheme; suspension of analogical reasoning and embrace of a master role.[44] Biographical reconstruction involves a dismantling of the past and its reconstitution within a new religious or ideological meaning-system and its vocabulary of motives.[45] However, the radical reorganization and reinterpretation of the past that is held to occur is not expressed in the present respondents' accounts, the nature of which suggest instead that identity is partially integrated into a new set of meanings. In this sense, the more general conception of Staples and Mauss, that conversion is primarily a process of self-transformation, a change in one's self-concept,[46] is more applicable than the four rhetorical indicators proposed by Snow and Machalek. However, the change that is most identifiable for the adherents concerned beyond the personal changes that they identify is that of the shift in worldviews. Following from this, of the two forms the view of alternation is better suited than is conversion to describe the observed nature of change, although I do not find this completely satisfactory because all indications are that adherents accept Buddhism as their primary interpretive frame of reference.

Making a commitment to Buddhism either privately or by taking refuge does not prohibit the utilization of other organizing principles or frameworks in the reinterpretation of subjective reality. While reference to other organizing frameworks is not prohibited, it seems typical that once practitioners have committed Buddhism becomes their primary if not only religious involvement, although I hesitate to use Travisano's phrase 'a change to one's sense of root reality' to describe this acceptance of the Buddhist worldview.[47] For this reason, the complexities of religious identity introduced by the phenomena of serial conversion and religious pluralism raised by Bryant and Lamb[48] do not apply here. Nevertheless, rather than use criteria suggested by American scholars—such as taking refuge or the five lay vows, holding certain beliefs, meditating and chanting or having active membership in a specific organization[49]—to indicate indentity as a Buddhist, I let the adherents answer for themselves the questions 'Are you a Buddhist?' and 'Why?'

A final look at the sense-of-self and its transformations

A strong influence on practitioners' decision to commit to Buddhism was their observation of the self-transformation effected by Buddhist study and practice. Discussion in Chapters 3 and 5 outlined three views of the self from the Buddhist perspective: the absolute and relative views and the imputed *I*. The absolute view is expressed by the Theravadin concept of anatta and the Mahayana view of sunyata, emptiness. Teachers at both Centres take great care to explain this central concept as unambiguously as possible. As Cush alludes, confusion is created in the Western understanding of emptiness of self by commentators who express it as *Self* with a *capital S*.[50] In writings pertaining to Budddhist–Christian interreligious dialogue we find comparisons between Christ and the Buddha-nature as representations of the *authentic Self* (i.e. capitalized).[51] I suspect that teachers are alert to the tendency of the Western mind to think in terms of reification when practitioners hear phrases such as the authentic Self, and to infer therefrom a transcendent, essentially-existent entity. The relative view of the self as the interplay of impersonal phenomena dependent on causes and conditions is reflected in doctrinal views such as the five aggregates, the satipatthanas, and the doctrine of dependent origination both in its twelve-stage formula and more generally as a characteristic of the samsaric world. Orru and Wang note that the tension between this-worldly and other-worldly at the root of much religious thought is expressed in Buddhism's treatment of the conditioned and the unconditioned, samsara and nibbana,[52] which cannot be taken as directly equivalent to the sacred-profane dichotomy familiar to the Western mind.

The imputed *I* is the sense of personal continuity that arises from this interplay. As outlined in Chapter 5, Geshe Acharya Thubten Loden divides the imputed *I* into two: the *I* imputed onto its base of the five aggregates having conventional existence as a dependent arising, and inherently empty but arising from the superposition of inherent existence onto the first.[53] The aim of practice is to shift awareness from the sense of personal continuity to the subjective field of impersonal phenomena. The aim of insight of vipassana practice and the *special insight* of Gelugpa analytical practice is the view of the self as inherently devoid of essential existence.[54] In vipassana, with the establishment of mindfulness one observes objects within the phenomenal field in terms of their arising and ceasing. Practitioners typically report experiences of dukkha, 'suffering' and anicca, 'impermanence', and occasionally some refer to the shifting sense-of-self in meditation. The emptiness meditation, the four-point analysis of Ascertaining the Non-Existence of a Personal Self discussed in Chapters 4 and 5, consists of identifying the I as the object to be refuted, utilizing the *imputed self* as the initial meditation object.[55] In both practices, the shift in experiential understanding involves a shift of experiential location from the imputed *I* onto the impersonal phenomenal field.

The target of self-transformative practice is the imputed *I*. Both Buddhist and Western psychologies agree that the sense of personal continuity, the self we take to be 'me' constructed out of our experience of objects and the interactions we have with them, is an internalized image or concept.[56] A variety of terms has been used to denote facets of, or ideas related to this self-concept, for instance James' notion of *me-the-known*,[57] the sociological concept of self,[58] and Berger and Luckmann's concept of identity as objective location in the world.[59] I have conceived self-transformation generated in meditation as reflexive movement between the objectified self-concept and the functional, processual sense-of-self[60] which James calls *I-the-knower*. Changes in the way practitioners wish to see themselves, for instance as calm, patient, accepting and compassionate, are authenticated by changes to their habitual mental and emotional functioning that are at once objectified and owned by the individual as they are integrated into the self-concept. Engler has expressed the difference between the concerns of Western psychotherapy and Buddhism as 'regrowing the self versus dis-identifying from a self-structure'. With the former the concern is for a self-image that is functional in terms of the world's expectations, while the latter's concern is to deconstruct this very self-image but not to eliminate it. As Engler expresses it, self is a pre-condition of no-self.[61]

A *last word*

One final point about the nature of this sense-of-self in transformation is worthy of mention. The kinds of changes that individuals willingly undergo reflect something of the values that are important to them. The point has been made about the appeal of Buddhist practice in both efficacy and value. One of the values held by practitioners to emerge consistently throughout discussion is their concern for living an ethical life. Keown sees Buddhism as a response to an ethical problem, viz. about the best kind of life for humanity to lead,[62] and practitioners adopt Buddhism as an answer to that problem. However, in considering that an ethical motivation seems to support one's desire for self-transformation there arises the problem of how a Western Buddhist fulfils the urge for personal growth within a religious culture that advocates renunciation. As highlighted above, Buddhism has appeal to Westerners through the combination of meditation and ethics that it supports. Western Buddhism, through its focus on self-growth alongside the development of compassion and the view of not-self can be seen as both a furtherance of individualistic humanism[63] and a reaction against the excesses of that view.

Appendices

Appendix 1: Interview-Respondents

At the Blue Mountains Insight Meditation Centre

Respondent	Sex	Age	Occupation	Interviewed on
BM	M	early 30s		30.05.2003
KT	F	38	Architect	30.05.2003
KN	F	37	Office Assistant	01.06.2003
HR	F	early 50s	Academic	01.07.2003
HD	F	early 50s	Dentist	04.08.2003
DN	M	late 50s	Psychologist	19.08.2003
RN	F	mid 50s	TAFE Teacher	19.08.2003
KBN	M	early 60s	Academic	05.09.2003
SI	F	58	Housewife	16.09.2003
LP	F	45	Psychologist	13.11.2003
KBT	M	late 30s	Geologist	13.11.2003
EJ	F	early 50s	Public Servant	16.11.2003
MV	M	early 40s	Artist	31.01.2004
EBS	M	47	Psychologist	15.07.2004
FV	F	40s		09.08.2004
KM	F	early 50s	Aged-Care Worker	13.08.2004
RL	M	mid 50s	Dhamma Teacher	18.08.2004
EC	F	53	Administrative Officer	17.11.2004
JD	M	late 50s	Biologist	25.11.2004
HU	M	50	Solicitor	30.11.2004

At Vajrayana Institute

Respondent	Sex	Age	Occupation	Interviewed on
NJ	F	early 30s		15.01.2004
CR	F	50	Business Manager	03.03.2004
AN	M	26	Administrative Officer	08.03.2004
MM	F	early 50s	TAFE Teacher	15.03.2004
RI	M	36	Archeologist	24.03.2004

(Continued)

Respondent	Sex	Age	Occupation	Interviewed on
MVR	F	early 70s	Buddhist Nun	26.03.2004
MW	F	41	Corporate Executive	19.06.2004
KI	F	48	Corporate Executive	08.08.2004
EF	F	early 60s	Accountant	14.08.2004
NM	M	30	Construction Worker	20.08.2004
MF	F	50	Carer	14.09.2004
KD	F	50	Carer	14.09.2004
ML	F	early 50s		11.11.2004
MN	F	late 50s	Buddhist Nun	22.11.2004
ER	F	50s	Psychologist	03.12.2004
WR	F	48	Business Manager	06.12.2004
NC	M	36	Gym Instructor	07.12.2004
DE	F	early 50s	Actress	08.12.2004
MC	M	40	Web Designer	14.12.2004

Appendix 2: Schedule for Beginners Weekend Meditation Workshop, 29–30 May 2004

Saturday

9.30-10.00 am	Introductory Talks
10.00-11.15 am	Awareness Exercise
11.15-11.45 am	Morning Tea
11.45-12.45 pm	Meditation
12.45-2.00 pm	Lunch and Rest
2.00-3.30 pm	Meditation/Awareness
3.30-4.00 pm	Afternoon Tea
4.00-5.30 pm	Meditation, Questions and Answers
5.30 -7.00 pm	Supper
7.00-8.00 pm	Dhamma Talk
9.00 pm	Tea
9.30 pm	Bed

Sunday

7.00-8.30 am	Meditation/Awareness
8.30-10.00 am	Breakfast and Chores
10.00-11.00 am	Awareness
11.00-12.30 pm	Meditation
12.30-2.00 pm	Lunch
2.00-3.30 pm	Meditation
3.30-4.00 pm	Questions and Answers
4.00-4.30 pm	Cleanup and Finish

Appendix 3: Schedule for Long-Weekend Retreat, 12–15 June 2004

Friday

7.45-8.00 pm	Manager's Talk
8.00-9.00 pm	Introductory Talk, Precepts and Preliminary Instruction
9.00 pm	Bed or Further Practice

Saturday

6.00-6.45 am	Wake Up and Walking
6.45-7.30 am	Sitting
7.30-8.30 am	Breakfast
8.30-9.30 am	Instruction/Precepts
9.30-10.15 am	Walking
10.15-11.00 am	Sitting
11.00-11.30 am	Walking
11.30-12.30 pm	Sitting
12.30-2.00 pm	Lunch and Rest
2.00-2.45 pm	Walking
2.45-3.30 pm	Sitting
3.30-5.30 pm	Group Interview in Interview Room
5.30-6.30 pm	Supper
6.30-7.00 pm	Walking
7.00-8.00 pm	Dhamma Talk
8.00-8.30 pm	Walking
8.30-9.15 pm	Sitting
9.15 pm	Bed or Further Practice

Sunday

6.00-6.45 am	Wake Up and Walking
6.45-7.30 am	Sitting
7.30-8.30 am	Breakfast
8.30-9.30 am	Instruction/Precepts
9.30-10.15 am	Walking
10.15-11.00 am	Sitting
11.00-11.30 am	Walking
11.30-12.30 pm	Sitting
12.30-2.00 pm	Lunch and Rest
2.00-2.45 pm	Walking
2.45-3.30 pm	Sitting
3.30-4.30 pm	Walking (Individual Interviews, 3.30 to 5.30)
4.30-5.30 pm	Sitting

(Continued)

5.30-6.30 pm	Supper
6.30-7.00 pm	Walking
7.00-8.00 pm	Dhamma Talk
8.00-8.30 pm	Walking
8.30-9.15 pm	Sitting
9.15 pm	Bed or Further Practice

Monday

6.00-6.45 am	Wake Up and Walking
6.45-7.30 am	Sitting
7.30-8.30 am	Breakfast
8.30-9.00 am	Walking
9.00-10.00 am	Sitting
10.00-10.30 am	Walking
10.30-11.30 am	Dhamma Talk and Questions
11.30-12.30 pm	Manager's Closing Talk and Cleanup
12.30 pm	Lunch and Finish

Appendix 4: Daily Schedule for 15–16 February during Four-Day Retreat, 14–17 February 2004

6.00 am	Wake
6.30 am	Posture and Flexibility Session
7.30 am	Sitting
8.30 am	Breakfast
9.30 am	Practice Talk
10.00 am	Walking
10.30 am	Sitting
11.00 am	Walking
11.30 am	Sitting
Midday	Walking
12.30 pm	Lunch and Rest
2.30 pm	Walking
3.00 pm	Sitting
3.30 pm	Walking
4.00 pm	Sitting
4.30 pm	Walking
5.00 pm	Sitting or Beginner's Mind Group
5.30 pm	Walking
6.00 pm	Supper
7.30 pm	Dhamma talk
8.30 pm	More Practice or Bed

Interviews of those who wished for them were scheduled mainly in the afternoon.

Appendix 5: Schedule for Days 3–9, 25 April– 1 May, during Nine-Day Retreat, 23 April to 2 May 2004

5.00 am	Wake Up
5.45 am	Sitting
6.30 am	Walking
7.00 am	Sitting
7.30 am	Breakfast
9.30 am	Walking
10.00 am	Talk given by the Teachers and Sitting
10.45 am	Sitting or Standing
10.55 am	A Talk
11.00 am	Walking
11.30 am	Lunch
1.30 pm	Walking
2.15 pm	Sitting or Standing
3.15 pm	Walking
4.00 pm	Sitting
4.45 pm	Sitting or Standing
5.00 pm	Walking
5.45 pm	Light Dinner
7.15 pm	Sitting
7.45 pm	Standing or Walking
8.15 pm	A Talk
afterwards	Optional Meditation or Sleep

Appendix 6: Prayers for Before and After Teachings

1 Seven-Limb Prayer

Reverently I prostrate with my body, speech and mind,
And present clouds of every type of offering, those actually performed and
  mentally transformed.
I declare all my negative actions accumulated since beginningless time
And rejoice in the merit of all holy and ordinary beings.
Please remain until samsara ends
And turn the wheel of dharma for all sentient beings.
I dedicate the merit created by myself and others to the great enlightenment.

2 Outer Mandala

This ground, anointed with perfume, strewn with flowers,
Adorned with Mount Meru, four continents, the sun and the moon.
I imagine this as a buddha-field and offer it.
May all living beings enjoy this pure land.

3 Mandala Offering (Inner Mandala)

The objects of my attachment, aversion and ignorance—friends, enemies
  and strangers
And my body, wealth and enjoyments;
Without any sense of loss I offer this collection.
Please accept it with pleasure and bless me with freedom from the three
  poisons.

4 Refuge and Bodhicitta Prayer

I go for Refuge until I am enlightened
To the Buddha, the Dharma, and the Supreme Assembly
By the merit I create by listening to the Dharma,
May I become a Buddha to benefit all sentient beings.

5 Dedication of Merit

Through this virtuous action
May I quickly attain the state of a guru-buddha
And lead every living being without exception,
Into that pure land.

6 Bodhicitta Prayer

May the supreme jewel bodhicitta
That has not arisen, arise and grow;
And may that which has arisen not diminish
But increase more and more.

7 Long Life Prayer for His Holiness

In the land encircled by snow mountains
You are the source of all hapiness and good;
All-powerful Chenrezig, Tenzin Gyatso,
Please remain until samsara ends.

Appendix 7: Refuge Teachings, 19 June 2005

Going for Refuge

Refuge is the door by which we enter the Buddhist teachings. It is important to
know from the beginning what Refuge is. The process of taking Refuge is common to all spiritual traditions. However, the way in which you go for Refuge,
and the objects of Refuge are different. In other traditions, the Refuge objects

are external to ourselves, separate from us, and different from our own mental continuum, for example, a creator god. The Buddhist object of Refuge is not separate from our own mindstream. How is the way of going for Refuge different from other traditions? They have causes of fear, faith, belief, but only this faith is not enough to serve as the protection. Where there is no understanding of the causes, there is no protection. We must understand the causes for protection. The causes are fear and conviction or belief. The first, fear, is fear of suffering, samsara and lower rebirth. The second, conviction, is the conviction that the objects of Refuge can protect us from suffering and lower rebirth. The quality of Refuge depends on how well we understand the causes.

We can have different types of Refuge in our minds dependent on causes. An example of such a cause is the fear of suffering. Then this is a lower scope Refuge, the belief that the triple gem can protect us. The cause of fear of all suffering is a middle scope Refuge. The cause of fear of suffering of samsara, and abiding in nirvana for peace for oneself, then this is a large scope Refuge. If you change the cause, then you will change the result. In order to understand Refuge, you must understand the causes; you must also understand the objects. The Buddha is one who eliminated all faults, and achieved all good qualities. A reference is 'Compendium of Valid Cognition'. In this, Dharmakirti says that the Buddha is a being who is enlightened, who understands all phenomena. The point of transforming, through practice enlightenment and omniscience came about. Transformation comes about through great compassion, emptiness through this, eliminating all faults and cultivating good qualities. Dharmakirti says, 'to this being I prostrate'.

This marks Buddhism out as distinct. The Buddha started out like us, but was transformed. In other traditions the object of Refuge is a god who was always a god, who has not passed through a transformation. This enlightened being teaches the Refuge. The actual Refuge is the Dharma, the truth of cessation, the truth of the path. When realizations of this are generated in the mind, these act as our Refuge. The Refuge is the generation of these realizations in our own mind. The dharma is the real Refuge. The Sangha are friends, helpers, but not the actual Refuge. The Arya beings have direct realizations of the path in their own mindstream. Knowing what these objects are is important; recognizing the way they provide the causal and the resultant Refuge. The causal Refuge is the three jewels in the mindstream of someone external to us, not the actual Refuge. For example, the causal Buddha is the Buddha himself. The actual Buddha Refuge, the Buddha we will become, is the resultant Refuge. When we say 'I go for Refuge to the Buddha', we mean by generating the Buddha in our mindstream, we take Refuge in this. By going for Refuge in the dharma, we mean we will achieve those realizations. By going for Refuge in the Sangha, I am saying I will become that Arya being myself.

When we generate the Buddha in our mindstream, then we will have achieved a state of protection from all suffering and achievement of nirvana only for ourselves. By saying that we have this Buddha potential or buddha-nature in our mindstream, this mind has this clear light nature; delusions and obstructions are pollutants that can be removed. The reason that we can know that delusions and faults are not inherent is if they were, they would always be there, and we can see their arising and ceasing. Because they are not truly existent within the mind, then it is possible to remove or purify them; there is a more fundamental nature of the mind.

Normally, we would discuss other sections of the Refuge teaching such as why the objects are worthy, and things in more detail, but there is no time today. I will give advice that comes with taking Refuge; great benefit comes from taking the advice.

First, this is what not to do, to abandon.

1. After having taken Refuge in the Buddha, take no refuge in other gods. If we believe that other gods can stop suffering, it weakens the reason for [taking] Refuge [i.e. to stop suffering]. Our conviction that the three jewels can protect us from the causes of suffering is also weakened.
2. Having taken Refuge in the dharma, then we should abandon harming all sentient beings. We should abandon the ten non-virtuous actions; abandoning in body, speech, and mind.
3. Having taken Refuge in the Sangha, we should abandon the company of negative friends, and give up non-Buddhist practices.

This is what to do, what to cultivate.

1. Treat all images of the Buddha as the actual Buddha. Treat them with respect, make offerings to them. This increases our own merit.
2. With respect to the Dharma, treat scriptures, even one word, like the actual Dharma. Lama Tsong Khapa said every word of teaching is a way to lead every sentient being to a realization of Dependent Arising, and lead them to enlightenment.
3. With respect to the Sangha, see all ordained people as Arya beings. This will increase our merit.

This is general advice that refers to all of the jewels.

1. Go for Refuge, then you should remember the good qualities of the jewels. Remember the difference between Buddhist and non-Buddhist objects of Refuge.
2. Remember the great kindness of the three jewels. Make offerings; whatever action we do, if we make offerings, we increase merit.

3. Remember the positive qualities of leading others to take Refuge; we stop others from performing negative actions.
4. In the morning and evening, recite the Refuge prayer three times, 'I go for Refuge until I am enlightened'. This contains both the Refuge and bodhicitta prayer.
5. No matter what, do not give up Refuge.
6. Whatever we do, make it a positive action. When we do it, rely on the three jewels. In doing this, it removes obstacles and becomes a virtuous action.

There are eight benefits of having remembered the good qualities.

1. We become a Buddhist.
2. We become a suitable base for future commitments and vows.
3. Our Refuge becomes the cause to purify negativities.
4. You are able to increase merit.
5. Humans and non-humans have no power to harm you. Taking Refuge puts a stop to others generating harmful thoughts toward us. Follow the path of non-harm shortcircuits others.
6. Refuge prevent the causes for being born in the lower realms.
7. Refuge creates the causes for us to be born as humans or gods (abandoning the ten non-virtuous actions can be a cause for 6 or 7).
8. It is easy to achieve temporary and ultimate goals, a better rebirth as in 7, and the ultimate goal of enlightenment respectively.

Appendix 8: Medicine-Buddha Practice Day, 28 May 2005

First Session

Mahayana Precepts and Prayers
Practice: Medicine Buddha Sadhana

Second Session

Prostrations to the thirty-five Buddhas
Medicine Buddha Sadhana

Third Session

Prostrations to the thirty-five Buddhas
Medicine Buddha Sadhana

Fourth Session

Medicine Buddha Sadhana: concentrating more on the visualization

After Lunch

Medicine Buddha Puja: making offerings to the Medicine Buddha

Notes

Chapter 1

1 P. Croucher. (1989), *Buddhism in Australia 1848–1988*. Sydney: New South Wales University Press.

2 E. Adam and P. J. Hughes. (1996), in K. Waters (ed), *The Buddhists in Australia*. Canberra: Australian Government Publishing Service.

3 P. Sherwood. (2003), *The Buddha Is in the Street: Engaged Buddhism in Australia*. Bunbury: Edith Cowan University.

4 M. Spuler. (2000), 'Characteristics of Buddhism in Australia', *Journal of Contemporary Religion* 15 (1), 29.

5 See A. Schutz. (1967), G. Walsh and F. Lehnert (trans.), *The Phenomenology of the Social World*. Evanston: Northwestern University Press, p. 74. This term is used by Schutz to mean the level of experience 'not in need of further analysis'. Also see D. Preston. (1988), *The Social Organization of Zen Practice: Constructing Transcultural Reality*. Cambridge: Cambridge University Press, pp. 65–66.

6 T. Tweed. (2011), 'Theory and Method in the Study of Buddhism: Toward "Translocative" Analysis', *Journal of Global Buddhism* 12, 17–32.

7 M. Baumann. (1997), 'Culture Contact and Valuation: Early German Buddhists and the "Creation of a Buddhism in Protestant Shape"', *Numen* 44 (3), 270–95.

8 H. Waterhouse. (1997) *Buddhism in Bath: Adaptation and Authority*. Monograph Series: Community Religions Project. Leeds: Department of Theology and Religious Studies, University of Leeds.

9 S. Bell. (1998), 'British Theravada Buddhism: Otherworldly Theories, and the Theory of Exchange', *Journal of Contemporary Religion* 13 (2), 149–70; S. Bell. (2000), 'Being Creative with Tradition: Rooting Theravada Buddhism in Britain', *Journal of Global Buddhism* 1, 1–23.

10 D. Kay. (2004), *Tibetan and Zen Buddhism in Britain: Transplantation, Development and Adaptation*. London and New York: Routledge Curzon.

11 Kay, *Tibetan and Zen Buddhism in Britain:* p. 37; C. Rocha. (2006), *Zen in Brazil: The Quest for Cosmopolitan Modernity*. Honolulu: University of Hawai'i Press, p. 192.

12 R. Sharf. (1995), 'Buddhist Modernism and the Rhetoric of Meditative Experience', *Numen* 42, 228.

13 J. W. Coleman. (1999), 'The New Buddhism: Some Empirical Findings', in D. R. Williams and C. S. Queen (eds), *American Buddhism*. Richmond: Curzon Press, p. 92; E. M. Layman. *Buddhism in America*. Nelson-Hall, p. xvi; P. D. Numrich.

(2000), 'How the Swans Came to Lake Michigan: The Social Organization of Buddhist Chicago', *Journal for the Scientific Study of Religion* 39 (2), 195; C. S. Prebish. (1998), 'Introduction', in C. S. Prebish and K. Tanaka (eds), *The Faces of Buddhism in America*. Berkely, Los Angeles and London: University of California Press, p. 1; A. Rawlinson. (1997), *The Book of Enlightened Masters: Western Teachers in Eastern Traditions*. Chicago and La Salle: Open Court Publishing, p. 13.

[14] E. Conze. (1980), *A Short History of Buddhism*. London: George Allen and Unwin, p. 131; Prebish, 'Introduction', in *The Faces of Buddhism in America*, p. 1; Coleman, 'The New Buddhism: Some Empirical Findings', p. 98; C. Rocha. *Zen in Brazil*, p. 153.

[15] Rocha, *Zen in Brazil*, pp. 153, 192.

[16] Coleman, 'The New Buddhism: Some Empirical Findings', p. 92.

[17] G. Fronsdal. (1998), 'Insight Meditation in the United States: Life, Liberty, and the Pursuit of Happiness', in C. S. Prebish and K. Tanaka (eds), *The Faces of Buddhism in America*. Berkeley, Los Angeles and London: University of California Press, p. 176; Rawlinson, *The Book of Enlightened Masters*; Coleman, 'The New Buddhism', pp. 97–8.

[18] Fronsdal, 'Insight Meditation in the United States', p. 176.

[19] Coleman, 'The New Buddhism: Some Empirical Findings', pp. 96–8.

[20] See Layman, *Buddhism in America*, p. 275.

[21] Coleman, 'The New Buddhism: Some Empirical Findings', p. 91; Numrich, 'How the Swans Came to Lake Michigan', 194–95; Prebish, 'Introduction', p. 1. Also see Sherwood, *The Buddha Is in the Street*, p. 29.

[22] M. Baumann. (2002), 'Protective Amulets and Awareness Techniques, or How to Make Sense of Buddhism in the West', in C. S. Prebish and M. Baumann (eds), *Westward Dharma: Buddhism Beyond Asia*. Berkeley, Los Angeles, London: University of California Press, p. 53; Rocha, *Zen in Brazil*, pp. 153–54.

[23] W. Cadge. (2005), *Heartwood: The First Generation of Theravada Buddhism in America*. Chicago and London: University of Chicago Press, p. 157.

[24] See M. D. Bryant and C. Lamb. (1999), 'Introduction: Conversion: Contours of Controversy and Commitment in a Plural World', in C. Lamb and M. D. Bryant (eds), *Religious Conversion: Contemporary Practices and Controversies*. London and New York: Cassell, pp. 9–11.

[25] See Layman, *Buddhism in America*, p. xiv; J. Nattier. (1998), 'Who is a Buddhist? Charting the Landscape of Buddhist America', in C. S. Prebish and K. Tanaka (eds), *The Faces of Buddhism in America*. Berkely, Los Angeles and London: University of California Press, p. 185; T. Tweed. (1999), 'Night-Stand Buddhists and Other Creatures: Sympathizers, Adherents, and the Study of Religion', in D. R. Williams and C. S. Queen (eds), *American Buddhism*. Richmond: Curzon Press, pp. 71–2, 74–5.

[26] Nattier, 'Who is a Buddhist? Charting the Landscape of Buddhist America', pp. 183–95.

[27] Prebish, 'Introduction', in *The Faces of Buddhism in America*, pp. 1–10; Numrich, 'How the Swans Came to Lake Michigan', 195; Tweed. 'Night-Stand Buddhists and Other Creatures', p. 75.

[28] P. L. Berger. (1974), 'Some Second Thoughts on Substantive Versus Functional Definitions of Religion', *Journal for the Scientific Study of Religion* 13 (2), 125.

29 J. W. Coleman. (2001), *The New Buddhism: The Western Transformation of an Ancient Tradition*. New York: Oxford University Press, p. 97.

30 Fronsdal, 'Insight Meditation in the United States: Life, Liberty, and the Pursuit of Happiness', p. 172. In this chapter Fronsdal discusses both vipassana meditation and Western psychotherapy as strands of western individualism that focus on personal experience and change.

31 H. Urban. (2003), *Tantra: Sex, Secrecy, Politics, and Power in the Study of Religion*. Berkeley: University of California Press.

32 D. Lyon. (2000), *Jesus in Disneyland: Religion in Postmodern Times*. Cambridge: Polity Press, pp. 76–7.

33 P. Heelas. (1996), *The New Age Movement: The Celebration of the Self and the Sacralization of Modernity*. Oxford and Cambridge, MA: Blackwell Publishers.

34 H. A. Berger. (1999), *A Community of Witches: Contemporary Neo-Paganism and Witchcraft in the United States*. Columbia: University of South Carolina Press, p. 8; S. Pike. (2001), *Earthly Bodies, Magical Selves: Contemporary Pagans and the Search for Community*. Berkeley, Los Angeles and London: University of California Press, p. 221.

35 This was largely by use of Buddhanet, at www.buddhanet.net.

36 See Coleman, 'The New Buddhism: Some Empirical Findings', p. 92.

37 Rigpa is an international network of meditation centres under the guidance of Sogyal Rinpoche. Its website for the Sydney centre is at www.rigpa.com.au/sydney.htm.

38 The Sydney Buddhist Centre in Newtown, Sydney, is the Sydney centre for the FWBO. Its website at www.sydneybuddhistcentre.org.au states that the FWBO draws upon the entire Buddhist tradition.

39 Rawlinson, *The Book of Enlightened Masters*, pp. 98–9.

40 Rawlinson, *The Book of Enlightened Masters*, p. 103. See diagram 4: The Different Kinds of Buddhism.

41 Rawlinson, *The Book of Enlightened Masters*, p. 100.

42 Mahasi Sayadaw (1971), U Pe Thin and Myanaung U Tin (trans.), *Practical Insight Meditation: Basic and Progressive Stages*. Kandy: Buddhist Publication Society, pp. 20–38. Also see chapter 3 in this work, *Mahasi's Thirteen Stages of Insight Knowledge*.

43 Tsong-kha-pa. G. Newland (ed), The Lam Rim Chen Mo Translation Committee (trans.), *The Great Treatise on the Stages of the Path to Enlightenment*. New York: Snow Lion Publications, vols. 1 (2000), 2 (2004), and 3 (2002).

44 Bhikkhu Bodhi (ed). (2001), 'Satipatthana Sutta', in B. Nanamoli (trans.), *Majjhima Nikaya (The Middle Length Discourses of the Buddha)*, revised ed. Boston: Wisdom Publications, pp. 145–55.

45 See M. Baumann. (2001), 'Global Buddhism: Developmental Periods, Regional Histories, and a New Analytic Perspective', *Journal of Global Buddhism* 2, 3–4; M. Baumann. 'Protective Amulets and Awareness Techniques', p. 55. Also see S. McAra. (2007), *Land of Beautiful Vision: Making a Buddhist Sacred Place in New Zealand*. Honolulu: University of Hawai'i Press, pp. 24–5.

46 See I. Jordt. (2007), *Burma's Mass Law Meditation Movement: Buddhism and the Cultural Construction of Power*. Ohio: Centre for International Studies, Ohio University.

47 L. Rambo and C. Farhadian. (1999), 'Converting: Stages of Religious Change', in C. Lamb and M. D. Bryant (eds), *Religious Conversion: Contemporary Practices and Controversies*. London and New York: Cassell, p. 23.

[48] L. Rambo. (1993), *Understanding Religious Conversion*. New Haven and London: Yale University Press, p. 165; R. Paloutzian (1996), *Invitation to the Psychology of Religion*. Boston: Allyn and Bacon; P. Granqvist. (2003), 'Attachment Theory and Religious Conversions: A Review and Resolution of the Classic and Contemporary Paradigm Chiasm', *Review of Religious Research* 45 (2), 173.

[49] L. Rambo. (1989), 'Conversion: Toward a Holistic Model of Religious Change', *Pastoral Psychology* 38 (1), 47–63; Rambo, *Understanding Religious Conversion*. The seven steps are context, crisis, quest, encounter, interaction, commitment and consequences. Rambo states that the stages are not linear; they are cumulative and interactive. The stages have similarities to Lofland and Stark's seven stages of their world-saver model, which Rambo states he uses as a heuristic guide. However, his approach allows for more self-directed action on the part of the subject. See J. Lofland and R. Stark. (1965), 'Becoming a World-Saver: A Theory of Conversion to a Deviant Perspective', *American Sociological Review* 30 (6), 862–75.

[50] See Lofland and Stark, 'Becoming a World-Saver: A Theory of Conversion to a Deviant Perspective', 862–75. This is the most well-known.

[51] P. L. Berger and T. Luckmann. (1966), *The Social Construction of Reality: A Treatise in the Sociology of Knowledge*. New York: Doubleday & Company, p. 144. Also see T. Pilarzyk. (1978), 'Conversion and Alternation Processes in the Youth Culture: A Comparative Analysis of Religious Traditions', *Pacific Sociological Review* 21 (4), 382–83.

[52] J. Lofland and N. Skonovd. (1981), 'Conversion Motifs', *Journal for the Scientific Study of Religion* 20 (4), 373–85.

[53] P. Stromberg. (1993), *Language and Self-transformation: A Study of the Christian Conversion Narrative*. Cambridge: Cambridge University Press, p. 18.

[54] C. L. Staples and A. L. Mauss. (1987), 'Conversion or Commitment? A Reassessment of the Snow and Machalek Approach to the Study of Conversion', *Journal for the Scientific Study of Religion* 26 (2), 137.

[55] M. Heirich. (1977), 'Change of Heart: A Test of Some Widely Held Theories about Religious Conversion', *American Journal of Sociology* 83 (3), 674.

[56] R. Travisano. (1970), 'Alternation and Conversion as Qualitatively Different Transformations', in G. P. Stone and H. A. Farberman (eds), *Social Psychology Through Symbolic Interaction*. Waltham: Xerox College Publishing, pp. 600–01.

[57] Heirich, 'Change of Heart: A Test of Some Widely Held Theories about Religious Conversion', 673–74.

[58] See Lofland and Skonovd, 'Conversion Motifs', 375, as an example.

[59] A. Nock. (1998), *Conversion: The Old and the New in Religion from Alexander the Great to Augustine of Hippo*. Baltimore and London: John Hopkins University Press.

[60] Travisano, 'Alternation and Conversion as Qualitatively Different Transformations', 594–606.

[61] See D. Gordon. (1974), 'The Jesus People: An Identity Synthesis', *Urban Life and Culture* 3 (2), 165–6; J. T. Richardson. (1980), 'Conversion Careers', *Society* 17 (3), 47–50, for discussions of such schemes and their derivations.

[62] D. A. Snow and R. Machalek. (1984), 'The Sociology of Conversion', *Annual Review of Sociology* 10, 168–69. J. T. Richardson. (1978), 'Conversion Careers: In and Out of the New Religions', in J. T. Richardson (ed), *Conversion Careers: In and*

Out of the New Religions. Beverly Hills and London: Sage Publications, p. 7. Also see S. Wilson. (1984), 'Becoming a Yogi: Resocialization and Deconditioning as Conversion Processes', *Sociological Analysis* 45 (4), 301.

[63] C. M. Cusack. (1996), 'Towards a General Theory of Conversion', in L. Olsen (ed), *Religious Change, Conversion and Culture.* Sydney: Sydney Association for Studies in Society and Culture, p. 3.

[64] W. James. (2002), E. Taylor and J. Carrette (eds), *The Varieties of the Religious Experience: A Study in Human Nature,* centenary edition. London and New York: Routledge, pp. 163–64. James credits Starbuck with this distinction.

[65] J. T. Richardson. (1985), 'The Active vs. Passive Convert: Paradigm Conflict in Conversion/Recruitment Research', *Journal for the Scientific Study of Religion* 24 (2), 166–68.

[66] Granqvist, 'Attachment Theory and Religious Conversions', 172.

[67] J. V. Downton. (1980), 'An Evolutionary Theory of Spiritual Conversion and Commitment: The Case of Divine Light Mission', *Journal for the Scientific Study of Religion* 19 (4), 381–82.

[68] R. E. Gussner and S. D. Berkowitz. (1988), 'Scholars, Sects, and Sanghas, 1: Recruitment to Asian-Based Meditation Groups in North America', *Sociological Analysis* 49 (2), 136.

[69] E. Volinn. (1985), 'Eastern Meditation Groups: Why Join?', *Sociological Analysis* 46 (2), 147–48.

[70] Richardson, 'Conversion Careers', 49. See also B. Kilbourne and J. T. Richardson. (1985), 'Social Experimentation Self-Process or Social Role', *The International Journal of Social Psychiatry* 31 (1), 13. Here Lifton's protean man concept is used to describe a pattern of social experimentation with role change in new religious and self-growth groups in contemporary American society.

[71] L. Dawson. (1990), 'Self-Affirmation, Freedom, and Rationality: Theoretically Elaborating "Active" Conversions', *Journal for the Scientific Study of Religion* 29 (2), 141–63. See B. Kilbourne and J. T. Richardson. (1989), 'Paradigm Conflict, Types of Conversion, and Conversion Theories', *Sociological Analysis* 50 (1), 1–2; and Cusack. 'Towards a General Theory of Conversion', pp. 1–21, for discussions of the Pauline experience as the model for the old conversion paradigm.

[72] C. Glock. (1964), 'The Role of Deprivation in the Origin and Evolution of Religious Groups', in R. Lee and M. E. Marty (eds), *Religion and Social Conflict.* New York: Oxford University Press, pp. 24–36.

[73] R. J. Lifton. (1993), *The Protean Self: Human Resilience in an Age of Fragmentation.* New York: Basic Books.

[74] J. Hall. (1988), 'Social Organization and Pathways of Commitment: Types of Communal Groups, Rational Choice Theory, and the Kanter Thesis', *American Sociological Review* 53, 679–92.

[75] Lofland and Stark, (1965) 'Becoming a World-Saver: A Theory of Conversion to a Deviant Perspective', 862–75.

[76] See Kilbourne and Richardson, 'Paradigm Conflict, Types of Conversion, and Conversion Theories', 3–8, for an outline of their *2 × 2 typology* conceived along two axes: the passive or active role of the convert, and the intraindividual or inter-individual mechanism for change.

77 See Lofland and Skonovd, 'Conversion Motifs', 375–82, for description of their six conversion motifs: intellectual, mystical, experimental, affectional, revivalist and coercive. Also see Gussner and Berkowitz. 'Scholars, Sects, and Sanghas', 138, who acknowledge Lofland and Skonovd's conversion motifs as a recognition of the different forms of conversion generated by the interplay of structural circumstances and the actors.

78 Lofland and Skonovd, 'Conversion Motifs', 374.

79 Lofland and Skonovd, 'Conversion Motifs', 378–79.

80 R. Balch and D. Taylor. (1976), 'Salvation in a UFO', *Psychology Today* 10 (5), 58–66; R. W. Balch and D. Taylor. (1978), 'Seekers and Saucers: The Role of the Cultic Milieu in Joining a UFO Cult', in J. T. Richardson (ed), *Conversion Careers: In and Out of the New Religions*. Beverly Hills: Sage Publications, pp. 43–64.

81 C. Campbell. (1972), 'The Cult, the Cultic Milieu and Secularization', in M. Hill (ed.), *A Sociological Yearbook of Religion in Britain* 5. London: SCM Press, pp. 120–22.

82 R. Ellwood. (1973), *Religious and Spiritual Groups in Modern America*. Englewood Cliffs: Prentice-Hall, pp. 42–3.

83 See H. T. Buckner. (1968), 'The Flying Saucerians: An Open Door Cult', in M. Truzzi (ed), *Sociology and Everyday Life*. Englewood Cliffs: Prentice-Hall, pp. 223–30; D. Jorgensen. (1982), 'The Esoteric Community: An Ethnographic Investigation of the Cultic Milieu', *Urban Life* 10 (4), 383–408.

84 C. Lamb. (1999), 'Conversion as a Process Leading to Enlightenment: The Buddhist Perspective', in C. Lamb and M. D. Bryant (eds), *Religious Conversion: Contemporary Practices and Controversies*. London and New York: Cassell, pp. 75–88. Lamb discusses two approaches to conversion within Buddhism: the formal ceremony or the quiet transition to the Buddhist perspective.

85 Lofland and Skonovd, 'Conversion Motifs', 383.

86 James. *The Varieties of the Religious Experience*, p. 164.

87 See P. Stromberg. (1985), 'The Impression Point: Synthesis of Symbol and Self', *Ethos* 13 (1), 56–74.

88 Stromberg, 'The Impression Point: Synthesis of Symbol and Self', 61.

89 J. A. Beckford. (1978), 'Accounting for Conversion', *British Journal of Sociology* 29 (2), 249–62.

90 See C. L. Staples and A. L. Mauss. 'Conversion or Commitment? A Reassessment of the Snow and Machalek Approach to the Study of Conversion' and D. A. Snow and R. Machalek. 'The Sociology of Conversion', 167–90.

91 Lofland and Skonovd, 'Conversion Motifs', 383.

92 N. Smart. (1997), *Dimensions of the Sacred: An Anatomy of the World's Beliefs*. London: Harper Collins. Smart's dimensional analysis of worldviews is outlined in pp. 8–11.

93 Granqvist, 'Attachment Theory and Religious Conversions', 172.

94 Smart, *Dimensions of the Sacred*, p. 1.

95 Smart, *Dimensions of the Sacred*, pp. 1–2.

96 See G. H. Mead. (1934), C. W. Morris (ed), *Mind, Self, and Society: From the Standpoint of a Social Behaviourist*. Chicago and London: University of Chicago Press.

[97] See T. Shibutani. (1955), 'Reference Groups as Perspectives', *The American Journal of Sociology* 60 (6), 562–69; A. Greil. (1977), 'Previous Dispositions and Conversion to Perspectives of Social and Religious Movements', *Sociological Analysis* 38 (2), 115–25.

[98] See D. Preston. (1988), *The Social Organization of Zen Practice: Constructing Transcultural Reality.* Cambridge: Cambridge University Press. See pp. 3–4 for his discussion of interpretive vs explanatory approaches within the social sciences. Various schools of thought such as phenomenological sociologies and symbolic interaction comprise the interpretive approach.

[99] Berger and Luckmann, *The Social Construction of Reality*, p. 120. Also see P. L. Berger. (1963), *Invitation to Sociology: A Humanistic Perspective.* Harmondsworth: Penguin Books, pp. 116, 140; W. Wentworth. (1980), *Context and Understanding: An Inquiry into Socialization Theory.* New York: Elsevier North Holland Inc, p. 85.

[100] P. L. Berger. (1969), *The Sacred Canopy: Elements of a Sociological Theory of Religion.* New York: Anchor Books, pp. 3–4. This external facticity is often referred to as taken-for-granted reality, defined as the level of experience not in need of further analysis. See A. Schutz. (1967), G. Walsh and F. Lehnert (trans.), *The Phenomenology of the Social World.* Evanston: Northwestern University Press, p. 74.

[101] Berger and Luckmann, *The Social Construction of Reality*, p. 144.

[102] Berger, *Invitation to Sociology*, p. 68.

[104] Berger and Luckmann, *The Social Construction of Reality*, p. 144.

[105] See Paloutzian, *Invitation to the Psychology of Religion*, 146.

[106] Dawson. 'Self-Affirmation, Freedom, and Rationality: Theoretically Elaborating "Active" Conversions', pp. 150–1. See Wentworth, *Context and Understanding: An Inquiry into Socialization Theory*, p. 2, for his discussion of two extreme positions within sociology and particularly influential on socialization theory: individualism and sociologism, mirroring the determinism versus freedom issue within the social sciences.

[107] See the following discussions. D. Preston. (1981), 'Becoming a Zen Practitioner', in *Sociological Analysis* 42(1), 48. Preston refers to Suzuki's comment that it is impossible for Western categories of thought to grasp Zen adequately. S. Bedford. (1996), 'Crying out of Recognition: Experiences with Meditative Practices in a New Religious Movement', *ARC, Journal of the Faculty Religious Studies, McGill* 24, 119–32. Bedford observes that it is difficult to find language to describe phenomena that are not generally part of a culture. Also see C. Campbell. (1999), 'The Easternization of the West', in B. Wilson and J. Cresswell (eds), *New Religious Movements: Challenge and Response.* London: Routledge, pp. 35–48. Although Campbell argues for a movement towards Eastern understandings in the West, he does not indicate how deeply these notions, for instance karma, are held by Western people. Also see A. Gilgen and J. Cho. (1979), 'Questionnaire to Measure Eastern and Western Thought', *Psychological Reports* 44, 835–41.

[108] Heirich, 'Change of Heart: A Test of Some Widely Held Theories About Religious Conversion', 674.

[109] Heirich, 'Change of Heart: A Test of Some Widely Held Theories About Religious Conversion', 654.

[110] M. Harrison. (1974), 'Preparation for Life in the Spirit: The Process of Initial Commitment to a Religious Movement', *Urban Life and Culture* 2(4). Harrison distinguishes between commitment as a renewal of faith, and conversion as the adoption of new beliefs.

[111] Snow and Machalek, (1984), 'The Sociology of Conversion', 170.

[112] Berger and Luckmann, *The Social Construction of Reality*, pp. 144–45.

[113] See Shibutani, 'Reference Groups as Perspectives', 568; Wilson, 'Becoming a Yogi: Resocialization and Deconditioning as Conversion Processes'; Greil, 'Previous Dispositions and Conversion to Perspectives of Social and Religious Movements', 123.

[114] Rambo, *Understanding Religious Conversion*, p. 56.

[115] Berger, *The Sacred Canopy*, p. 15.

[116] Wentworth, *Context and Understanding: An Inquiry into Socialization Theory*, pp. 8, 64, 83.

[117] M. Spiro. (1987), 'Collective Representations and Mental Representations in Religious Symbol Systems', in B. Kilborne and L. L. Langness (eds), *Culture and Human Nature: Theoretical Papers of Melford E. Spiro*. Chicago and London: University of Chicago Press, pp. 162–64.

[118] R. D'Andrade. (1995), *The Development of Cognitive Anthropology*. Cambridge: Cambridge University Press, p. 227.

[119] Spiro, 'Collective Representations and Mental Representations in Religious Symbol Systems', pp. 163–64.

[120] Spiro, 'Collective Representations and Mental Representations in Religious Symbol Systems', p. 163.

[121] R. Strauss. (1979), 'Religious Conversion as a Personal and Collective Accomplishment', *Sociological Analysis* 40 (2), 163; R. Balch. (1980), 'Looking Behind the Scenes in a Religious Cult: Implications for the Study of Conversion', *Sociological Analysis* 41, 142; Wilson, 'Becoming a Yogi: Resocialization and Deconditioning as Conversion Processes'; Shibutani. *Society and Personality: An Interactionist Approach to Social Psychology*, 46. Shibutani's definition of a conventional role is 'a prescribed pattern of behaviour expected of a person in a given situation by virtue of his position in the transaction'.

[122] Dawson, 'Self-Affirmation, Freedom, and Rationality: Theoretically Elaborating "Active" Conversions'. Dawson believes that a role-theoretical approach is too limited, as it fails to adequately differentiate between active and passive phenomena, hence his position of combining it with rational choice theory.

[123] Wilson, 'Becoming a Yogi: Resocialization and Deconditioning as Conversion Processes'.

[124] Preston, 'Becoming a Zen Practitioner'; 'Meditative Ritual Practice and Spiritual Conversion-Commitment: Theoretical Implications Based on the Case of Zen'; *The Social Organization of Zen Practice: Constructing Transcultural Reality*.

[125] Volinn, 'Eastern Meditation Groups: Why Join?', 147–56.

[126] Wilson, 'Becoming a Yogi: Resocialization and Deconditioning as Conversion Processes'.

[127] Preston, 'Becoming a Zen Practitioner'; 'Meditative Ritual Practice and Spiritual Conversion-Commitment: Theoretical Implications Based on the Case of Zen'; *The Social Organization of Zen Practice: Constructing Transcultural Reality*.

[128] J. McIntyre. (1997), 'On Becoming a Meditator: Adult Learning and Social Context', in P. Willis and B. Neville (eds), *Qualitative Research Practice in Education*. Melbourne: David Lovell Publishing, pp. 33–48.

[129] C. Soanes., A. Stevenson, and S. Hawker (eds) (2004), *Concise Oxford English Dictionary*, 11th ed. Oxford: Oxford University Press, pp. 64, 294.

[130] Greil, 'Previous Dispositions and Conversion to Perspectives of Social and Religious Movements', 115–16.

[131] See Smart, *Dimensions of the Sacred: An Anatomy of the World's Beliefs*, pp. 8–11. I used his set of dimensions as a guide for the formulation of my initial questions.

[132] D. A. Snow., L. Zurcher and G. Sjoberg. (1982), 'Interviewing by Comment: An Adjunct to the Direct Question', *Qualitative Sociology* 5 (4), 285–311.

[133] R. McCutcheon. (1999), *The Insider/Outsider Problem in the Study of Religion: A Reader*. London and New York: Cassell. McCutcheon draws attention to the differences between four methodological approaches within the Discipline of Religious Studies: the empathetic, explanatory, agnostic, and the reflexive. Also see Rambo. *Understanding Religious Conversion*, pp. 18–19, for his six-stage methodology for studying religious conversion: observation, description, empathy, understanding, interpretation, and explanation.

[134] See Stromberg, 'The Impression Point: Synthesis of Symbol and Self'.

[135] McCutcheon, *The Insider/Outsider Problem in the Study of Religion*.

[136] A. Faivre. (1998), 'Questions of Terminology Proper to the Study of Esoteric Currents in Modern and Contemporary Europe', in A. Faivre and W. J. Hanegraaff (eds), *Gnostica 2: Western Esotericism and the Science of Religions*. Bondgenotenlaan, Belgium: Peeters, pp. 1–10.

[137] H. Spencer Lewis. (1978), *Rosicrucian Manual*, 25th ed. San Jose: Rosicrucian Press. See pp. 161, 171, and 192 for definitions of key terms such as divine mind, inner self, and soul personality.

[138] C. Queen. (1998), 'Professing Buddhism: The Harvard Conference on Buddhism in America', *Buddhist-Christian Studies* 18, 217–20.

Chapter 2

[1] S. Wilson. (1984), 'Becoming a Yogi: Resocialization and Deconditioning as Conversion Processes', *Sociological Analysis* 45 (4), 301.

[2] T. Shibutani. (1955), 'Reference Groups as Perspectives', *The American Journal of Sociology* 60 (6), 562–69.

[3] Greil refers to a body of thought that sees conversion as a process of accepting the opinions of one's new reference group, citing the work of Shibutani and Lofland and Stark's notion of strong affective bonds to adherents of the new perspective. See A. Greil. (1977), 'Previous Dispositions and Conversion to Perspectives of Social and Religious Movements', *Sociological Analysis* 38 (2), 115–125; J. Lofland and R. Stark. (1965), 'Becoming a World-Saver: A Theory of Conversion to a Deviant Perspective', *American Sociological Review* 30 (6), 862–75; Shibutani, 'Reference Groups as Perspectives'.

⁴ W. Wentworth. (1980), *Context and Understanding: An Inquiry into Socialization The-ory*. New York: Elsevier North Holland Inc., p. 65; p. 85.

⁵ The acceptance of the constructivist view was influenced by the work of Katz in the 1970s. See S. Katz. (1978), 'Language, Epistemology and Mysticism', in *Mysticism and Philosophical Analysis*. London, Sheldon Press, pp. 22–73; S. Katz. (1985), 'Recent Work on Mysticism', *History of Religions* 25 (1), 76–86.

⁶ R. Forman. (1990), 'Introduction: Mysticism, Constructivism, and Forgetting', in R. K. C. Forman (ed.), *The Problem of Pure Consciousness*. Oxford: Oxford University Press, pp. 3–49; R. Forman. (1998), 'Mystical Consciousness, the Innate Capacity, and the Perennial Psychology', in R. Forman (ed.), *The Innate Capacity: Mysticism, Psychology, and Philosophy*. New York: Oxford University Press, pp. 3–41.

⁷ Bhikkhu Bodhi. (2001), 'Satipatthana Sutta', in Bikkhu Nanamoli (trans.), *Majjhima Nikaya (The Middle Length Discourses of the Buddha)*, revised ed. Boston: Wisdom Publications, pp. 145–55.

⁸ M. Walshe (trans.). (1995), 'Mahasatipatthana Sutta', in the *Digha Nikaya*. Boston: Wisdom Publications, pp. 335–50. Also see Nyanaponika, Thera. (1965), *The Heart of Buddhist Meditation: A Handbook of Mental Training Based on the Buddha's Way of Mindfulness*. San Francisco and Newburyport: Weiser Books, pp. 8–9. Also see U Silananda. (1990), R. Heinze (ed.), *The Four Foundations of Mindfulness*. Boston: Wisdom Publications.

⁹ At www.meditation.asn.au.

¹⁰ See Nyanaponika Thera, *The Heart of Buddhist Meditation*, 8.

¹¹ Mahasi Sayadaw. (1971), U Pe Thin and Myanaung U Tin (trans.), *Practical Insight Meditation: Basic and Progressive Stages*. Kandy: Buddhist Publication Society, p. 20.

¹² Bhikkhu Bodhi. (1999), 'Message', in Soma Thera. *The Way of Mindfulness: the Satipatthana Sutta and Its Commentary*, 6th ed. Kuala Lumpur: Buddhist Publication Society, p. v.

¹³ J. Kornfield. (1979), 'Intensive Insight Meditation: A Phenomenological Study', *Journal of Transpersonal Psychology* 2(1), 42.

¹⁴ See Nyanaponika Thera, *The Heart of Buddhist Meditation*, 30–56.

¹⁵ See Soma Thera. (1999), *The Way of Mindfulness: The Satipatthana Sutta and Its Commentary*, 6th revised ed. Kuala Lumpur: Buddhist Publication Society, p. 133. Also see G. Deatherage. (1975), 'The Clinical Use of 'Mindfulness' Meditation Techniques in Short-Term Psychotherapy', *Journal of Transpersonal Psychology* 7 (2), 134. Deatherage refers to the fourth of four object types employed in clinical applications of vipassana 'the objects of one's thought processes'.

¹⁶ Nyanaponika Thera. (1998), Bhikkhu Bodhi (ed.), *Abhidhamma Studies: Buddhist Explorations of Consciousness and Time*, 4th ed. Boston: Wisdom Publications, Kandy: Buddhist Publication Society, p. xvi; Analayo. (2003), *Satipatthana: The Direct Path to Realization*. Birmingham: Windhorse Publications, p. 19; U Silananda. (1990), R. Heinze (ed.), *The Four Foundations of Mindfulness*. Boston: Wisdom Publications, p. 95.

¹⁷ Bhikkhu Bodhi, ' Satipatthana Sutta', p. 145.

¹⁸ Nyanaponika Thera, *The Heart of Buddhist Meditation*, p. 8.

19 J. Engler. (1984) ,'Therapeutic Aims in Psychotherapy and Meditation: Developmental Stages in the Representation of Self', *Journal of Transpersonal Psychology* 16 (1), 27.

20 Deatherage, 'The Clinical Use of 'Mindfulness' Meditation Techniques in Short-Term Psychotherapy', 133.

21 Nyanaponika Thera, *The Heart of Buddhist Meditation*, p. 89; P. Williams with A. Tribe. (2000), *Buddhist Thought: A Complete Introduction to the Indian Tradition.* London and New York: Routledge, p. 81–2.

22 Kornfield, 'Intensive Insight Meditation: A Phenomenological Study', 42.

23 These instructions are a synthesis of the main points outlined in two publications by Mahasi Sayadaw: (1958), U Pe Thin (trans.), *Discourse on the Basic Practice of the Satipatthana Vipassana.* Printed at the Burma Art Press (no publisher given); (1971), U Pe Thin and Myanaung U Tin (trans.), *Practical Insight Meditation: Basic and Progressive Stages.* Kandy: Buddhist Publication Society.

24 Bhikkhu Bodhi. (2001), 'Anapanasati Sutta', in Bikkhu Nanamoli (trans.), *Majjhima Nikaya.* Boston: Wisdom Publications, pp. 941–48.

25 Several series of these classes were held during the period of my fieldwork with BMIMC. One series, held on Wednesday nights between August and September 2004, focused on some key suttas from the *Majjhima Nikaya.*

26 See Appendices 2 to 5, the schedules for: the Beginners' Weekend Workshop, 29–30 May 2004; the Long-Weekend Retreat, 12–15 June 2004; the Four-Day Retreat, 14 to 17 February, 2004; the Nine-day Retreat Schedule, 23 April- 2 May 2004. Also see R. and S. Weissman. (1999), *With Compassionate Understanding: A Meditation Retreat.* St Paul, Minnesota: Paragon House, p. xiv; J. McIntyre. (1997), 'On Becoming a Meditator: Adult Learning and Social Context', in P. Willis and B. Neville (eds), *Qualitative Research Practice in Education.* Melbourne: David Lovell Publishing, for discussions of typical daily retreat schedules.

27 G. Fronsdal. (1998), 'Insight Meditation in the United States: Life, Liberty, and the Pursuit of Happiness', in C. S. Prebish and K. Tanaka (eds), *The Faces of Buddhism in America.* Berkeley, Los Angeles and London: University of California Press, pp. 172–74. Fronsdal maintains that Vipanassa and metta practices are seldom mixed when taught in Asia.

28 P. Harvey. (2000), *An Introduction to Buddhist Ethics: Foundations, Values, and Issues.* Cambridge: Cambridge University Press, p. 61.

29 See the following publications for an outline of the five lay precepts. J. W. Coleman. (2001), *The New Buddhism: The Western Transformation of an Ancient Tradition.* New York: Oxford University Press, p. 30; J. Kornfield. (1994), *A Path with Heart: A Guide Through the Perils and Promises of Spiritual Life.* London: Rider, p. 297.

30 These other three precepts are outlined in Harvey, *An Introduction to Buddhist Ethics*, 87.

31 See Coleman, *The New Buddhism: The Western Transformation of an Ancient Tradition*, p. 30, for a discussion of the relation between Sila and precepts.

32 See Appendix 2: Beginners' Weekend Workshop Schedule, 29–30 May 2004.

33 See Bhikkhu Bodhi, 'Satipatthana Sutta', p. 150–51.

34 Bhikkhu Bodhi, 'Satipatthana Sutta', p. 149.

35 See Appendix 3: Long-Weekend Retreat Schedule, 12–15 June 2004.

[36] The retreat schedule followed a standard retreat pattern, akin to those outlined in Appendices 2 and 3.

[37] See Nyanaponika Thera, *The Heart of Buddhist Meditation*; Deatherage, 'The Clinical Use of 'Mindfulness' Meditation Techniques in Short-Term Psychotherapy', 133.

[38] Mahasi Sayadaw, *Discourse on the Basic Practice of the Satipatthana Vipassana*, pp. 20–22.

[39] Nyanaponika Thera, *The Heart of Buddhist Meditation*, pp. 36–37.

[40] Engler, 'Therapeutic Aims in Psychotherapy and Meditation: Developmental Stages in the Representation of Self', 27.

[41] Engler, 'Therapeutic Aims in Psychotherapy and Meditation: Developmental Stages in the Representation of Self', 27–8.

[42] Bhikkhu Bodhi. (2005), *In the Buddha's Words: An Anthology of Discourses from the Pali Canon.* Boston: Wisdom Publications, p. 228.

[43] U Silananda, *The Four Foundations of Mindfulness*, pp. 20–21.

[44] Bhikkhu Bodhi, 'Satipatthana Sutta', p. 151.

[45] See Appendix 2: Beginners' Weekend Workshop Schedule, 29–30 May 2004.

[46] See Appendix 4: Four-Day Retreat Schedule, 14–17 February, 2004.

[47] See Appendix 5: Nine-day Retreat Schedule, 23 April to 2 May 2004.

[48] See Bhikkhu Bodhi. (2001), 'Salayatanavibhanga Sutta', in Bikkhu Nanamoli (trans.), *Majjhima Nikaya (The Middle Length Discourses of the Buddha)*, revised ed. Boston: Wisdom Publications, p. 1067. Here desire, grief, and equanimity are contemplated as three satipatthanas with reference to the six senses. Also see Analayo, *Satipatthana: The Direct Path to Realization*, p. 269; U Silananda, *The Four Foundations of Mindfulness*, pp. 22–3. He notes that the phrase in the Satipatthana Sutta, 'covetousness and grief in the world' is a reference to desire and aversion, the two grosser of the five hindrances, where 'in the world' refers to the body, the five aggregates.

[49] U Silananda, *The Four Foundations of Mindfulness*, pp. 123–26.

[50] Mahasi Sayadaw, *Discourse on the Basic Practice of the Satipatthana Vipasanna*, and *Practical Insight Meditation: Basic and Progressive Stages.*

[51] Mahasi Sayadaw, *Discourse on the Basic Practice of the Satipatthana Vipasanna*, and *Practical Insight Meditation: Basic and Progressive Stages.*

[52] Bhikkhu Bodhi (ed.). (2005), *In the Buddha's Words: An Anthology of Discourses from the Pali Canon.* Boston: Wisdom Publications, p. 225; D. Keown. (2003), *A Dictionary of Buddhism.* Oxford: Oxford University Press, p. 84. Bhikkhu Bodhi, *In the Buddha's Words: An Anthology of Discourses from the Pali Canon*, p. 225.

[53] This view was outlined in a Sutta Study weekend facilitated by Patrick Kearney on 30–31 August, 2003, at BMIMC.

[54] Greil, 'Previous Dispositions and Conversion to Perspectives of Social and Religious Movements'.

[55] See McIntyre, 'On Becoming a Meditator: Adult Learning and Social Context'.

[56] A. Schutz. (1967), G. Walsh and F. Lehnert (trans.), *The Phenomenology of the Social World.* Evanston, Illinois: Northwestern University Press, p. 74.

[57] L. Dawson. (1990) 'Self-Affirmation, Freedom, and Rationality: Theoretically Elaborating 'Active' Conversions', *Journal for the Scientific Study of Religion* 29 (2), 141–63.

Chapter 3

1 W. Wentworth. (1980), *Context and Understanding: An Inquiry into Socialization Theory*. New York: Elsevier North Holland Inc.

2 P. Stromberg. (1993), *Language and Self-transformation: A Study of the Christian Conversion Narrative*. Cambridge: Cambridge University Press, p. 18; C. L. Staples and A. L. Mauss. (1987), 'Conversion or Commitment? A Reassessment of the Snow and Machalek Approach to the Study of Conversion', *Journal for the Scientific Study of Religion* 26 (2), 133–47.

3 See S. Bedford. (1996), 'Crying Out of Recognition: Experiences with Meditative Practices in a New Religious Movement', *ARC, The Journal of Religious Studies* 24, 125. Similarly, Bedford reported that three out of thirteen informants from the i and I Art of Living Foundation, described experiences that were sometimes characterized by flow states.

4 M. Walshe (trans.). (1995), 'Mahasatipatthana Sutta', in the *Digha Nikaya*. Boston: Wisdom Publications, pp. 335–50.

5 G. Watson. (2002), *The Resonance of Emptiness: A Buddhist Inspiration for a Contemporary Psychotherapy*. Richmond: Curzon Press, p. 154.

6 E. M. Layman. (1976), *Buddhism in America*. Chicago: Nelson-Hall, p. 287. Layman's observation that some Westerners try Transcendental Meditation (a well-known samatha technique that employs a mantra as the concentration object), and then come to Buddhism in search of a more demanding practice, warrants further investigation thirty-five years on and in the Australian context.

7 Nyanaponika Thera. (1998), 'The Four Sublime States' (1958), in *The Four Sublime States*, Nyanaponika Thera, and *The Practice of Lovingkindness*, Nanamoli Thera, combined ed. Kandy: Buddhist Publication Society, pp. 11–21, 30.

8 See Nyanaponika Thera, *The Four Sublime States*, pp. 3–6.

9 D. Keown. (2003), *A Dictionary of Buddhism*. Oxford: Oxford University Press, p. 212.

10 Nyanaponika Thera, *The Four Sublime States*, p. 6.

11 Nanamoli Thera, *The Practice of Lovingkindness*, p. 31.

12 G. Fronsdal. (1998), 'Insight Meditation in the United States: Life, Liberty, and the Pursuit of Happiness', in C. S. Prebish and K. Tanaka (eds), *The Faces of Buddhism in America*. Berkeley, Los Angeles and London: University of California Press, pp. 173–74.

13 Keown, *A Dictionary of Buddhism*, 212.

14 See K. Valham (compiler). (1997), *Lam Rim Outlines: Beginners' Meditation Guide*. Boston, Wisdom Publications, pp. 58–72.

15 See D. Goleman. (1978), *The Varieties of the Meditative Experience*. London: Rider and Company, p. 12; S. Shaw. (2006), *Buddhist Meditation: An Anthology of Texts from the Pali Canon*. London and New York: Routledge, p. 18. Their comments indicate that they consider initial concentrative states to be accessible during everyday activities.

16 The satipatthanas are listed in Bhikkhu Bodhi. (2001), 'Satipatthana Sutta', in Bikkhu Nanamoli (trans.), *Majjhima Nikaya (The Middle Length Discourses of the Buddha)*, revised ed. Boston: Wisdom Publications, pp. 145–55. A comprehensive

diagram of the objects listed in the *Satipatthana Sutta* is to be found in Analayo. (2003), *Satipatthana: The Direct Path to Realization.* Birmingham: Windhorse Publications, p. 19.

[17] See Analayo, *Satipatthana: The Direct Path to Realization,* p. 153.

[18] Shaw, *Buddhist Meditation: An Anthology of Texts from the Pali Canon,* p. 78.

[19] Nyanaponika Thera, *The Heart of Buddhist Meditation,* p.68.

[20] Analayo, *Satipatthana: The Direct Path to Realization,* p. 157.

[21] S. Hamilton. (1996), *Identity and Experience: The Constitution of the Human Being According to Early Buddhism.* London: Luzac Oriental, p. xviii.

[22] J. Rubin. (2001), 'A New View of Meditation', *Journal of Religion and Health* 40 (1), 124.

[23] Rubin. 'A New View of Meditation', 124.

[24] Bhikkhu Bodhi , 'Satipatthana Sutta' p. 150.

[25] U Silananda. (1990), *The Four Foundations of Mindfulness.* Ruth-Inge Heinze ed. Boston: Wisdom Publications, p. 93; Soma Thera. (1999), *The Way of Mindfulness: the Satipatthana Sutta and Its Commentary,* 6th revised ed. Kuala Lumpur: Buddhist Publication Society, p. 128.

[26] Bhikkhu Bodhi, *Majjhima Nikaya,* p. 1193 (footnote 154).

[27] Bhikkhu Bodhi, 'Satipatthana Sutta', pp. 151–54. See also Analayo, *Satipatthana: The Direct Path to Realization,* pp. 19, Fig. 1.2.

[28] Bhikkhu Bodhi, *Majjhima Nikaya,* p. 1194 (footnote 157).

[29] See Nyanaponika Thera, *The Heart of Buddhist Meditation,* p. 73.

[30] Analayo, *Satipatthana: The Direct Path to Realization,* pp. 19–21. See Fig. 1.2 on p. 19.

[31] Bhikkhu Bodhi, *Majjhima Nikaya,* p. 1193, (note 52).

[32] Analayo, *Satipatthana: The Direct Path to Realization,* p. 20. Bhikkhu Bodhi, 'Satipatthana Sutta', pp. 150, 1193 (note 155).

[34] Bedford, 'Crying Out of Recognition: Experiences with Meditative Practices in a New Religious Movement', 126.

[35] Nyanaponika Thera, *The Heart of Buddhist Meditation,* p. 73.

[36] P. Griffiths. (1981), 'Concentration or Insight: The Problematic of Theravada Buddhist Meditation-Theory', *Journal of the American Academy of Religion* 49 (4), 614.

[37] H. F. De Wit. (1992), 'Transmitting the Buddhist View of Experience', in J. D. Gort, H. M. Vroom, R. Fernhout, and A. Wessels (eds), *On Sharing Religious Experience: Possibilities of Interfaith Mutuality.* Grand Rapids, MI: William B. Eerdmans Publishing Company, p. 199.

[38] Griffiths, 'Concentration or Insight: The Problematic of Theravada Buddhist Meditation-Theory', 612–13.

[39] Mahasi Sayadaw. (1971), U Pe Thin and Myanaung U Tin (trans.), *Practical Insight Meditation: Basic and Progressive Stages.* Kandy: Buddhist Publication Society, pp. 20–38.

[40] This talk is the last in a series of thirteen dhamma-talks by Venerable Chanmay Sayadaw Ashin Janakabhivamsa (U Janaka), which can be downloaded from the Centre's website at www.meditation.asn.au/talks/html.

[41] Griffiths, 'Concentration or Insight: The Problematic of Theravada Buddhist Meditation-Theory', p. 611.

[42] Nyanaponika Thera, *The Heart of Buddhist Meditation,* p. 8.

[43] P. Harvey. (1990), *An Introduction to Buddhism: Teachings, History, and Practices*, Cambridge University Press, p. 244.

[44] Bedford, 'Crying Out of Recognition: Experiences with Meditative Practices in a New Religious Movement', 126.

[45] D. J. MacPhillamy. (1986), 'Some Personality Effects of Long-Term Zen Monasticism and Religious Understanding', *Journal for the Scientific Study of Religion* 25 (3), 304.

[46] D. Burns and R. J. Ohayv. (1980) 'Psychological Changes in Meditating Western Monks in Thailand', *Journal of Transpersonal Psychology* 12 (1), 15.

[47] De Wit, 'Transmitting the Buddhist View of Experience', p. 196.

[48] Nyanaponika Thera, *The Heart of Buddhist Meditation*, p. 57.

[49] J. Engler. (1984), 'Therapeutic Aims in Psychotherapy and Meditation: Developmental Stages in the Representation of Self', *Journal of Transpersonal Psychology* 16 (1); Watson, *The Resonance of Emptiness*; J. Welwood. (2002), *Toward a Psychology of Awakening: Buddhism, Psychotherapy, and the Path of Personal and Spiritual Transformation*. Boston and London: Shambala; Thupten Jinpa. (2000), 'The Foundations of a Buddhist Psychology of Awakening', in G. Watson, S. Batchelor, and G. Claxton (eds), *The Psychology of Awakening*. York Beach, Maine: Samuel Weiser, 10–22.

[50] Watson, *The Resonance of Emptiness*, p. 94.

[51] Watson, *The Resonance of Emptiness*, p. 116.

[52] W. James. (1983), *Principles of Psychology*. Cambridge Massachusets: Harvard University Press. Also see G. Eddy. (2007c), 'The Application of James' Model of the Self to the Understanding of Self-Transformative Experience in Vipassana Meditation', in *Spirituality in Australia: Psychological, Social and Religious Perspectives*, proceedings of the UWS Psychology and Spirituality Society Annual Conference 20 July 2007, Centre for Human Interaction, Learning and Development (CD-Rom).

[53] D. Leary. (1990), 'William James on the Self and Personality: Clearing the Ground for Subsequent Theorists, Researchers, and Practitioners', in M. G. Johnston and T. B. Henley (eds), *Reflections on the Principles of Psychology: William James After a Century*. New Jersey: Lawrence Erlbaum Associates, pp. 101–37.

[54] Watson, *The Resonance of Emptiness*, p. 110.

[55] R. N. Walsh. (1977), 'Initial Meditative Experiences: Part 1', *Journal of Transpersonal Psychology* 9 (2), 158–62.

[56] Walsh, 'Initial Meditative Experiences: Part 1' , 162.

[57] Walsh, 'Initial Meditative Experiences: Part 1', 158–62; R. N. Walsh. (1978), 'Initial Meditative Experiences: Part 2', *Journal of Transpersonal Psychology* 10 (1), 7.

Chapter 4

[1] During the period of my fieldwork, Vajrayana Institute (VI) relocated from 22 Linthorpe St, Newtown, to 9 Victoria Square, Ashfield. Information about VI can be found on its website at www.vajrayana.com.au. For information about the FPMT, visit its website at www.fpmt.org.

[2] J. Powers. (1995), *Introduction to Tibetan Buddhism*. New York: Snow Lion Publications, p. 315.

[3] Powers, *Introduction to Tibetan Buddhism*, p. 416. See Chapter 15, for the treatment of the Lam Rim in the writings of Lama Tsong-kha-pa.

[4] Powers, *Introduction to Tibetan Buddhism*, p. 418; Geshe Tsultrim Gyeltsen, in the Foreword to Tenzin Gyatso. (2002), R. McClen, Thupten Jinpa, and N. Ribush (eds), Thupten Jinpa (trans.), *Illuminating the Path to Enlightenment*. Long Beach California: Thubten Dhargye Ling Publications. The translation of the root text, by Ruth Sonam in Dharamsala in 1997, consists of 68 verses typically of four lines each. In the unpublished version of the root text used in teachings at VI, Atisha's dates are given as 982–1054.

[5] J. Cutler. (2000), 'Preface', in Tsong-kha-pa. G. Newland (ed.), The Lam Rim Chen Mo Translation Committee (trans.), *The Great Treatise on the Stages of the Path to Enlightenment*, volume 1. New York: Snow Lion Publications, pp. 9–11.

[6] Tsong-kha-pa. G. Newland (ed.), The Lam Rim Chen Mo Translation Committee (trans.), *The Great Treatise on the Stages of the Path to Enlightenment*. New York: Snow Lion Publications; vol. 1 (2000); vol. 2 (2004); vol. 3 (2002).

[7] K. Valham (compiler). (1997), *Lam Rim Outlines: Beginners' Meditation Guide*. Boston: Wisdom Publications. The preface in this publication serves the purpose of outlining the three scopes.

[8] See also Valham, *Lam Rim Outlines*.

[9] P. Williams. (1989), *Mahayana Buddhism: The Doctrinal Foundations*. London and New York: Routledge, p. 43.

[10] Tenzin Gyatso. (2002), Geshe Thupten Jinpa (ed./trans.), *Essence of the Heart Sutra: The Dalai Lama's Heart of Wisdom Teachings*. Boston: Wisdom Publications. See pp. 59–61 for the text of the Heart Sutra.

[11] See the Lama Yeshe Wisdom Archive at http://lamayeshe.com, for teachings by Lama Yeshe and Lama Zopa, which is linked to the FPMT website.

[12] R. Balch. (1980), 'Looking Behind the Scenes in a Religious Cult: Implications for the Study of Conversion', *Sociological Analysis* 41, 142; S. Wilson. (1984), 'Becoming a Yogi: Resocialization and Deconditioning as Conversion Processes', *Sociological Analysis* 45 (4), 302.

[13] D. Preston. (1981), 'Becoming a Zen Practitioner', *Sociological Analysis* 42(1), 47–56; (1982), 'Meditative Ritual Practice and Spiritual Conversion-Commitment: Theoretical Implications Based on the Case of Zen', *Sociological Analysis* 43 (3), 257–70; (1988), *The Social Organization of Zen Practice: Constructing Transcultural Reality*. Cambridge: Cambridge University Press.

[14] Current information about the Discovering Buddhism course can be found on the FPMT's website, at http://www.fpmt.org/education/programs/discovering-buddhism.html

[15] The introductory booklet, called *Discovering Buddhism*, printed in 2001 by the FPMT Education Department, is distributed at the information night held before the commencement of every module.

[16] They are also outlined in K. McDonald. (1984), *How to Meditate: A Practical Guide*. Robina Courtin ed. Massachusets: Wisdom Publications, pp. 150–51.

[17] See Appendix 6 for the text of these prayers. See also *Essential Buddhist Prayers: Kopan Prayer Book* (2001), pp. 4–23; McDonald, *How to Meditate: A Practical Guide*. Pages 148–155 explain why these introductory prayers are done.

[18] McDonald, *How to Meditate: A Practical Guide*, p. 150.

[19] This translation is given in Thubten Yeshe and Thubten Zopa Rinpoche. (2003), 'The Yoga Method of the Glorious Supreme Heruka Vajrasattva', in *The Preliminary Practice of Vajrasattva*. FPMT inc., p. 37.

[20] McDonald, *How to Meditate: A Practical Guide*, p. 154.

[21] McDonald, *How to Meditate: A Practical Guide*, p. 155.

[22] See McDonald, *How to Meditate: A Practical Guide*, p. 154, for her description of the Outer Mandala's composition in terms of Abhidharma cosmology, in which Mount Meru is a jewelled mountain in the centre of the universe, and the four continents are realms of human life.

[23] McDonald, *How to Meditate: A Practical Guide*, p. 155.

[24] These practices are outlined in Valham, *Lam Rim Outlines*, pp. 53–81.

[25] McDonald, *How to Meditate: A Practical Guide*, p. 8.

[26] McDonald, *How to Meditate: A Practical Guide*, p. 19.

[27] McDonald, *How to Meditate: A Practical Guide*, p. 111.

[28] McDonald, *How to Meditate: A Practical Guide*, pp. 19–20.

[29] Gen Lamrimpa. (1992), H. Sprager (ed.), B. A. Wallace (trans.), *Samatha Meditation: Tibetan Buddhist Teachings on Cultivating Meditative Quiescence*. Ithaca, New York: Snow Lion Publications, p. 146.

[30] Tsong-kha-pa, *Lam Rim Chen Mo* vol. 3, p. 14.

[31] McDonald, *How to Meditate: A Practical Guide*, p. 56.

[32] Gen Lamrimpa. (2002), E. P. (ed.), B. A. Wallace (trans.), *Realizing Emptiness: Madhayaka Insight Meditation*, 2nd ed. Ithaca, NY, Boulder, CO: Snow Lion Publications, pp. 47–48, for a discussion of how such construction processes occur.

[33] E. Wortz. (1982), 'Application of Awareness Methods in Psychotherapy', *Journal of Transpersonal Psychology* 14 (1), 61–2.

[34] Geshe Acharya Thubten Loden. (1993), *Path to Enlightenment in Tibetan Buddhism*. Melbourne: Tushita Publications, p. 849.

[35] Gen Lamrimpa, *Realizing Emptiness*, pp. 47–48.

[36] See McDonald, *How to Meditate*, pp. 60–61, and Valham, *Lam Rim Outlines*, 77–80. See Geshe Acharya Thubten Loden, *Path to Enlightenment in Tibetan Buddhism*, pp. 849–60, for the background theory and reasoning to the meditation.

[37] Also see R. Preece. (2006), *The Psychology of Buddhist Tantra*. New York: Snow Lion Publications, p. 140. Preece describes this practice as it is done in Kriya, Action Tantra, the lowest of the four classes.

[38] Valham, *Lam Rim Outlines*, pp. 1–4, contains a Sakyamuni Buddha visualization used as a Lam Rim preliminary practice.

[39] P. L. Berger and T. Luckmann. (1966), *The Social Construction of Reality: A Treatise in the Sociology of Knowledge*. New York: Doubleday & Company.

[40] The concept of *karmic imprints* is discussed towards the end of this chapter, in the consideration of the acquired and apprehended framework that one begins to construct with time and experience.

[41] Valham, *Lam Rim Outlines*, p. 58. This meditation is classed as a practice for generating *bodhicitta*.

[42] *Introduction to Tantra* began on 27 January 2004. The Saturday afternoon teachings, by Geshe Samten, were on *The Three Principal Aspects of the Path* in January, and on *The Thirty Seven Practices of the Bodhisattva* in February of that year.

[43] Powers, *Introduction to Tibetan Buddhism*, pp. 416–29. In his section on distinctive Gelugpa practices, Powers discusses the same doctrinal points in some detail: the three principals of the path, how to develop compassion, and the nature of mind.

[44] Powers, *Introduction to Tibetan Buddhism*, p. 417.

[45] This initiation took place on 30 April 2005, at the Buddhist Library in Camperdown, Sydney.

[46] Powers, *Introduction to Tibetan Buddhism*, p. 426.

[47] A. Gilgen and J. Cho. (1979), 'Questionnaire to Measure Eastern and Western Thought', in *Psychological Reports* 44, 835.

[48] See Appendix 7: *Refuge Teachings, 19 June 2005*, for comments made about the differences between objects of refuge in the Buddhist and other traditions.

[49] Examples are: *Buddhism and Western Psychology*, 2003, and *Mind and Mental Events*, 8 September to 27 October 2003, which studied traditional Awareness and Knowledge texts, the *Lo Rig*, as presented in *Mind in Tibetan Buddhism* by Venerable Lati Rinpoche.

[50] See Thubten Yeshe. (2004), N. Ribush (ed.), *Becoming Vajrasattva: The Tantric Path of Purification*. Boston: Wisdom Publications, pp. 131–32. Geshe Dawa's commentary on the Lam Rim, given over two-and-a-half days during the second annual *Lam Rim and Four-Armed Chenrezig* retreat in January 2004, discussed the purification of negative karma and the accumulation of merit as significant aspects of the path to enlightenment.

[51] See N. Ribush in the 'Editor's Introduction', Thubten Yeshe, *Becoming Vajrasattva: The Tantric Path of Purification*, pp. 1–3. See also Thubten Zopa Rinpoche, *Wish-Fulfilling Golden Sun* (2000), 10; McDonald, *How to Meditate: A Practical Guide*, p. 150.

[52] C. Campbell. (1999), 'The Easternization of the West', in B. Wilson and J. Cresswell (eds), *New Religious Movements: Challenge and Response*. London: Routledge, pp. 35–48.

[53] The four opponent powers are explained in Thubten Yeshe, *Becoming Vajrasattva: The Tantric Path of Purification*, pp. 11–14. These comments were made as part of Geshe Dawa's teaching during the Lam Rim retreat, in January 2004.

Chapter 5

[1] See M. Baumann. (2001), 'Global Buddhism: Developmental Periods, Regional Histories, and a New Analytic Perspective', *Journal of Global Buddhism* 2, 3–4; (2002), 'Protective Amulets and Awareness techniques, or How to Make Sense of Buddhism in the West', in C. S. Prebish and M. Baumann (eds), *Westward Dharma: Buddhism Beyond Asia*. Berkeley, Los Angeles, London: University of California Press, p. 55.

[2] Sections of this chapter have been previously published as G. Eddy. (2007a), 'A Strand of Contemporary Tantra: Its Discourse and Practice in the FPMT', *Journal of Global Buddhism* 8, 81–106.

[3] J. Powers. (1995), *Introduction to Tibetan Buddhism*. New York: Snow Lion Publications, p. 80.

4 See Powers, *Introduction to Tibetan Buddhism*, 80–85, for a discussion of the five Buddhist paths: *accumulation, preparation, seeing, meditation*, and *no more learning*. See especially page 80 for his discussion of the *Path of Accumulation*. Also see J. Hopkins. (1999), Anne C. Klein (ed.), *The Tantric Distinction: A Buddhist's Reflections on Compassion and Emptiness, revised ed.* Boston: Wisdom Publications, p. 39.

5 This is a reference to one of the purification practices, the *nine round breathing* meditation, where one visualizes clearing the body's energy channels.

6 Tsong-kha-pa. (2002), G. Newland (ed.), The Lam Rim Chen Mo Translation Committee (trans.), *The Great Treatise on the Stages of the Path to Enlightenment*, volume 3. New York: Snow Lion Publications, p. 14.

7 The meditation is outlined in J. Hopkins. (1996), *Meditation on Emptiness*, revised ed. Boston: Wisdom Publications, pp. 44–6.

8 The four opponent powers, the power of reliance, regret, the opponent force, and promise, form part of preliminary Vajrasattva practices. See K. Magnussen, (ed.). (2003), 'A Simple Vajrasattva Practice', in *The Preliminary Practice of Vajrasattva: Practice and Instructions for Retreat*. FPMT inc. pp. 128–33; K. McDonald. (1984), *How to Meditate: A Practical Guide*. Robina Courtin ed., Boston: Wisdom Publications, pp. 179–86.

9 P. Heelas (1996), 'Introduction: Detraditionalization and Its Rivals', in P. Heelas, S. Lash, and P. Morris (eds), *Detraditionalization: Critical Reflections on Authority and Identity*. Oxford: Blackwell Publishers, pp. 1–18.

10 See N. Ribush in Thubten Yeshe. (2004), N. Ribush (ed.), *Becoming Vajrasattva: The Tantric Path of Purification*. Boston: Wisdom Publications, pp. 1–4. See also Thubten Zopa. (2000), *The Wish-Fulfilling Golden Sun of the Mahayana Thought Training*, original publication details unknown, republished for Kachoe Zung Juk Ling Nunnery, p. 10; McDonald. *How to Meditate: A Practical Guide*, p. 150.

11 See Geshe Acharya Thubten Loden. (1993), *Path to Enlightenment in Tibetan Buddhism*. Melbourne: Tushita Publications, Chapter 5. The recommended text for the Discovering Buddhism module is A. Berzin. (2000), *Relating to a Spiritual Teacher: Building a Healthy Relationship*. New York: Snow Lion Publications.

12 See S. Bell. (2002), 'Scandals in Emerging Western Buddhism', in C. S. Prebish and M. Baumann (eds), *Westward Dharma: Buddhism Beyond Asia*. Berkeley, Los Angeles, London: University of California Press, pp. 230–31; D. Capper. (2004), 'Enchantment with Tibetan Lamas in the United States', *Journal of Contemporary Religion* 19 (2), 137–53. While Capper's paper focuses on the constructive aspects of guru devotion, Bell cites several instances of problems caused by misuse of authority by teachers in organizations such as these. It is noteworthy that students are encouraged to use discrimination when choosing a teacher.

13 Gen Lamrimpa. (1992), H Sprager (ed.), B. A. Wallace (trans.), *Samatha Meditation: Tibetan Buddhist Teachings on Cultivating Meditative Quiescence*. Ithaca, New York: Snow Lion Publications, p. 20; Tashi Tsering. (2002), *The Theory and Practice of Mahamudra: A Teaching Given by Venerable Tashi Tsering*, Voula Zarpani (interpreter). Eudlo: Chenrezig Institute Publications, p. 37.

14 Gen Lamrimpa, *Samatha Meditation*, p. 16.

15 Tashi Tsering, *The Theory and Practice of Mahamudra*, p. 37.

16 See Gen Lamrimpa, *Samatha Meditation*, p. 20.

17 Hopkins, *Meditation on Emptiness*, pp. 9; 11. Also see Gen Lamrimpa. (2002), E. P. (ed.), B. A. Wallace (trans.), *Realizing Emptiness: Madhayaka Insight Meditation*, 2nd ed. Ithaca, Boulder: Snow Lion Publications, pp. 99–100, for his discussion of the Middle Way as the avoidance of the extremes of substantialism and nihilism.

18 This meditation is outlined in Hopkins, *Meditation on Emptiness*, pp. 44–46. See also p. 10 for the reasoning and sets of reasonings used to reflect on the impossibility of inherent existence. The meditation is also referred to in Gen Lamrimpa, *Realizing Emptiness*, p. 99.

19 R. Ray. (2001), *Secret of the Vajra World: The Tantric Buddhism of Tibet.* Boston and London: Shambala, p. 95.

20 G. Samuel. (2005), *Tantric Revisionings: New Understandings of Tibetan Buddhism and Indian Religion.* Aldershot and Burlington: Ashgate. Samuel identifies two orientations within Western Tibetan Buddhism, the textual and the yogic, in contrast to the *shamanic* and the *clerical* he identifies in Tibetan societies.

21 A. Wayman. (1974), *The Buddhist Tantras: Light on Indo-Tibetan Esotericism.* London: Routledge and Kegan Paul, p. 4.

22 See Hopkins, in Tenzin Gyatso, Tsong-ka-pa, and J. Hopkins. (1987), J. Hopkins (trans./ed.), *Deity Yoga in Action and Performance Tantra.* New York: Snow Lion Publications, p. 207. Hopkins expresses the view that 'Tantra Is the Six Perfections Plus Deity Yoga'.

23 Kelsang Gyatso. (2002), *The Meditation Handbook.* New Delhi: New Age Books, pp. 6–7.

24 Tsong-kha-pa. (1995), *Preparing for Tantra: The Mountain of Blessings.* Howell, New Jersey: The Mahayana Sutra and Tantra Press.

25 Tulku Thondup. 'Foreword', in Ray, *Secret of the Vajra World*, pp. viii–ix.

26 See H. Urban. (2003), *Tantra: Sex, Secrecy, Politics, and Power in the Study of Religion.* Berkeley: University of California Press; H. Guenther. (1972), *The Tantric View of Life.* Berkeley and London: Shambala Publications, p. 2. I have made this point elsewhere in Eddy, 'A Strand of Contemporary Tantra: Its Discourse and Practice in the FPMT', 81–106.

27 Ray, *Secret of the Vajra World*, pp. 91–2.

28 Wayman, *The Buddhist Tantras: Light on Indo-Tibetan Esotericism*, pp. 3–4.

29 See Tenzin Gyatso, *Deity Yoga in Action and Performance Tantra*, pp. 15–16. Here the Dalai Lama outlines the vows for each of the four classes of Tantra. Those engaged in Action and Performance Tantra take the Bodhisattva vows: eighteen root vows and maintenance of the aspirational mind of enlightenment, while those engaged in Yoga and Highest Yoga take Tantric Vows.

30 See Tsong-kha-pa. (2005), G. Sparham (trans.), *Tantric Ethics: An Explanation of the Precepts for Buddhist Vajrayana Practice.* Boston: Wisdom Publications, pp. 115–31. Chapter 5 of this book, *How to Keep a Tantric Ordination*, is a commentary on the consideration of thinking about the benefits of protecting, and the penalties of not protecting the vows.

31 Hopkins, *Deity Yoga in Action and Performance Tantra*, p. 210. Hopkins refers to techniques revolving around and using the bliss arising from the desire for male–female union, which can be seen as an extension of the 'smiling' and

'looking with desire' metaphor used to describe action and performance tantra respectively.

32 For an example of a practice that utilizes the imagery of the body's channels, see the *Inner Heat Meditation* in McDonald, *How to Meditate*, pp. 134–38.

33 See Wayman, *The Buddhist Tantras: Light on Indo-Tibetan Esotericism*. His table on page 33 contains this kind of information.

34 Guenther, *The Tantric View of Life*, p. ix; Wayman, *The Buddhist Tantras: Light on Indo-Tibetan Esotericism*, p. 62.

35 Ray, *Secret of the Vajra World*, p. 113.

36 One such booklet is Ngawang Losang Tempa Gyaltsan. (2002), Lama Thubten Zopa Rinpoche (trans.), *Medicine Buddha Sadhana*, revised edition. Taos New Mexico: FPTM Education Services.

37 See Wayman, *The Buddhist Tantras: Light on Indo-Tibetan Esotericism*, especially pp. 41, 55 and 60. In this vein, he also says that the sexual symbolism itself is not the secret.

38 Thubten Yeshe, *Becoming Vajrasattva: The Tantric Path of Purification*, p. 287. Vajrasattva is the male meditational deity symbolizing the inherent purity of all Buddhas. His practice is held to remove obstacles created by negative karma and breaking vows.

39 See Wayman, *The Buddhist Tantras: Light on Indo-Tibetan Esotericism*, pp. 54, 20–1. Here Wayman refers to a correspondence between the five Dhyani Buddhas, the five aggregates and five corporeal centres.

40 See Appendix 8: Medicine Buddha Practice Day, 28 May 2005. This practice day followed a Medicine Buddha initiation given by Geshe Dawa at the Buddhist Library, Camperdown on 30 April 2005.

41 Ray, *Secret of the Vajra World*, p. 114; pp. 198–99.

42 P. Harvey. (2000), *An Introduction to Buddhist Ethics: Foundations, Values, and Issues*. Cambridge: Cambridge University Press, p. 141.

43 Thubten Yeshe, *Becoming Vajrasattva: The Tantric Path of Purification*.

44 See Wayman, *The Buddhist Tantras: Light on Indo-Tibetan Esotericism*, pp. 110–11 for these comments, and Ray, *Secret of the Vajra World*, p. 177.

45 Tenzin Gyatso, *Deity Yoga in Action and Performance Tantra*, 15.

46 Harvey, *An Introduction to Buddhist Ethics: Foundations, Values, and Issues*, p. 141.

47 See Harvey, *An Introduction to Buddhist Ethics: Foundations, Values, and Issues*, pp. 9–17.

48 Tulku Thondup, in Ray, *Secret of the Vajra World*, p. viii–ix.

49 Guenther, *The Tantric View of Life*, p. 6, pp. 8–9.

50 McDonald, *How to Meditate: A Practical Guide*, p. 8; 19.

51 Tsong-kha-pa, *The Great Treatise on the Stages of the Path to Enlightenment*, vol. 3.

52 M. Csikszentmihalyi. (1991), *Flow: The Psychology of Optimal Experience*. New York: HarperPerennial, p. 41; S. Bedford. (1996), 'Crying out of Recognition: Experiences with Meditative Practices in a New Religious Movement', *ARC, Journal of the Faculty Religious Studies, McGill* 24, 126. Here Csikszentmihalyi explains that flow experience has an integrating effect on the self because consciousness is unusually well-ordered during states of concentration.

53 Csikszentmihalyi, *Flow: The Psychology of Optimal Experience*, p. 144.

[54] G. Watson. (2000), 'I, Mine, and Views of the Self', in G. Watson, S. Batchelor, and G. Claxton (eds), *The Psychology of Awakening*. York Beach, Maine: Samuel Weiser, p. 31; (2002), *The Resonance of Emptiness: A Buddhist Inspiration for a Contemporary Psychotherapy*. Richmond: Curzon Press, pp. 96–7.

[55] Geshe Acharya Thubten Loden, *Path to Enlightenment in Tibetan Buddhism*, pp. 851–52.

[56] Watson, *The Resonance of Emptiness*, p. 110.

[57] Geshe Acharya Thubten Loden, *Path to Enlightenment in Tibetan Buddhism*, pp. 851–52.

[58] Here, I refer the reader to the section *A Contemporary Western View of the Self* in Chapter 3 in this work. Also see Watson, *The Resonance of Emptiness*, p. 110.

[59] J. Engler. (1984), 'Therapeutic Aims in Psychotherapy and Meditation: Developmental Stages in the Representation of Self', in *The Journal of Transpersonal Psychology* 16 (1), 26; Watson, *The Resonance of Emptiness*, p. 93.

[60] Watson, *The Resonance of Emptiness*, p. 121, p. 159.

[61] Watson agrees with Epstein's view that the contradiction between ego and Buddhist self is easily negated once it is understood that the 'target of Buddhist insight is not the ego in a Freudian sense, but the self-concept, the representational component of the ego'. See Watson, *The Resonance of Emptiness*, p. 116. See also R. Imamura. (1998), 'Buddhist and Western Psychotherapies: An Asian American Perspective', in C. S. Prebish and K. Tanaka (eds), *The Faces of Buddhism in America*. Berkely, Los Angeles and London: University of California Press, p. 235.

[62] P. Berger and T. Luckmann. (1966), *The Social Construction of Reality: a Treatise in the Sociology of Knowledge*. New York: Doubleday & Company.

[63] K. Horney. (1970), *Neurosis and Human Growth: The Struggle Toward Self-Realization*. New York and London: Norton, p. 17.

[64] The teacher drew our attention to pride as one of the Six Root-Delusions, the other five being desirous attachment, anger, ignorance, doubt and deluded view. These are described in Geshe Acharya Thubten Loden, *Path to Enlightenment in Tibetan Buddhism*, pp. 417–37.

[65] Harvey, *An Introduction to Buddhist Ethics: Foundations, Values, and Issues*, p. 141.

Chapter 6

[1] J. Lofland and N. Skonovd. (1981), 'Conversion Motifs', *Journal for the Scientific Study of Religion* 20 (4), 378–79.

[2] L. Rambo. (1993), *Understanding Religious Conversion*. New Haven and London: Yale University Press, p. 59.

[3] T. Pilarzyk. (1978), 'Conversion and Alternation Processes in the Youth Culture: A Comparative Analysis of Religious Traditions', *Pacific Sociological Review* 21 (4), 398.

[4] J. Lofland and R. Stark. (1965), 'Becoming a World-Saver: A Theory of Conversion to a Deviant Perspective', *American Sociological Review* 30 (6), 862–75.

5 See E. Puttick. (2004), 'Gurdjieff and Ouspenski Groups', in C. Partridge (ed.), *Encyclopedia of New Religions*. Oxford: Lion Publishing, p. 327. Puttick refers to Gurdjieff's technique for achieving awakening as self-remembering, a close observation of inner states.

6 E. Volinn. (1985), 'Eastern Meditation Groups: Why Join?', *Sociological Analysis* 46 (2), 148. Volinn makes this comment in connection with his twelve months of research in an ashram in the New England countryside in the US. The *movement towards* that he discusses is the desire for an experience of a meditative state, or a sense for the experiential, which he found to be a significant motivator for ashram residents.

7 J. Goldstein. (1976), *The Experience of Insight*, Shambala Publications.

8 Volinn, 'Eastern Meditation Groups: Why Join?', 147–56.

9 A. Nock. (1998), *Conversion: The Old and the New in Religion from Alexander the Great to Augustine of Hippo*. Baltimore and London: John Hopkins University Press, p. 7; D. A. Snow and R. Machalek. (1984), 'The Sociology of Conversion', *Annual Review of Sociology* 10, 169.

10 J. W. Coleman. (2001), *The New Buddhism: The Western Transformation of an Ancient Tradition*. New York: Oxford University Press, p. 125. Coleman notes that in Shikantaza, the attempt is made to see experience as it is without imposing an interpretation onto it.

11 M. Heirich. (1977), 'Change of Heart: A Test of Some Widely Held Theories about Religious Conversion', *American Journal of Sociology* 83 (3), 653–80.

12 M. Abe. (1998), Faith and Self-Awakening: A Search for the Category Covering All Religious Life, *The Eastern Buddhist* XXXI (1), 15. Abe contrasts this specifically Buddhist sense of faith as awakening to dharma or self-realization of Nirvana, with Wilfred Cantwell Smith's essentialist notion of faith as a spiritual orientation of the personality and the capacity to relate to the transcendent.

13 Abe, 'Faith and Self-Awakening: A Search for the Category Covering All Religious Life', 16–17. Faith is the first of five, the others being assiduous striving, mindfulness, concentration, and wisdom, in that order.

14 G. Fronsdal. (1998), 'Insight Meditation in the United States: Life, Liberty, and the Pursuit of Happiness', in C. S. Prebish and K. Tanaka (eds), *The Faces of Buddhism in America*. Berkeley, Los Angeles and London: University of California Press, pp. 169–77. This is in much the same way as people sometimes use the word spiritual in preference to the term religious, because they feel that the latter implies a dogmatic approach and subservience to an outer religious authority. Fronsdal observed that the early American vipassana students, many of whom were part of the counter-culture movement of the 60s and 70s, distanced themselves from mainstream religion, and described their involvement with Buddhist practice as spiritual rather than religious.

15 K. McDonald. (1984), *How to Meditate: A Practical Guide*. Robina Courtin ed. Boston: Wisdom Publications.

16 See T. Tweed. (1999), 'Night-Stand Buddhists and other Creatures: Sympathizers, Adherents, and the Study of Religion', in D. R. Williams and C. S. Queen (eds), *American Buddhism*. Richmond: Curzon Press, pp. 74–75. Tweed maintains that many in the West fit the profile of the night-stand Buddhist, a sympathizer who

reads Buddhist material and incorporates some practices into their life, without any formal affiliation with Buddhism.

[17] See Lofland and Stark, 'Becoming a World-Saver: A Theory of Conversion to a Deviant Perspective', 862–75.

[18] C. L. Staples and A. L. Mauss. (1987), 'Conversion or Commitment? A Reassessment of the Snow and Machalek Approach to the Study of Conversion', *Journal for the Scientific Study of Religion* 26 (2), 145. Snow and Machalek, 'The Sociology of Conversion', 167–90. The former paper is a critique of the position outlined in the latter paper.

[19] The rest of this excerpt dealing with the opening up of a sense of spaciousness felt by NC on performing his refuge commitments is discussed in Chapter 5.

[20] See S. Wilson. (1984), 'Becoming a Yogi: Resocialization and Deconditioning as Conversion Processes', *Sociological Analysis* 45 (4), 305.

[21] P. L. Berger and T. Luckmann. (1966), *The Social Construction of Reality: a Treatise in the Sociology of Knowledge*. New York: Doubleday & Company.

[22] Lofland and Stark, 'Becoming a World-Saver: A Theory of Conversion to a Deviant Perspective', 862–75. Possession of a religious problem-solving perspective as opposed to another type, for instance a political one, was one of the predisposing factors to religious conversion, according to their Worldsaver model, generated by their research on the Divine Precepts, the early form of the Unification Church.

[23] E. Hedges and J. A. Beckford. (2000), 'Holism, Healing, and the New Age', in S. Sutcliffe and M. Bowman (eds), *Beyond New Age: Exploring Alternative Spirituality*. Edinburgh: Edinburgh University Press, p. 172. They believe the label to be appropriate for the alternative forms of spirituality that encourage practitioners to rely on inner guidance rather than on external texts and authorities.

[24] S. Sutcliffe and M. Bowman. (2000), 'Introduction', in S. Sutcliffe and M. Bowman (eds), *Beyond New Age: Exploring Alternative Spirituality*. Edinburgh: Edinburgh University Press, p. 8.

[25] R. Sharf. (1995), 'Buddhist Modernism and the Rhetoric of Meditative Experience', in *Numen* 42, 228.

[26] See R. S. Ellwood. (1979), *Alternative Altars: Unconventional and Eastern Spirituality in America*. Chicago and London: University of Chicago Press, p. 10.

[27] For instance, Tingay outlines a taxonomy of movements related to Theosophy. See K. Tingay. (2000), 'Madame Blavatsky's Children: Theosophy and Its Heirs', in S. Sutcliffe and M. Bowman (eds), *Beyond New Age: Exploring Alternative Spirituality*. Edinburgh University Press, p. 40.

[28] P. Heelas. (1996), *The New Age Movement: The Celebration of the Self and the Sacralization of Modernity*, Oxford: Blackwell Publishers p. 18. Heelas comparison between EST seminars and Gurdjieffs approach highlights their common focus on placing lived experience above dogma.

[29] S. Sutcliffe. (2000), 'Wandering Stars: Seekers and Gurus in the Modern World', in S. Sutcliffe and M. Bowman (eds), *Beyond New Age: Exploring Alternative Spirituality*. Edinburgh University Press, p. 29.

[30] Fronsdal, 'Insight Meditation in the United States: Life, Liberty, and the Pursuit of Happiness', p. 76; A. Rawlinson. (1997), *The Book of Enlightened Masters: Western Teachers in Eastern Traditions*. Chicago and La Salle, Illinois: Open Court

Publishing; J. W. Coleman. (1999), 'The New Buddhism: Some Empirical Findings', in D. R. Williams and C. S. Queen (eds), *American Buddhism*. Richmond: Curzon Press, pp. 97–98.

[31] Geshe Acharya Thubten Loden. (1993), *Path to Enlightenment in Tibetan Buddhism*. Melbourne: Tushita Publications, pp. 480–84. Also see Gen Lamrimpa. (2002), E. Posman (ed.), B. A. Wallace (trans.), *Realizing Emptiness: Madhayaka Insight Meditation*, 2nd ed. Ithaca, New York, Boulder, Colorado: Snow Lion Publications, p. 108.

[32] Tsong-kha-pa. *The Great Treatise on the Stages of the Path to Enlightenment*, Snow Lion Publications, volume 2 (2004); volume 3 (2002).

[33] Preliminary research with the Friends of the Western Buddhist Order had shown ethics to be highly important to that group also. See Chapter 1: *The Western Buddhist Ethnographic Field*, for the reasons why this group was not included in the study.

[34] See D. Keown. (1992), *The Nature of Buddhist Ethics*. New York: St Martin's Press, p. 107, and Gen Lamrimpa, *Realizing Emptiness*, pp. 108–09.

[35] J. W. Coleman. (2001), *The New Buddhism: The Western Transformation of an Ancient Tradition*. New York: Oxford University Press, p. 110.

[36] T. Pilarzyk. (1978), 'Conversion and Alternation Processes in the Youth Culture: A Comparative Analysis of Religious Traditions', *Pacific Sociological Review* 21 (4), 398; 403. Pilarzyks attention to shock experiences arises from his perception that sociological perspectives on conversion grounded in structural functionalism have stressed the importance of social processes, and not paid attention to those experiences that appear to disrupt the routine aspect of everyday life.

[37] Pilarzyk, 'Conversion and Alternation Processes in the Youth Culture: A Comparative Analysis of Religious Traditions', 382.

[38] Those of Vipassana meditators HD, HU, and EBS, and Vajrayana students CR, AN and RI are in this category.

[39] Neither do these situations fit Pilarzyk's description of the antecedents of conversion, attempts to reinterpret a period prior to contact as one of partial or total discontentment, crisis, alienation, or suffering. See Pilarzyk. 'Conversion and Alternation Processes in the Youth Culture', 380.

[40] Berger and Luckmann, *The Social Construction of Reality*, p. 144.

[41] R. Travisano. (1970), 'Alternation and Conversion as Qualitatively Different Transformations', in G. P. Stone and H. A. Farberman (eds), *Social Psychology Through Symbolic Interaction*. Waltham: Xerox College Publishing, pp. 594–606.

[42] Pilarzyk, 'Conversion and Alternation Processes in the Youth Culture', p. 383.

[43] Pilarzyk, 'Conversion and Alternation Processes in the Youth Culture'.

[44] D. A. Snow and R. Machalek. (1983), 'The Convert as a Social Type', in R. Collins (ed.), *Sociological Theory*. San Francisco and London: American Sociological Association, pp. 266–70; D. A. Snow and R. Machalek. (1984), 'The Sociology of Conversion', *Annual Review of Sociology* 10, 173–74. Also see Staples and Mauss, 1987, 'Conversion or Commitment? A Reassessment of the Snow and Machalek Approach to the Study of Conversion'.

[45] Snow and Machalek, 'The Convert as a Social Type', 173; P. L. Berger. (1963), *Invitation to Sociology: A Humanistic Perspective*. Harmondsworth: Penguin Books,

pp. 75–6; J. A. Beckford. (1978), 'Accounting for Conversion', *British Journal of Sociology* 29 (2).

[46] Staples and Mauss, 'Conversion or Commitment? A Reassessment of the Snow and Machalek Approach to the Study of Conversion', 137. They use the term self-transformation to distinguish self-concept change from other, more routine changes to self-concept, such as role changes and life-cycle changes.

[47] Travisano, 'Alternation and Conversion as Qualitatively Different Transformations', pp. 594–606; Heirich, 'Change of Heart: A Test of Some Widely Held Theories about Religious Conversion', 653–80.

[48] M. D Bryant and C. Lamb. (1999), 'Introduction: Conversion: contours of controversy and commitment in a plural world', in C. Lamb and M. D. Bryant (eds), *Religious Conversion: Contemporary Practices and Controversies.* London and New York: Cassell, pp. 9–11.

[49] J. Nattier. (1998), 'Who is a Buddhist? Charting the Landscape of Buddhist America', in C. S. Prebish and K. Tanaka (eds), *The Faces of Buddhism in America.* Berkely, Los Angeles and London: University of California Press, pp. 183–195. T. Tweed. (1999), 'Night-Stand Buddhists and other Creatures: Sympathizers, Adherents, and the Study of Religion', in D. R. Williams and C. S. Queen (eds), *American Buddhism.* Richmond: Curzon Press, pp. 79–80.

[50] D. Cush. (1996), 'British Buddhism and the New Age', *Journal of Contemporary Religion,* 11 (2), 205. Her comments suggest that the writings of Christmas Humphreys, criticized for their Theosophical slant, especially the interpretation of no-self as Self with a Capital S, were instrumental in creating this confusion (although she does not suggest that this was deliberate).

[51] See S. Kaza. (2000), 'Buddhist Views on Ritual Practice: Becoming a Real Person', *Buddhist-Christian Studies* 20, 46; Y. Seiichi. (2001), 'The Distinction Between ego (e) and ego-Self (e/S): Notes Upon Religious Practice Based Upon Buddhist-Christian Dialogue', *Buddhist-Christian Studies* 21, 96–7.

[52] M. Orru and A. Wang. (1992), 'Durkheim, Religion, and Buddhism', *Journal for the Scientific Study of Religion* 31 (1), 55–56.

[53] Geshe Acharya Thubten Loden, *Path to Enlightenment in Tibetan Buddhism,* pp. 851–52.

[54] Geshe Acharya Thubten Loden, *Path to Enlightenment in Tibetan Buddhism,* p. 849. Also see Gen Lamrimpa, *Realizing Emptiness: Madhyamaka Insight Meditation,* p. 86. Tsong-kha-pa, *The Great Treatise on the Stages of the Path to Enlightenment* volume 3, p. 14.

[55] See J. Hopkins. (1996), *Meditation on Emptiness,* revised ed. Boston: Wisdom Publications pp. 44–46. Gen Lamrimpa, *Realizing Emptiness,* pp. 99; McDonald, *How to Meditate,* pp. 60–61, and K. Valham (compiler). (1997), *Lam Rim Outlines: Beginners Meditation Guide,* Boston, Wisdom Publications pp. 77–80. See Geshe Acharya Thubten Loden, *Path to Enlightenment in Tibetan Buddhism,* pp. 849–60, for the background theory and reasoning to the meditation.

[56] J. Engler. (1983), 'Vicissitudes of the Self According to Psychoanalysis and Buddhism: A Spectrum Model of Object Relations Development', *Psychoanalysis and Contemporary Thought* 6, 29–72.

[57] W. James. (1983), *Principles of Psychology.* Cambridge MA: Harvard University Press.

58 G. P. Stone and H. A. Farberman. (1970), 'The Self', in G. P. Stone and H. A. Farberman (eds), *Social Psychology Through Symbolic Interaction.* Xerox College Publishing, pp. 367–68.

59 Berger and Luckmann, *The Social Construction of Reality,* p. 122.

60 Geshe Acharya Thubten Loden, *Path to Enlightenment in Tibetan Buddhism,* p. 116. G. Watson. (2002), *The Resonance of Emptiness: A Buddhist Inspiration for a Contemporary Psychotherapy,* Richmond: Curzon Press, p. 110.

61 Engler, 'Vicissitudes of the Self According to Psychoanalysis and Buddhism', 30–31.

62 Keown, *The Nature of Buddhist Ethics,* 1.

63 S. King. (1991), *Buddha Nature.* New York: State University of New York Press, pp. 69–71.

References

Abe, M. (1998), 'Faith and Self-Awakening: A Search for the Category Covering All Religious Life', *The Eastern Buddhist* XXXI (1), 12–24.

Adam, E. and Hughes, P. J. (1996), K. Waters (ed.), *The Buddhists in Australia*. Canberra: Australian Government Publishing Service.

Analayo (2003), *Satipatthana: The Direct Path to Realization*. Birmingham: Windhorse Publications.

Anthony, D., Robbins, T., Doucas, M., and Curtis, T. E. (1978), 'Patients and Pilgrims: Changing Attitudes Toward Psychotherapy of Converts to Eastern Mysticism', in J. T. Richardson (ed.), *Conversion Careers: In and Out of the New Religions*. Beverly Hills: Sage Publications, pp. 65–90.

Balch, R. (1980), 'Looking Behind the Scenes in a Religious Cult: Implications for the Study of Conversion', *Sociological Analysis* 41, 137–43.

Balch, R. W. and Taylor, D. (1976), 'Salvation in a UFO', *Psychology Today* 10 (5), 58–66; 106.

Balch, R. W. and Taylor, D. (1978), 'Seekers and Saucers: The Role of the Cultic Milieu in Joining a UFO Cult', in J. T. Richardson (ed.), *Conversion Careers: In and Out of the New Religions*. Beverly Hills: Sage Publications, pp. 43–64.

Baumann, M. (1997), 'Culture Contact and Valuation: Early German Buddhists and the "Creation of a Buddhism in Protestant Shape" ', *Numen* 44 (3), 270–95.

Baumann, M. (2001), 'Global Buddhism: Developmental Periods, Regional Histories, and a New Analytic Perspective', *Journal of Global Buddhism* 2, 1–43.

Baumann, M. (2002), 'Protective Amulets and Awareness Techniques, or How to Make Sense of Buddhism in the West', in C. S. Prebish and M. Baumann (eds), *Westward Dharma: Buddhism Beyond Asia*. Berkeley, Los Angeles, London: University of California Press, pp. 51–64.

Becker, H. (1960), 'Notes on the Concept of Commitment', *American Journal of Sociology* 66 (1), 32–40.

Beckford, J. A. (1975), *The Trumpet of Prophecy: A Sociological Study of the Jehovah's Witnesses*. Oxford: Basil Blackwell.

Beckford, J. A. (1978), 'Accounting for Conversion', *British Journal of Sociology* 29 (2), 249–62.

Bedford, S. (1996), 'Crying out of Recognition: Experiences with Meditative Practices in a New Religious Movement', *ARC, Journal of the Faculty Religious Studies, McGill* 24, 119–32.

Bell, S. (1998), 'British Theravada Buddhism: Otherworldly Theories, and the Theory of Exchange', *Journal of Contemporary Religion* 13 (2), 149–70.

Bell, S. (2000), 'Being Creative with Tradition: Rooting Theravada Buddhism in Britain', *Journal of Global Buddhism* 1, 1–23.

Bell, S. (2002), 'Scandals in Emerging Western Buddhism', in C. S. Prebish and M. Baumann (eds), *Westward Dharma: Buddhism Beyond Asia*. Berkeley, Los Angeles, London: University of California Press, pp. 230–44.

Berger, H. A. (1999), *A Community of Witches: Contemporary Neo-Paganism and Witchcraft in the United States*. Columbia: University of South Carolina Press.

Berger, P. L. (1963), *Invitation to Sociology: A Humanistic Perspective*. Harmondsworth: Penguin Books.

Berger, P. L. (1969), *The Sacred Canopy: Elements of a Sociological Theory of Religion*. New York: Anchor Books.

Berger, P. L. (1974), 'Some Second Thoughts on Substantive Versus Functional Definitions of Religion', *Journal for the Scientific Study of Religion* 13 (2), 125–33.

Berger, P. L. and Luckmann, T. (1966), *The Social Construction of Reality: A Treatise in the Sociology of Knowledge*. New York: Doubleday & Company.

Berger, P. L., Berger, B., and Kellner, H. (1973), *The Homeless Mind: Modernization and Consciousness*. Harmondsworth: Penguin Books.

Berzin, A. (2000), *Relating to a Spiritual Teacher: Building a Healthy Relationship*. New York: Snow Lion Publications.

Bhikkhu Bodhi (1999), 'Message', in Soma Thera (ed.), *The Way of Mindfulness: The Satipatthana Sutta and Its Commentary*, 6th ed. Kuala Lumpur: Buddhist Publication Society, pp. v–vii.

Bhikkhu Bodhi (ed.) (2001), 'Anapanasati Sutta', in B. Nanamoli (trans.), *Majjhima Nikaya*. Boston: Wisdom Publications, pp. 941–48.

Bhikkhu Bodhi (ed.) (2001a), 'Satipatthana Sutta', in B. Nanamoli (trans.), *Majjhima Nikaya (The Middle Length Discourses of the Buddha)*, revised ed. Boston: Wisdom Publications, pp. 145–55.

Bhikkhu Bodhi (ed.) (2001b), 'Salayatanavibhanga Sutta', in B. Nanamoli (trans.), *Majjhima Nikaya (The Middle Length Discourses of the Buddha)*, revised ed. Boston: Wisdom Publications, pp. 1066–73.

Bhikkhu Bodhi (ed.) (2005), *In the Buddha's Words: An Anthology of Discourses from the Pali Canon*. Boston: Wisdom Publications.

Bryant, M. D. and Lamb, C. (1999), 'Introduction: Conversion: Contours of Controversy and Commitment in a Plural World', in C. Lamb and M. D. Bryant (eds), *Religious Conversion: Contemporary Practices and Controversies*. London and New York: Cassell, pp. 1–22.

Buckner, H. T. (1968), 'The Flying Saucerians: An Open Door Cult', in M. Truzzi (ed.), *Sociology and Everyday Life*. Englewood Cliffs, NJ: Prentice-Hall, pp. 223–30.

Burns, D. and Ohayv, R. J. (1980), 'Psychological Changes in Meditating Western Monks in Thailand', *Journal of Transpersonal Psychology* 12 (1), 11–24.

Cadge, W. (2005), *Heartwood: The First Generation of Theravada Buddhism in America*. Chicago and London: University of Chicago Press.

Campbell, C. (1972), 'The Cult, the Cultic Milieu and Secularization', in M. Hill (ed.), *A Sociological Yearbook of Religion in Britain* 5. London: SCM Press, pp. 119–36.

Campbell, C. (1999), 'The Easternization of the West', in B. Wilson and J. Cresswell (eds), *New Religious Movements: Challenge and Response*. London: Routledge, pp. 35–48.

Capper, D. (2004), 'Enchantment with Tibetan Lamas in the United States', *Journal of Contemporary Religion* 19 (2), 137–53.

Coleman, J. W. (1999), 'The New Buddhism: Some Empirical Findings', in D. R. Williams and C. S. Queen (eds), *American Buddhism*. Richmond: Curzon Press, pp. 91–99.

Coleman, J. W. (2001), *The New Buddhism: The Western Transformation of an Ancient Tradition*. New York: Oxford University Press.

Conze, E. (1980), *A Short History of Buddhism*. London: George Allen and Unwin.

Croucher, P. (1989), *Buddhism in Australia 1848–1988*. Sydney: New South Wales University Press.

Csikszentmihalyi, M. (1991), *Flow: The Psychology of Optimal Experience*. New York: HarperPerennial.

Cusack, C. M. (1996), 'Towards a General Theory of Conversion', in L. Olsen (ed.), *Religious Change, Conversion and Culture*. Sydney: Sydney Association for Studies in Society and Culture, pp. 1–21.

Cush, D. (1996), 'British Buddhism and the New Age', *Journal of Contemporary Religion* 11 (2), 195–208.

D'Andrade, R. (1995), *The Development of Cognitive Anthropology*. Cambridge: Cambridge University Press.

Dawson, L. (1990), 'Self-Affirmation, Freedom, and Rationality: Theoretically Elaborating "Active" Conversions', *Journal for the Scientific Study of Religion* 29 (2), 141–63.

Deatherage, G. (1975), 'The Clinical Use of "Mindfulness" Meditation Techniques in Short-Term Psychotherapy', *Journal of Transpersonal Psychology* 7 (2), 133–43.

De Wit, H. F. (1992), 'Transmitting the Buddhist View of Experience', in J. D. Gort, H. M. Vroom, R. Fernhout, and A. Wessels (eds), *On Sharing Religious Experience: Possibilities of Interfaith Mutuality*. Grand Rapids, MI: William B. Eerdmans Publishing Company, pp. 189–202.

Downton, J. V. (1980), 'An Evolutionary Theory of Spiritual Conversion and Commitment: The Case of Divine Light Mission', *Journal for the Scientific Study of Religion* 19 (4), 381–96.

Eddy, G. (2007a), 'A Strand of Contemporary Tantra: Its Discourse and Practice in the FPMT', *Journal of Global Buddhism* 8, 81–106.

Eddy, G. (2007b), 'Western Buddhist Experience: The Journey from Encounter to Commitment in Two Forms of Western Buddhism', Ph.D. Thesis, Department of Studies in Religion, University of Sydney, pp. ix + 293.

Eddy, G. (2007c), 'The Application of James' Model of the Self to the Understanding of Self-Transformative Experience in Vipassana Meditation', in *Spirituality in Australia: Psychological, Social and Religious Perspectives*, Proceedings of the UWS Psychology and Spirituality Society Annual Conference 20 July 2007, Centre for Human Interaction, Learning and Development (CD-Rom).

Eddy, G. (2009), 'The Applicability of James' Model of the Self to the Western Buddhist Experience of Self-Transformation', in K. McPhillips and J. Johnston (eds), *Refereed Conference Papers of the AASR Sessions of the SBL International Congress*, Auckland, New Zealand, 6–11 July, 2008. Sydney: Australian Association for the Study of Religion, pp. 88–100.

Ellwood, R. S. (1973), *Religious and Spiritual Groups in Modern America.* Englewood Cliffs, New Jersey: Prentice-Hall.

Ellwood, R. S. (1979), *Alternative Altars: Unconventional and Eastern Spirituality in America.* Chicago and London: University of Chicago Press.

Engler, J. (1983), 'Vicissitudes of the Self According to Psychoanalysis and Buddhism: A Spectrum Model of Object Relations Development', *Psychoanalysis and Contemporary Thought* 6, 29–72.

Engler, J. (1984), 'Therapeutic Aims in Psychotherapy and Meditation: Developmental Stages in the Representation of Self', *Journal of Transpersonal Psychology* 16 (1), 25–61.

Faivre, A. (1998), 'Questions of Terminology Proper to the Study of Esoteric Currents in Modern and Contemporary Europe', in A. Faivre and W. J. Hanegraaff (eds), *Gnostica 2: Western Esotericism and the Science of Religions.* Bondgenotenlaan, Belgium: Peeters, pp. 1–10.

Fields, R. (1992), *How the Swans Came to the Lake: A Narrative History of Buddhism in America,* 3rd ed. Boston and London: Shambala.

Fields, R. (1998), 'Divided Dharma: White Buddhists, Ethnic Buddhists, and Racism', in C. S. Prebish and K. Tanaka (eds), *The Faces of Buddhism in America.* Berkely, Los Angeles and London: University of California Press, pp. 196–206.

Forman, R. (1990), 'Introduction: Mysticism, Constructivism, and Forgetting', in R. K. C. Forman (ed.), *The Problem of Pure Consciousness.* Oxford: Oxford University Press, pp. 3–49.

Forman, R. (1993), 'Mystical Knowledge: Knowledge by Identity', *Journal of the American Academy of Religion* 61 (4), 705–38.

Forman, R. (1998), 'Mystical Consciousness, the Innate Capacity, and the Perennial Psychology', in R. Forman (ed.), *The Innate Capacity: Mysticism, Psychology, and Philosophy.* New York: Oxford University Press, pp. 3–41.

Fronsdal, G. (1998), 'Insight Meditation in the United States: Life, Liberty, and the Pursuit of Happiness', in C. S. Prebish and K. Tanaka (eds), *The Faces of Buddhism in America.* Berkeley, Los Angeles and London: University of California Press, pp. 164–80.

Gen Lamrimpa (1992), H Sprager (ed.), B. A. Wallace (trans.), *Samatha Meditation: Tibetan Buddhist Teachings on Cultivating Meditative Quiescence.* Ithaca, NY: Snow Lion Publications.

Gen Lamrimpa (2002), E. Posman (ed.), B. A. Wallace (trans.), *Realizing Emptiness: Madhayaka Insight Meditation,* 2nd ed. Ithaca, NY and Boulder, CO: Snow Lion Publications.

Geshe Acharya Thubten Loden (1993), *Path to Enlightenment in Tibetan Buddhism.* Melbourne: Tushita Publications.

Gilgen, A. and Cho, J. (1979), 'Questionnaire to Measure Eastern and Western Thought', *Psychological Reports* 44, 835–41.

Glock, C. (1964), 'The Role of Deprivation in the Origin and Evolution of Religious Groups', in R. Lee and M. E. Marty (eds), *Religion and Social Conflict.* New York: Oxford University Press, pp. 24–36.

Goldstein, J. (1976), *The Experience of Insight.* Boston: Shambala Publications.

Goldstein, J. (1994), *Insight Meditation: The Practice of Freedom.* Boston and London: Shambala.

Goldstein, J. (2002), *One Dharma: The Emerging Western Buddhism.* London: Rider.

Goleman, D. (1978), *The Varieties of the Meditative Experience.* London: Rider and Company.

Gordon, D. (1974), 'The Jesus People: An Identity Synthesis', *Urban Life and Culture* 3 (2), 159–78.

Granqvist, P. (2003), 'Attachment Theory and Religious Conversions: A Review and Resolution of the Classic and Contemporary Paradigm Chiasm', *Review of Religious Research* 45 (2), 172–87.

Greil, A. (1977), 'Previous Dispositions and Conversion to Perspectives of Social and Religious Movements', *Sociological Analysis* 38 (2), 115–25.

Griffiths, P. (1981), 'Concentration or Insight: The Problematic of Theravada Buddhist Meditation-Theory', *Journal of the American Academy of Religion* 49 (4), 605–21.

Griffiths, P. (1983), 'Buddhist Jhana: A Form-Critical Study', *Religion* 13, 55–68.

Griffiths, P. (1990), 'Pure Consciousness and Indian Buddhism', in R. K. C. Forman (ed.), *The Problem of Pure Consciousness.* Oxford: Oxford University Press, pp. 71–96.

Guenther, H. (1972), *The Tantric View of Life.* Berkeley and London: Shambala Publications.

Gussner, R. E. and Berkowitz, S. D. (1988), 'Scholars, Sects, and Sanghas, 1: Recruitment to Asian-Based Meditation Groups in North America', *Sociological Analysis* 49 (2), 136–70.

Hall, J. (1988), 'Social Organization and Pathways of Commitment: Types of Communal Groups, Rational Choice Theory, and the Kanter Thesis', *American Sociological Review* 53, 679–92.

Hamilton, S. (1996), *Identity and Experience: The Constitution of the Human Being According to Early Buddhism.* London: Luzac Oriental.

Hamilton, S. (2000), *Early Buddhism: A New Approach (The I of the Beholder).* Richmond: Curzon Press.

Hammond, P. and Machacek, D. (1999), 'Supply and Demand: The Appeal of Buddhism in America', in D. R. Williams and C. S. Queen (eds), *American Buddhism.* Richmond: Curzon Press, pp. 100–114.

Harrison, M. (1974), 'Preparation for Life in the Spirit: The Process of Initial Commitment to a Religious Movement', *Urban Life and Culture* 2 (4), 387–414.

Harvey, P. (1990), *An Introduction to Buddhism: Teachings, History, and Practices.* Cambridge: Cambridge University Press.

Harvey, P. (2000), *An Introduction to Buddhist Ethics: Foundations, Values, and Issues.* Cambridge: Cambridge University Press.

Hedges, E. and Beckford, J. A. (2000), 'Holism, Healing, and the New Age', in S. Sutcliffe and M. Bowman (eds), *Beyond New Age: Exploring Alternative Spirituality.* Edinburgh: Edinburgh University Press, pp. 169–87.

Heelas, P. (1996), *The New Age Movement: The Celebration of the Self and the Sacralization of Modernity.* Oxford and Cambridge, MA: Blackwell Publishers.

Heelas, P. (1996), 'Introduction: Detraditionalization and Its Rivals', in P. Heelas, S. Lash, and P. Morris (eds), *Detraditionalization: Critical Reflections on Authority and Identity.* Oxford: Blackwell Publishers, pp. 1–18.

Heirich, M. (1977), 'Change of Heart: A Test of Some Widely Held Theories About Religious Conversion', *American Journal of Sociology* 83 (3), 653–80.

Henepola Gunaratana (1985), *The Path of Serenity and Insight: An Explanation of the Buddhist Jhanas*. Delhi: Motilal Banarsidass.

Henepola Gunaratana (1992), *Mindfulness in Plain English*. Boston: Wisdom Publications.

His Holiness the Dalai Lama, Tsong-kha-pa, and Hopkins, J. (1987), J. Hopkins (ed. and trans.), *Deity Yoga in Action and Performance Tantra*. New York: Snow Lion Publications.

Hopkins, J. (1996), *Meditation on Emptiness*, revised ed. Boston: Wisdom Publications.

Hopkins, J. (1999), Anne C. Klein (ed.), *The Tantric Distinction: A Buddhist's Reflections on Compassion and Emptiness*, revised ed. Boston: Wisdom Publications.

Horney, K. (1970), *Neurosis and Human Growth: The Struggle Toward Self-Realization*. New York and London: Norton.

Imamura, R. (1998), 'Buddhist and Western Psychotherapies: An Asian American Perspective', in C. S. Prebish and K. Tanaka (eds), *The Faces of Buddhism in America*. Berkely, Los Angeles and London: University of California Press, pp. 228–37.

James, W. (1970), 'The Social Self', in G. P. Stone and H. A. Farberman (eds), *Social Psychology Through Symbolic Interaction*. Waltham, Massachusetts: Xerox College Publishing, pp. 373–82.

James, W. (1983), *Principles of Psychology*. Cambridge, MA: Harvard University Press.

James, W. (2002), E. Taylor and J. Carrette (eds), *The Varieties of the Religious Experience: A Study in Human Nature*, centenary edition. London and New York: Routledge.

Jordt, I. (2007), *Burma's Mass Law Meditation Movement: Buddhism and the Cultural Construction of Power*. Ohio: Centre for International Studies, Ohio University.

Jorgensen, D. (1982), 'The Esoteric Community: An Ethnographic Investigation of the Cultic Milieu', *Urban Life* 10 (4), 383–408.

Katz, S. (1978), 'Language, Epistemology and Mysticism', in *Mysticism and Philosophical Analysis*. London: Sheldon Press, pp. 22–73.

Katz, S. (1985), 'Recent Work on Mysticism', *History of Religions* 25 (1), 76–86.

Kay, D. (2004), *Tibetan and Zen Buddhism in Britain: Transplantation, Development and Adaptation*. London and New York: RoutledgeCurzon.

Kaza, S. (2000), 'Buddhist Views on Ritual Practice: Becoming a Real Person', *Buddhist-Christian Studies* 20, 45–69.

Kelsang Gyatso (2000), *Tantric Grounds and Paths: How to Enter, Progress On, and Complete the Vajrayana Path*. Delhi: Motilal Banarsidass.

Kelsang Gyatso (2002), *The Meditation Handbook*. New Delhi: New Age Books.

Keown, D. (1992), *The Nature of Buddhist Ethics*. New York: St Martin's Press.

Keown, D. (2003), *A Dictionary of Buddhism*. Oxford: Oxford University Press.

Kilbourne, B. and Richardson, J. T. (1985), 'Social Experimentation Self-Process or Social Role', *The International Journal of Social Psychiatry* 31 (1), 13–22.

Kilbourne, B. and Richardson, J. T. (1989), 'Paradigm Conflict, Types of Conversion, and Conversion Theories', *Sociological Analysis* 50 (1), 1–21.

King, S. (1991), *Buddha Nature*. New York: State University of New York Press.

Komito, D. (1983), 'Tibetan Buddhism and Psychotherapy: A Conversation with the Dalai Lama', *Journal of Transpersonal Psychology* 25 (1), 1–11.

Kornfield, J. (1979), 'Intensive Insight Meditation: A Phenomenological Study', *Journal of Transpersonal Psychology* 2 (1), 41–58.

Kornfield, J. (1994), *A Path with Heart: A Guide Through the Perils and Promises of Spiritual Life.* London: Rider.

Kornfield, J. (1996), *Living Dharma: Teachings of Twelve Buddhist Masters.* Boston and London: Shambala.

Lamb, C. (1999), 'Conversion as a Process Leading to Enlightenment: The Buddhist Perspective', in C. Lamb and M. D. Bryant (eds), *Religious Conversion: Contemporary Practices and Controversies.* London and New York: Cassell, pp. 75–88.

Lavine, A. (1998), 'Tibetan Buddhism in America: The Development of American Vajrayana', in C. S. Prebish and K. Tanaka (eds), *The Faces of Buddhism in America.* Berkely, Los Angeles and London: University of California Press, pp. 100–115.

Layman, E. M. (1976), *Buddhism in America.* Chicago: Nelson-Hall.

Leary, D. (1990), 'William James on the Self and Personality: Clearing the Ground for Subsequent Theorists, Researchers, and Practitioners', in M. G. Johnston and T. B. Henley (eds), *Reflections on the Principles of Psychology: William James After a Century.* New Jersey: Lawrence Erlbaum Associates, pp. 101–37.

Lifton, R. J. (1993), The Protean Self: Human Resilience in an Age of Fragmentation. New York: BasicBooks.

Lofland, J. (1978), 'Becoming a World-Saver' Revisited, in J. T. Richardson (ed.), *Conversion Careers: In and Out of the New Religions.* Beverly Hills and London: Sage Publications, pp. 10–23.

Lofland, J. and Skonovd, N. (1981), 'Conversion Motifs', *Journal for the Scientific Study of Religion* 20 (4), 373–85.

Lofland, J. and Stark, R. (1965), 'Becoming a World-Saver: A Theory of Conversion to a Deviant Perspective', *American Sociological Review* 30 (6), 862–75.

Lopez, D. (1996), *Elaborations on Emptiness: Uses of the Heart Sutra.* Princeton and Chichester: Princeton University Press.

Lyon, D. (2000), *Jesus in Disneyland: Religion in Postmodern Times,* Cambridge: Polity Press.

MacPhillamy, D. J. (1986), 'Some Personality Effects of Long-Term Zen Monasticism and Religious Understanding', *Journal for the Scientific Study of Religion* 25 (3), 304–19.

Magnussen, K. (ed.). (2003), *The Preliminary Practice of Vajrasattva: Practice and Instructions for Retreat.* FPMT inc.

Mahasi Sayadaw (1958), U Pe Thin (trans.), *Discourse on the Basic Practice of the Satipatthana Vipassana.* Printed at the Burma Art Press.

Mahasi Sayadaw (1971), U Pe Thin and Myanaung U Tin (trans.), *Practical Insight Meditation: Basic and Progressive Stages.* Kandy: Buddhist Publication Society.

McAra, S. A. (2007), *Land of Beautiful Vision: Making a Buddhist Sacred Place in New Zealand.* Honolulu: University of Hawai'i Press.

McCutcheon, R. (1999), *The Insider/Outsider Problem in the Study of Religion: A Reader.* London and New York: Cassell.

McDonald, K. (1984), *How to Meditate: A Practical Guide.* Robina Courtin ed. Massachusets: Wisdom Publications.

McIntyre, J. (1997), 'On Becoming a Meditator: Adult Learning and Social Context', in P. Willis and B. Neville (eds), *Qualitative Research Practice in Education.* Melbourne: David Lovell Publishing, pp. 33–48.

Mead, George H. (1934), C. W. Morris (ed.), *Mind, Self, and Society: From the Standpoint of a Social Behaviourist*. Chicago and London: University of Chicago Press.

Mead, George H. (1970), 'Self as Social Object', in G. P. Stone and H. A. Farberman (eds), *Social Psychology Through Symbolic Interaction*. Waltham, Massachusetts: Xerox College Publishing, pp. 383–86.

Nanamoli Thera (1998a), 'The Practice of Lovingkindness' (1958), in *The Four Sublime States*, Nyanaponika Thera, and *The Practice of Lovingkindness*, Nanamoli Thera, combined edition. Kandy: Buddhist Publication Society, pp. 3–26.

Nanamoli Thera (trans.). (1998b), *Mindfulness of Breathing (Anapanasati): Buddhist Texts from the Pali Canon and Commentaries*, 6th ed. Kandy: Buddhist Publication Society.

Nattier, J. (1998), 'Who Is a Buddhist? Charting the Landscape of Buddhist America', in C. S. Prebish and K. Tanaka (eds), *The Faces of Buddhism in America*. Berkely, Los Angeles and London: University of California Press, pp. 183–95.

Ngawang Losang Tempa Gyaltsan (2002), Lama Thubten Zopa Rinpoche (trans.), *Medicine Buddha Sadhana*, revised edition. Taos New Mexico: FPTM Education Services.

Nock, A. (1998), *Conversion: The Old and the New in Religion from Alexander the Great to Augustine of Hippo*. Baltimore and London: John Hopkins University Press.

Numrich, P. D. (1998), 'Theravada Buddhism in America: Prospects for the Sangha', in C. S. Prebish and K. Tanaka (eds), *The Faces of Buddhism in America*. Berkely, Los Angeles and London: University of California Press, pp. 147–61.

Numrich, P. D. (2000), 'How the Swans Came to Lake Michigan: The Social Organization of Buddhist Chicago', *Journal for the Scientific Study of Religion* 39 (2), 189–203.

Nyanaponika Thera (1965), *The Heart of Buddhist Meditation: A Handbook of Mental Training Based on the Buddha's Way of Mindfulness*. San Francisco and Newburyport: Weiser Books.

Nyanaponika Thera (1998a), Bhikkhu Bodhi (ed.), *Abhidhamma Studies: Buddhist Explorations of Consciousness and Time*, 4th ed. Boston: Wisdom Publications, Kandy: Buddhist Publication Society.

Nyanaponika Thera (1998b), 'The Four Sublime States' (1958), in *The Four Sublime States, Nyanaponika Thera, and The Practice of Lovingkindness*, Nanamoli Thera, combined ed. Kandy: Buddhist Publication Society, pp. 29–57.

Oliver, I. (1979), *Buddhism in Britain*. London: Rider & Company.

Orru, M. and Wang, A. (1992), 'Durkheim, Religion, and Buddhism', *Journal for the Scientific Study of Religion* 31 (1), 47–61.

Paloutzian, R. (1996), *Invitation to the Psychology of Religion*. Boston: Allyn and Bacon.

Pike, S. (2001), *Earthly Bodies, Magical Selves: Contemporary Pagans and the Search for Community*. Berkeley, Los Angeles and London: University of California Press.

Pilarzyk, T. (1978), 'Conversion and Alternation Processes in the Youth Culture: A Comparative Analysis of Religious Traditions', *Pacific Sociological Review* 21 (4), 379–405.

Powers, J. (1995), *Introduction to Tibetan Buddhism*. New York: Snow Lion Publications.

Prebish, C. S. (1998), 'Introduction', in C. S. Prebish and K. Tanaka (eds), *The Faces of Buddhism in America*. Berkely, Los Angeles and London: University of California Press, pp. 1–10.

Prebish, C. S. (1999), *Luminous Passage: The Practice and Study of Buddhism in America*. Berkeley: University of California Press.

Preece, R. (2006), *The Psychology of Buddhist Tantra*. New York: Snow Lion Publications.

Preston, D. (1981), 'Becoming a Zen Practitioner', in *Sociological Analysis* 42 (1), 47–56.

Preston, D. (1982), 'Meditative Ritual Practice and Spiritual Conversion-Commitment: Theoretical Implications Based on the Case of Zen', *Sociological Analysis* 43 (3), 257–70.

Preston, D. (1988), *The Social Organization of Zen Practice: Constructing Transcultural Reality*. Cambridge: Cambridge University Press.

Proudfoot, W. and Shaver, P. (1975), 'Attribution Theory and the Psychology Religion', *Journal for the Scientific Study of Religion* 14 (4), 317–30.

Puttick, E. (2004), 'Gurdjieff and Ouspenski Groups', in C. Partridge (ed.), *Encyclopedia of New Religions*. Oxford: Lion Publishing, pp. 327–29.

Queen, C. (1998), 'Professing Buddhism: The Harvard Conference on Buddhism in America', *Buddhist-Christian Studies* 18, 217–20.

Rambo, L. (1989), 'Conversion: Toward a Holistic Model of Religious Change', *Pastoral Psychology* 38 (1), 47–63.

Rambo, L. (1993), *Understanding Religious Conversion*. New Haven and London: Yale University Press.

Rambo, L. and Farhadian, C. (1999), 'Converting: Stages of Religious Change', in C. Lamb and M. D. Bryant (eds), *Religious Conversion: Contemporary Practices and Controversies*. London and New York: Cassell, pp. 23–34.

Rawlinson, A. (1997), *The Book of Enlightened Masters: Western Teachers in Eastern Traditions*. Chicago and La Salle: Open Court Publishing.

Ray, R. (2001), *Secret of the Vajra World: The Tantric Buddhism of Tibet*. Boston and London: Shambala.

Ribush, N. (2004), 'Editor's Introduction', in Thubten Yeshe, N. Ribush (ed.), *Becoming Vajrasattva: The Tantric Path of Purification*. Boston: Wisdom Publications, pp. 1–3.

Richardson, J. T. (1978), 'Conversion Careers: In and Out of the New Religions', in J. T. Richardson (ed.), *Conversion Careers: In and Out of the New Religions*. Beverly Hills and London: Sage Publications, pp. 5–9.

Richardson, J. T. (1980), 'Conversion Careers', *Society* 17 (3), 47–50.

Richardson, J. T. (1985), 'The Active vs. Passive Convert: Paradigm Conflict in Conversion/Recruitment Research' *Journal for the Scientific Study of Religion* 24 (2), 163–79.

Richardson, J. T., Harder, M., and Simmonds, R. (1972), 'Thought Reform and the Jesus Movement', *Youth and Society* 4 (2), 185–202.

Richardson, J. T. and Stewart, M. (1978), 'Conversion Process Models and the Jesus Movement', in J. T. Richardson (ed.), *Conversion Careers: In and Out of the New Religions*. Beverly Hills and London: Sage Publications, pp. 24–42.

Rocha, C. (2006), *Zen in Brazil: The Quest for Cosmopolitan Modernity*. Honolulu: University of Hawai'i Press.

Rubin, J. (2001), 'A New View of Meditation', *Journal of Religion and Health* 40 (1), 121–28.

Samuel, G. (2005), *Tantric Revisionings: New Understandings of Tibetan Buddhism and Indian Religion*. Aldershot and Burlington: Ashgate.

Schutz, A. (1967), G. Walsh and F. Lehnert (trans.), *The Phenomenology of the Social World*. Evanston: Northwestern University Press.

Seiichi, Y. (2001), 'The Distinction Between ego (e) and ego-Self (e/S): Notes Upon Religious Practice Based Upon Buddhist-Christian Dialogue', *Buddhist-Christian Studies* 21, 95–99.

Shapiro, D. H. (1983), 'Meditation as an Altered State of Consciousness: Contributions of Western Behavioural Science', *Journal of Transpersonal Psychology* 15 (1), 61–81.

Sharf, R. (1995), 'Buddhist Modernism and the Rhetoric of Meditative Experience', *Numen* 42, 228–83.

Shaw, S. (2006), *Buddhist Meditation: An Anthology of Texts from the Pali Canon*. London and New York: Routledge.

Sherwood, P. (2003), *The Buddha Is in the Street: Engaged Buddhism in Australia*. Bunbury: Edith Cowan University.

Shibutani, T. (1955), 'Reference Groups as Perspectives', *The American Journal of Sociology* 60 (6), 562–69.

Smart, N. (1997), *Dimensions of the Sacred: An Anatomy of the World's Beliefs*. London: Harper Collins.

Snow, D. A. and Machalek, R. (1983), 'The Convert as a Social Type', in R. Collins (ed.), *Sociological Theory*. San Francisco and London: American Sociological Association, pp. 259–92.

Snow, D. A. and Machalek, R. (1984), 'The Sociology of Conversion', *Annual Review of Sociology* 10, 167–90.

Snow, D. and Phillips, C. (1979), 'The Lofland-Stark Conversion Model: A Critical Reassessment', *Social Problems* 27, 430–47.

Snow, D., Zurcher, L., and Sjoberg, G. (1982), 'Interviewing by Comment: An Adjunct to the Direct Question', *Qualitative Sociology* 5 (4), 285–311.

Soanes, C. Stevenson, A., and Hawker, S. (eds). (2004), *Concise Oxford English Dictionary*, 11th ed. Oxford: Oxford University Press.

Soma Thera (1999), *The Way of Mindfulness: the Satipatthana Sutta and Its Commentary*, 6th revised ed. Kuala Lumpur: Buddhist Publication Society.

Spencer Lewis, H. (1978), *Rosicrucian Manual*, 25th ed. San Jose: Rosicrucian Press.

Spiro, M. (1987), 'Collective Representations and Mental Representations in Religious Symbol Systems', in B. Kilborne and L. L. Langness (eds), *Culture and Human Nature: Theoretical Papers of Melford E. Spiro*. Chicago and London: University of Chicago Press, pp. 161–86.

Spuler, M. (2000), 'Characteristics of Buddhism in Australia', *Journal of Contemporary Religion* 15 (1), 29–44.

Staples, C. L. and Mauss, A. L. (1987), 'Conversion or Commitment? A Reassessment of the Snow and Machalek Approach to the Study of Conversion', *Journal for the Scientific Study of Religion* 26 (2), 133–47.

Stone, G. P. and Farberman, H. A. (1970), 'The Self', in G. P. Stone and H. A. Farberman (eds), *Social Psychology Through Symbolic Interaction*. Waltham, Massachusetts: Xerox College Publishing, pp. 367–72.

Strauss, R. (1979), 'Religious Conversion as a Personal and Collective Accomplishment', *Sociological Analysis* 40 (2), 158–65.

Stromberg, P. (1985), 'The Impression Point: Synthesis of Symbol and Self', *Ethos* 13 (1), 56–74.

Stromberg, P. (1993), *Language and Self-transformation: A Study of the Christian Conversion Narrative*. Cambridge: Cambridge University Press.

Sutcliffe, S. (2000), 'Wandering Stars: Seekers and Gurus in the Modern World', in, S. Sutcliffe and M. Bowman (eds), *Beyond New Age: Exploring Alternative Spirituality*. Edinburgh: Edinburgh University Press.

Sutcliffe, S. and Bowman, M. (2000), 'Introduction', in S. Sutcliffe and M. Bowman (eds), *Beyond New Age: Exploring Alternative Spirituality*. Edinburgh: Edinburgh University Press.

Tashi Tsering (2002), *The Theory and Practice of Mahamudra: A Teaching Given by Venerable Tashi Tsering*, Voula Zarpani (interpreter). Eudlo: Chenrezig Institute Publications.

Tenzin Gyatso (2001), Geshe Lobsang Jordhen, Losang Choephel Ganchenpa and J. Russell (trans.), *Stages of Meditation: Training the Mind for Wisdom*. London: Rider.

Tenzin Gyatso (2002a), Geshe Thupten Jinpa (ed./trans.), *Essence of the Heart Sutra: The Dalai Lama's Heart of Wisdom Teachings*. Boston: Wisdom Publications.

Tenzin Gyatso (2002b), R. McClen, T. Jinpa, and N. Ribush (eds), Thupten Jinpa (trans.), *Illuminating the Path to Enlightenment*. Long Beach California: Thubten Dhargye Ling Publications.

Tenzin Gyatso, Tsong-ka-pa, and Hopkins, J. (1987), J. Hopkins (trans./ed.), *Deity Yoga in Action and Performance Tantra*. New York: Snow Lion Publications.

Tenzin Gyatso, Tsong-ka-pa, and Hopkins, J. (2005), J. Hopkins (trans./ed.), *Yoga Tantra: Paths to Magical Feats*. New York: Snow Lion Publications.

Thubten Yeshe (2001), J. Landaw (ed.), *Introduction to Tantra: The Transformation of Desire*, revised ed. Somerville Massachusets: Wisdom Publications.

Thubten Yeshe (2004), N. Ribush (ed.), *Becoming Vajrasattva: The Tantric Path of Purification*. Boston: Wisdom Publications.

Thubten Yeshe and Thubten Zopa Rinpoche (2003), 'The Yoga Method of the Glorious Supreme Heruka Vajrasattva', in *The Preliminary Practice of Vajrasattva*. FPMT inc.

Thubten Zopa (2000), *The Wish-Fulfilling Golden Sun of the Mahayana Thought Training*, original publication details unknown, republished for Kachoe Zung Juk Ling Nunnery.

Thubten Zopa (2001), *A Daily Meditation on Shakyamuni Buddha*, revised ed. Taos, New Mexico: FPMT Education Services.

Thupten Jinpa (2000), 'The Foundations of a Buddhist Psychology of Awakening', in G. Watson, S. Batchelor, and G. Claxton (eds), *The Psychology of Awakening*. York Beach, Maine: Samuel Weiser, pp. 10–22.

Tingay, K. (2000), 'Madame Blavatsky's Children: Theosophy and Its Heirs', in S. Sutcliffe and M. Bowman (eds), *Beyond New Age: Exploring Alternative Spirituality*. Edinburgh: Edinburgh University Press, pp. 37–50.

Travisano, R. (1970), 'Alternation and Conversion as Qualitatively Different Transformations', in G. P. Stone and H. A. Farberman (eds), *Social Psychology Through Symbolic Interaction.* Waltham, Massachusetts: Xerox College Publishing, pp. 594–606.

Tsong-kha-pa (1995), *Preparing for Tantra: The Mountain of Blessings.* Howell, New Jersey: The Mahayana Sutra and Tantra Press.

Tsong-kha-pa (2000), G. Newland (ed.), The Lam Rim Chen Mo Translation Committee (trans.), *The Great Treatise on the Stages of the Path to Enlightenment,* vol. 1. New York: Snow Lion Publications.

Tsong-kha-pa (2002), G. Newland (ed.), The Lam Rim Chen Mo Translation Committee (trans.), *The Great Treatise on the Stages of the Path to Enlightenment,* vol. 3. New York: Snow Lion Publications.

Tsong-kha-pa (2004), G. Newland (ed.), The Lam Rim Chen Mo Translation Committee (trans.), *The Great Treatise on the Stages of the Path to Enlightenment,* vol. 2. New York: Snow Lion Publications.

Tsong-kha-pa (2005), G. Sparham (trans.), *Tantric Ethics: An Explanation of the Precepts for Buddhist Vajrayana Practice.* Boston: Wisdom Publications.

Tulku Thondup (2001), 'Foreword', in R. A. Ray, *Secret of the Vajra World: The Tantric Buddhism of Tibet.* Boston and London: Shambala.

Tweed, T. (1999), 'Night-Stand Buddhists and Other Creatures: Sympathizers, Adherents, and the Study of Religion', in D. R. Williams and C. S. Queen (eds), *American Buddhism.* Richmond: Curzon Press, pp. 71–90.

Tweed, T. (2011), 'Theory and Method in the Study of Buddhism: Toward "Translocative" Analysis', *Journal of Global Buddhism* 12, 17–32.

U Silananda (1990), R. Heinze (ed.), *The Four Foundations of Mindfulness.* Boston: Wisdom Publications.

Urban, H. (2003), Tantra: Sex, Secrecy, Politics, and Power in the Study of Religion. Berkeley: University of California Press.

Valham, K (compiler). (1997), *Lam Rim Outlines: Beginners' Meditation Guide.* Boston: Wisdom Publications.

Volinn, E. (1985), 'Eastern Meditation Groups: Why Join?', *Sociological Analysis* 46 (2), 147–56.

Walsh, R. N. (1977), 'Initial Meditative Experiences: Part 1', *Journal of Transpersonal Psychology* 9 (2), 151–92.

Walsh, R. N. (1978), 'Initial Meditative Experiences: Part 2', *Journal of Transpersonal Psychology* 10 (1), 1–28.

Walshe, M. (trans.). (1995), 'Mahasatipatthana Sutta', in the *Digha Nikaya.* Boston: Wisdom Publications, pp. 335–50.

Watson, G. (2000), 'I, Mine, and Views of the Self', in G. Watson, S. Batchelor, and G. Claxton (eds), *The Psychology of Awakening.* York Beach, Maine: Samuel Weiser, pp. 30–39.

Watson, G. (2002), *The Resonance of Emptiness: A Buddhist Inspiration for a Contemporary Psychotherapy.* Richmond: Curzon Press.

Wayman, A. (1961), 'Totemic Beliefs in the Buddhist Tantras', *History of Religions* 1 (1), 81–95.

Wayman, A. (1974), *The Buddhist Tantras: Light on Indo-Tibetan Esotericism.* London: Routledge and Kegan Paul.

Weissman, R. and Weismann, S. (1999), *With Compassionate Understanding: A Meditation Retreat.* St Paul, Minnesota: Paragon House.

Welwood, J. (2000), 'Realization and Embodiment: Psychological Work in the Service of Spiritual Development', in G. Watson, S. Batchelor, and G. Claxton (eds), *The Psychology of Awakening.* York Beach, Maine: Samuel Weiser, pp. 137–66.

Welwood, J. (2002), *Toward a Psychology of Awakening: Buddhism, Psychotherapy, and the Path of Personal and Spiritual Transformation.* Boston and London: Shambala.

Wentworth, W. (1980), *Context and Understanding: An Inquiry into Socialization Theory.* New York: Elsevier North Holland Inc.

Williams, P. (1989), *Mahayana Buddhism: The Doctrinal Foundations.* London and New York: Routledge.

Williams, P. and Tribe, A. (2000), *Buddhist Thought: A Complete Introduction to the Indian Tradition.* London and New York: Routledge.

Wilson, S. (1984), 'Becoming a Yogi: Resocialization and Deconditioning as Conversion Processes', *Sociological Analysis* 45 (4), 301–14.

Wortz, E. (1982), 'Application of Awareness Methods in Psychotherapy', *Journal of Transpersonal Psychology* 14 (1), 61–8.

Wuthnow, R. (1976), 'The New Religions in Social Context', in C. Y. Glock and R. N. Bellah (eds), *The New Religious Consciousness.* Berkeley and Los Angeles: University of California Press, pp. 267–93.

Index